INVISIBLE STARS

MEDIA, COMMUNICATION, AND CULTURE IN AMERICA

Michael C. Keith and Donald A. Fishman, Series Editors

INVISIBLE STARS

A Social History
of Women in
American Broadcasting

DONNA L. HALPER

M.E. Sharpe
Armonk, New York
London, England

Library of Congress Cataloging-in-Publication Data

Halper, Donna L.
    Invisible stars : a social history of women in American broadcasting / Donna L. Halper.
      p. cm. — (Media, communication, and culture in America)
    Includes bibliographical references and index.
    ISBN 0-7656-0581-3 (alk. paper)
      1. Women in the broadcasting industry—United States. I. Title. II. Series.

PN1990.9.W64 H35 2001   00-049676
791.44′028′082—dc21   CIP

Printed in the United States of America

The paper used in this publication meets the minimum requirements of
American National Standard for Information Sciences
Permanence of Paper for Printed Library Materials,
ANSI Z 39.48-1984.

BM (c)   10   9   8   7   6   5   4   3   2   1

Table of Contents

Foreword

The role of women in broadcasting has been a vastly neglected subject. The most well-known and celebrated pioneers of radio have all been men: David Sarnoff, Lee DeForest, Frank Conrad, and Edwin H. Armstrong. Traditional textbooks on the history of broadcasting seldom mention a woman's name in connection with the early developments of the industry. Moreover, there have been no large archival collections available to draw upon to discuss the role of women either as performers, writers, program directors, or station owners. Unfortunately, existing materials on women in broadcasting have been scattered and difficult to locate.

Donna Halper's book, *Invisible Stars: A Social History of Women in Broadcasting,* is designed to remedy this gap. Halper's emphasis is on a social history of women in broadcasting, and she skillfully explains how the changing role of women in different eras influenced their participation in broadcasting.

Halper directly connects societal values and social trends to the achievements of women in broadcasting. During the era when radio began to emerge, the lives of most women largely revolved around the family, religion, and household management. Career women were the exception, not the rule. Traditional careers for women were restricted to fields such as teaching, nursing, and clerical assistance. Those few women who embarked upon a career in broadcasting entered a very male-dominated atmosphere. Radio had begun primarily as a male hobby by ham radio operators and broadcast engineers, and it retained many of the vestiges of this male culture as it matured. But there also was an egalitarian quality to early radio. The low pay and small budgets for programming created opportunities for women as vocalists and musicians. And the need for programming material allowed women who had special talents, especially those with musical backgrounds, to prosper.

Halper is at her best in discussing the early female pioneers of radio. None of these figures is widely known: Eunice Randall, Eleanor Nesbitt Poehler, Bertha Brainard, Ada Morgan O'Brien, and Corinne Jordan. Typically, these women had either strong organizational skills or backgrounds in music. Halper observes that many of the female pioneers of broadcasting gained entry into the field because of their musical talents, and there is a strong correlation between musical skills and opportunities for women in early radio. But during the 1930s and 1940s, Americans continued to be ambivalent about women in radio. Broadcasting or performing was a role at odds with society's definition of femininity. Yet some women such as Corinne Jordan, the program director at KSTP in St. Paul, Minnesota, were accepted—and even praised—for their skills. Moreover, the "women's hour," or specially designed programs for women, increasingly became a popular segment for listeners. In addition, World War II provided a myriad of opportunities for women to enter broadcasting as engineers, announcers, studio pages, and assorted functionaries.

After the war, however, women found it difficult to retain prominent positions in broadcasting. The reigning social trends favored the stay-at-home mother. In fact, this became the dominant ideology of the post-war period. Halper traces the gradual change in the status of women during the 1950s and 1960s, highlighting the careers of those women who proved to be exceptional and surveying the opportunities that television provided for women. By the 1970s, the changing role of women in society—spearheaded by the feminist movement—led to increased status for women in broadcasting. Finally, Halper intelligently discusses the successes of women in broadcasting during the 1980s and 1990s and the special gender-related problems that they encountered, such as ageism.

Overall, Halper has blended together the historical context, the contents of broadcasting, and the achievements of individual women into a highly readable account of the past eighty years. This book is likely to become the major point of departure for readers and scholars who want to investigate the role of women in broadcasting during the twentieth century.

Donald A. Fishman
Boston College

INVISIBLE STARS

Introduction

Although you can't see Eunice Randall's house from the highway, it is still standing. A long, unpaved (and very bumpy) road takes you there, and if you are patient, and have a vehicle with good shock absorbers, you arrive at a place where it is still 1918. The house hasn't changed much since Eunice left. Electricity was added, and relatives put in a telephone, but for the most part, things remain the way they were when she lived there—a wood-burning stove, a pump for drawing water, and a seemingly endless expanse of land for farming. Back then, a farmer's daughter could finish high school, and then the rest of her life would revolve around religion, family, and the domestic tasks women were expected to perform. But Eunice didn't want that life, much to her father's surprise. Ahead of her time, she probably had no role models to encourage her. Yet despite the fact that she seldom met businesswomen, somehow she knew her future was not in the small town of Mattapoisett, but, rather, in the big city of Boston. Getting there meant an eighty-mile trip, at a time when few women traveled alone and fewer sought out careers. But Eunice knew she had to make that journey, even if her father disapproved.

In Boston, she found her answer in a very unlikely place: a factory that manufactured radio receivers. In 1918, she was the first and only women the American Radio and Research Company (AMRAD) had ever hired. She started there doing technical drawings for the engineers, but that soon changed because AMRAD also operated radio station 1XE. Radio was an amateur activity back then, and members of the AMRAD staff kept the station running. Soon, Eunice was learning to build ham radio equipment and taking her turn behind the microphone. She graduated from working with blueprints, moved into testing new equipment, and was asked to join the engineers who demonstrated AMRAD's products at trade shows. In early 1922,

1XE became commercial station WGI. And while her announcing skills won her many fans, more important to Eunice was earning the respect of her AMRAD colleagues, who accepted her as a team member and a friend.

Her father, meanwhile, expected her to come home. However, when she did, it was only for a visit and to build a radio set so her family could hear her on the air. George Randall did not understand his daughter's need for a career, and there is evidence that when she returned to Boston, he never spoke to her again. But her mother and relatives were proud of her; even years later, they would recall how much radio had meant to Eunice.

Today, the house is empty. A niece stops by occasionally, and thanks to her, I was able to go inside. Standing in what was Eunice's bedroom, I pictured her building that radio receiver and listening to distant stations. I wondered how she put up with the loneliness of being the only woman in the factory, how she handled the insults and practical jokes the men played on her, and how she managed to have a successful life despite all that. I also wondered why this amazing woman—the first female announcer in New England radio, one of the few women engineers, and a licensed ham radio operator—is not mentioned in any History of Broadcasting textbook. In fact, such books tend to ignore the vast majority of the women of early broadcasting, even though so many of them overcame great odds to achieve what women today take for granted—the right to be on the air.

When I became the first woman announcer at my college station in 1968, I wanted to know about the women who preceded me, so I could thank them for what they had accomplished. But it wasn't until 1992 that I learned that women like Eunice Randall existed, when, entirely by chance, I found an article about her in an old newspaper. This started me on a journey of my own, uncovering the names and stories of other forgotten women in early radio and television, as well as examining what their society thought about the proper role of women. The more I learned about them, the more I came to believe that these pioneering women broadcasters played an important part in changing our culture: not only did they expand society's expectations of what women could do, but they also provided a forum for the issues that affected the lives of housewives, children, and "career girls." As a result of talk shows, quiz shows, and even the ubiquitous cooking shows, there emerged an entirely new form of public discourse in America, a discussion about what was said on the radio. And in this conversation, women were active participants.

Throughout this social history of women in broadcasting, I will be exploring how radio and television became so influential in shaping society's attitudes about women. Some media critics believe this process was nothing more than hegemony, and they accuse radio and television of persuading generations of women to follow certain behaviors, buy certain products, and accept a certain standard of beauty. I can see some validity in that assessment, but there is also a positive side that often gets lost in the criticism. In today's media-saturated world, it is easy to take for granted how dramatically the arrival of broadcasting changed the society, and how it created a new popular culture.

From its earliest days, radio made an immediate impact. Unlike print, which required reading skills, or film, which required people to have the money and the transportation to get to a movie theater, radio just required the ability to relax and listen from the comfort of the room where the radio was located. (Early radios were neither small nor portable, and some families set aside one room just for radio listening.) Staying home to listen to radio, as opposed to going out to a movie or a play, became such a popular trend that sociologists and critics began writing essays about how radio might make people antisocial. Entertainment-oriented newspapers like *Variety* were worried that radio would mean the death of movies and theater: a page 1 headline in the March 3, 1922, issue stated, "Vaudeville and Musicians Declare Against Radiophone." In this and other subsequent articles, *Variety* editorialized against radio (or "radiophone" as it was often called in the early 1920s), commending those performers who pledged not to participate in it. It was a common belief among big-name entertainers during those early years that performers who appeared on radio would diminish the public's desire to go and see them live. But the rapidly growing popularity of radio listening also inspired a new magazine, called *Radio in the Home.* This publication was as much about style as it was about radio, as it described the radio rooms and the homes of celebrities and executives, showing how radio had improved their quality of life.

Radio also made the social classes more equal: now, everyone who had a radio had access to what previously was the domain of the wealthy—the so-called *good music.* Prior to radio, opera and the classics were appreciated mainly by those people who could afford to attend the theater or own a top-quality phonograph—there was no other way to hear the great singers like Enrico Caruso or Amelita Galli-Curci. But when radio came along, even the poor could enjoy the music of the most admired vocalists. And for the first time, people living in rural towns, where famous opera singers seldom traveled, were able to enjoy the same entertainers that people in the big cities did. Even those who did not yet own a radio had an opportunity to listen. In the early 1920s, a number of department stores opened up a radio section, and in order to promote the merchandise, managers began putting up loudspeakers and playing the broadcasts of local stations. Crowds gathered at the store to listen and were amazed at hearing a baseball game or an important singer. This gimmick was supposed to encourage shoppers to buy a new radio set, and many did. Prices ranged from as little as $10 for a simple crystal set, up to about $280 for a name-brand, state-of-the-art receiver. Some people preferred to buy the parts and build their own sets. It didn't take long for radio to move from a fad to an obsession—by late 1922, it seemed that everybody wanted a radio of his or her own. Once the radio was installed, any person could hear the biggest sporting events and enjoy the latest dance bands with minimal inconvenience. Listeners were also able to hear broadcasts from distant cities, places where many in the audience had never been. And, at a time when America was still racially segregated, people who had previously never heard much black music suddenly had the opportunity to listen to Eubie Blake, Duke Ellington, Dewey Washington, Lottie Gee, and numerous others. In all too many cities, even the most highly acclaimed black performers were still restricted in where they were allowed to appear. But thanks to radio, both black and white listeners all over the country could hear their talents.

The ability of radio to transmit to a wide range of cities was not valuable only for performers of color. A number of women performers who would have been limited to entertaining at local venues suddenly were receiving fan mail from distant locations. It may not have resulted in any new job offers, but in early radio, which was largely a volunteer effort, the ego gratification of suddenly being critically acclaimed by more than the hometown fans had to be a thrill.

This was, as mentioned earlier, the era when more women were entering the public sphere to work or attend school. There had always been a belief in upper-class circles that an educated woman was supposed to be the arbiter of good taste and refinement. As far back as the Victorian era, it was women, for the most part, who bought the sheet music and played the songs on the piano to teach music appreciation to their children.[1] Until the arrival of radio, performing for the family, singing in the choir, or perhaps doing some local concerts under the auspices of the bigger music schools was all a woman was expected to do with her talent or her training. But as soon as the first commercial stations began in 1920–21, the need for performers gave some of these women an opportunity to be heard outside of the confines of the old expectations. Now, a woman with talent had a new option: radio singer or accompanist. Newspapers covering the rise of radio were soon commenting that certain female vocalists were developing a following thanks to their radio work. This article in the *Brooklyn (NY) Eagle* of April 4, 1922 is typical. The headline said, "Aunt Jean, Sally Hamlin, and H.V. Kaltenborn Will Be Heard by Wireless Fans." The article discussed the work of Kaltenborn, the famous print journalist; talked about the "story lady" Aunt Jean; and then told readers that station WVP was pleased to bring back

Sally Hamlin. "Miss Hamlin, who has entertained over the radiophone before, has arranged a program of her most popular numbers . . . her earlier [performances] have shown that her voice is unusually well suited for radio transmission . . . Of the younger entertainers of today, few show as great promise as Miss Hamlin does, and the *Eagle* is glad that the demand for 'more recitations by Miss Sally Hamlin' can be answered."

In researching this book, I found quite a few grandchildren who recalled stories that their grandmother had related about singing on a local radio station in broadcasting's early years. It is unfortunate that audiotape had not yet been invented, as it would be fascinating to hear what these women sounded like as they performed for the "unseen audience." In today's world of instant publicity, we can only imagine how amazing it was for these women to go from being known mainly in their community to receiving fan letters and newspaper adulation.

As time passed, radio also helped to create national hit songs and, with the rise of the networks, hit programs. This truly gave Americans a shared popular culture; where in the late 1800s, vaudeville or traveling theater companies achieved popularity one city at a time, over a duration of many months, the new medium could spread a hit from coast to coast within hours. Now, despite some regional differences, Americans liked many of the same stars, enjoyed many of the same hit songs, and read many of the same celebrity-oriented magazines.

Radio gave talented local performers national exposure, and many women benefited from this as much as men did. It is true that men hosted most of the sports and variety shows, and they would later in the 1920s comprise the majority of the network announcers, but a number of women did manage to became highly paid and well-respected stars in their own right, idolized by millions of fans. It is also true that in those early days, everyone at the station had to do whatever was needed, so a woman would sometimes read the news headlines or introduce the guests; Eunice Randall often read the nightly police reports of stolen cars. And because radio was theater of the imagination, what a woman looked like was not as important as how she related to the audience. A warm personality, a sense of humor, and the ability to hold the listener's interest resulted in popularity. Unfortunately, the early microphones distorted the higher pitched voices, so only those women who had learned to keep their voice in the low- to mid-range sounded good on the air. But to the audience, as long as female announcers sounded pleasant, that seemed to matter most.

When television came along, there was a fear that only the attractive women would do well in this new visual medium. But although some women (and some men, too) certainly were hired mainly because they were good

looking, many women also achieved success on TV by being talented entertainers. And although it took a while, women gradually moved beyond being automatically typecast as singers, story ladies, weather girls, and cooking
show hosts. Today, it is quite common to see TV's women anchoring at the
news desk, interviewing major celebrities, announcing sports, and directing
documentaries; there are also a number of women managers. And as for
radio, women hold just about every job, from sales to publicity to owning a
chain of stations. But none of this would have been possible without the
efforts of so many women from broadcasting's early years—the women
who contributed their talent and energy to the audience for no pay, the women
who worked hard to gain acceptance and who broke down a number of
barriers, the women who won over even the most skeptical male critics and
proved that women do belong on the air.

Today, society is not as stratified as it was in the 1920s, and nearly everyone has TV and radio in their home. While computers and the Internet have
changed the way people get information, many people still rely on radio and
TV. There are still people who idolize their favorite disc jockey or wish they
could be a talk show host. (As I write this, two of the most widely known—
and wealthiest—people in media are women who interview celebrity guests:
Barbara Walters and Oprah Winfrey.) For good or for ill, radio and television continue to provide a useful context for examining women's changing
roles, demonstrating that even during the most conformist times, some unique
voices have found a way to be heard.

* * *

In the three years that I researched this book, I encountered some wonderful
librarians, and I wish I had the space to list every one of them. Reference
librarians are often unappreciated, but the ones who assisted me have my
eternal gratitude because without them, this book would have taken much
longer to write. I especially want to thank the staff in the Microtext Room
of the Boston Public Library, as well as the staff in the reference department
at the Quincy (MA) Public Library. These hard-working professionals went
out of their way for me many times. I found some very useful information
at the Seattle Public Library, the Minneapolis Public Library, and the New
Bedford (MA) Public Library. I also want to thank the many record collec-
tors and scholars on the 78–L Internet discussion group (Professor Mike
Biel and Elizabeth McLeod especially), Lou Genco of the Old Time Radio
pages, and Barry Mishkind of the Broadcast Archives. Bob Fleming, the
archivist at Emerson College, was very helpful, as were media historian
Professor J. Michael Kittross and Lisa Tuite in the Boston Globe Library.

My thanks also go out to the Pavek Museum, for its resources on the history of radio and phonograph technology, as well as to the Museum of Steam and Wireless, for its tribute to Eunice Randall and its collection of wireless equipment. Both museums helped me to understand what the early days of broadcasting must have been like, and the curators answered my many questions patiently. I am eternally grateful to the relatives of some of the women pioneers, who shared memorabilia with me (Mrs. Eunice Stolecki especially) and encouraged my research. And above all, my thanks to Peter Coveney, Michael Keith, and the other good people at M.E. Sharpe for believing in this project and for giving me the opportunity to write the women of broadcasting back into history.

I dedicate this book to the memory of my parents, Bea and Sam Halper; to my husband and colleague, Jon Jacobik; and, of course, to the memory of Eunice Randall.

Chapter 1

The Early 1920s:
The Radio Adventure Begins

Bertha Brainard did not expect to become a role model, assuming there was such a concept in 1920. She had driven an ambulance for the Red Cross during World War I, but she really wanted to be involved with theater and was looking for a job writing reviews for a newspaper. Marie Ciesielski had married Robert Zimmerman and was undoubtedly planning to work on her family's farm in Jessup, Iowa. Eleanor Nesbitt Poehler's husband was a wealthy doctor; they had a baby boy, and Eleanor enjoyed doing volunteer work and singing in her church choir. Eunice Randall had played basketball in high school, but professional sports for girls was not a possibility in those days, and besides, she really hoped to be an artist. It is doubtful that any of these women envisioned a radio career as they were growing up, and they probably had no idea that radio would soon change their lives.

What we know as radio was still called *wireless* during the first two decades of the 1900s, and it was not yet a career path. Radio was the domain of amateur hobbyists and engineers, and nobody expected to make a living at it. To be on the air usually meant sending and receiving Morse code. Hams, most of whom were boys or young men, spent many hours building and modifying their equipment, improving on the technology until they were not only sending code, but even speaking to other amateurs in far-off cities. By the middle of the second decade of the 1900s, some hams had also begun to play phonograph records or read sports scores for their audiences. And while the word *broadcasting* did not yet conjure up images of beautiful studios, famous dance bands, or glamorous celebrities, for the growing number of fans attracted to the amateur game, it was both educational and fun.

Given that ham radio required a solid knowledge of mathematics and engineering principles, as well as some skill at carpentry, it is not surprising that the majority of the early amateur radio operators were male, since these particular subjects had not been commonly taught to girls. For many men, that was exactly as it should be. Carroll Pursell's essay, "The Long Summer of Boy Engineering," suggests that as women had gradually broken down barriers in society and begun to participate more in the public sphere, some men were not happy about it, even though gender roles per se had not changed all that much. The arrival of the new radio technology enabled men to recapture the public sphere for themselves. "Public space—politics, commerce, war, engineering—was the special place of men, which they not only controlled, but from which women were excluded."[1] Advanced scientific training, which was almost exclusively reserved for white males, gave status to those who possessed it; few women (and even fewer minorities) were encouraged to take any advanced science courses in school. The proliferation of after-school ham radio clubs also tended to be overwhelmingly white and male. And, in page after page of science and hobby magazines, boys were being invited to join the adventure of electronics. Advertisements stressed the benefits of learning the new technology; girls, if portrayed at all, were typically shown watching in amazement as brother and father built something together. The "boy engineer," resourceful, innovative, and clever, quickly became a familiar character in books (as in the popular *Radio Boys* adventure series), as well as in magazines. His hobby was not only exciting, but it afforded him useful skills that could serve him well when it came time for a career.

Yet, despite the fact that girls and women were not expected to enjoy ham radio except as passive observers, there were a few enterprising females who found their way into the hobby and managed to persuade a father or a brother to teach them more about it. While ham radio call books from that era listed very few women's names, magazines like *QST* and *Radio Amateur News* had pictures of some girls and young women who operated their brother's or father's station, even though the license was held by the male. But it is certainly true that females comprised only a small number of the participants in amateur radio during the first two decades of the 1900s. And since it was mainly the amateurs who created what became commercial broadcasting, it is not surprising that the names associated with radio's beginnings all belong to men: David Sarnoff, Lee DeForest, Frank Conrad, Harold Power, Charles "Doc" Herrold, and Edwin Howard Armstrong, just to name a few.

Women's Place in 1920

But while its founders may indeed have been men, it would be inaccurate to say that early radio was all male, or even that broadcasting had traditional gender roles. The newness of commercial radio allowed for considerable experimentation, and with an all-volunteer staff, whoever knew how to do a certain job would be expected to help, be that person male or female. In 1920, when commercial radio first began, the subject of women's proper place was still being hotly debated, and a number of changes had already occurred. After years of marches, demonstrations, and parades, 1920 was the year the women's suffrage movement finally saw passage of the Nineteenth Amendment, giving women the right to vote in national elections. But prior to that, in 1917, a woman from Montana, Jeanette Rankin, had already been elected to Congress (a few states had given women the vote before the Nineteenth Amendment was finally ratified). And women had also achieved considerable visibility as a result of their ongoing efforts to ban alcoholic beverages. From the late 1800s, when Frances Willard of the Women's Christian Temperance Union and the crusading Carry Nation led the fight, on through the early 1900s when women from religious and civic organizations took up the challenge, women were the ones who spoke the most eloquently about the negative impact of liquor. Thanks to a strong media campaign filled with tragic stories of children abandoned by alcoholic fathers and wives left destitute as a result, a majority of Americans gradually came to accept the need for Prohibition; the Eighteenth Amendment finally became law in January of 1919.

Women were also becoming more visible in aspects of public life other than those typically associated with the female gender, such as volunteering for charitable or religious causes. More and more women were now working for pay; so many of them had entered the job market that the U.S. Department of Labor established a Women's Bureau to "promote the welfare of wage earning women."[2] Also, as the new decade opened, a steadily increasing number of women were going to college: by the early 1920s, 40 percent of college enrollment was female.[3] During the recently concluded World War I, American women had joined the military and served as wireless operators, freeing up men for combat duty. Some of these women had come from privileged backgrounds, yet in their desire to serve their country, they took courses in subjects that women had never been asked to study. The Signal Corps found that the new female recruits quickly mastered wireless telegraphy, and several of them rose to the rank of captain of their unit.[4]

In daily life, young women were rejecting long hair in favor of much more practical styles, and their choice of clothing reflected a preference for more comfortable dresses and varied styles. The Sears Roebuck catalog now carried over ninety illustrated pages of women's clothing. As for married life, syndicated columnist Dorothy Dix was instructing the husband to treat his wife like a partner rather than a servant, and she did not condemn the woman who wanted a career.[5] Some newspapers of the time still questioned whether a married woman should work outside the home, but no longer were all the writers in agreement that she should not.

The young women entering the workforce found that there were jobs, but the choices were not very glamorous. One woman, quoted in *Literary Digest,* spoke of the problems women working in factories encountered, including foremen who refused to explain the job or answer questions and a lack of sinks so that women doing dirty jobs could wash their hands before lunch.[6] There had already been a series of workers' strikes during 1919 to protest low wages and poor working conditions; as many as 4 million workers, some of whom were women, took part. This included a strike at the New England Union of Telephone Operators, one of the few that had a positive outcome for the workers.[7] Despite previous labor problems, most women still preferred being a telephone operator to working in the factories. But although the work was certainly much cleaner and not as strenuous, the job itself remained strictly regulated, to the point where an operator was only allowed to use certain phrases, which she had to speak in a certain tone of voice.[8] Those women who aspired to professional careers, such as nursing or teaching, had somewhat more freedom, but even late in the second decade of the 1900s, articles were being written lamenting the low salaries that schoolteachers were given.[9] Although it is true that more American women than ever before were in the public sphere, still only certain career fields were considered appropriate. However, one occupation that accepted women almost immediately was radio.

Women as Radio Pioneers

It was not because radio was inherently egalitarian that the new medium welcomed female participation. It was actually a very practical reason that caused owners to make the studios available to not only women but, in some cities, minorities as well. Early stations had small budgets with which to pay for talent. The original vision of owners had been that their station would be a vehicle for promoting their own business, so they seem to have assumed their own workers would provide the entertainment. This, however, was not always a wise assumption. The majority of the employees at Westinghouse or AMRAD or General Electric were men with an electronics background. They built the radio studio and designed the equipment the station used, but they probably had not been hired with the expectation that they would also perform for a radio audience. Given the times, some engineers undoubtedly did have musical ability, since it was much more expected in the early 1900s that any educated person should know how to play a musical instrument, and music courses were taught even in the public schools. In commercial radio's first few months, the engineers who manufactured the radio equipment during the day then operated the company's station at night, and it was up to them to find people to entertain. Since audiotape had not been invented, and there were problems getting phonograph records to sound good when played through very primitive amplification, there was an immediate and constant need for live performers, some of whom were recruited from the company and from friends or relatives who enjoyed singing. The engineers tried their best to keep the station functioning: Eunice Randall recalls working her shift in the AMRAD factory, and then taking her turn announcing on station 1XE, as well as doing some engineering and repairing anything that broke. When guests could not be found, she and another engineer would sing duets to entertain the audience.[10] But even though some engineers and their friends could sing fairly well, it was evident that this was not the ultimate solution. As radio's popularity increased and its audience appeal widened, there were not enough singing engineers to go around. Someone needed to be assigned the task of finding talent and making sure a variety of performers was available. The person chosen for this important role was often a woman.

Again, the reason was not necessarily that early owners believed in feminism. What they believed in was having somebody on the staff who had good contacts with musicians and other performers. Women ran many of the music schools (another occupation that society considered appropriate for them was that of music teacher or vocal coach), and a number of these women also sang in church choirs or for their local symphony orchestra. As we will see, some of the first program directors in radio were women whose background was in music, and who could bring in a number of up-and-coming students (also female in many cases) to perform for free. Also, it was commonly believed that women were by nature good at organizing, making them ideal for tasks that involved scheduling and arranging the talent. In subsequent decades, this would be the reason given for restricting women to working as secretaries, rather than as executives: the theory was that women's skills were only organizational, and they lacked the ability to make independent decisions. Yet the women program directors of the 1920s made many decisions and kept their stations operating as a result.

Because so few cities had a commercial radio station and because these first stations did not receive much publicity from the print media, it is probable that the average person in 1920–21 was still relatively unaware of radio. When a local performer appeared on one of the few broadcasting stations, the appearance was heard only by a very limited audience, most of whom were still involved with amateur radio. A couple of department stores did install speakers so that people on the street could listen, but this was not typical. (These stores sold radio equipment, and their hope was that once people heard this new invention, they would want one for their very own.) But in 1921, radio was not widely listened to, even in large cities like Boston, New York, and Pittsburgh, where some of the early stations were located. And if a radio fan opened the newspaper, there was little evidence that radio existed. Newspapers still regarded the new medium as competition, since radio could bring an event to people immediately, whereas a newspaper could not. Few newspapers in 1921 wrote much about radio as a result, perhaps hoping that if they ignored it, radio might go away.

The Radio Craze Expands

But radio did not go away; in fact, in 1922, interest in radio exploded, as a handful of stations grew to several hundred, and a number of new magazines devoted to radio appeared, including *Radio Digest, Radio World,* and *Radio Broadcast.* Even serious news magazines like *Literary Digest* inserted a page about radio, and newspapers were forced to add a radio page whether they wanted to or not. By mid-1922, what had once been regarded as a fad was a major trend in American life. Even books for young people reflected the fascination with radio: the *Radio Boys* was a popular series for the boy engineer, and each new book featured a different adventure involving the use of radio to save lives, capture criminals, or solve a mystery. And while not as many radio books were aimed at girls, there was a 1922 series written by Margaret Penrose: the *Radio Girls* series featured a group of friends who were interested in radio and had some exciting adventures as a result of their new hobby.

All kinds of magazines began running advertisements showing where radios could be bought (since not everyone knew how to build their own), as companies moved away from marketing exclusively to ham radio operators and started to reach out to the average family. In 1922, there was a growing audience of consumers who wanted a radio for entertainment and information. By year's end, nearly $60 million worth of radio receiving equipment was sold.[11] Newspapers not only inserted a radio page with program listings, many even created the new position of "radio editor," sending this person out to interview local performers and station personnel. Most of the first radio editors were men who came from ham radio and knew the technology, but in subsequent decades, some of the editors would be women who knew many of the performers. Certain newspapers even became directly involved with a station, which they either owned or operated (the *Detroit News* and WWJ and the *Los Angeles Times* and KHJ are two of many examples). Journalists from the newspaper read news for the radio stations their company owned, enabling the audience for the first time to hear the people whose columns they had read. Gwen Wagner of WPO in Memphis was not only a columnist for the *Memphis News-Scimitar,* but she also read news, was radio editor, and scheduled the talent for the station.[12]

Women Managers in Early Radio

As the number of stations grew, the need for performers intensified. By the middle of 1922, new owners were hiring a specific person to find guests and train prospective new talent. The job of program director, unlike today, was not so much a management position as a hands-on job, requiring a person who booked all the performers and speakers, and literally kept the programming on the air. As with the early days, if a guest failed to show up, the program director was supposed to entertain, another good reason for hiring somebody who was known for having musical abilities. In Minneapolis, for example, Eleanor Nesbitt Poehler found herself pressed into service by the owners of WLAG. She was a well-known classical vocalist, as well as someone with ties to a music school. Thanks to her efforts, WLAG constantly had performances by some of the area's better classical musicians. Getting them proved to be no problem at the beginning: even though there was no paycheck, there was an obvious benefit to an up-and-coming entertainer. With a limited number of stations on the air, all of which were on the AM band only, signals traveled much farther; thus, a singer in Pittsburgh could be heard in Boston, and a singer in Boston might be heard in England if atmospheric conditions were right.[13] Appearing on radio when it was still a novelty also offered performers a way to get publicity. There were still newspapers that hesitated to mention the new medium too frequently, but they might publish a press release from a music school—especially one that was an advertiser—about an upcoming performance on the "radiotelephone." And on the rare occasions when a celebrity was willing to perform on the radio (such as when comedian Ed Wynn appeared on WJZ in New York in February of 1922, or the times when popular vocalist Vaughn DeLeath, known as "The Original Radio Girl," gave a concert on WDT, the New York station where she was hired as program manager in 1923), there was a good chance a newspaper would report the story.

Early radio provided an immediate opportunity for anyone, male or female, who had a good idea for something to put on the air. While few of the pioneer stations were on the air for more than a couple of hours a night, those hours needed to be filled, and as the novelty wore off, listeners were beginning to expect something interesting. A number of women with ideas about being on the air volunteered their talents. Among them was Bertha Brainard, who had by this time become a theater critic. She offered radio her expertise in theater (as well as her friendships with many of the actors and actresses themselves). She began doing a program on WJZ called "Broadcasting Broadway," where she not only gave her reviews, but she also did interviews with the people performing on stage. For the average person who could not afford a theater ticket, this show, and others like it, offered an insight into what was happening in theater and made the audience feel more knowledgeable.

As mentioned earlier, station owners who selected women to direct the programming in the early 1920s chose them because middle- and upper-class women of that time were often associated with a music school and knew plenty of classical musicians. This preference was not accidental: one of radio's earliest battles was over whether it should educate or entertain. Some owners felt very strongly about offering only "good music." One Chicago station, KYW, went on the air in 1921 determined to play only opera, an experiment that did not prove successful. Other station owners, perhaps because they themselves preferred classical or opera, refused to play jazz or popular music until they were absolutely forced to by listener demand. For these owners, popular music was vulgar, and they saw their station's role as educating the mass audience. Many of the women they hired agreed with this role, since they made their living teaching music. Ada Morgan O'Brien, for example, was a well-respected pianist and mezzo-soprano who programmed several stations in San Francisco during the early to mid-1920s. Like Eleanor Poehler in Minneapolis, she disliked popular music intensely, preferring to expose her audience to only "good music." Mrs. O'Brien also believed that music education was something women could do best. In an interview with *Radio Digest,* she said, "I feel that musical program direction of radio is a woman's work. It requires tact. The woman can best deal with the temperamental artist or the phlegmatic plodder. The woman arranges details; she can best plan a balanced program for her listeners, of whom many today are women. Radio is no longer a man's game."[14]

The idea of keeping radio an educational medium also received support from newspaper and magazine columnists, especially the music critics, who applauded the work of Eleanor Poehler and Ada O'Brien and lamented the fact that some stations were playing jazz. Since a number of music critics had come from classical backgrounds or were former musicians themselves, it was understandable that they wanted radio to provide exposure for the great composers and vocalists. Writing reviews and critiques of what they heard on the air was another area open to women: *Radio News*, *Radio Digest*, and *Radio Broadcast* all hired women reporters and critics throughout the early to mid-1920s, as did a few of the newspapers. During 1922 and 1923, *Radio World* featured a weekly column titled "Radio and the Woman"; the columns not only had gossip about female performers at various stations, but also mentioned women doing programs that were unique or interesting, and they advocated for more women to play an active role as radio expanded. *Radio Broadcast*'s music critic, Jennie Irene Mix, was equally outspoken in defending women's participation in broadcasting, and she frequently praised stations with women program directors. Like Ada O'Brien, Mix believed that stations that offered opera or the classics were performing a valuable service.[15]

Another role filled by women in early radio was story lady, but in fairness, there were men who read stories to children, too. Eunice Randall, when not engineering or announcing at AMRAD's station WGI, read bedtime stories three nights a week. But then, so did some of the male engineers, two of whom inherited the names "Uncle David" and "Uncle Eddie." There is no evidence that Eunice was "Aunt Eunice," but perhaps she used some other invented name, as many children's hosts did (one male Philadelphia announcer took the name "Dream Daddy"). It was typical of early radio for a staff member to spend time at a number of different jobs, although going from story lady to climbing the tower and making engineering repairs, as Eunice often had to do, might strike the modern professional as a bit extreme. But most of the women of early radio, Eunice among them, loved their work because there was never a dull moment. In an interview with *Wireless Age* in 1924, Eleanor Poehler (whose job included managing station WLAG, hiring and training announcers, booking all the guests, often playing piano for the vocalists, and sometimes performing selections from her own extensive repertoire) was still enthusiastically discussing "my happy radio career" and talking about "the life of excitement which any broadcasting station develops."[16] For obvious reasons, the more versatile a women was, the greater her value to the radio station, especially when a crisis arose.

In addition to theater critics, story ladies, singers, program managers (or directors), and announcer/engineers, there was at least one female station owner in the early 1920s. Not all stations were owned by corporations, although as it turned out, the stations that survived had some financial backing, which usually meant a business ran them. But 1922 and 1923 were when a number of young and eager entrepreneurs put their own station on the air. In Vinton, Iowa, the first woman to own a station was Marie (Mrs. Robert) Zimmerman. Her husband was fascinated by ham radio and engineering, while she became interested in business. He built WIAE in mid-

1922, but it was Marie who ran it and got the guests for it, and it was she whose name was on the station's license. The little station lasted barely a year, and in her later years, she never spoke of her radio days with any of her relatives,[17] but the fact remains that Marie Zimmerman was the first American woman to ever own a radio station.

The early 1920s was an exciting time in radio, a time when there were few rules and stations felt free to innovate. Not many stations had commercial advertising yet, and the quality of the programming varied. Some cities had better music schools and better singers than others. Some cities rejected the "good music" idea and went ahead with popular vocalists and dance bands. Others aired college professors (the majority of whom were still men) giving talks on their specialties. And some stations gave the forum to clubwomen, who were involved with civic and philanthropic organizations. A number of women got on the air by this means. They gave a weekly talk on the activities of their particular club and invited guests to discuss some topic related to the club. Among these clubs was the new League of Women Voters, which had been organized in 1920. By 1922, the league was offering radio stations educated and articulate spokeswomen (including the league's founder, Carrie Chapman Catt) who discussed current events and helped the voting public (especially the newly enfranchised female electorate) to become better informed. Several chapters of the league also offered educational courses on issues that might be coming up for a vote in the near future.

Radio may have started off as a mainly male hobby, but by the end of 1922, women were very involved and very interested. A number of cities held radio shows where manufacturers showed off the newest radio sets and station personnel made appearances and offered entertainment (and prizes) to everyone who attended. The newspaper reporters who covered these shows all noted with surprise how many members of the crowd were women.[18] No doubt some of these women went to the radio show in hopes of meeting a Eunice Randall or a Bertha Brainard. But others went because they were genuinely excited about the new medium. They enjoyed listening, and they wanted to become more knowledgeable. *Literary Digest,* quoting from the New York newspapers about the 1923 radio show there, observed that the large number of women in attendance were as devoted to radio as the men were. Explaining radio's popularity with women, the article stated:

> Radio is even more popular in the homes of women who reside on isolated farms and in small towns at a distance from the great urban centers of music, entertainment and general culture. To women thus situated, radio is not merely a joy; it is rapidly becoming a necessity. Radio has a

universal appeal to all classes of women. For every woman, housewife or lady of leisure, there is a program in the air somewhere which will appeal to her.[19]

Audience Reaction to Women on the Air

And so it was in radio's early years that nearly every city had women performers, women announcers, and women lecturers. Women gave talks on traditional subjects like fashion and food, but they also gave talks on politics and current events. The response to women on the air was generally quite positive. Eunice Randall's announcing was regularly praised by male columnists at all the Boston newspapers, and she received considerable fan mail from listeners. She was not the only one, as we will see. And although the majority of announcers continued to be male, it does appear that the female announcers were generally accepted; in some cases, despite a station's efforts to keep them anonymous, they developed their own following. Some of them even received marriage proposals from male listeners who had fallen in love with the sound of their voice.[20]

Of course, there were letters from men to various radio magazines criticizing some of the subjects that female guests discussed. But this is not surprising when we consider that many towns still had only one station, so a woman talking about the latest style of hats (even for only fifteen minutes) was irritating when the men were hoping for the sports scores. Programs seem to have been arranged in accordance with society's beliefs about men's and women's interests: women were supposed to prefer shows related to homemaking, and men were supposed to want sporting events like boxing or baseball. While that seems stereotypic to us in a world where many women love sports and many men can cook, the 1920s were still quite traditional on many levels, despite all the new freedoms we associate with the Roaring Twenties. Homemaking occupied a large part of the average woman's life, and although more women were developing diverse interests, advice about home and family was still eagerly sought; radio stations made the experts accessible to even the most distant listeners. Of course, early stations had to do a complicated balancing act as they tried to make both the male and female radio fans happy. While some programs pleased both genders—popular music, for one example—stations had to try to find speakers who could reach the woman listener, as well as speakers whom the men would find interesting. Complaints about the programs were thus inevitable—not everybody liked every show, and also not every speaker was good at performing for an invisible audience. The critics frequently mentioned speakers of both genders who sounded terrified by the microphone as well as those who were easy to listen to. And while men were writing to complain that women speakers talked about boring subjects, women, too, wrote to the radio editor, often complaining that their husband or male relatives obsessively tinkered with the radio set rather than just listening and enjoying the programs. However, in my reading of numerous early radio columns, I found very few men complained about the existence of women announcers; it was mainly some of the "women's programmes" that the men disliked.

In addition to putting women in very visible roles, radio was having one other interesting effect on the culture of the early 1920s: it contributed to changes in the English language. New words emerged, old words acquired new meanings, long words were shortened. First there was *wireless,* then *radio-telephone,* then *radiophone,* and finally, circa 1923, the word *radio* was commonly used. In similar fashion, *sending* would be replaced by *broadcasting;* radio station signals that first "came through the ether" were soon "heard on the air," and the British spelling of *programme,* which many U.S. publications still used in the early 1920s, would be replaced by the American spelling of *program.* The new radio vocabulary that was created had lasting effects on the English we speak today. The expression "stay tuned," (as well as to "tune in") for example, once referred to the procedure of correctly positioning the elaborate number of knobs and dials on early radios in order to receive the best possible signal; yet despite the fact that contemporary radios no longer have knobs or dials and most sets adjust for the frequency automatically, we still hear announcers advising us of an upcoming feature and asking us to "stay tuned," just as they did in radio's formative years.

Looking back at the first several years of commercial broadcasting in the United States, there seems to have been a general acceptance of women on the air. No matter what city a radio fan might visit, women like "Miss V.A.L. Jones" (whose first name, Virginia, was seldom revealed) of KSD in St. Louis, Judith Waller, program director of WMAQ in Chicago, Gwen Wagner of WPO in Memphis, and Helen Hann of WBAY (later WEAF) in New York were popular and respected announcers. And while there was some consternation from certain newspaper columnists about the changing roles of women in society, women radio broadcasters were not criticized, nor even mentioned as a problem (off-key singers, however, both male and female, were an ongoing complaint). It is thus somewhat surprising that over the next few years, critical acceptance of women announcers would gradually disappear, replaced by a heated debate about the proper place, if any, for women in radio. The discussion occupied the pages of many newspapers and magazines in the mid-1920s. And by the end of the decade, opportunities for women in broadcasting would be severely curtailed as the role of the radio woman was totally redefined.

Chapter 2

The Late 1920s:
A Time of Contradictions

Jessie Koewing was popular. Most people did not know her full name, but they knew they liked the woman known as "JEK." In those early years, few announcers were permitted to use their real name; as had been the custom in ham radio, from whence many of them came, the operator of the equipment used only initials or a brief nickname. Media historian Erik Barnouw has suggested that the station owners preferred initials only because they hoped to prevent the announcers from developing a big following and then asking for a big salary.[1] So, Bertha Brainard, when she first began announcing, was known as ABN: *A*nnouncer *B*rainard *N*ewark. Everyone at WJZ, male or female, was given a set of initials to use. There were exceptions—there is no evidence that Eleanor Poehler or Eunice Randall used initials—but the vast majority did, including even some of the owners themselves, who believed the performers were the ones deserving of attention, not the announcer. John Shepard III, who owned a large department store as well as stations WNAC in Boston and WEAN in Providence, sometimes enjoyed getting behind the microphone, but he always did so as "JS."[2] Yet despite the owners' belief that the talent was the main attraction, early announcers did in fact develop large numbers of fans, many who demanded to know the names of the people they were hearing. By mid-1925, the policy had ended and most announcers were allowed to go on the air using a name rather than just initials. But in 1922–23, Jessie Koewing was "JEK" more often than not. She was also a very talented violinist (part of an ensemble of entertainers who had performed for the troops overseas during the recently concluded World War); when she performed for station WOR, which was then in Newark, New Jersey, she was so well received that the owners asked her to come back. Soon, they hired her, and not long after, she became the program manager. It was a good choice: not only did her skill as an announcer win her large amounts of fan mail, but she quickly showed an ability to book famous guests. Among the biggest was the legendary magician Houdini, who came to WOR to speak out against mediums and fortune-tellers.[3] And despite the fact that women were generally expected to quit working after they married, when Jessie Koewing announced her engagement, she told the interviewer that she had no intention of giving up the radio career that she enjoyed so much.[4]

Jessie Koewing was by no means unique in 1923. Just about every station had at least one woman announcer, and women frequently served as accompanists to the vocalists who performed. Officials from the League of Women Voters, as well as leaders of women's civic clubs, continued giving educational talks. But some station owners, responding to letters from female listeners, decided they should devote more time to the housewives in the audience.

Expanding the Women's Shows

When commercial radio first began, stations had typically broadcast only for an hour or two, several nights a week. But by 1923, many stations were also broadcasting during daytime hours, and that meant reevaluating the programming. Although more women were in the workforce, many remained at home, raising their children and doing all the domestic chores that society still believed were "women's work." This was especially true in rural areas where farmers' wives wrote to their local stations, saying how isolated they often felt and how much they valued their new friends on the radio. In states like Nebraska, Kansas, and Iowa (which in June of 1922 already had ten stations, while some states only had one), radio was becoming an essential part of the day for numerous members of the farming community. One Nebraska station had begun to offer agriculture courses by radio, while another gave daily market information from the Omaha Grain Exchange.[5] These midwestern stations also offered church services, talks about the best way to raise baby chicks, and experts giving advice on the latest trends in farming; when time permitted, local performers entertained with band concerts or country and western music. But it became obvious that the homemaker who was a farmer's wife needed a very specific kind of program, a show that offered useful information and taught her something new, while still being entertaining.

By the mid-1920s, such programs were no longer just a good idea; they were a necessity. At KMA in Shenandoah, Iowa, women's programming began in late 1925 with a series called *Domestic Science Talks* given by LeOna Teget, Ormah Carmean, and June Case. KMA, which was known to its fans as "the Cornbelt Station in the Heart of the Nation," got so much favorable response about this type of program that owners Earl and Gertrude May decided to expand it. By 1927, Bernice Currier was broadcasting a *Home Hour* of household hints and recipes, and an additional show called the *Stitch and Chat Club* was hosted by Mrs. Jessie Young.[6] These programs were very folksy and casual by our modern standards. The hostess, usually a woman from the Shenandoah area, would talk about her kids, what she did today, what she was cooking for dinner, etc. If she played an instrument or sang (as Bernice did), she might pause for a musical interlude, but these shows were mostly about how a typical farmer's wife spent the day. The friendly women on the air answered questions that listeners sent in, and they also gave advice and helpful hints about running the home more efficiently.

Because these shows were very unsophisticated and often unscripted, I am sure critics must have disliked them; the women's shows that ran on NBC and CBS in the late 1920s were certainly done in a more structured and polished manner. But to the listeners, these local shows provided some much-needed companionship, and the fact that the announcers came from the community made the audience feel like part of an extended radio family. In January of 1925, *Radio World* magazine asked listeners to write in and discuss what they liked about radio. A number of farmers' wives responded, and this letter from Mrs. G.W. Fitch of Yankton, South Dakota, was typical. "Few people realize how lonely it is in winter on the wind swept prairies. . . . We live on a ranch 20 miles from town and 2 miles from a neighbor. . . . But since installing a radio set, the loneliness is gone and we seem to be living in the center of the world. We are no longer isolated. . . ."[7]

In the August 1926 issue of *Radio Broadcast*, the results of an extensive survey by the National Farm Radio Council showed that while most male farmers preferred to hear music on the radio, their wives had different preferences, especially in the East and Midwest: "41% [of farm women] like the household homemakers' programs the best . . . [because of] hints on economics and the new recipes." The farmers' wives also said they found educational programs very useful, with 37 percent of the women saying they often seek out such programs to learn something new.[8]

The "women's hour" was not a midwestern phenomenon. In New York City, Bertha Brainard, now assistant program manager at WJZ, had decided that urban housewives deserved a show aimed at their interests and concerns. WJZ (which had moved from Newark to New York) first started with a series of talks about interior decorating called *The Home Beautiful*. Miss Brainard also enlisted some editors of women's magazines to give talks on various subjects related to homemaking. And she brought in visiting nurses to discuss how to raise healthy children.[9] In our age of easy access to information, this doesn't sound so valuable, but in the early 1920s, a time when many homes still lacked a telephone and movies were still silent, immigrant women, poor women, and women with large families came to rely on radio; the medium's ability to offer free advice from so many experts was greatly appreciated. As Golda M. Goldman, a freelance writer for several radio magazines, explained, "At ten o'clock in the morning, mother sits down, with a basket of [clothes to be mended] . . . and enjoys [her own] special lecture course in home economics. And let it be understood that this has come to be one of the most important features in [her] life . . . [S]uddenly, in a literally magic fashion, from out of the air [comes] a friend who [doesn't] interfere but who help[s] to reinvest the prosaic drudgery of the household tasks with . . . glamour, who [gives] variety and [brings] fresh ideas into the little world of home."[10] By 1924, WJZ's female audience could hear a daily broadcast from Mrs. Julian Heath, founder and president of the National Housewives League and editor of *Housewives Magazine*. Mrs. Heath shared her expertise in how to save money, how to live on a budget, how to plan interesting meals, and other topics related to the running of a typical home. Speaking on radio had a very positive effect on Mrs. Heath's career. She had been a clubwoman for many years and had founded the National Housewives League in 1911. But scandal marred the organization: Mrs. Heath had claimed her group was neutral and consumer oriented, but it turned out there were serious conflicts of interest regarding her enthusiastic endorsements of food manufacturers who, coincidentally she claimed, placed big advertisements in league publications. By 1919, revelations of such cozy relationships cast doubt on the league's credibility and rendered it nearly defunct.[11] But thanks to her appearances on WJZ, Mrs. Heath, and the Housewives League, got a second chance. By 1925, she was once again writing magazine articles and was frequently referred to as an expert on home economics.[12]

Another popular woman heard on WJZ was Mrs. Sarah F. Hitchcock, from the staff of *Women's Wear Daily*. Along with other experts, Mrs. Hitchcock discussed the latest fashion news, from what the designers in Paris were showing, to what society people were seen wearing at the theater, to fashion mistakes that women should avoid. While only a few women could afford the latest fashions from Paris, listeners undoubtedly enjoyed these programs for the opportunity to vicariously experience the lifestyles and activities of the rich and famous. And while a number of cartoonists took women to task for their interest in clothing, demographic studies showed some interesting new buying patterns. With more women working, there was more disposable income, some of which was being spent on clothes. Statistics showed the average woman in the early 1920s spent only about 5 to 6 percent of total income on wearing apparel, but there were some women who were spending much more. It was not the stereotypic wealthy clubwomen, or the debutantes; rather, as a survey by R.H. Macy discovered, "the young business woman spends more on her clothes than her married sister, because part of her stock in trade is a smart, trim, neat appearance."[13]

Women and Radio Sets

In addition to women making their presence felt as consumers of clothing, they were also having an effect on the radio manufacturers. As discussed earlier, radio fans (most of whom were men) originally built their own sets. There were women who built sets, too, as the newspapers and magazines liked to point out, but the vast majority of women, and probably quite a few men, had no idea how to make sense of the electronics, the tubes, the dials, and all the diagrams. Even though sets could be purchased, women let stores know these sets were still too complicated and difficult to operate, and they were too cumbersome to put in the typical living room. Gradually, the message got through, and some manufacturers began to offer sets that looked more like a nice piece of furniture. But of greater importance was that these new receivers could be operated without taking a course in engineering. Said one manufacturer in late 1925, "The lady of the house exercises a dominant influence on the purchase of radio receivers, as well she should. Her choice is a set that will tune in stations by turning only one dial."[14]

By 1927, Bertha Brainard, now an executive with NBC, stated that, "I believe women were largely responsible for the improvements in receiving apparatus because I know that . . . women . . . purchase 75% of the total merchandise sold at retail. Naturally, they have demanded receivers of good appearance which were simple to operate."[15] And so it was that the aesthetics of radio sets became an important factor, as demand increased for receivers that looked good, sounded good, and did not have too many dials or wires to contend with. Also, women had become involved in the manufacturing process: the Atwater Kent company placed magazine ads in 1928 showing industrious-looking women seated at their benches, assembling radio sets. The text noted that the coils for the receivers were wound by this all-female workforce because their "sharper eyes, nimbler fingers, and quicker reflexes" ensured the accuracy and precision such tasks required.

With a growing number of women listening to radio each day, most stations had begun to create programming for them. But depending on the city and the program director, the women's show could be a traditional hour of chat and recipes, or it could be somewhat more varied. At WHT in Chicago, for example, the women's show included what one might expect, except there were several unique elements: advice for women with careers and advice to husbands on how to help around the home.[16] Other women's shows featured musical guests or offered segments on travel. What determined the direction of the show was usually the women who hosted it. The majority of the hostesses had not been in radio before; rather, they had been teachers of home economics, writers for women's magazines, or presidents of important women's clubs, so their shows revolved around their own areas of expertise. A few women had come from advertising agencies or public relations firms, and it reflected in the kinds of shows they produced. Bertha Mitchell (the first "Jean Sargent" at WNAC in Boston), who was working for WHT in late 1925, was one of the few women's show hosts with prior radio experience, but she also had a strong background in business and advertising.[17] By the late 1920s, many stations had a new position called women's show director (or director of women's programming); this woman was responsible for booking the guests and finding out what subjects the audience wanted to know about. Some directors also tested the recipes and household hints before sharing them with the listeners.

The Rise of Sponsorship

Most male station owners undoubtedly thought the women's shows were boring, but something new was happening in radio in the mid-1920s, and it involved sponsorship, which the owners did not find boring at all. Since radio's earliest days, how to pay for the programs had been an ongoing problem. The Department of Commerce, led by Herbert Hoover, frowned on "direct advertising" (what we would call commercials), yet the owners were having increasing difficulty finding good talent that was willing to perform for free. Sponsorship could provide a way to pay the musicians and allow the station to make some money from the broadcasts. As it became more obvious to advertisers that radio was a viable medium with a large number of women listeners, it was only a matter of time before commercials would find their way into the broadcast day. At first, advertisers tended to sponsor the performers themselves, rather than buying individual minutes of advertising time. Thus, the Cliquot Club Eskimos did not come from the frozen North: led by Harry Reser (who was born in Ohio), they were New York–based musicians sponsored by a soft drink company. The sponsorship agreement meant the group was expected to dress in pseudo-Eskimo costumes and make appearances to promote Cliquot Club beverages. On the air, such groups sang their sponsor's jingle and did their commercials. The trend toward creating an identity for sponsored musicians began even be-

fore there were national networks. Among the best-known examples were
Jones and Hare, the "Happiness Boys," whose sponsor was a candy company. Much later, when their sponsor changed, so did their name—they became the "Interwoven Pair," working for a company that manufactured socks.
By the time the two major networks emerged (NBC in November of 1926
and CBS in September of 1927), all sorts of companies, selling everything
from toothpaste to shampoo to groceries, had hired performers as their radio
spokespeople. And so it was that the women's shows began to find many
advertisers eager to link up with them. In the case of the women's shows,
however, the sponsorship agreements were not with musicians, but with
homemaking experts, radio cooks, and story ladies. And then, there was the
sponsorship of a well-known woman who had never even existed.

In 1921, the icon of the ideal homemaker, "Betty Crocker," first appeared.
The idea of having a mythical person to answer reader mail was already
used by newspapers: Hearst's *New York American* invented "Miss Margery
Rex" for that job, and also offered a syndicated column of household hints,
which answered reader queries in the name of "Prudence Penny."[18] Newspapers frequently used a woman's name for answering mail or giving homemaking advice, undoubtedly because of the popular belief that women were
more polite and conciliatory than men, and thus more suited to soothing an
upset reader or helping to solve a problem. In fact, readers seemed convinced that Margery and Prudence were real people, and the newspapers
were perfectly happy to contribute to that impression. In one advertisement
promoting the homemaker column, the copy read in part, "Come to Prudence Penny with confidence! Your letter [is] not departmentalized, rubber-
stamped, or form-letter-answered. If you have never received a letter from
Prudence Penny, you have a sweet experience before you!"[19] Some of the
women who worked in the "Margery Rex" or "Prudence Penny" departments went on to jobs in radio, where, ironically, they were still known by
"house names." (When the announcers were finally allowed to use names
instead of initials, many followed the custom of the movies and invented a
name to protect their privacy and create the character they wanted their
audience to remember. In Boston, for example, WNAC's radio homemaker
was also station owner John Shepard III's secretary. When WNAC's first
women's show went on the air, Shepard assigned its hostess the radio name
"Jean Sargent"; in real life, the woman behind that name was the previously
mentioned Bertha Mitchell. She left WNAC in 1925 for a better-paying job,
but "Jean Sargent" lived on, because the next woman to do the women's
show was still known as "Jean Sargent," as was the one who came after her.

On competitor WEEI, Genevieve Sherlock, the station's radio homemaker,
took the name "Caroline Cabot," and it, too, never changed for as long as

the show was on the air. But WEEI, owned by the Edison Electric Illuminating Company, did something more to promote consumerism: the management put a modern, all-electric kitchen in the same building where their radio station was located. Visitors could watch the radio homemakers at work in the "Friendly Kitchen," and, of course, if they were interested in buying some of the new electric appliances, that could easily be arranged.

As for Betty Crocker, the representation of the perfect homemaker was created by the Washburn-Crosby Company of Minneapolis; it had a successful flour milling business and was seeking ways to reach the new woman consumer of the early 1920s. When Washburn-Crosby merged with General Mills in the late 1920s, the character of Betty Crocker had long been used as a house name for answering customer inquiries. Washburn-Crosby felt the character had great advertising possibilities, and a woman executive with the company, Marjorie Child Husted, hired one of the most respected illustrators, a woman who had successfully designed numerous magazine covers, Neysa McMein, to give Betty Crocker a visual image for use in print advertisements. That image would later get a voice when the Washburn-Crosby radio station, WCCO in Minneapolis, put a woman on the air to play the role of Betty Crocker and do a women's show.

After the merger of Washburn-Crosby and General Mills, the Betty Crocker show was broadcast over CBS, making the mythical lady of the kitchen famous all over the United States, and enabling her to teach her audience new recipes, which, of course, utilized General Mills's fine assortment of products. No doubt the listeners thought that Betty was just a nice lady giving helpful advice, as opposed to a paid pitchwoman extolling the virtues of the company that sponsored her. Betty even sponsored baking contests, and in 1925–26, the show began offering on-air courses as part of a Radio Cooking School. Those who completed the course even received a certificate.[20]

It is ironic that Betty Crocker, the symbol of perfect feminine domesticity, was the legacy of two businesswomen who had achieved their success in male-dominated fields, Marjorie Husted and Neysa McMein. As historian Christine Lunardini observes, "[Betty Crocker's] appearance changed over the decades . . . but [it] was always carefully designed to reinforce the impression that a woman could be stylish and a homemaker, up-to-date and yet fulfilled in her traditional role. She reflected . . . the ambivalence many American women felt toward their dual role in society, their desire to be fresh and independent and their duty to home and family."[21]

Both Michele Hilmes and Susan Smulyan have pointed out how radio executives joined up with advertisers, and how this relationship served to reinforce and encourage women's traditional role as homemaker (or, if the woman worked, she was at least encouraged to be a good consumer). Radio was able to carve out a niche as an excellent way for companies to reach the female listener and persuade her to spend money. Wrote Professor Hilmes, "[A]s the commercial possibilities of radio came to be realized in the mid- to late 1920s, the economic role of women as the primary purchasing agents for the family increased women's appeal as audience members. Advertising studies confirmed that 85% of household purchases were made by women, making them the obvious target for radio's increasingly commercialized address."[22]

As a result, sponsors began to establish very close ties with their chosen radio homemaker; as part of the contractual agreement, she was expected to give glowing testimonials about the sponsor's products at various points during the show. Ida Bailey Allen, for example, was already well known: she had written homemaking columns that were syndicated in a number of newspapers, authored several popular cookbooks, and had been on the air since the early 1920s, starting in St. Louis. When the networks came along, she became the voice of the National Radio Homemakers Club on CBS in the fall of 1928. Her show did so well that it was soon expanded to two hours; she also put out a weekly newsletter. Those who subscribed not only received columns that Mrs. Allen and guests from her show had written, but they also received some of the recipes from the show. And, of course, Mrs. Allen recommended that women use only Crisco when shortening was needed, and Pillsbury flour was enthusiastically suggested, too.

Today, in our more cynical and media-wise era, we would see these mentions as plugs, but it is quite likely that back then, given how new radio was, people took the speaker at her word and believed she had their best interest at heart. The testimonials from such credible figures as Ida Bailey Allen and other network experts helped boost sales for the sponsors and enabled these programs to remain on the air. It was a symbiotic relationship that worked. And while even back then there were critics who accused advertisers of manipulating the audience and accused radio of selling out to those advertisers,[23] there was a benefit that should not be overlooked: for the first time, women with skills in cooking and sewing and running a household were being rewarded with large salaries for sharing their expertise with radio listeners. While in real life, a housewife did not get paid for all her hard work, the radio homemaker was not only paid well, but she had the opportunity to meet interesting people, sample free products, and even become a celebrity. And where radio singers and actresses were often young and attractive, some of the most respected radio homemakers were older women with degrees in home economics who were hired not for their looks, but for their credibility and their familiarity with the domestic arts.

As the networks became more powerful, they began to require a more professional-sounding program that met the standards the sponsors demanded; some of the local radio homemakers were eclipsed by the women chosen by the networks and the sponsors. However, locally produced women's shows did not go away, and for women in many markets, these shows became a haven, since by the late 1920s, many stations were no longer hiring women as announcers or program directors. The end result, as we will see, is that by the 1930s, women on radio were mainly singers, studio hostesses, or radio homemakers.

Women's New Roles in Society

While the rise of networks meant that a particular women's hour could be heard nationally, there was much more happening in the lives of women than just exchanging new recipes. As mentioned before, the 1920s was a decade of great social change, with more women entering college or beginning to work for pay. And while it is true that the majority of women gravitated toward jobs that we today would consider gender-stereotyped (working as secretaries, switchboard operators, nurses, teachers, maids), nearly every day, newspapers would publish yet another column about a woman who was succeeding in an occupation previously closed to females. There was Lizzie Murphy, one of the first women baseball players, who even played on several men's professional teams in the early to mid-1920s.[24] Nina Belle Hurst was a woman umpire in Los Angeles around the same time,[25] as was Mrs. Deana Ernest in Toledo, Ohio.[26] Mildred Elizabeth Trask was not a farmer's wife—she was a farmer who ran her parents' sixty-acre farm and was planning a business career.[27] There was Marie Raith, a civil engineer from New York, whose hobby was playing amateur hockey,[28] and inventor and radio engineer Gail Savage was written up in newspapers and magazines such as *Radio News.*[29] There were women judges, police officers, astronomers, biologists, telegraphers, a bank vice president, a physicist, and several women who worked in construction. The presence of women could even be seen in the field of religion, where the controversial evangelist Aimee Semple McPherson put her own radio station, KFSG, on the air in Los Angeles.[30] But while print journalists found good story ideas in the unusual occupations of the "new woman," newspapers also demonstrated that ambivalence Dr. Lunardini referred to—it was not uncommon for the article about a woman doctor or inventor to be juxtaposed with an article about a woman who loved decorating her home and derived her greatest joy from baking for her family. For every story about a modern career-oriented woman (most of whom were still called "girls" or "gals" in the language of that time), there was a column that expressed concern that the new woman had too much freedom and lacked the proper values.[31]

One example of the uncertainty society felt about the way a woman ought to behave was in the area of athletics. Not that long ago, the common wisdom was that women were too delicate for athletic pursuits. But by the 1920s, many young women, especially those in college, had taken an interest in sports. Some sociologists and psychologists felt this was quite healthy, a way for women to get exercise. But there were also those who regarded women's athletics as "mannish," and the print media became the battleground for various columns either praising or condemning women's sports. While I have not seen many studies on this, common sense says that radio had a hand in making sports more accessible to women—especially men's professional sports. As the radio craze swept America in the early to mid-1920s, many of the first live broadcasts were of sporting events such as the World Series or college football. It is certainly possible that women who might never have attended a baseball game now heard the play-by-play when a husband, boyfriend, or brother turned on the radio to listen to the big game. Hearing sports on the radio may well have encouraged women to learn more about the subject, even if the only reason at first was to be polite to the males in the family. Also a likely scenario is that sporting events were a part of college social life; if a girl had a boyfriend who was on a team, she had even more reason to follow that team and learn something about that sport.

While most sports fans back then probably were men, some women had begun attending the games, and they even became loyal fans. It was still relatively new for women to go to places perceived by society as for men only, such as boxing matches, but slowly, more and more areas of the public sphere were being opened to women, including ballparks and sports arenas. And even though there were no professional women's basketball or soccer teams back then, there were some sports in which women took part: competitive tennis, swimming, golf, and track were popular at most of the women's colleges. By the 1920s, there were even a few star athletes who were female. Popular women's tennis champion Helen Wills, later Helen Wills Moody, won her first U.S. tournament in 1923 and went on to win eight Wimbledon singles titles during the 1920s and into the 1930s. And in the mid-1920s, swimmer Gertrude Ederle captured the public's attention with her efforts to swim the English Channel.

Yet, despite their many fans, I doubt that Ederle or Wills were as well known as Babe Ruth or some of the other famous male athletes. Men's sports garnered most of the attention in newspaper columns and radio broadcasts; it was boys, rather than girls, who were expected to try out for the school team and who were regarded as heroes if they helped that team win. And although there were certainly new freedoms for women in the 1920s, there was ambivalent advice about taking advantage of those freedoms, especially where athleticism was concerned. A girl who liked sports too much was warned not to be a tomboy. Little girls who tried to play sports with the boys were usually treated with mild amusement, since most of them weren't able to hit homeruns or catch a long pass. But as girls grew older, a desire to play sports with the boys would certainly have been stigmatized; most girls did not fight it—they simply accepted that they weren't good enough, and with no organized women's teams to help them improve, they gave up. To complicate matters for the girl who wanted to participate in sports, the culture still held the belief that menstruation rendered women unable (or unfit) for athletic activity, and numerous magazine articles of the day warned against too much strenuous exercise.

Despite this, in the ubiquitous early 1920s newspaper articles about women in unusual occupations, one of the most frequently mentioned scenarios was a young girl who persisted in her attempt to break into an all-boys' sport or join a boys' team (since few if any girls' teams existed). Long before Little League finally allowed girls to play baseball, there were a few boys' teams that did permit an occasional girl to join them, but only if she had exceptional skill, as Lizzie Murphy was said to possess.[32]

Women, Politics, and Radio

It was not only sports that was being debated in the mid-1920s. Now that women had the vote, the question was whether they would fundamentally change American politics. The conventional wisdom of the time was that women were somehow more polite, compassionate, and refined;[33] sociologists wondered if they would make the political landscape kinder and gentler. The early 1920s was the first time when political candidates and their spokespeople could be heard on the radio, rather than just read about in newspapers; suddenly the quality of a candidate's voice became important, as did the ability to express ideas in a credible and compelling way. Modern audiences are often bored by political talks, but in the early 1920s, such talks were a novelty, and the listeners seemed eager to hear what the candidates had to say. Meanwhile, the League of Women Voters served as a resource for clarifying the issues. Led by Carrie Chapman Catt, the League provided guest speakers for radio, as well as information about all the candidates. It was something very new to include women in political discourse, and by doing it in such a public way (radio stations in the 1920s could be heard for hundreds of miles), Catt and others hoped to dispel the stereotype that women could not understand politics. Members of other women's organizations, such as the League of American Pen Women, also saw radio as an excellent way to demonstrate that many women kept up with current events and could speak knowledgeably about them. The Pen Women, whose membership included some of the best-known female authors and poets, made speakers available to a number of stations in major cities like New York, Washington, and Chicago.

When the results of the first elections since suffrage were tallied, the critics immediately weighed in with their views about what changes the "women's vote" had wrought. Founder of the National Women's Party Alice Paul was bitterly disappointed by early results, which showed that no women were elected to Congress in 1922 (one woman, Rebecca Felton of Georgia, had been appointed to the Senate in October of 1922 to complete the term of a senator who had died; she had only served for one day). Alice Paul was especially upset that women did not support women candidates, and she felt this lack of solidarity had hurt the women running for office.[34] However, Minnie Fisher Cunningham of the League of Women Voters responded that electing women candidates would take time, and the greater the number of qualified women candidates, the sooner prejudices against women in politics would be overcome.[35]

A New York women's political magazine, *The Woman Citizen*, assessed what had occurred in the most recent elections and decided the results so far were mixed. Having surveyed officials in all the chapters of the League of Women Voters, the author concluded that even though it was still an uphill battle to get women elected to national office, on the local level, women had been elected in increasing numbers. Eighty women in thirty-one states now held an elected office: these included some state senators, county commissioners, mayors, judges, and state superintendents of education. Also, the support of women's clubs had influenced passage of certain legislation to protect children and to allow married women to be independent citizens whose legal and political rights were not controlled by their husband. The article's conclusion was that women had gotten off to a fairly good start since achieving the vote.[36] But a journalist and historian of that time, Frederick Lewis Allen, suggested that while women had battled long and hard to achieve the right to vote, once that right had been won, many women seemed to decide that politics was not worth the effort after all; they found that it was "a sordid and futile business," and to the disappointment of the league and many other civic groups, they decided not to get involved with it, preferring instead to concentrate on matters that they felt more directly affected their lives.[37] Mrs. Emily Newell Blair disputed this viewpoint, however. Writing in *Harper's* magazine in 1925, she reminded readers that there was no such thing as "the women's vote," since women did not stick together any more than men did when it came to the issues. "The early suffragists were rationalists. They knew that women would vote their own interests, and that women were as easily and as foolishly led as men were."[38]

The common wisdom had been that women would support any and every piece of social welfare legislation, but they did not. Certain causes appealed to them, while others failed to attract their loyalty. As for the warnings by foes of women's suffrage that women would become corrupted by the harshness and unfairness of politics, this, too, turned out to be a myth. One woman governor (Miriam "Ma" Ferguson of Texas) did become enmeshed in scandal and controversy,[39] but most women who ran for office and got elected did not seem any the worse for the experience; they did their jobs and performed their duties professionally.

As women began to achieve in politics, they were asked to speak on the radio about those achievements. It certainly must have been a new experience for men to hear a woman mayor or legislator, and undoubtedly the women themselves were not accustomed to speaking on the air, but it would not be long before radio became an integral part of campaigning. As early as February 1921, a woman candidate made use of the airwaves: Alice M. Robertson, who had just been elected to Congress from the state of Oklahoma, gave a talk over KDKA in Pittsburgh; she was speaking at a banquet of the Pittsburgh Press Club. (The event took place at the William Penn Hotel and was carried by a special remote pickup, a relatively new technique that enabled guests to broadcast from a location other than a radio studio.) As they became more accustomed to broadcasting, some women politicians did more than just give speeches. A few even seemed to have fun being on the air. When Miss Elizabeth Ries, the recently elected mayor of Shakopee, Minnesota, spoke over WCCO in Minneapolis in early 1926, she served as a sort of mistress of ceremonies, bringing with her an orchestra of local musicians called the Shakopee Serenaders and a vocal group of three male singers known as The Lady Mayor's Trio.[40]

On the other hand, some women found that Frederick Allen was right: politics could indeed be a sordid business, and radio only served to amplify it. In Boston in the late 1920s, one member of the school committee was a lawyer and feminist named Jennie Loitman Barron. She was happily married and had three children; she also seems to have had a very supportive husband. One night, Mrs. Barron gave a speech on local radio station WNAC, after which she became the object of an unexpected (and quite nasty) political attack from her more experienced male opponent. While intense debate is nothing new in politics, it must have been a shock for a 1929 audience to hear a woman being subjected to the kind of brutal political discourse that had previously occurred only among male candidates.[41]

Women and Social Behavior

How the new woman should behave and what she should or should not do was provoking an often contentious debate. Parents were puzzled by the rebelliousness of their daughters (and their sons, too, since young men were also seeking some of the new freedoms). It seemed that everything the older generation was accustomed to, the younger generation rejected. The new dance crazes, the fads, the fashions seemed scandalous and vulgar to older people. And worse yet, radio stations had begun playing this dance music, instead of music that was sedate and traditional. With such a visible generation gap and so much social change, it was the perfect opportunity for somebody to come along and offer a guide for how to behave correctly in any situation. Emily Post, capitalizing on the uncertainty of the times, first wrote her famous book of etiquette in 1922, and then updated it on a regular basis. She also made guest appearances on radio, becoming known as the ultimate authority on good manners.

But not everybody could find a solution for social change by consulting a book of etiquette. Society was still very old-fashioned about certain customs, and young, college-educated adults found some of these traditions outmoded. A few newly married businesswomen began waging a legal battle to be allowed to keep their maiden name if they chose to, only to find that the courts and the clergy would not cooperate. In 1922, Ruth Hale, wife of journalist Heywood Broun, was denied a passport unless she took her husband's last name, which she refused to do.[42] In 1923, author and publicist Doris Fleischman, wife of Edward L. Bernays, finally became the first married woman in America to obtain a passport in her maiden name, but not many of the women who tried to keep their own name had much success. Other customs were also being challenged, such as the wedding vow that made a woman say she would love, honor, and *obey* her husband (who had only to vow he would love, honor, and *cherish* his wife). The Episcopal church had decided in 1919 to remove the word *obey*, but by the end of 1922, nothing had changed and the controversy between the church's traditionalists and its modernists showed no sign of abating.[43]

As some women were trying to do away with certain traditions, a new one was being created—the beauty pageant. It was nothing new for men to judge women by their physical appearance, but now a woman could compete with other women and win prizes just for being considered the most beautiful. In September of 1921, the precursor to the Miss America Pageant had first taken place, scandalizing some of the crowd by allowing the contestants to show their bare knees and putting them in bathing suits that hugged their skin.[44] With each subsequent year, young women in bathing suits competed for the title and the fame that went with it. And, as if to demonstrate that radio had become an essential part of the modern young woman's life, the 1925 Miss America, Miss California Fay Lamphier, was proudly photographed wearing headphones, which were still needed to listen to radio back then. She remarked that she loved to tune in distant stations whenever she got the chance.[45] A beauty queen who operated a radio was just one more odd juxtaposition, in a decade that had many.

In 1925, the first Radio World's Fair crowned Rena Jane Frew "Miss Radio," not for wearing a bathing suit, but for being "the most enthusiastic female radio fan" and for receiving the most distant stations on her radio set.[46] Frew, a teacher, had been a ham radio operator since her high school days.[47] But although there were plenty of avid female radio fans, by the late 1920s, the fair's organizers had changed the concept of "Miss Radio" entirely; the crown now belonged to a beauty queen or a female celebrity.

Some women wanted their own name and their own career; other women just wanted to be pretty and adored because of it. The traditional images of women as passive objects of beauty, dignity, and grace were being challenged by images of the new woman, the so-called flapper, who wore bobbed hair, danced to jazz music, and preferred practical clothing instead of long skirts. She used vulgar language, and she even smoked cigarettes. In a time when the health hazards of smoking were not widely known, smoking was one more male privilege, and many wanted to do it just to show they were equal. The debate that ensued even reached popular music, where the vaudeville team of Gallagher and Shean had a novelty hit song in 1922 in which they lamented several things they found scandalous about the modern woman, including her demand for the right to smoke in public.

Public Debate About the "New Woman" Continues

There was also a continuing debate about whether mothers who worked outside the home were harmful to their children. This was one of the most popular topics in newspapers and magazines of the early 1920s, with many male social workers and psychologists saying wives should not work,[48] while a number of clubwomen and professional women defended married women working at least part time. In January of 1925, *Literary Digest* announced that the Bureau of Vocational Information was doing a study, the purpose of which was to determine how best a wife could combine a career with raising children. The bureau had already gathered considerable anecdotal evidence that educated women who continued working after marriage gained considerable satisfaction from work, and they did not want to abandon their career entirely when children came along.[49] The reevaluation of a married woman's role had been ongoing since the turn of the century. In fact, whether a woman should go to college or have a career had been discussed for several decades as well. But something was different now: what would previously have been a conversation held privately among women friends at home or perhaps at a club meeting was suddenly out in the open, discussed on the radio for anyone to hear. It was fortuitous for women's show hosts that their new programs were taking place at a time of so much to talk about; this was probably the first era in American history when opinions about the treatment of women or analysis of their role in society occupied such a public forum, and when even people who could not read were able to be part of the discussion.

It is difficult to ascertain what the average listener thought about hearing so many educated women on the air, since few surveys of listener attitudes would be taken until 1930, when the Crossley ratings began. But we may assume that for many male listeners, the concept of a woman talking politics or expressing opinions on current events was somewhat disconcerting. Change often creates discomfort, as we can see from the numerous articles that spoke out against women cutting their hair or wearing shorter skirts or attending college.[50] And yet, it would have been difficult to avoid women speakers, even if listeners wanted to do so. Since radio's earliest days, most stations welcomed anyone, male or female, who would volunteer to speak knowl-edgeably about a subject in which they had expertise. Some colleges were sending professors to the local station to offer lectures in a variety of subjects, from agriculture to zoology. The majority of these professors were men, but in perusing the programming schedules of stations in 1922–25, the era when volunteers were still being actively sought, I noticed that about 10 to 15 per-cent of the lectures were by women. Because most women who went to col-lege in the 1920s majored in music or theater or home economics, subjects they were encouraged to study (since these were considered useful for women to learn), it is not surprising that a large number of the radio talks by women involved these subjects. However, there were also some women whose exper-tise was in topics other than homemaking. In addition to speakers from the League of Women Voters or the Pen Women, individual authors and poets spoke or read from their latest works. Amy Lowell, a great fan of radio, read her poetry on the air in Boston as early as 1922.[51] Press agent to the stars Nellie Revell spoke from several New York stations, telling stories about the celebrities she knew. Singer, recording artist, and for a brief time program director Vaughn DeLeath talked about what went on behind the scenes in the music industry; and Grace Hazen of the Bureau of Standards Radio Labora-tory in Washington, D.C., discussed principles of engineering and how radio signals worked, just to give a few examples.

Hearing such a diverse group of female speakers must have somewhat dispelled the myth that women cared only about cooking and fashion. Then, later in the decade, when flying airplanes across the ocean became a national obsession, and Charles Lindbergh's long-distance flight made him a national hero, some of the women flyers were also guests on radio. This included everybody's favorite, Amelia Earhart, who even spoke via a network hookup, giving fans from all over the country the chance to hear her. While today we take celebrities for granted, the listeners of the 1920s, especially those in out-of-the-way places, must have been thrilled to turn on the radio and hear somebody as famous as Amelia. On the other hand, it should be noted that some of the women flyers felt as ambivalent about how to present themselves as certain women of the 1980s and 1990s did when they espoused a strong belief in equality for women yet were quick to point out, "but I'm not a feminist." Ruth Elder, whose exploits as an "aviatrix" (as women flyers were called) later led to roles in Hollywood, captivated the public with her flights in her specially built plane, the *American Girl*. Yet, in Paris, she told United Press International that she could not wait to discard her flying uniform (which the newspapers described as "mannish") and change into something more feminine. "I'm sick and tired of breeches, you know. They call me [a] Tomboy, but I'm a woman after all." She told reporters she was eager to do some shopping, and when she returned to the United States, she would mull over the movie offers, once she consulted with her husband.[52]

Negative Comments About Women Announcers

But despite all the speeches by famous women (radio guest speakers of the mid- to late 1920s included foreign dignitaries, internationally known opera singers, and a number of women in business), despite all the women who still served as announcers and program directors, and despite even the women who did traditional homemaking shows, there was a segment of the population that was not persuaded that women belonged on the air. Whereas in the early days of radio, women had by and large escaped critical comment, now suddenly, there was a new debate, concerning whether women sounded good as speakers and announcers. This discussion heated up around 1924, which was the year most major cities finally had their own professionally run stations.

Until late 1923, radio was still a novelty in many areas of the United States, so the critics did not say much about either the male or the female air talent. Some columnists had been ham radio operators themselves and were big fans of broadcasting; they seemed delighted that their town had a station, and they hesitated to say anything bad about it. But as time passed and certain stations began to sound noticeably better than others, the critics became much more willing to offer opinions. With regard to women, those opinions were mixed. Some critics commented on how stiff and forced most women speakers were. But in fairness, these same critics also took some men speakers to task. One critic, John Wallace of *Radio Broadcast*, said that Thomas Edison had given the worst radio speech Wallace had ever heard. In other columns, Wallace regularly pointed out that certain male announcers were repetitious, inarticulate, and prone to using too many clichés.[53]

The women's hour was critiqued in *Radio Broadcast*, too, and the conclusion was not especially positive. But the issue was not whether women should be on the air—rather, what bothered the columnist was that these shows all sounded very similar. "Almost without exception, American broadcasting stations, when they have a program for women, have limited it to the obvious domestic things. No broadcaster has had the courage . . . to arrange a program to appeal to the intelligence of women. One wonders whether this failure is due to a belief that it would be useless to make the attempt, or because the program designers simply fail to appreciate the necessity."[54]

Perhaps the most frequently quoted, and among the first of the critical columns against the woman as announcer, was a discussion veteran journalist Jennie Irene Mix for *Radio Broadcast* in September 1924. While Miss Mix was absolutely in favor of women announcers, some of the people she interviewed were not. One notable program manager who was rather vehement in his disapproval of women announcers was Bertha Brainard's boss, Charles Popenoe of WJZ. Popenoe stated that women lacked the skill to be announcers, and if it were not for Bertha's reputation as a credible theater critic, he would have taken her off the air, too.[55] I can only imagine how Miss Brainard must have felt when she read these comments; it is a tribute to her own sense of dignity that she never responded to Mr. Popenoe's remarks. All of her published comments about him, and about those with whom she worked at WJZ, were always tactful. She even attributed some of her professional success to him, since she said in an interview with Doris Fleischman, it was Mr. Popenoe who had promoted her to manager of WJZ.[56] Bertha Brainard always seemed to look on the positive side whenever she was quoted. In a 1927 interview, for example, she said that, "the vast majority of men with whom I am in business contact during the course of a year think nothing of the fact that I am a woman." Further, she encouraged women to explore the technical and engineering end of broadcasting, and she expressed the belief that a woman "can fill practically any position [in radio], providing she is willing to concentrate her energies upon it and do the job exactly as a man would."[57]

But Miss Brainard's optimism was not shared by the men Jennie Irene Mix interviewed for her *Radio Broadcast* article; most did not speak any more favorably about women on the air than Charles Popenoe did. Typical of their comments was what W.W. Mr. Rogers of Westinghouse (parent company of pioneer stations KDKA and WBZ) said when he remarked that if it were left up to him, he would never allow women to give a radio lecture: "[F]ew women have voices with distinct personality . . . their voices are flat or they are shrill, and they are usually pitched far too high to be modulated correctly . . . most women before the microphone [are lacking] . . . a sense of humor . . . women who are heard by radio seem unable to let themselves go."[58]

Comments such as these incensed Miss Mix, who observed that while indeed some women were difficult to listen to, many of the men she heard on the air used an artificially "booming, aggressive tone" of voice; in their efforts to project, they spoke only in a loud monotone. Further, she felt that some men on the air did not articulate clearly and, worst of all, they mumbled. Said Miss Mix in conclusion, "if a woman knows her business when she speaks before the microphone, she can create a most favorable impression."[59] And as for the remark Mr. Rogers had made about women announcers lacking a sense of humor, in June of 1926, *Radio Broadcast*'s John Wallace accused male announcers and radio comedians of the same thing. He said that radio humor seldom came across well, and that most of the men who tried to be funny failed to create a good rapport with the listening audience.[60]

Charles Popenoe's Criticism of Women Announcers

An interesting thing to consider about the sudden criticism of women on the air was that one person, the previously mentioned Charles Popenoe of WJZ, seemed to be behind most of it. While he may indeed have helped Bertha Brainard (who began as his assistant) to move into a management position, Mr. Popenoe was especially outspoken on the subject of women who thought they could be announcers. Because he was an executive with a major New York radio station, and New York was where most of the magazines were published, his quotes frequently appeared in national publications. This was unfortunate, because his bias against women on the air received a disproportionate amount of media attention.

The 1926 WJZ survey that purported to show that, overwhelmingly, listeners preferred male announcers and disliked women announcers is worth a closer look. The results of this survey would often be cited later on by male columnists trying to explain why women announcers were no longer heard as much. But the survey was actually quite unscientific. The sample was approximately 10,000 listeners who had written to WJZ already. They received questionnaires, and about 4,000 of these listeners responded.[61]

Listeners who write to radio stations and who regard radio as a major part of their lives are called "actives." These active listeners pay much more attention to radio than the average person, letting announcers know when a mistake was made, writing or calling to complain about the station's programming, and having very definite ideas about how radio ought to sound. Actives are quick to react and very vocal about what they like. And as any contemporary announcer or market researcher knows, actives make up only about 5 to 7 percent of the typical radio audience, but because they write or call so much, it seems as if their numbers are much greater.

In 1926, long before scientific radio ratings would be taken, concepts like "random sample" or "active listeners" probably were not commonly discussed at radio stations. It may not have occurred to Mr. Popenoe that, according to surveys done by radio manufacturers in several cities during 1925, the typical owner of a radio set was a male, and the twenty-one to thirty-year-old male seemed especially devoted to radio. In fact, in Seattle, one survey showed that 71 percent of those who chose the programming and operated the radio set were men.[62] That being the case, it is likely that mostly men, and mostly "actives," responded to the WJZ survey; it is doubtful that they liked the women's hour or the radio homemakers. Further, the WJZ survey showed that classical music was more popular than jazz, and news was more popular than sports, two results that received surprisingly little critical analysis, given that surveys conducted by other stations the same year showed that jazz was extremely popular and sporting events, especially baseball, were, too. Further, a 1927 survey done in Milwaukee showed that men preferred music played on the organ, while woman liked dance bands and orchestras; classical music was not in the top five for either men or women, although both groups said they enjoyed hearing a famous symphony orchestra.[63]

But unlike Jennie Irene Mix, who was not afraid to debate the people she interviewed, John Wallace just accepted what Charles Popenoe said; the statistic about the preference for male announcers was not questioned at all. And in November of 1926, Popenoe was back again in *Radio Broadcast* quoting his survey results, and once more revisiting his views on women announcers. This time, he claimed the results showed that one hundred to one, the public wanted male announcers, and that "men are naturally better fitted for the average assignment of the broadcast announcer." He said this was because women were too enthusiastic and sounded patronizing on the air; only male announcers knew how to strike the proper balance of emotions and sound appropriately friendly without overdoing it. Women were fine as singers, he concluded, but there was no demand for them as announcers.[64]

Women Announcers Are Replaced

Unfortunately, it seems that early radio technology, especially the micro-phones, really did distort women's voices, making them sound more shrill or higher pitched. Some women, like Eunice Randall, had naturally low and pleasant voices, and so the microphones did not adversely affect them. But even some female vocalists were victims of microphone distortion. *Radio Broadcast*'s engineers wrote several articles about how the transmitting and receiving apparatus distorted higher-pitched tones (and, by implication, higher voices), and how this affected even certain musical instruments such as the flute and the clarinet.[65]

A 1928 article in *Scientific American* explained why listeners were find-ing sopranos difficult to endure, no matter how talented they might be.[66] Radio simply did not bring out the best in the higher registers. Vocalist Vaughn DeLeath developed a style of "crooning" to make herself more listenable, and other women tried their best to keep their voices in the lower range, but the debate continued.

Some listeners seemed to have no objection to women announcers—when *Radio World* did a poll in 1925 (which they repeated a year later), asking listeners what they most objected to about radio, women announcers were not mentioned at all. The pet peeve was announcers who talked too much or did not say the call letters of the station.[67] And contrary to the 1926 WJZ survey, an article from *Variety* later that year stated that women announcers who did the women's shows on WJZ were now in big demand to do commercials, since these women were perceived by the audience as especially credible. Another New York station, WRNY, also weighed in, saying that its listeners had no problem at all with women announcers and it planned to hire more.[68]

To demonstrate that men were by no means united in their attitude about women announcers, there were male critics who liked certain women air personalities and wrote favorably about them. One example of this was in Chicago, where Halloween Martin became very popular. Miss Martin broad-cast a morning show in 1929 on station KYW, one of the very few women doing a show in that time slot. A former journalist (she had even been a "Prudence Penny" for a while prior to radio), her show, *The Musical Clock*, was praised in *Radio Digest* and also received compliments from newspa-per critic Yank Taylor of the *Chicago Daily Times*.[69]

Halloween Martin's success and critical acclaim, however, were the ex-ception. For the most part, from the mid-1920s to the decade's end, owners evidently decided that women did not belong as announcers and began mov-ing them into only the women's hour programs. It is doubtful that research played much of a part in the decision. Michele Hilmes and other feminist scholars have suggested that a woman speaker seemed unnatural to the more conservative men, who believed a woman's place was not as a public spokesperson; men were supposed to speak, and women were supposed to listen.[70] Whether it was sexism or whether it reflected how the microphone adversely carried the female voice, the end result was that by 1929, there were fewer and fewer women serving as announcers.

The same effort to limit women's opportunities was occurring in print journalism, too. One of the few American women to cover international news, Dorothy Thompson lamented that talented, college-educated women journalists were being restricted to covering "women's stuff," as in society, women's clubs, and the domestic arts, rather than being given a chance to break free and learn to cover hard news.[71] Miss Thompson would go on to a successful radio career and make the cover of *Time* magazine in 1939, but when news on radio was expanded, she was one of a very few female commentators not relegated to only the women's hour. And despite the fact that by the mid-1920s the radio editor was not expected to be an expert on technology, it would not be until the mid-1930s that more women became radio editors.

As the stereotypic newspaper reporter was a white man who let nothing stand in his way as he pursued the next big scoop, so the accepted standard for radio became a white male with a deep voice and excellent diction. In promoting this as the ideal, one station, WBZ in Boston, even went so far as to replace its female homemaker with a male announcer, stating, "It has long been known . . . that male voices are more easily understood than are the voices of women. In line with this knowledge, WBZ has inaugurated a new feature, known as 'The Radio Chef and Householder.'"[72] Perhaps WBZ's management underestimated the audience's acceptance of having women do these programs, because within a few months, the Radio Chef was gone and a female homemaker had returned. A few stations did invite a male chef to give some cooking tips during the women's hour, but the show itself was still moderated by a woman. One notable exception was the NBC *Women's Magazine of the Air.* A West Coast production, it was hosted by a man named Bennie Walker, who had considerable expertise in baking. Walker's two assistants, Helen Webster and Ann Holden, were experts in various other aspects of homemaking. According to *Radio Digest*, the audience not only accepted Bernie Walker as host, but he often received the most fan mail of anyone on the program.[73]

Some broadcast historians have theorized that women were gradually replaced as announcers as a result of the network/sponsor relationship; despite all the new jobs women were entering, certain attitudes had not changed. Michele Hilmes and others suggest that it was not public disapproval at all, but, rather, sponsor preference. The sponsors seemed to believe a deep male voice conveyed more authority. Many ad agencies also believed that a woman was best suited for selling household products to other women.[74] These advertisers were paying for the talent, including the announcers, and they could audition and select whomever they wanted; the networks usually went along with the sponsor's decision. So, women were chosen only for the stereotypic roles such as giving recipes or reading bedtime stories, and men were chosen for everything else. As more affiliates depended on the networks for much of their programming, the voices from NBC or CBS became very familiar to the mass audience. Perhaps listeners thought that women wanted only to be radio homemakers, and they did not question why there were progressively fewer women announcers. Or perhaps they just did not notice, given that there were still a number of women performers.

Despite some of the social changes that had occurred in the newspapers and magazines of the late 1920s, there was still a definite double standard with regard to how male and female radio performers were discussed. Women radio announcers, singers, and even homemakers were often described in terms of how they dressed or how they looked, while men announcers were described in terms of their skill in describing events and were praised for their ability to make a broadcast come alive for the listener. Their physical appearance was mentioned in passing if they were particularly young and handsome, but, otherwise, it was not part of the article—their experiences and achievements were what mattered. But fan magazines seldom failed to give the height and weight of the female performers; and the writer nearly always reminded readers that even though a woman performer had become successful, she was still "feminine."

The Last Few Women Program Directors

By the end of the 1920s, a few female program directors still remained; among them were Marie Kieny of WOW in Omaha, whose work was praised in a *Radio Digest* article in December of 1929, and Jean Campbell Crowe of KPO in San Francisco, who would be hired away by NBC in the early 1930s. Corinne Jordan had been hired by KSTP in St. Paul in February 1928 as program director, and she told the local newspaper, the *Pioneer Press*, that she was eager to begin auditioning new talent for the station.[75] However, Jordan was one of the last women of the 1920s hired to be in charge of station programming.

As with women announcers, the number of women program directors and station managers was declining rapidly. Again, a case could be made for sexism—perhaps some owners never really wanted a woman in charge, and when the opportunity to remove her from that role presented itself, many owners took it, but there is also the issue of how the needs of radio stations had changed. In the early 1920s when radio was live, and all volunteer stations needed talent and lots of it. Women from music schools could often provide that talent, and they were hired to do so. But when the networks began to dominate, local stations no longer relied on a small music school or a group of eager volunteers. With sponsorship came the ability to pay musicians, some of whom were quite well known. Many stations by the late 1920s even had their own house orchestra, led by a popular local bandleader. Stations that had trouble attracting talent could simply rely upon the big stars the network provided. What women like Eleanor Poehler did so well in 1922 was no longer required by late 1926. Not only that, but while classical music was still beloved by the critics and by a number of radio fans (and by the WJZ survey), dance music was even more popular. Because of that, it was no longer necessary to find an endless parade of sopranos or violinists. When Mrs. Poehler's original station, WLAG in Minneapolis, went off the air in 1924, she was eventually hired by its successor, WCCO—but as the musical director, not the program director. By 1927, she had left radio for good and taken a job directing a church choir.

Many of the women program directors of the early 1920s found that by the mid-1920s, they were being offered jobs as studio hostesses rather than program directors. As the job of program director became more of a management function, the old beliefs against women as bosses seemed to resurface. Women directing volunteers was okay; women running a company of paid employees seemed to make some owners uncomfortable. Bertha Mitchell, the first "Jean Sargent," quit WNAC when her boss, John Shepard III, refused to allow her to do anything other than either secretarial work or a women's show, even though she had years of experience in business. Her new job at a Chicago station gave her more flexibility and let her do some of the programming. As for many of the other women, they appeared to be willing to give up their program director job and accept a lesser position. To a contemporary feminist, it might look as though these women acquiesced too easily; perhaps they should have fought for their jobs as Bertha Mitchell seems to have done. But the reality of the 1920s was that the majority of women did not have executive jobs, nor did they expect to have them. Bertha Brainard and Judith Waller were the exceptions, rather than the rule, and even they were limited in how far they could advance. Many of the women who had been suddenly thrust into the role of program director may have been relieved when they no longer had to handle the constant pressure and responsibility. Eager to remain in radio, they accepted what was in some ways a demotion—they went from a job with considerable authority to one where they basically gave tours, showed guests around the station, answered fan mail, and helped musicians to get ready to perform. But again, we cannot apply modern criteria to life in the 1920s. There are many interesting career options for female college graduates today; back then, a studio hostess had a far more glamorous job than most women did. Unlike telephone operators or factory workers, studio hostesses still got to meet famous people, and there was always something happening around the station. Sometimes, if an announcer was late, they were asked to fill in temporarily. And a few also became part of their station's women's hour.

Of course, for every station where women no longer were allowed to broadcast, there were some that continued to have popular female announcers, although by the late 1920s, these were usually the ones who hosted the women's shows. But an interesting experiment occurred in Boston in 1927, when WNAC's controversial but innovative owner John Shepard III created an all-female radio station. WASN (All Shopping News) tried years ahead of its time to do home shopping, and while the experiment lasted only six months, it seems to have been technological problems (not as many people had telephones as Mr. Shepard thought) rather than a dislike of women announcers that ended the experiment. In fact, nearly all of the women on the staff (which included a woman program director, a woman news director, and even a woman in the sales department, something very unusual in 1927) continued on in radio; one (Grace Lawrence) went on to announce for the Yankee Network, and another (Claire Crawford) was promoted to assistant sales manager for that network by the early 1930s.

One might ask why Mr. Shepard was willing to have an all-female station when several years earlier he had refused to allow Bertha Mitchell to be in management. Perhaps it was because the format, shopping news and consumer information, plus phonograph records (available for purchase in the Shepard Stores, naturally) and friendly chats about fashion, went along with his beliefs about for what positions women were best suited. And yet, WASN was one more example of something unique that women did, and from all the evidence I have been able to gather, the women did in fact operate the station.[76] Interestingly, the Boston newspaper critics, all of whom were male, were complimentary toward the female announcers of WASN; these critics were not especially fond of the shopping part, but they liked the professional way the women did their jobs. And when women were vanishing from the air in most cities, Boston continued to have a few female announcers who did more than just the women's hour.

Radio and Diversity

By the end of the 1920s, much of the programming on the air came from NBC or CBS (other networks did not exist yet). There was a new agency to oversee radio—the Federal Radio Commission had been created by the Radio Act of 1927. By 1928, the commission would issue General Order 32, a plan to reduce crowding on the airwaves by eliminating a number of the smaller stations. Radio had changed from a hobby to a necessity and had undergone numerous technological improvements in its nine years of being available to the public. Along with the automobile, radio had truly enhanced the lives of millions of Americans, making them feel less alone and less isolated.[77]

Unfortunately, radio also reflected the stereotypes and beliefs of the times, meaning it was predominantly white, and most stations were reticent to hire minorities. A few black musicians such as Duke Ellington had network shows, but these were usually scheduled for late at night; there was only one black announcer, a Chicago businessman and concert promoter named Jack L. Cooper. Other ethnic minorities were not much more visible, although in Los Angeles, some Mexican-American vocalists performed occasionally. Radio would be slow to embrace diversity, even though there would be public affairs and educational programs that spoke in favor of it. And yet, radio did make some room for the "new woman" of the 1920s. Granted, the majority of the opportunities went to white, middle- or upper-class women, many of whom were arbitrarily assigned shows as radio homemakers or given jobs as receptionists. But a surprising number of women performed in supervisory roles, and even receptionists got the chance to play a character in a radio play or read an occasional commercial. And in the music industry, while most bandleaders were men, there was at least one popular jazz orchestra of the late 1920s led by a woman—Thelma Terry and her Playboys. Among the women vocalists who were making hit records were Ruth Etting and Helen Morgan, both of whom were torch singers (specializing in emotional performances of songs about lost love); each was a guest performer on CBS's variety show, the *Majestic Theater of the Air.* Also making hit records was Sophie Tucker, who billed herself as the "Last of the Red Hot Mamas"; she was an outspoken and flamboyant performer whose career had begun in vaudeville, and many of her fans were convinced by her singing style that she was black (and were shocked to find out she was not). In reality, it would be the mid-1930s before any minority women were given their own network programs—most notable among these was vocalist Ethel Waters.

In assessing the 1920s, even if it was not a trendsetter in breaking down racial barriers, radio did provide a number of average, middle-class women with extraordinary jobs. Many of radio's first women performers and managers were local residents who had never expected to be involved in the new medium, and in many cases, it changed their life: suddenly, they were well known in cities far beyond their hometown and being interviewed by editors of national publications. Of course, not every radio performer became famous; many went back to the life they had been living before, carrying with them the memories of what it had been like to be part of the radio adventure even for a little while. There were also a few women who had never planned to be on the air, yet who became involved with broadcasting by way of the music industry. One songwriter, Mabel Wayne, even wrote two big hits, "In a Little Spanish Town" in 1926 and "Ramona" in 1927. Around the same time, another young woman, Dorothy Fields, was beginning her own career in songwriting; she had her first hit in 1928 with "I Can't Give You Anything but Love." The new freedoms for women helped make Tin Pan Alley more receptive to women who brought their songs to publishers; but another factor was that radio orchestras and singers constantly needed new material to perform, and whether a hit was written by a male or a female was of little consequence.

Unfortunately, by the decade's end, many opportunities for women in broadcasting had vanished and others were limited. In fairness, it should also be said that some opportunities for men vanished as well. General Order 32 took over one hundred radio stations off the air, and many of the men who had owned these small stations were unable to get another job in broadcasting. Meanwhile, although women were no longer as numerous in announcing or in management as they had been in radio's first few years, they were becoming more prominent as performers. In the 1930s, women would also make their mark in a number of behind-the-scenes radio jobs. The national conversation about women's proper place showed no sign of stopping, but it was soon eclipsed by a different conversation, about the terrible effects of the stock market crash in late 1929. As the Great Depression dominated the lives of most average Americans and the economy worsened, the issue of whether women should be in the workplace at all began all over again.

Timeline: The 1920s

1920	1XE, WWJ (8MK), and KDKA are broadcasting
	KDKA broadcasts presidential election returns
	Women get the vote
	Eunice Randall is among first women to broadcast
1921	WBZ, WJZ, KYW, and others now on the air
	Congresswoman-elect Alice M. Robertson speaks on KDKA
	"Betty Crocker" character first appears
1922	Explosion in number of radio stations
	Marie Zimmerman is first woman to own a station

Several stations, including WEAF (NY), air commercials
First black hit Broadway musical performed on radio
Amateurs forbidden to broadcast music
1923   Singer Vaughn DeLeath becomes manager of WDT
Bertha Brainard becomes assistant program director at WJZ
1923–24 Most stations have women announcers and singers;
many stations have women program managers
1926   NBC radio network established
1927   CBS radio network established
First all-female radio station, WASN
Bertha Brainard promoted to executive post at NBC
Radio Act of 1927 creates Federal Radio Commission
1928   Songwriter Dorothy Fields has her first big hit
1929   Halloween Martin first woman to do a morning show
The Women Flyers found the Ninety-Nines
WMAQ program manager Judith Waller brings "Amos 'n' Andy"
to NBC after CBS turns the show down

Chapter 3

The 1930s:
The Women Behind the Men

In May 1929, the American Academy of Political and Social Science devoted an entire issue to the progress women had made and how their roles had changed. Among the changes were a list of "odd and unusual fields of work" in which women could now be found. Included in this list of occupations were women explorers, women biologists, women inventors, women electrical and civil engineers, women business owners, women mechanics . . . and women in broadcasting. And although the author of the article spelled her last name wrong, Bertha Brainard's many contributions to current broadcasting were very accurately detailed: by this time, she was program director for the entire NBC chain, responsible for coming up with new ideas for programs and hiring the talent for the network.[1]

However, what had not changed was women's salary. While more women had gone to college and entered some nontraditional fields of work during the 1920s, statistics showed that, in general, women were not making substantially higher wages, even though they had more education. A brief item in *The Survey* in late 1930 noted that while men with more education tended to receive higher wages, women did not. And although college-educated women did earn more than women who had only finished high school, ". . . [most women] tend, however, to concentrate in lower paid fields of work, such as teaching and clerical work . . . Seventy per cent of these college women are in the employ of educational, social or welfare organizations . . . Are the inherent satisfactions of the work itself more important to her than financial returns?"[2] And another study reported that black women earned twenty cents and white women sixty-one cents for every dollar that a white male earned.[3]

Opposition to Working Women

Surprisingly, many articles in the print media of the era continued to express a positive attitude about women in the workforce. But there were some notable exceptions. Among the most misogynistic of these was a syndicated full-page article by novelist Rex Beach in the spring of 1929. His basic point was that women's efforts to enter sports and business were doomed to failure because women were just not meant to be equal with men. "In sport, the average girl . . . plays a game for display, and not for the game's sake, but merely as a chance to show off. But a man plunges into every [contest], motivated by a sheer desire to win and make a real game of it . . . A woman has one interest—love. Man has fifty, [among them] adventure, sports, and business . . . men have too many interests to talk about romance. [T]he emancipated Eve of today suffers from the ancient illusion that love is all. And when she [fails to get] her man in marriage, she is utterly without a reserve of a diversity of interests." He also reminded the readers that women who tried to have careers were really petty, vindictive people who were too emotional to make a logical decision, and who were only working until they found a husband.[4]

There was also the view of Martin Branner, expressed in a popular comic strip that was syndicated in many newspapers across the country. He created a story line about a "working girl" named Winnie Winkle. This comic strip was called *Winnie Winkle the Breadwinner* when it first appeared in 1920; the name would be shortened to *Winnie Winkle* in 1943. Looking at this humorous view of the working woman's life, a modern reader can get a good idea of how Mr. Branner felt about the changing role of women in American society. Like Rex Beach, Martin Branner believed that women were born shoppers, interested in displaying their newly acquired goods. As Professor Ian Gordon observes:

> Branner was not alone in regarding consumption as a feminine activity. In the 1920s, a consensus existed among advertisers that women purchased between 70 and 85 percent of manufactured commodities . . . [A]dvertisers depicted consumption as a social movement through which women could exercise their rights. Although couched in a language of political entitlement, the rights advertisers envisaged for women were often limited to product selection . . . But whereas advertisers employed the [images] of women as consumers to sell products, Branner incorporated the notion into a nascent criticism of consumer culture.[5]

Winnie was a lower-middle-class girl who hoped to move into a higher social class and wanted to own what the upper-class person owned. And while she was holding down a job, her main worries were finding the right clothes, having the right hairstyle (should she get a bob or not?), and, of course, marrying the right man so she could improve her station in life. Granted, some of the men characters in the strip were not paragons of virtue —Winnie's father, Rip, was too lazy to get a job, for example—but the recurring subject of the strip's humor was Winnie's endless striving to shop and her need to buy things as a way to improve her self-image. To Branner, and we may assume this also applied to other men of that era, Winnie's obsession was amusing. Gordon pointed out how Branner gendered such qualities as vanity and excessive consumerism; these were regarded as exclusively female traits that the men in the comic strip often laughed at or made jokes about.[6]

Joking about women must have struck a responsive chord in the culture, since many vaudeville and radio comedians constructed skits (and even entire programs) around the foibles of the "typical female"; one-liners in which women were the object of the jest were frequently reprinted in magazines like *Radiolog* and *Radio Spotlight*.

Ambivalence About Working Women

A decade of social change had passed, yet there was still no consensus on the "new woman"; some columnists were highly critical of her, and not all of those columnists were disgruntled men. It was not uncommon to find articles written by women about how happy they were to have given up their business career and returned to their proper role as homemaker.[7] And yet, nearly every publication, from *Good Housekeeping* to *Literary Digest,* also printed positive articles about women achievers, often in the same issue as articles about why women were better off at home. The women's shows on radio exhibited the same ambivalence as the newspapers and magazines. Some followed the path of recipes and fashions only, avoiding talk about potentially divisive social issues. But others encouraged women with strong views to come on the show and express them.

As the Depression worsened and jobs for men grew scarce, the question of whether a woman really "needed" a job was raised more frequently. The common wisdom was still that women worked only for "pin money," to buy the little extras, whereas men worked to support a family. The idea that a married woman might want to work had not caught on with the general population. It was still expected that when a woman married, she would quit her job and be supported by her husband. The problem with this expectation was that now, more labor-saving devices existed, cutting down on the time it took to do housework. There were also more interesting jobs opening up to women, especially women who had graduated from college. As a result, not every woman wanted to work for a little while and then quit. But with fewer jobs for men, companies focused on their women employees and decided that the married ones should give up their jobs so that a single woman or a man with a family could work. This was nothing new in some professions: there had long been school districts that demanded that women teachers remain single. But during the Depression, even many office jobs were declared off-limits for married women. In the Edison Electric Company employee manual, it stated that a woman who got married would have to resign, and it reiterated that the company policy was not to hire married women at all.[8] By the mid- to late 1930s, a number of companies imposed similar rules; several states even tried to pass laws forbidding any married woman from taking a job unless she could prove economic need.[9] But here again, there was no consensus. Some businesses continued to employ married women, and there were married women in politics, law, and government.

Married Women in Radio

Radio was another occupation where a woman's marital status was seldom a barrier to whether she kept her job, no matter how bad the economy got. During the Depression's worst days, a few performers—men included— took temporary pay cuts, but if a show was popular, and the sponsors were selling their products, nobody seemed to care if the women on that show were single or married. In fact, if a woman was on a radio homemaker show, being married was a plus because she could talk knowingly about raising a family and caring for a husband. Listeners did not seem to find it odd that a working woman was telling them about how to be better stay-at-home house-wives. In an era when jobs were hard to find and married women were being ordered to leave the workforce (or not being hired at all for certain jobs), none of this seemed to affect radio at all. Broadcasting had numerous female singers and accompanists who were married; some even had children, as their profiles in the fan magazines mentioned. But to my knowledge, no stations demanded that stars like Gertrude Berg quit their jobs in favor of somebody single. Given the fact that the debate over working women was growing more contentious, it is interesting that the entertainment industry was relatively untouched. (This also included the movies, where some of the most popular female stars were married, and some were even divorced; but if a star's movies did well at the box office, somehow her marital status was not an issue.)

As traditional as the sponsors may have been about using female voices, they seemed to have no problem with husband-and-wife radio comedy teams such as George Burns and Gracie Allen or Fibber McGee and Molly (Jim and Marian Jordan). As long as the show remained popular, these stars did not have to worry about being replaced. In fact, one of the most popular shows of the early 1930s featured a married women and her daughter— *Myrt and Marge*. Myrtle Spear (in real life Myrtle Vail) and Margie Minter (Donna Damerel, her daughter) portrayed chorus girls, and the story was based on some of Myrtle Vail's experiences—she had been a successful vaudevillian, along with her husband, but the stock market crash wiped out their savings and left the family struggling to make ends meet. Myrtle decided to go back to work, and radio seemed like a good place for a performer with vaudeville experience. She wrote much of *Myrt and Marge* and also took a starring role. The show, which definitely fell into the soap opera genre, first went on the air in November 1931. Myrtle Vail had created a story of romance, adventure, and excitement—there were gangsters, danger, intense dialog—set in the world of show business. Critics praised it as one of the more innovative shows of the early 1930s, and it got excellent ratings from the new Crossley ratings service.[10]

The fact that Myrtle was married, and her daughter was in the show, too, was not considered a negative at all. In fact, when married radio stars had a new baby, the "blessed event" was often noted by the radio gossip columnists, and fans sent letters of congratulations. The use of her maiden name by a married female performer (or sometimes, a house name that was not the same as her husband's) may have also helped to maintain the illusion that a woman performer could keep her independence while she was entertaining the audience; her real name and her real identity were who she was as a wife and mother in private life.

But then, there was that same ambivalence I mentioned earlier. There were numerous women—many of whom were married—writing hit shows, acting, singing, and becoming very popular; yet the fan magazines of the 1930s ran countless stories in which the female star said she felt conflicted about working, or in which she was shown relaxing at home with her husband and children, looking every bit the devoted mother.[11] Part of the image many women stars tried to project was that they were perfectly normal people, just like you and me (only much more prosperous), and that their family meant more to them than having a big hit song or touring with a famous band. In other words, being famous did not mean they had lost their "femininity." Just as years later, gay male performers would often be given a mythical fiancé because it was believed that being openly gay was a career destroyer, so the women performers of the 1930s probably agreed with their publicists that a female celebrity should still be portrayed in ways that fit with society's expectations. A woman who said publicly that she did not want to marry would have been considered strange; it might have alienated her female fans. Yes, there were a few women who were known for doing things their own way, such as movie star Mae West and singer Kate Smith (whose first network show debuted in 1931 and who had become one of America's favorite vocalists); their independent streaks were incorporated in stories about them. But it was rare to find many stars in the 1930s who openly questioned the status quo.

Women in the Fan Magazines

Most of the articles about women stars were about their personal tragedies and triumphs, and, of course, how they found true love. Since magazines like *Radio Stars* and *Radio Mirror* were aimed at the woman radio fan, this was not unusual; romance was an integral part of most fiction in women's magazines. (Readers were probably unaware that most of the allegedly factual stories about the stars were created by publicists.) As might be expected, the articles avoided anything that might be controversial. Now and then, an article would mention a star's views on a social issue or a favorite charity, but most of the focus was on relationships and family.

Typical stories revolved around some personal crisis in a performer's life and how it all ended happily. There was "The Romance of George Olsen and Ethel Shutta," which began when Ethel was singing with a band; the orchestra leader was George, and the music his band played was so loud that it drowned out her singing. From their ensuing quarrel emerged a great love affair, which resulted in marriage.[12] Or, there was "If You Want a Radio Husband," in which two of radio's eligible bachelors discussed why they had not married yet.[13] There were also numerous stories in which a radio star invited the readers into his or her beautiful and opulent home for a guided tour. Some magazines also had a monthly feature in which radio stars discussed their favorite foods and gave tips on how to prepare a particular dish. Some radio magazines offered fiction, sometimes based on radio soap operas; the stories often had plots in which our heroine gave up her radio or show business career for the man she loved, or decided to put her career on hold to help with his.[14] This was to be expected; as mentioned before, magazines and newspapers had exhibited ambivalence about the "new woman" in the 1920s, running articles about how women were meant to be homemakers and also running articles about women engineers like Eunice Randall, who did not mind climbing a radio tower to make repairs.

But in a bad economy, the radio fan magazines were caught in an interesting dilemma. Some of the most popular radio stars were working women, female vocalists like Jessica Dragonette, Gladys Swarthout, or Jane Froman.

There was often an attractive woman singer featured on the cover of *Radio Digest, Radio Stars, Radioland, Popular Songs, Radio Guide,* and *Radio Mirror.* But while society (and many literary magazines) had begun expressing antipathy to the idea of married women working, the radio magazines needed to praise the biggest stars, many of who were in fact married women. And so, while the articles about these women seemed positive at first glance, a closer look revealed that the story line seldom portrayed a happy, independent women; it was a truism that the women of broadcasting were either married, about to be married, or wishing they were married. If a woman performer was single, like Kate Smith, the story was about her heartbreak at not finding a man who would accept the fact that she was overweight. If she was married, the story was about how the woman performer helped her husband, or how even though she loved singing, she also loved her family and wished she could be with them more.[15] Perhaps the editors, nearly all of whom were men, could not imagine a woman being happy by herself. After all, this was still a time when being a "spinster" or an "old maid" was considered a terrible fate, and when women feared giving their true age because they might be perceived as too old.

Although the fan magazines gave eager readers a chance to see pictures of their favorite stars, too often the articles also reinforced every negative stereotype about women. One example was an article about a female performer who recommended "playing dumb" in order for women to get whatever they wanted from men.[16] As mentioned earlier, comedians frequently made jokes about women, and the archetype of the "stupid woman" was among the most prevalent. But it is disconcerting for a modern reader to find that often it was women themselves back then who portrayed every possible stereotype of female helplessness and foolishness. And while it is also true that certain male comedians had a "stupid act," if I were a critic back then, I might have asked women like Gracie Allen or Jane Ace (whose character in the show *The Easy Aces* provided much of the comedy with her convoluted way of speaking English) why they wanted to encourage what was already a popular (and problematic) belief in the culture—that women were not very bright and caused men endless problems. Granted, Jane and Gracie in real life were quite intelligent and made good salaries, but just as black comedians would be criticized by a later generation for having played demeaning roles, so I must admit I cringe a little when I study some of the female roles that involved the "dumb little wife." In a culture where male bosses were already reticent to hire women, these comic routines certainly reinforced the common wisdom that women were indeed too scatterbrained for important jobs. The character of the bewildered and somewhat daffy woman gained wide acceptance in 1930s radio and movies. Along with the gold digger (the woman whose only goal in life was to find a rich husband), it was a stereotype that endured well into the television age.

The Women Pioneers in the 1930s

Meanwhile, as the 1930s began, a few of radio's pioneering women, in addition to Bertha Brainard, were still working in the industry. Eunice Randall was not: she was working for the New England Power Company doing technical drawings; occasionally, she was a guest on a Boston radio station, talking about the early days of broadcasting, but her work behind the microphone was mainly as a ham radio operator. Marie Zimmerman was not in radio either. She had moved into retail sales as a buyer for a midwestern department store; her relatives told me she never spoke about her 1922 radio adventure, evidently believing that what she and her husband had done was not that special. But Judith Waller was still very active on the Chicago radio scene. She was working for NBC and was still heavily involved in her first love, advocating for more educational radio programs. Since the early 1920s, when she had programmed WMAQ, Miss Waller had a long history of bringing educational features to her station. She helped to promote and then broadcast the first Woman's World's Fair in 1925. This was an exhibition featuring the achievements of women in over seventy different occupations. She worked with the Board of Education to develop lessons for public school children, and attempted on several occasions to create a radio school. Miss Waller wrote several journal articles about radio's ability to educate and in the 1930s was serving as NBC's educational director for the Midwest. Vaughn DeLeath was no longer program directing as she had for a brief while in the early 1920s, but she was still a popular singer with her own network show and a number of hit recordings. Another woman whose radio career began in the early 1920s was author and publicist Nellie Revell; she was now one of the editors of *Radio Digest* and for several years had been doing a Wednesday night program of interviews and celebrity gossip for NBC. There were other women (excluding the radio homemakers) whose careers on radio began in the 1920s and who were still broadcasting. Mrs. Jean Campbell Crowe, a former concert pianist, had long been active in promoting music education. She had been named program director of KPO in San Francisco in the mid-1920s, and she dedicated much of her time to putting quality programs on the air. In the early 1930s, she was hired away by NBC to work with the network's artist bureau, hiring the best musical talent for West Coast programming. Rosaline Greene had made her name with WGY in Schenectady, New York, as an announcer and an actress; contrary to the myth about women's voices being unpleasant, people liked hers so much that she won several awards during the 1920s. In the 1930s, the former elementary school teacher was one of radio's most in-demand dramatic actresses. One article guessed that she had portrayed over 1,000 characters during her career, including 25 of the most famous women in history.[17] There were two other women pioneers, Ida McNeil and Edythe Meserand, who will both be discussed later in this chapter.

New Opportunities in Broadcasting

Although the term was not commonly used during the 1930s, historians writing about that decade years later named it the "Golden Age of Radio." It was an era when, because of the Depression, people became dependent on radio for escape and for information, and some of the most innovative shows with the biggest stars were on the air to take people's minds off their troubles. President Franklin D. Roosevelt became known for his "Fireside Chats" during this time. Huge audiences heard these radio talks, in which he reassured the public and kept them apprised of what the government was doing to solve the national crisis. The First Lady, Eleanor Roosevelt, was also on radio fairly often, and she very much liked to give press conferences. One unique feature of her press conferences was her insistence that the media send women journalists to do the reporting; those outlets that did not have a female journalist naturally hired one so as not to be shut out from covering a woman who often made news.[18] The Roosevelts were both very much aware of how radio gave them the opportunity to reach out to the average American, and they frequently made use of the airwaves.

In spite of the Depression, radio, especially at the network level, managed to survive quite nicely. Unlike the phonograph record business, which was having financial woes, people already owned a radio and the music it provided was free, assuming listeners were willing to put up with various commercial announcements. In fact, the Depression brought even more commercials to radio, since many national advertisers had come to believe radio was the best way to reach the mass audience.

But radio was not just doing commercials, although it may have seemed that way sometimes. As the medium matured, it began offering more varied types of programs. One genre with great appeal was the radio drama. There had been plays broadcast on radio since the early days—the previously mentioned WGY in Schenectady, New York, was among the first to do them on a regular basis. But in the hours when local stations were not offering network programs and not doing a women's hour, radio dramas became popular; people enjoyed a good play, and with the Depression, the vast majority lacked the money to attend the theater. Radio stepped in, offering comedy sketches, serious dramas, and even a musical or two. Stations usually recruited the players from their own staffs: at WBZ in Boston, the WBZ Players were all employees in sales, engineering, and programming during the day, but several nights a week, they hurriedly rehearsed and then put on a dramatic presentation. The same was true with the KSTP Players in St. Paul, where program director Corinne Jordan directed her talented group of employees, getting the station considerable good publicity as a result of their performances. Sometimes, a station hired actors and actresses from community theater or from local colleges to augment its own staff. The programming department was usually in charge of finding the right plays and making sure the presentations went well. Radio dramas received such favorable response locally that the networks began doing them. And from these beginnings emerged a genre that would become known as soap operas, since they were sponsored by a company that sold soap and detergents. One network comedy/drama that quickly became a hit when it first appeared in late 1929 on NBC was *The Rise of the Goldbergs,* written by Gertrude Berg, who also played Mollie, the lead character in the program.

Radio dramas and soap operas were escapist entertainment, loved by women listeners, but they also provided more opportunity for women performers. At a time when women were discouraged from announcing or management, talented women (especially those who did not want to be confined to homemaking shows) could make money in dramatic roles and get on the air regularly. Among the popular actresses of the Golden Age were Alice Frost (*Big Sister*), Agnes Moorhead (who portrayed numerous radio roles, but was critically acclaimed for her work in "Sorry, Wrong Number" on the CBS crime show, *Suspense*), Virginia Payne (*Ma Perkins*), Dorothy Lowell (*Our Gal Sunday*), and Vivian Fridell (*Backstage Wife*). Also, many of the soap operas were written by women. The "Queen of the Soaps" was Irna Phillips, a former Chicago schoolteacher whose first radio job was as an actress for station WGN. Several years later, Phillips began to write scripts for radio dramas. A prolific writer, she single-handedly plotted and arranged as many as six soap operas at a time, with only the assistance of a secretary. Best known for *The Guiding Light,* at the height of her career, she made as much as $5,000 a week.[19] Years later, one of her protegées, Agnes Nixon, would bring the genre to television, where it would be equally popular.

But not everybody could be an Irna Phillips or an Anne Hummert, who, along with her husband Frank (and a large staff of assistants), wrote many other network soaps (including *Backstage Wife*). Local radio stations desperately needed more good plays to perform, as interest in radio drama increased. Since very few program directors had the time or the talent to write their own plays, they began to seek out scripts that could be performed on the air. In September 1930, Ruth Jeffreys wrote an article for *The Author and Journalist*. In it, she spoke of how writing for radio could be a potentially lucrative endeavor, and she gave advice to would-be writers about how to create a script that a radio station would want to buy. Miss Jeffreys had sold her first radio play to a station in Kansas City in April of 1929, and since then, had found that station managers were eager to receive good scripts. The pay, she noted, could range from five to twenty-five dollars per script, which in a time of economic hardship, was a respectable sum. The experienced writers could make more than that. Plus, once a writer had gotten a play accepted at a station, this often led to an ongoing relationship. Writing for radio was also very egalitarian—if you could create an interesting plot and some good characters, it did not matter whether you were male or female.[20] By the mid-1930s, there was intense competition for script-writing jobs. A literary agent remarked that several thousand scripts were submitted to studios or radio stations in an average month, but only a few hundred showed any potential, and even fewer stood a chance of getting final acceptance and being put into production. The best scripts were usually from the experienced and established writers.[21]

Protests Against Women Announcers

In March 1931, a rather vehement article appeared in *Variety*. It criticized those women who were still doing any announcing. Using some extremely harsh rhetoric, the article, entitled "Women Fall Down on the Air," contained a number of negative quotes, not just about women as announcers, but about women as people. The unnamed author, citing unnamed sources, accused women in radio of being vain, self-centered, and temperamental, unlike men, who were much more professional. "Women announcers [and actresses] are without . . . voice lure on the air, but are difficult to handle . . . most are general nuisances." According to the article, program directors are forced to let women do beauty talks or other "freak things," but they are now refusing to put up with women in any other type of announcing.[22] As with the comments of Charles Popenoe a few years earlier, no proof was given for these sentiments, but the print media treated them as factual and did not call upon any women announcers to challenge what had been said.

In July of 1932, an article in *Collier's* reinforced the fact that women had indeed been moved from the foreground to behind the scenes in radio. The author, John B. Kennedy, put a positive spin on this, however. He noted that women had been "barred by tradition from the microphone" and then went on to profile some of what he called the ". . . small army of young women [who have] invaded the studios in the past two or three years, [making] good not only as artists but as executives and directors."[23] Most of the women in his article were involved in children's programming (another area felt to be suitable for women), writing scripts, doing radio home-maker shows, and providing the piano or organ accompaniment for net-work vocalists. However, several had very unusual jobs, which were unique to radio. Minnie Blauman was a musical arranger for radio orchestras, while Sallie Belle Cox was known for her radio voices, especially the crying baby.[24] In June 1933, *Radio Stars* did a feature article about this unusual aspect of radio employment, with part of the story about a man named Bradley Barker, whose radio specialty was animal noises (and, yes, one of his skills was barking like a dog), and the rest on Sallie Belle Cox. It turns out that Sallie acquired her skill accidentally—she was working with chil-dren in an orphans' home, and to amuse them when they were cranky, she began to imitate the sounds babies made, including crying. When she read an article that said NBC was having trouble finding a way to create the sound of a baby for radio scripts, she wrote to them and said she knew how to do that. She was hired, and thus began her successful career of being a "radio baby."[25]

Another woman with an important job behind the scenes was Vida Ravenscroft Sutton, who taught speech and diction to all of the NBC an-nouncers. She also brought her techniques for being a better speaker to an education program called "The Magic of Speech." Interestingly, Miss Sutton was quoted as telling women not to attempt to become announcers; she suggested instead that they go into radio drama, writing, or producing, where she felt their voices fit better. And although she was not a fan of women announcers, she also said that most men did not have the right voice or good enough diction for radio announcing either.[26]

In 1934, when the editors of *Radio Stars* attempted to select the most important women in radio, one name that came up was Ora D. Nichols. Mrs. Nichols had another of those unique radio jobs—as head of the Sound Department at CBS, she was an expert at creating any kind of sound a drama needed, from a fire to a lawn mower. Her special effects were ad-mired by her colleagues, yet the average listener was totally unaware that she existed.[27] Of course, Bertha Brainard was included among the most important women in radio, and the author was quick to point out that Brainard was "feminine but efficient," as if the two qualities were mutually exclu-sive.[28] Also on the list was the First Lady, Mrs. Eleanor Roosevelt, who had been on the radio before she was the wife of a president, and who frequently gave radio talks on social issues that were of concern to her (the fee she would normally be paid for appearing on the air was always donated to charity).[29] Most of the other women chosen for the article were singers, dramatic actresses, or comediennes. (Someone who could easily have been on the list was Margaret "Maggie" Cuthbert, who was director of women's programming for NBC, and who, like Judith Waller in Chicago, worked tirelessly to keep a certain amount of educational programming on the network, even in the face of increasing commercialization. Marian S. Carter also deserved a mention; she was CBS's assistant national program director and helped to determine which programs for women were put on the network.)

Looking at the world through the eyes of the radio columnists of the 1930s, it would have been easy to assume there was no Depression. There were over 13 million unemployed by the end of 1932, total wages declined to 60 percent less than in 1929, and more banks closed. Yet, *Radio Digest*'s October issue opened with the following: "These are the days when Radioland is all agog over new programs, ambitious auditions, new faces and new voices, old stars in new roles and new stars in old roles." The essay went on to discuss network performer Russ Columbo, who was making $5,000 a week.[30] The audience was probably living vicariously through these celebrities, because the average American was certainly not making a huge salary, assuming he or she still had a job. In fact, few people made $5,000 a year, let alone $5,000 a week.

Some Women Who Advanced in Radio

There probably were many young girls who dreamed of a job assisting a famous man, especially one who was an eligible bachelor. It would have been unusual back then for the average girl, especially during the Depression, to have aspirations of owning a company or being the big boss. For many, finding a job as a secretary was perfectly acceptable. Whether their boss was famous or not, the job of confidential secretary was essential to many businesses, and many of the women in those positions had considerable responsibility. In radio, a few of the women who became managers in the 1940s started by doing secretarial work at a station. And some of the famous women of radio, especially executives like Judith Waller and Bertha Brainard, had their own secretaries, too. Even some of the women's show hosts depended on their female support staff. Mary Margaret McBride, whose successful career began at WOR in New York City in 1934, frequently pointed out that she would not have been able to do her job as effectively had it not been for her assistant and long-time friend Stella Karn. Karn did everything from clerical tasks like answering phones and responding to mail to more advanced duties like helping to produce the show, booking the guests, and arranging travel for McBride. Karn even helped decide about good topics to discuss and then found experts who could discuss them.[31] She held down a very important position, which, although classified then as secretarial, today would be considered more like a producer.

But for every young woman who was content to be the assistant to the great man (or sometimes to the great woman), there was also the young woman who developed the desire to move up. Edythe Meserand, who went on to become a publicist and a newswoman, was at first only encouraged to learn typing and shorthand, since the assumption was that for girls, office work would be their usual means of employment until they married. So, Edythe came to radio with few aspirations other than making a living; she was first hired to answer phones and compile information so that the man for whom she worked could write press releases. But gradually, she proved she was a skilled writer, and she was allowed to write some of the press releases herself. Working in such a visible department at the network, she met some of the women who were radio editors for the newspapers or press agents for the stars. She also learned from the other women who worked at NBC, including Bertha Brainard, whom she admired greatly and tried to emulate (she recalled in one interview how she even tried to dress as stylishly as Miss Brainard). From answering the phones and typing, Edythe Meserand moved up to being press liaison for NBC, setting up interviews, arranging photo shoots, and making sure the print journalists all were informed about the latest achievements of NBC performers. And although few of the listeners knew she existed, nearly every celebrity who appeared on NBC interacted with her on a regular basis.[32]

But most of the stories in fan magazines were not about women like Edythe Meserand, who found a radio career she had not really expected and then advanced in it. So while some women were moving up the ladder into more important and responsible jobs despite the obstacles thrown in their paths, this fact was seldom mentioned in the mainstream press; even the radio magazines like *Broadcasting* did not regard what women were doing as especially noteworthy. Now and then, a woman in advertising or a woman who did a women's show would be mentioned, but these mentions were definitely few and far between compared to the articles about what men in radio were doing. Even the school books about careers in broadcasting seemed to accept the idea that men were actively involved in radio and women were on the sidelines. And it was not just the male editors who put forth the belief that women were not suited for certain jobs or that their abilities were limited. One popular textbook, *Radio Workers,* part of a late 1930s series about careers, was edited by a woman; it contained thirty-five illustrations, every one of which showed a white male. A couple of the pictures showed females who seemed to be assisting the men, but even in those jobs that we know women held, such as writing and researching, the photograph was of a man. As for women on the air, the text that listed a woman as one of the writers said: "Women's voices, unless they are trained for radio, are likely to be high and squeaky. Women announcers who have been tried from time to time did not go over. . . . But now television is coming and women are being trained to be announcers, for in television, the announcer will be seen as well as heard."[33]

The message to young girls reading this book was that in radio, you would assist the men and watch them do exciting things. And someday, when TV came along, if you were pretty, you might have a chance of getting hired. (Experiments with TV were ongoing in the 1930s; the Radio World's Fair of 1931 even featured a demonstration of TV. Several well-known and attractive women, most notably Dorothy Knapp for NBC and Natalie Towers for CBS, were hired to appear on the new medium. But for all the predictions that TV was just about ready, it would not be until the late 1940s that television finally became an important part of the average person's life.)

Where Women in Radio Worked

Although they may not have gotten nearly as much publicity as their male colleagues, not every woman in radio had been relegated to working behind the scenes. As mentioned earlier, a few program directors of the 1920s were still around in the 1930s, and there is evidence that at least one of them got pay equal with men, highly unusual in those days. I was allowed to see the ledger with the staff payroll for the early 1930s at station KSTP in St. Paul, Minnesota, and it showed that program director (and sometimes singer and accompanist) Corinne Jordan was paid more than many of the men on the staff; only the general manager and sales manager made a higher salary than she did. (For those who wonder, Jordan made $200 a month as program director, which was probably good money during the Depression. In the mid-1930s, she was given a raise to $275 a month.)

But Corinne Jordan and women like Helen Margaret O'Neill—after being a successful program director at KTAB in San Francisco, Miss O'Neill was now producing the *NBC Matinee,* a network variety show for women, with everything from comedy to radio drama to famous guest performers— were by now the exceptions. If the 1920s were about middle-class women getting more freedom, the 1930s saw a certain backlash, no doubt made worse by the severe economic times. Women who wanted radio jobs were usually steered toward producing educational shows or children's programming, and, of course, there was always a demand for more radio homemakers. Women who wanted to work within those areas, as undoubtedly many did, found that their aspirations were encouraged. And while network announcing (other than women's shows) may have been declared off-limits, a few young women of the early 1930s, such as Grace Lawrence of WAAB in Boston, found opportunities at local stations. Several also ventured into such mostly male areas as engineering. One example was Helen Klein, a Phi Beta Kappa graduate of Wellesley (Massachusetts) College, who was hired in 1930 by the Crosley Radio Corporation of Cincinnati to be the assistant to the chief engineer, with duties that were technical, not clerical.[34] And while the retail sales aspect of radio too was mostly all men, there were a few women merchants: one was Grace Baker, part of a family business in St. Louis that sold radio sets and equipment.[35]

For the most part, however, women in radio in the early to mid-1930s were more likely to be found in safe and nonthreatening roles such as reading bedtime stories to the kids; and just about every station had at least one woman who played piano or organ and sang popular songs. A Kentucky station even had a new twist on the female advice giver: Tremlette Tully, a former newspaperwoman, was hired in 1930 by WCKY in Covington (the station later moved to Cincinnati) to be women's director, but she decided to use part of her show to discuss issues that concerned her audience. She invited listeners to send in their questions about home or family problems, and if she could not come up with an answer, she would find an expert to address it. Tully became well known for her ability to find answers to a wide range of listener queries, from how to adopt a child to how to handle grief over the loss of a loved one; several national radio magazines praised her work.[36]

While many women broadcasters of the 1930s were limited to traditional roles, they made the most of those jobs, earning the respect of their audiences; they were also relied upon by their sponsors. But a few women's show hosts spoke out about their genre and how they felt it ought to sound. Helen O'Neill was very upset by programs that treated women as if they were children. "If you want to please women [listeners], don't talk down to them!" she told an interviewer.[37] And Ida Bailey Allen, even though she did a very old-fashioned women's show and espoused beliefs in traditional gender roles (in one of her newsletters, she stated that men should never help with the housework), felt strongly that women were not being given enough training so that they could become successful announcers.[38] To help the next generation of women's show hosts sound more professional, she began offering classes twice a week. With the assistance of Adele Holt, who specialized in teaching diction, Allen's goal was to provide the networks with more women who could produce and announce their own shows.

Another woman who maintained her on-air popularity despite the Depression was Nellie Revell. She was best known for doing a celebrity gossip program, another area considered appropriate for female broadcasters. But because of her many years of media experience, Miss Revell had become a good interviewer; she did not use a script, preferring to just talk with her guests. Listeners felt as if they were part of a conversation among friends when she sat down with her celebrity guests.[39] That ability to ad-lib and sound comfortable was also part of Mary Margaret McBride's expertise. When Miss McBride came to radio from journalism in 1934, the management at WOR gave her the house name of Martha Deane, and she was told to sound like a grandmotherly type. But she soon began using her own name and sounding like herself. She, too, never used a script, preferring to just have conversations with her guests. Besides chatting about traditional matters like recipes or child rearing, she often featured guests with strong opinions, such as feminist author Fanny Hurst, with whom she would discuss issues that affected working women.[40] But although both Nellie Revell and Mary Margaret McBride were very well known, Miss Revell was seldom the object of criticism from the radio columnists, whereas Miss McBride was frequently criticized. Perhaps Miss Revell got more of a free ride because of her many years as a publicist and an author, as well as the fact that she was not broadcasting as part of a "women's hour" (she was on the air late Wednesday nights). But McBride was the woman the male critics loved to hate. They found her and her show far too talkative and unstructured; one said she "gabs aimlessly,"[41] and another accused her show of being silly and trivial, saying her announcer deserved sympathy for having to endure the entire hour.[42] But her fans, and her sponsors, adored her. She had an ability to sell a product, and her women's hour was as much about interesting people in the news as it was about the domestic arts. It was said that her greatest skill was her ability to ask her guests the questions the listeners wished they could ask.

Changing Women's Shows

Network women's shows were changing somewhat; many no longer relied exclusively on just recipes and household chat, although sponsor plugs were a major part of these shows. But during the 1930s, some hosts had added radio dramas or talks about important social issues from leaders of civic groups; spokeswomen from the government's Women's Bureau as well as the Children's Bureau frequently kept the audience up to date on what each agency was doing. Even Ida Bailey Allen added segments unrelated to the domestic arts: she began bringing in more culture, such as inviting classically trained actors and actresses who performed scenes from Shakespeare. Many local women's shows added musical interludes by the station's house orchestra, and some experimented with contests and trivia questions. Claudine

Macdonald had been doing her own unique version of a women's show over WEAF (New York) and NBC since May 1930, and five years later, the show continued to provide the audience with both entertainment and information. *The Women's Radio Review* was almost like a magazine, featuring segments on music (sometimes written or performed by women artists), literature, art, travel, news . . . and no recipes. Miss Macdonald was often able to get the big-name guest speakers—men and women who had best-selling books or were well known in some area of culture. She, too, was opposed to the type of women's show that talked to women as if they were stupid. She tried to provide both intellectual stimulation and entertainment.[43] Alma Kitchell, also on NBC, had already done some traditional midday chat shows and had even been a vocalist on the *Women's Radio Review* in the late 1930s. She created a dinnertime show called *Brief Case,* in which she answered listener queries about radio and explained some of what went on behind the scenes. And a CBS network feature that began in 1936 starred one of the few newswomen, commentator Kathryn Cravens. Her show, *News Through a Woman's Eyes,* took her listeners into what today would be called the human interest aspect of news stories.[44]

Women Station Owners

There were several more women who owned stations in the 1930s. Since Marie Zimmerman's brief foray into station ownership in 1922, an Arizona woman named Mary Costigan had put a station on the air in Flagstaff in the autumn of 1925. And in Medford, Oregon, Mrs. Blanche Virgin (later Blanche Virgin Randle) inherited her husband William's station when he died in 1928. Rather than sell it, she decided to operate it herself. For six months, she ran the station alone, before hiring an assistant and then gradually expanding the staff of station KMED.[45] But nobody else was doing anything to equal the work of Ida McNeil, who ran a one-woman radio station for several decades. In the early 1920s, owners were often the only official employees of their stations, and if they could not find volunteer guests, they had to keep the station on the air themselves; as mentioned earlier, that is why so many of the early station operators had musical talent. Legendary vaudeville star Eddie Cantor recalls how Vaughn DeLeath, who was already a successful recording artist, ended up as manager and chief operator of station WDT in 1923; because the station had no budget for talent, ". . . [Miss DeLeath sometimes] sang on the air for three and a half to four hours straight . . . A singer went on the air until someone arrived at the studio to take over."[46]

But Ida McNeil was one of a kind. She continued to single-handedly run a radio station for many years, much of the time from her own home. Her radio career had started rather inauspiciously in those pioneering days of the early 1920s. Her husband, Dana, had operated an amateur station in Pierre, South Dakota, and Ida had sometimes helped out. She broadcast local community events such as births and deaths, and slowly, she built up a following of shut-ins and people who lived in isolated, rural areas. The amateur station was renamed KGFX in 1927, and even after her husband passed away, Ida McNeil continued to operate it as a friendly, folksy hometown station that broke every rule of so-called "professional" broadcasting. Mrs. McNeil gave birthday greetings over the air, said hello to various listeners, took requests, talked about what was going on in the local stores (the station began accepting commercial advertising in the early 1930s), talked about how various patients at local hospitals were doing (she went to visit many of them), and made sure the farmers got the most up-to-date weather available.[47] It should not have worked; when the networks came along, the audience should have insisted on the big-name stars and smooth announcers. But they did not. They insisted on Ida McNeil, who was the entire staff of KGFX (except for a chief engineer), and who became one of the most beloved people in town. KGFX, or perhaps more accurately, Mrs. McNeil, came to be known as "the Voice of the Prairie," and her little station was even written about in both *Broadcasting* and *Time*. By the end of the 1930s, KGFX was still pretty much in the capable hands of Ida, although now sometimes her son helped her, as she had once helped her husband.[48]

Women Station Managers

Broadcasting magazine had made its debut in October 1931. Its intent was to be for radio (and later TV) what the magazine *Editor & Publisher* was for print.[49] This new magazine covered all aspects of the industry, from management to programming to engineering, concentrating on the individuals who were the major executives and leaders in radio and in broadcast advertising. If its first several volumes were any indication, the people it concentrated on were male executives, especially those active in the National Association of Broadcasters. Granted, a number of these men had done some amazing things in radio and advertising, but anyone reading the magazine would have assumed the entire industry was comprised of only older white males. *Broadcasting* began doing weekly profiles of the most successful men of the radio industry, under the heading "We Pay Our Respects To _____." It was not until 1934 that there were any regular tributes to women achievers. One of the first women to be profiled came from broadcast advertising—Margaret Elisabeth Jessup, in charge of station relations for ad agency McCann-Erickson. And speaking of 1934, that was the year a new station went on the air in New York, which in and of itself was not so unusual; what was different about WNEW was that its general manager would make quite a name for herself. *Broadcasting* did not do its tribute to her until 1941, but Bernice Judis had already established herself as one of radio's most effective executives. Working at WNEW was the first radio job she ever had, and she only made $15 a week doing general office work and assisting several of the managers. But it quickly became obvious that Bernice had an inherent understanding of how a station should operate and what the public wanted. Within a year, she had been promoted to management. Her first move was to dramatically change the way so-called women's shows were done. She believed that there were too many melodramatic soap operas and too many cooking shows on the air, and women deserved something different. She began concentrating on a music format, where announcers played hit records and communicated with the female listener in a friendly and conversational style; she is credited with hiring Martin Block, who became one of the first disc jockeys on the air. She also expanded WNEW's news coverage, and unlike other stations that signed off at midnight or 1:00 A.M., WNEW remained on all night, which shift workers felt was a wonderful idea.[50]

Another woman given a full-page profile was Hyla Kiczales, who ran two stations, one in New York and the other in Philadelphia. As general manager of the International Broadcasting Corporation, her specialty was creating and implementing foreign language and ethnic programming. She also helped to design foreign language programs for an eight-station network. When the tribute to her was published in the fall of 1938, "Miss K" was managing three stations and had just been given a prestigious award for public service by the Dante Alighieri Society, the first time a non-Italian had won.

By 1939, not only were women from major markets being profiled, but *Broadcasting* was taking note of women from smaller markets in a short feature called "Meet the Ladies," which singled out what the magazine called "lady executives" in radio. The first one chosen was Maxine Chaffin, assistant manager of KID in Idaho Falls, Idaho, who the writer assured us was not only an executive, but also pretty.[51] It is also interesting to note that many of the successful women executives were unmarried, devoting their lives entirely to their career in broadcasting. But whether married or single, radio was the top priority for these women executives. Bernice Judis, for example, had radios in every room of her house, a portable in her purse, and radios in every office at the station. Her staff had the perception that she listened to WNEW from early morning until late at night, and she might even call to correct an announcer at 3:00 A.M. One staff member, commenting about her pervasive influence on the station, said that ". . . she challenged you, she dared you, she rewarded you, she complimented you, and she understood . . . she got the best out of you."[52]

The Women Flyers

In addition to the women radio executives whose exploits were mainly discussed in industry trade publications, there were some women newsmakers who were very much in the public eye, even during the Depression's most difficult days. Celebrities could always be counted on for a good story: vaudevillian and singer Belle Baker took part in an interesting publicity stunt in late March of 1932 when she did her network radio show from a moving train, the first time such a thing had been done.[53] That same year, champion swimmer Gertrude Ederle was persuaded to wear a new and very small portable microphone, with which she gave reports to the listeners while she was in an aquaplane.[54] Women aviators remained in the headlines during the 1930s, as they set a number of speed and distance records; the fact that they were female was about to provide the fledgling commercial aviation industry with a boost. As one historian pointed out, the common wisdom persisted that women tended to be frail, timid, and unmechanical. In marketing air travel, advertising agencies decided to utilize the women flyers to prove that air travel could be fun and was not dangerous at all. The message to the public seemed to be "if flying is so easy that a woman can do it, then the average would-be traveler has nothing to worry about." The general public was still nervous about flying, the success of Amelia Earhart and Charles Lindbergh notwithstanding.

But there was something reassuring about these attractive and perfectly normal-looking young women who were breaking all kinds of records in their planes.[55] In an interview with *Radio Digest* in 1931, aviatrix Ruth Nichols stated that "[e]very woman should learn to fly!" She also said that flying was easier than driving a car in traffic, and that she depended on radio because it gave her up-to-the-minute weather reports, which she needed when making decisions about whether it was a good day for a flight. The author was quick to point out Miss Nichols's "feminine charm" and described the "pretty silk frock" the woman flyer wore to the interview, which proved to the author that flyers need not be masculine.[56] The plane she used in her exploits was loaned to her by radio executive Powell Crosley Jr. of WLW in Cincinnati, which made for another tie-in with broadcasting. Few if any broadcast history books mention the phenomenon of the women flyers, but surely many girls and young women who heard them, or heard about them, on the radio must have been influenced to consider flying; or perhaps, similar to how the fan magazines depicted the glamorous lives of the radio singers, the typical woman of the early 1930s vicariously experienced the excitement of flying and was happy to know that these women aviators had such interesting lives.

When commercial flying became more popular, however, the jobs women were offered were only those of "air hostesses," later called stewardesses. One article inviting women to apply explained that most women did not yet have enough flying experience to become pilots, but this new job offered adventure. It also offered rigid qualifications, among them that the female candidates must stand no more than five feet five inches tall and weigh no more than 121 pounds; married women need not apply, and a college degree was preferred. The air hostess must also be "charming, with some knowledge of practical nursing, dignified, [and] able to answer passenger questions . . ." The salary was $110 a month.[57]

Amelia Earhart persistently expressed her disappointment that women were not being given the chance to become commercial pilots. Since the late 1920s, she had spoken out against women being relegated to the "fringes of aviation" rather than being allowed to get the training that would elevate them to pilot status.[58] But now, even those women who had the skill to fly were not given the opportunity by the airline industry, which must have been infuriating to the growing number of women aviators.

A Lack of Role Models

Today, when women avoid certain occupations and gravitate toward the lower-paying jobs traditionally associated with the female gender, a lack of positive role models is sometimes suggested as a factor. Yet as I discussed earlier with Bertha Brainard and Eunice Randall, the women flyers, who included Ruth Nichols, Bobbi Trout, Louise Thaden, Gladys O'Donnell, and Amelia Earhart, seem to have been drawn to flying despite having no female mentor; not only did they all enter the new field of aviation, but contrary to the myth that women could not work together because they are jealous or "catty," they banded together to form their own club, enduring the ridicule and insults of some of the male flyers in the process. The club that they and other women aviators started in 1929, the Ninety-Nines, still exists; in 1999, it had members from thirty-five countries who were all licensed pilots.[59]

As veteran journalist Ann Harris observed in a 1984 article about how times had changed since she entered the field many years earlier, ". . . before the term 'role model' had been invented, [we women] were actually in the labor market working in an environment that consistently reinforced our notion that professional success was open to us if we were willing and able to work for it . . . It is difficult for the young women of today to believe this because [of a] recurring myth that is dragged out with each new generation. Simply stated, it says 'Today's young women are doing totally new things; they are achieving what their mothers never dreamed of and what their daughters will take for granted.'"[60] But, of course, even in the 1920s and 1930s, women were somehow managing to achieve, with or without mentors and role models. How they did it is something that sociologists and psychologists have continued to discuss.

Not all of the women making headlines in the 1930s were aviators or radio singers. One was the heroine of a fairy-tale love story. People on both sides of the Atlantic Ocean stayed close to their radios to hear a memorable speech by the King of England on December 11, 1936, as he announced to the radio audience that he was giving up his throne for "the woman I love." That woman was Wallis Simpson, an American divorcée. While biographers have noted that their real-life marriage was not such a fairy tale after all, their romance captivated people on both sides of the Atlantic. In a decade where the women's magazines constantly wrote about the search for true love and soap opera women loved and lost on a daily basis, Wallis Simpson's story must have resonated with female radio listeners, who dreamed that one day somebody would do something that romantic for them.

Another woman was making headlines of an entirely different sort throughout the 1930s; she was one of the few women in the government. When Franklin Delano Roosevelt formed his Cabinet after he was elected president, he chose Frances Perkins to be his Secretary of Labor, the first woman ever chosen for a Cabinet post. Miss Perkins, who had been a suffragette and a strong supporter of women's rights, also had a long history of fighting for the rights of workers. As the Secretary of Labor, she fostered such legislation as the Social Security Act in 1935 and the Fair Labor Standards Act in 1938. Miss Perkins gave speeches on the radio to explain her views about social justice, as did President Roosevelt and First Lady Eleanor, with whom she was friends. Ironically, despite her image as a strong supporter of both women's rights and labor, she was rather traditional and accepted the belief that married women should not work.[61] However, one of the best-kept secrets regards Perkins's own personal life—she was a married woman, but presumably, she was not working for "pin money."

Hoping to Be Discovered

Despite the Depression, some women did find work in places other than factories or offices. There were still some jobs for entertainers, although most of these opportunities were local and did not offer big salaries. However, even a job singing in a local restaurant was often seen as the first step to something much bigger, a belief capitalized upon by the fan magazines, which frequently offered stories about another girl from a small town who was discovered by a talent scout and was now singing on a major network program. This was the era of the network talent shows, the best known of which was hosted by Major Edward Bowes; would-be stars came to his auditions from all over the country, praying they would become famous. Most never did. Yet, the fan magazine stories about ordinary people who were discovered and became network stars must have given thousands of local amateurs the belief that their dream might come true if they could just be seen by the right person. Where once young women had longed to be on the stage, now they wanted to be radio singers. Lucille Singleton, whose job at CBS was to audition potential new talent, said that perhaps one in 500 was good enough to sing on a national radio network; she said the vast majority of the singers she auditioned each week lacked confidence in front of a microphone and did not have a warm personality that came through on radio.[62] Yet despite the long odds, several hundred eager men and women showed up each week asking for an audition.

But no matter how many cautionary articles by radio executives appeared, warning of the difficulty in getting a network job, it did not stop people from dreaming and hoping that one day, they would get a lucky break and become famous. At a time when it seemed the economy would never improve, and only a very few women had exciting jobs, the fantasy of becoming the next Jessica Dragonette must have been very strong. Jessica had been orphaned at a very young age and raised in a convent by nuns who saw her talent and helped her to have a music career. Surely if somebody from such humble beginnings could go on to become one of the most beloved female vocalists of the 1930s, it could happen for almost anyone.

The young women who were not great singers could derive encouragement from the success story of Dorothy Fields. Her father Lew had been a star in vaudeville in the team of Weber and Fields, but Dorothy managed to have her own achievements, despite her father's vehement opposition to his daughter going into show business. Since her first hit song in 1928, she continued to write or cowrite a number of popular songs throughout the 1930s and into the 1940s. In 1937, she became the first woman to win an Oscar for songwriting, for her song "The Way You Look Tonight" from the movie *Swingtime*. In another predominantly all-male part of the music industry, Dorothy Fields earned the respect of her male colleagues, several of whom (most notably Jimmy McHugh and Jerome Kern) collaborated with her on hits that were frequently heard on the radio. Mabel Wayne, her songwriting compatriot, was still writing, too: Miss Wayne had come from a family of performers and musicians, but despite debuting on the stage at the age of sixteen, she found she preferred writing songs to singing them.[63] She too cowrote with some of the best, and in 1934, she had a big hit with "Little Man You've Had a Busy Day," and another hit in 1937 with "Why Don't You Fall in Love with Me?"

Stories about women who followed their dreams despite obstacles made inspiring reading, but the majority of the readers had no chance of breaking into show business. And although the movie and radio fan magazines seemed oblivious to the hard times, the average woman knew that her life would never be that of a celebrity. Still, it did not hurt to dream.

Avoiding Serious Analysis

Certain feminist critics have pointed out that the discussion about whether married women should work was really about whether married *middle-class white women* should work, since poor and minority women were working all along, and not many essays were written about whether this was right or wrong. In my research, I found few radio programs that addressed the subject of how social class affected society's expectations of women. There were even fewer that discussed racism in the workplace: occasionally, a speaker from the National Association for the Advancement of Colored People was a guest on an educational show, and the subject was mentioned in passing.[64] Now and then, a women's show would have speakers from an organization of business and professional women. But the networks did not see their role as providing analysis of why poverty existed, why women were paid less, or why a backlash against career women was taking place. In fact, network executives said in interviews that radio was about entertainment and escape; some even admitted it was mainly about selling products, Depression or not.[65]

So, with that context, while a number of the women's shows did mention the fact that there were hard times for women, the general trend of avoidance seemed to prevail; women's shows continued to present guests, often upper-class socialites, who had been to faraway places and had exciting adventures. The major way the Depression factored into programming was in the giving of helpful tips on how to stretch the budget or how to make meals that husbands would love even though the housewife had limited resources. The expectation was that a good wife would somehow continue presenting creative and interesting meals; the radio homemakers, especially those on the networks, seldom deviated from the belief that somehow the housewife should be able to find a way, no matter how small her budget. This attitude was undoubtedly influenced by the sponsors, who were paying the radio homemakers good money to boost consumerism; or it may be that these experienced veterans of domestic science genuinely believed that homemaking was a sacred duty, so even when times got tough, they could not accept anything less than 100 percent effort.

Jobs in Retail

One of the few industries receptive to hiring women even during the Depression was retail sales, including the copywriting and advertising departments of ad agencies. Unlike today when stores often hire untrained high school students, and a "sales clerk" is not seen as a high-status job, in the 1930s, department stores such as Macy's in New York were actively seeking women college graduates to train for jobs in retail, as well as to write advertising copy for print ads. Some stores had women buyers and department managers, and a few even had women in certain executive positions. Human resources (or personnel, as they called it then) was often managed by a woman. For young women who liked fashion, retail was a desirable way to make a living. Mrs. Helen Law, who was very satisfied with her retail career at Macy's, wrote a very positive magazine article about the numerous opportunities for women in retailing and encouraged young women to apply for them.[66] But another woman, Mabel Barbee Lee, offered a slightly more pessimistic view. Despite the few women who had succeeded and made it to the top in business, she noted that the majority of women workers had not been able to attain any measure of financial security or independence. "In comparatively rare instances can women earn enough to enable them to establish homes of their own. More often, they find it necessary to share an apartment with one or two other women. What luxuries they have are usually bought at the sacrifice of future security."[67]

But fair or not, advertising and retail were two of the few areas where women were welcomed; some women even combined their retail career with broadcasting, by writing or producing commercials on the women's shows. However, for every woman who did manage to rise to a better-paying position, the vast majority ended up in low-paying and low-prestige clerical jobs, typing and filing with little chance to move up. Of course the plight of women in the workplace was a concern of Mary Anderson, head of the Women's Bureau of the U.S. Department of Labor. Unfortunately, historians like Lois Scharf and others have noted that she was well meaning but not very effective, since the male power brokers in the government failed to take the Women's Bureau seriously.[68]

Members of the National Federation of Business and Professional Women's Clubs (BPW) also spoke out. They were appalled that women were arbitrarily being fired or being forced to take pay cuts to save companies money. Using their magazine (*Independent Woman*) and sending their better-known members like author Margaret Culkin Banning to speak on women's shows, they tried to call attention to the problems working women faced. Throughout the 1930s, the Women's Bureau, the League of Women Voters, and the BPW fought for better pay and more opportunities for women workers, but their efforts did not result in any substantial changes. And some critics have also pointed out that the policies of the New Deal, even though a woman, Frances Perkins, had helped to create them, kept women in gender-stereotyped work with no hope of advancement.

While it is true that some New Deal programs, such as the National Youth Administration (NYA), which enabled many young women to attend college, were helpful to women, Professor Sarah Jane Deutsch, discussing another New Deal program, the Works Progress Administration (WPA), observed considerable gender stereotyping. "Most women's [work] projects consisted . . . of sewing rooms, where workers made garments for relief recipients; food processing, such as canning factories; health care; and domestic-service training . . . New Deal policies focused on promoting domestic roles for women, such as sewing, cleaning, canning and nursing . . . [because] administrators tended to see women as temporary workers who were helping out in an emergency and would return to the home after the depression. Why teach them non-domestic skills they would never use again?"[69] She went on to explain that the WPA's official procedure, as might be expected, was to first find jobs for male heads of family; next, any adult male children were placed. "Only if a husband were absent or disabled and no adult sons lived at home could women receive a high priority . . . the WPA limited the proportion of jobs it opened to women to between 12 and 16%."[70] In a decade where even teaching and social work jobs were going to men, a job sewing probably seemed better than no job at all.

While broadcasting was not suffering as many financial losses as other industries, it is undoubtedly true that the small local stations had a more difficult time paying the bills than the networks, which relied largely on national advertising. While I do not have exact figures for every woman on the air, what I have seen shows that the best-paid women were those who worked for the networks; individual performers negotiated with their sponsors and some did quite well as a result of having a popular show. Jessica Dragonette and Kate Smith were making somewhere in the $2,000 to $5,000 a week range, certainly an impressive sum in any era. In 1938, *Variety* reported that Dorothy Thompson was being paid around $1,500 for a five-minute radio commentary. For the network superstars, such as Eddie Cantor or Major Bowes or George Burns and Gracie Allen, their salaries were tied to their ratings or their ability to sell their sponsor's product, and these performers made large salaries as a result. But the majority of the people employed in broadcasting were neither famous nor making large sums of cash. I doubt that the network pages and ushers (who tended to be male) were getting rich; but given the culture's bias against equal pay, it would be safe to assume that neither were the secretaries and studio hostesses who, no matter how much responsibility they had, were not paid accordingly. Much more will be said on this subject in a later chapter. When I went into radio in the late 1960s, equal pay was still an unresolved issue.

Hostility to Women in Media

Even though some women were finding work in retail or in offices during the Depression, there is a very real question about whether attitudes toward them had changed. The concept of the "new woman" was fairly recent, and from what I have read, it does not seem that the men, who were still the majority in most companies, took women employees very seriously. Many even seemed rather hostile to the idea of women doing anything other than support work. Ruth Cowan, who had covered politics for a Houston news-paper on a freelance basis (women were not supposed to be experts at politi-cal analysis), was first hired by United Press as "R. Baldwin Cowan," but quickly fired when the home office learned they had just hired a woman.[71] One advertising woman in the early 1930s used the masculine sounding name "Craig" for her first name, and several other women executives stated in interviews that they often signed only their first two initials so that people would not arbitrarily dismiss what they had written. (Lest people think that is old-fashioned, even in the 1990s, the successful author of the Harry Pot-ter books for children wrote under the name of J.K. Rowling because she was told by her editor that boys would not read a book written by a woman.)

Several women who became war correspondents during World War II recalled comments from male colleagues about how "girl journalists" were second-rate, because everybody knew covering hard news was a man's job.[72] And at *Time* magazine, there was a very specific arrangement of roles: women did all the research, while men went out and got the story. It was the same at sister magazines *Life* and *Fortune*. Many of the researchers were college educated and while a few had been hired because they came from wealthy families with good social contacts, most were hired for their knowledge and their ability to check facts thoroughly. Yet when the editors occasionally sent a woman researcher to get some background information from a newsmaker, she was treated with scorn. "When [researcher] Florence Horn telephoned Westinghouse Air Brake to say she was coming to research a

Fortune article, the incredulous response was, 'Did you say *Fortune* is send-ing down a *WOMAN?*'" The general perception was that women research-ers were seeking husbands and were not serious about journalism.[73]

Even winning awards did not necessarily mean that women would get the respect they deserved. In movies, prolific screenwriter Frances Marion had won an Oscar for the prison drama *The Big House* in 1930, and she also wrote the screenplay that featured silent film legend Greta Garbo in her first talking role. Miss Marion was known as the highest-paid writer in Holly-wood, making $3,000 a week as head of the story department at MGM. Yet despite writing hundreds of screenplays during her career, and winning an-other Oscar in 1932, she was given less and less work after her mentor, Irving Thalberg, died. She ultimately left MGM in total frustration.[74]

In radio, the lack of respect was more subtle. *Broadcasting* seldom asked women for quotes about industry issues, unless they pertained to a women's show. In January 1932, and again in 1933 and 1934, the magazine asked industry leaders from a variety of areas in radio, engineering, and advertis-ing to comment on what had happened the previous year and predict what they expected in the year to come. Not once were any of the prominent women in radio asked for their opinions. Perhaps one year the editors for-got, or perhaps the women were reticent to speak up. But this pattern of never including them recurred year after year, as if to say that women were not considered industry leaders. As for the broadcast organizations, they, too, were run by men and oriented around the opinions of their male mem-bers. The one woman who was an active participant in the National Associa-tion of Broadcasters was Judith Waller, and she was chair of a committee on education. Otherwise, on reading the yearly list of attendees at the NAB's annual convention, it was almost entirely male, even at stations where we know women were in management positions. And while it may well be that women were hesitant to travel alone back then, it may also be that these conventions did not make women feel as if they were part of the proceed-ings, so they stayed home and let the men have their get-together.

And as for Miss Waller, despite her having run WMAQ in Chicago dur-ing the station's first few years, and having first been its program director and eventually its vice president, in 1931 when the station was officially restructured and NBC became involved, Miss Waller was not promoted; she was kept on as the assistant to William Hedges, who had been named presi-dent and general manager. Granted, Mr. Hedges had an equally long career in journalism and broadcasting, including being elected president of the NAB in 1928. But had Judith Waller been male, I wonder if her years of managing WMAQ would have gotten her a better position than assistant to the manager. The only opportunity offered to her was directing the educational programs of

NBC in the Midwest, certainly no disgrace, but once again a role considered more suitable for a woman than station manager.

Dorothy Thompson's Dislike of Feminism

While many women wrote articles protesting the limits placed on opportunities for women or tried to encourage more equitable pay, one well-known journalist, Dorothy Thompson, caused quite a stir in 1936 when she published an article saying that feminism was causing men to feel resentful, and that working women were the reason for an increase in crime. She also agreed that women were taking away men's jobs, and accused the modern woman of not setting a moral example.[75] As she criticized the selfishness of other women, she, of course, did not mention her own two failed marriages, nor did she admit that she had seldom shown much interest in raising her son, having spent most of her life devoted to her career. Miss Thompson would write other antifeminist columns over the next several decades. However, her attitude about women, and especially working women, was definitely ambivalent; a number of women entering journalism recalled how supportive she was of their efforts and how she encouraged them to pursue their goals.[76] She also gave at least one radio talk in the mid-1930s—she often was a guest on chat shows—about whether women were happier as homemakers or career women (no, she did not believe women should arbitrarily be homemakers); and some of her news commentaries were about women who had achieved in their professions, for which she praised them.

Yet, in an article she wrote in September 1939 for *Ladies' Home Journal,* she stated that women should dedicate themselves to their husbands and accept the fact that a woman could not have both a happy marriage and a career.[77] She told her readers that the world needed good mothers more than it needed women lawyers or novelists. She also said she had come to believe that a woman could only be happy if she had a happy marriage (Miss Thompson would soon be married for a third time, making her perhaps an expert on this subject; from all accounts, this last marriage was indeed a happy one). And lest I seem dismissive of the content of her article blaming working women for society's problems, Dorothy Thompson was probably articulating the way many men of the 1930s did feel—while today we are much more accustomed to seeing women who have their own lives and their own careers, the idea of a woman making her own choices was still fairly new, and I am not surprised that there was resentment from men, most of whom had been raised to expect that a wife would obey and keep him happy in exchange for his financial support.

Male Critics of Feminism

John Bantry, who commented in the *Boston Post* about Miss Thompson's article, not only agreed with much of it but added his own personal grievances, including that women were terrible drivers, not able to do the difficult jobs, self-centered, and unappreciative of male chivalry; the world would be a much better place, he said, if women would just go back to their domestic roles.[78] This was also the general time period when men's magazines were going through some changes, reflecting that ambivalence about women as well as the confusion some men felt about the "new woman" and what she allegedly wanted from men.

Esquire, a magazine for middle- and upper-class men, began publishing in 1933. By 1936, the magazine was printing an ongoing series of misogynistic articles, criticizing the modern female and voicing some of the same resentments expressed by Dorothy Thompson and John Bantry. Evidently, criticizing women was good for business; the more vehemently *Esquire*'s articles did it, the more their circulation rose, in spite of the Depression.[79] If the editors at women's fan magazines knew what their readers wanted, the same could certainly be said about the editors at *Esquire.* Among the most frequent points the writers made were that modern women were gold diggers who liked men only for what expensive gifts they could bring. Women were not creative, yet were trying to expropriate and benefit from what men had created, and they did not appreciate the fact that men are biologically more intelligent. Women were "created to be helpers," yet they were now rebelling against what they had been designed to do. Women were seductresses, who destroyed relationships and could not remain faithful. And of course, "[m]en operate by reasoning. Women's minds work on instinct," and as a result of women's "wild emotionalism," they were unfit for most of the jobs they sought. Men were urged to beware, since the modern woman was not to be trusted.[80] And while the songs and the soap operas on radio might speak of pure and ideal love, in reality, romance was dead and the new woman had killed it.[81]

As for what message radio was giving to women about the gender wars, as mentioned earlier, the networks tried their best to avoid controversy, because it was bad for business. Sponsors expected women to fulfill the role assigned to them: doing testimonials about the wonders of various products. During the Depression, when money was hard to come by for the average family, there was no incentive for radio's women to rock the boat by calling attention to how stereotypic their roles often were. On the other hand, there was one place where relationship problems and the war between the sexes were frequently discussed—these were constant plot lines in soap operas.

Unfortunately, soap operas tended to feature women characters who fit every common female stereotype: there were gold diggers, devious home wreckers, women who were constantly dominated by their emotions, as well as some female characters who were incredibly long-suffering and saintly no matter what was done to them. Of course, it was not just women who were villains; there were some unsavory male characters, too, since the plot lines required constant conflict and melodrama. Some women in the soaps had careers (such as "Joyce Jordan, Girl Interne," later "Joyce Jordan, M.D."), which, of course, became a struggle as they tried to balance their work with their desire for a family. But serious discussion of how men and women got along was relegated to an occasional educational program; more often, it became a plot line in a comedy, or a network show where the subject was framed as entertainment. Two examples of this were *Battle of the Sexes,* hosted by husband-and-wife team Frank Crumit and Julia Sanderson beginning in 1938 on NBC Red; and *Husbands and Wives,* hosted by a man and a woman who had worked together on WOR in New York before getting a chance on the Mutual Broadcasting System in 1936.

Battle of the Sexes was a quiz show whose concept involved male contestants versus females, purporting to show who was more intelligent, men or women. As for *Husbands and Wives,* it was more of a fact-based soap opera, a precursor to the tell-all TV shows of the 1980s. The concept was simple: a team of husbands and a team of wives discussed real problems in their marriages, in sometimes heated fashion. Hostess Allie Lowe Miles, who had originally come up with the idea for the show, told *Radio Stars* magazine that she felt it was a good way for married couples to get things off their chest, and the audience could empathize or disagree as they wished. Co-host Sedley Brown concurred, explaining the neutral role that he and Miles played: ". . . [W]e never give advice. We never express an opinion or take sides in any of the problems that come before us . . . We believe the best way to help people is to let them help themselves . . . If you can talk about your troubles to somebody, it often clears up the situation. We've had thousands of letters of thanks from our audiences."[82] Evidently there was only so much catharsis a 1930s audience could take, because the show did not last more than a year.

Public Affairs and Controversy

Because all radio licensees were required to do public service and educational shows (the Federal Radio Commission had turned into the Federal Communications Commission in 1934, and it had very specific rules about how radio should serve the public), a certain amount of discussion on social issues did take place, although not as much as proponents of educational broadcasting would have liked. One of the first network programs to take on the controversial issues originated in New York and was later broadcast over the Mutual network (Mutual was founded in the autumn of 1934). *The American Forum of the Air,* which was first called the *Mutual Forum of the Air,* featured famous politicians and journalists debating the issues of the day. Another highly respected public affairs show was on NBC's Blue Network beginning in 1935—*America's Town Meeting of the Air.* Guest speakers gave their point of view on the week's topic (the show was usually oriented around current events), but so did the studio audience, which was free to heckle or disagree with the views of any speaker. The debates often became heated and the show received large amounts of fan mail. Guests included First Lady Eleanor Roosevelt, noted black author Langston Hughes, Socialist Norman Thomas, historian Will Durant, comedian Eddie Cantor, and journalists Heywood Broun and Dorothy Thompson, just to name a few. *Town Meeting* moderator George V. Denny chose guests from all walks of life and all political persuasions. He also turned down offers of sponsorship for fear that if the show became commercialized, it would not be as free and uninhibited in its discussions.[83]

Some controversial issues were more difficult to program than others, however. Network shows that were sponsored (most public affairs shows were not) tended to be cautious about subjects like racism, labor unrest, and sex education. The belief that these topics might offend or alienate the public persisted. Some local station managers sent memos to their news staff forbidding them from mentioning social issues, even if they were in the news.[84] It was an era of euphemism and circumlocution in movies as well as radio, as entire lists of banned words were issued, and songs that were perceived as having double entendres could be pulled from the air arbitrarily.[85] Even the fan magazines complained that radio was afflicted with too many censors worrying about too many inconsequential things.[86]

One issue that affected women in the 1930s was a very contentious subject: birth control. Ongoing efforts to reverse the Comstock Law were making slow progress; this law had, for quite some time, prevented women from receiving birth control information through the mail, even if they wanted to receive it. The ruling that contraceptive materials were no longer considered obscene was a victory for another outspoken woman, Margaret Sanger. Sanger had often talked to the print media on this subject, but radio was much more conservative about discussions that involved sex. One speaker found that he would not be allowed to say the word *syphilis* during a medical talk he was giving.[87] But Sanger and others in the birth control movement had mastered the art of getting publicity; and publicity made news, even when the subject matter was controversial. One technique Sanger used was to give educational talks about overpopulation in foreign countries, which would then lead to a discussion about the importance of family planning. She gave these talks in a number of cities, and radio stations in New York City; Richmond, Virginia; and even Havana, Cuba, aired them. CBS carried one of them as well, bringing the topic to a much wider audience than ever before.

Women in Orchestras

But most of the American public probably was content to let the soap operas, variety shows, and comedies entertain them, and while they found the occasional controversy interesting, there was still the Depression, and the economic hardships that affected the poor and lower middle class were slow to abate. Throughout the early to mid-1930s, the recording industry was especially hard hit, but one industry's problems meant benefits for radio. The networks capitalized on the fact that there were some excellent musicians around, some of whom might have been hesitant to perform on the air, but with record sales off dramatically and concert dates not as numerous, now they needed the work. Despite all of the female vocalists on radio, there were certainly visible gender roles in the big bands of that time. Bandleaders were always men, as were the members of the orchestra. There had been small groups that were all female, and in the 1920s, many were heard playing chamber music on local stations. But now, dance music and orchestras were popular, and none of the well-known big bands or the smaller jazz groups hired any women musicians. However, many bands had a female vocalist (or a "canary" as some of the music magazines called them), and these women became well known in their own right, even if they were only called upon to sing an occasional song.

Where many of the radio singers were mainly heard (unless a fan magazine did a story about one of them and included a photo), the women vocalists with the bands were also meant to be seen. They stepped in front of the microphone attractively dressed and looking confident as they sang about lost love or about finding Mr. Right. A woman as a vocalist was acceptable, yet despite a number of women who accompanied individual male performers on radio, the idea of women in orchestras was not encouraged at all. The usual stereotypes were given for excluding them: women were not team players, women were not as dedicated or as talented, women were too emotional, etc. Musicologist Lewis A. Erenberg suggests another possible reason. Men, feeling emasculated by the inability to find work, identified with the all-male bands the same way that women vicariously identified with a glamorous movie star or vocalist. The small jazz group or swing band represented freedom and adventure for men; these groups traveled to exciting places and received public acclaim.

[S]wing bands were nearly all-male teams of musicians who countered de-pression-era worries about masculine weakness . . . With work scarce and love and domesticity potentially entrapping for men, there was little interest on their part in integrating women musicians into swing or jazz bands be-fore World War II . . . [These men] immerse[d] themselves in . . . teams who took pride in their work habits and musical abilities and who were led by patriarchal fathers . . . Such bands offered a model of male group strength that avoided the entanglements of home, family and women.[88]

As for the female vocalist, Erenberg theorizes that she served a very spe-cific function. "While male musicians represented public values [of hard work, creativity, and skillfulness], women singers articulated private emo-tions. Many [band] leaders would have been content to function without vocalists, but they needed singers of romantic songs and iconic models of femininity to appeal to a heterosexual youth culture."[89] Helen Ward, who was the first vocalist bandleader Benny Goodman hired, remarked that Goodman saw female singers as "a necessary evil."[90] Interestingly, many gained a grudging acceptance by becoming the band's unofficial "mom," handling some of the cooking and sewing and doing the errands the men needed done. And the few male bandleaders (such as Guy Lombardo, Ray Noble, and Sammy Kaye) who refused to hire female vocalists were taken to task by *Radio Stars,* which half-jokingly suggested that Secretary of La-bor Frances Perkins ought to do something about it.[91]

But female musicians found an unlikely champion in bandleader Phil Spitalny. In the early 1930s, he formed what he called an "all-girl orches-tra," along with violinist Evelyn Kaye Klein, whom he later married. The *Hour of Charm* was first heard on CBS in May of 1934. Spitalny's attitude towards his "girls" was by modern standards very paternalistic. He defended the musicianship of his band and fought for them to be treated with respect; yet he also chose their clothes and their hairstyles, made them sign a con-tract that would not allow them to marry for two years, and nobody in his band could weigh more than 122 pounds.[92] Still, the members of his band, while under a control far more rigid than that of any male band member, were able to carve out a niche for themselves and prove that they were in fact good musicians. Whether the audience perceived the *Hour of Charm* as anything more than a novelty is difficult to say, but the show did have spon-sors, and for many of the women in the band, the regular work they got was worth the rules they were expected to follow.

When the print media wrote about the band, every stereotype about women found its way into the story: Mel Adams, paying tribute to the All-Girl Or-chestra in *Radio Guide,* suggested that Phil Spitalny was an amazing man because he was able to get "twenty eight girls to play together in one band with unity and precision . . . his diplomacy, tact, and understanding . . . [is needed] to achieve the herculean feat of an all-girl orchestra."[93] That twenty-eight men might be even more egocentric or hard to handle evidently never occurred to Mr. Adams, who several more times mentioned how great an achievement it was that Spitalny got along with the "girls" and was able to get them to cooperate. (The belief that women are petty and unwilling to work as a team would endure well into the 1990s.)

Successful Women in the Arts

If women had been encouraged, or in some cases forced, to return to the traditional role of homemaker during the 1930s, there were an increasing number of women starring in popular films, singing hit songs, and writing best-selling books or plays. Pearl Buck's novel *The Good Earth* won a Pulitzer Prize for fiction in 1932. In 1933, author Fanny Hurst wrote *Imitation of Life*, which was made into a popular movie a year later. And when Hurst appeared on her friend Mary Margaret McBride's chat show to talk about current events, she would sometimes mention that she hoped someday to do an issues-oriented show of her own, because she believed radio had the ability to educate women about what was going on in the world.[94]

Beginning in 1934, playwright Lillian Helman's *The Children's Hour* enjoyed a long and successful run on Broadway. In 1936, Claire Booth Luce had similar Broadway success with her social satire, *The Women,* later a hit movie with an all-female cast. Margaret Mitchell wrote *Gone with the Wind,* which won the Pulitzer Prize in 1937 and then became a major motion picture in 1939. Eleanor Roosevelt and Margaret Sanger both published their autobiographies in 1938.[95] It was yet another decade when women received conflicting messages about their proper role. Cosmetics advertising was at an all-time high despite the Depression; women were told that how they looked was crucial to keeping a husband or being popular, and the right cosmetics could help. And despite the ad agencies not wanting women to be announcers, where a product aimed at women was concerned, attractive female singers and movie stars were chosen to do testimonials on why every woman should buy the particular item. NBC vocalist Dorothy Page, who had been voted a "Radio Beauty Queen" in 1935, was featured in one of a series of articles, ostensibly paying tribute each month to a lovely female radio singer, but the articles were really about how women listeners could "Keep Young and Beautiful" by using the right cosmetics. Everyone who sent a self-addressed stamped envelope to *Radio Stars* magazine would receive a free pamphlet with helpful beauty tips and the names of these recommended products. Whether the end result was that those who emulated Page in her choice of makeup magically became beauty queens, too, is debatable, but this approach was frequently utilized when advertising to the female consumer.[96] Even male stars were called upon to help persuade women. One example was a magazine ad for a certain brand of lipstick that movie and radio star Dick Powell praised because he said women looked more natural when they wore it. And in an article that would probably get him sued for discrimination today, popular radio bandleader Leo Reisman vehemently stated that he hated fat women and could not stand the sight of them on the dance floor. He suggested that a woman who is not lithe and slender will never inspire matrimonial thoughts. He then launched into a discussion of how a woman who wears make-up that is too obvious also offends him. Rather than taking him to task for being so judgmental, the interviewer (the magazine's beauty editor), took the opportunity to plug a new "milk diet" and to recommend that women use Lady Esther cosmetics, which were, of course, never too obvious.[97]

It seems as if the only time that strong views about women's issues were discussed occurred when the author of a best-selling book was a guest on a women's show. Pearl Buck, who had expressed such outspoken ideas as that women who did not want to marry should not, and women should have the right to ask a man out on a date,[98] was always an interesting guest, as was feminist writer Fanny Hurst and, of course, Margaret Sanger inspired much debate. Even Eleanor Roosevelt polarized the audience, some of whom felt she should be more retiring and not call so much attention to her own views. Yet, while a few women did seem to march to the beat of their own drummer, the average woman of the 1930s probably did not feel she had the right to question the status quo too much. I recall a story my late mother told me about how her father arbitrarily decided her brother could go to college while she could not, even though she was the one who wanted to go and she was the one with the outstanding grades. Despite being disappointed, she accepted what her father said—that a male needed a college education more than a female did; she also accepted that her father had every right to make decisions about her future without asking her what she wanted. So, my mother went to work in an office, as a woman was supposed to. Years later, there were still men who believed a college education was a luxury for a woman, my late father among them; but by the time I was ready for college, I did not let my father's disapproval stop me from having both an education and a career, while in my mother's generation, she obviously felt it was not her place to disagree with what she was told. As we have seen, a few women of the 1930s did stand up for their rights, even during that extremely conservative and poverty-stricken era. Where they got their inner strength remains another of the mysteries of human behavior, since society as a whole did not tend to praise or reward women who were seen as too different.

As much as women were again told to withdraw from public life, there were still public figures who were greatly admired. One was sports heroine Mildred "Babe" Didrikson Zaharias, who won two gold medals and one silver in track and field events at the 1932 Olympics. Women's sporting events in the 1930s were sometimes covered by the networks. One example was the women's golf championships, which were carried by NBC. This may have been thanks to young Patty Berg, who was attracting considerable media attention as she won tournament after tournament, becoming the national women's champion when she was only twenty. Miss Berg was named Woman Athlete of the Year in 1938. And while not many women were network announcers, there were several women on the air doing sports commentary. In Cleveland in 1934, Marge Wilson was hired by an ad agency to do a sports program for station WHK, and according to the agency's spokesman, the listener response had been overwhelmingly positive.[99] And in 1938, General Mills hired another young woman, Helen Dettweiler, to do a sports interview show for CBS. *Time* magazine had a woman sportswriter for a time in the late 1930s and early 1940s. Pearl Kroll's biggest problem was not a lack of knowledge but, rather, old-fashioned attitudes about where women could and could not go—she was not allowed in the press box at baseball games because the press box was for men only.[100] Two of the most respected media women of the 1930s were award-winning photojournalist Margaret Bourke-White, whose pictures frequently appeared in *Life* and *Fortune,* two magazines where women were usually restricted to being researchers or secretaries, and photographer Dorothea Lange, whose unforgettable images of the poor during the Depression also appeared in magazines and to this day are displayed in museums. (Lange's success is even more amazing in light of the fact that not only was she one of the few women photographers of her era, but she also had a physical handicap—a childhood battle with polio left her with a noticeable limp, which did not deter her from her chosen career and which she felt helped to put her subjects at ease.)

As the Depression gradually ended and life began to improve again for many average Americans, radio continued to play an important part. Music fans waited patiently by their radio every Saturday night to find out what the top ten hits were as the popular show *Your Hit Parade* counted them down. Meanwhile, newspapers, which had long been in a rivalry with radio, were slowly coming to accept the popularity of the radio stars, and when a network was bringing one of them to town for a live broadcast, reporters would be right there to do an interview. Just how seriously people took what they heard on the radio was proven dramatically by Orson Welles in the autumn of 1938 when his dramatic performance of *War of the Worlds* convinced millions that Martians had invaded, and panic ensued in a number of cities. According to *Broadcasting,* in 1938, 82 percent of American homes had at least one radio, and over 4 million cars now had a radio installed.[101]

While music and melodrama were what listeners liked the best, events in Europe were growing more ominous, and people were asking for an increasing amount of information; as a result, by the late 1930s, most U.S. stations had expanded their news coverage and were sending reporters overseas. At home, the Fair Labor Standards Law established a twenty-five cents per hour minimum wage in many jobs, mandated a forty-four-hour work week, and officially abolished child labor. Kate Smith took a song that Irving Berlin had written years earlier and, in 1938, she turned it into a huge hit. With a possible war looming, the song "God Bless America" seemed especially appropriate. In fact, a number of women had hit songs—in 1939, for example, Martha Tilton (known as "Liltin' Martha Tilton"), a vocalist with Benny Goodman's band, had great success with "And the Angels Sing." Judy Garland appeared on several NBC radio shows in the summer of 1939, such as *Maxwell House Coffee Time* and the *Fred Waring Show,* performing the song "Over the Rainbow" from the hit movie *The Wizard of Oz.* Helen O'Connell, who was singing with the Jimmy Dorsey Band, would be named the top female vocalist of the year by 1940. And vocalists of color such as Billie Holliday and Ella Fitzgerald were becoming increasingly popular. Ella had a number one song in 1938 with "A-Tisket, A-Tasket," and *Downbeat* magazine named her a top female vocalist.

Children's Programming

As the 1930s ended, there were still the ubiquitous soap operas, as well as action dramas, police shows, and even shows with super heroes. As women's programming made money for radio, children were another very important audience for advertisers, and most stations had some programs for them. And just like today, some of these shows were criticized by parents and educators as too violent or too filled with gratuitous commercialism. Even the well-known comic strip *Little Orphan Annie,* which had been made into a radio show for kids, was accused of being too frightening, as Annie experienced a number of cliff-hanger plot twists. The show's sponsor, Ovaltine, was actively involved in the show, offering young listeners many premiums if they just purchased enough of the sponsor's product; children were encouraged to save up so they could get decoders and shake-up mugs—some of the commercials lasted as long as three minutes.[102]

But the women who were so much a part of children's programming produced many creative and imaginative programs. Some were even critically acclaimed, especially those produced by a woman named Nila Mack, who served as director of children's programming for CBS. It was she who trained and directed some of radio's best child performers, and her skill at finding innovative ways to keep children entertained was frequently praised. Starting with *The Adventures of Helen and Mary* in 1930 and continuing on with the show that was renamed *Let's Pretend* in 1934, Nila Mack taught the virtues of honesty, courtesy, and kindness. She did so with exciting stories that had a moral but did not preach at the young audience. *Let's Pretend* encouraged children to use the power of their imagination; given the show's excellent reputation, it is not surprising that in 1939, it was voted the best children's show by the annual *World-Telegram* newspaper poll of radio editors. Sponsored by Cream of Wheat cereal, *Let's Pretend* would last well into the early 1950s. A number of its child performers grew up to have successful careers in radio and in film.

Another fixture in children's radio in the 1930s was Ireene Wicker, the "Singing Lady," whose programs were heard on NBC Blue, sponsored by Kellogg's cereals, throughout most of the decade. She told stories, she sang, and she narrated musical skits, and parents loved her ability to hold their children's interest. There were also some men who did very successful children's programming, most notably "Big Brother" Bob Emery and "Uncle Don" Carney, both of whom had radio clubs that children could join. There were a number of other "uncles" and "big brothers" in cities all over the United States, as there were also numerous story ladies. In our visually oriented society, perhaps it is difficult to conceive of a time when kids sat eagerly by their radio, hearing the friendly voice of the host or hostess of their favorite show, going on whatever journey the show was taking that day, and learning about good manners or helping others or whatever the lesson for that day happened to be.

One other greatly respected woman in educational programming worked for CBS. Dorothy Gordon created a show called *Yesterday's Children* in 1939. On this program, famous adults, including Fannie Hurst, Eddie Cantor, and even President Roosevelt, talked about the books they had loved during their childhood. She was also involved with another critically acclaimed show, *The American School of the Air,* for which she was the musical director throughout most of the 1930s. And Dorothy Gordon also did a show known as the *Children's Corner* from May 1936 until January 1938. On this show, Miss Gordon, who was fluent in eight languages, read stories from around the world, and, according to media historian John Dunning, she was even able to convince her sponsor, Wheatena, to tone down the strident commercials and not offer any premiums, even though such tactics were the most common way to bribe kids into using a product.[103]

The late 1930s saw a few more women news commentators; they were usually restricted to the women's shows, but there they were, reporting on current events, as well as seeking out and reporting the stories of women and organizations that were making a positive difference in their community. And this was not just happening in the larger markets where the previously mentioned Kathryn Cravens or Dorothy Thompson were on the air. In smaller markets like Tulsa, Oklahoma, women could be heard more frequently in roles other than just giving new recipes. The General Manager of KVOO in Tulsa told *Broadcasting* that he had decided to try a female commentator and had been very pleased with the response. Dorothy McCune reported on special events in the area, including covering the recent local election. "We have found," said William B. Way, "[that] the use of Miss McCune's voice on the air . . . pleases our listeners, especially our women listeners . . . We have found that her pleasing voice personality adds a long needed touch to some types of special events broadcasts, which have heretofore used only masculine, rapid-fire types of voices."[104]

Conflicting Messages for Women

If we are trying to make sense out of the trends that occurred for women in the 1930s, once again there are many contradictions. Some scholars I have read express the belief that women lost ground in the 1930s, and certainly many women, especially those who were poor, unskilled, or minority, did suffer. The haunting faces in the photographs of Dorothea Lange are dramatic proof of the difficult times rural women endured. And yet, even in small towns, radio and movies tried to cheer people up and help them to forget their troubles for a while. People like Ida McNeil with her one-woman station even reached out to the listeners directly, encouraging them and talking to them as her friends, telling them things would get better.

Despite the fact that a number of married middle-class women did find themselves persona non grata in certain jobs, statistics do not show a drastic loss of jobs for women, even though there was massive unemployment in some parts of the country. Yes, middle-class women found that in fields like medicine, law, and even teaching, they were indeed losing ground. But over all, the number of married women in the labor force increased during the 1930s, even though the types of jobs available may not have been as varied, and the work they did was often temporary or part time. In spite of the increasing number of women holding down jobs, the woman who worked for pay was also expected to run the home, do all the housework, raise the children, and fulfill all the duties the culture assigned to women. Men were not yet expected to help, and the belief that a working woman should still do everything that a full-time housewife did was seldom questioned by the media.

The one social change the Depression did bring to the middle class was a drastic slowdown in how much money could be spent on clothing, leisure activities, cosmetics, and even food. Many American families had to learn to live on a budget, whether they wanted to or not; on this subject, it seems radio tried to have it both ways, encouraging consumerism at the same time as the women's shows were encouraging the need for budgeting. And while women's roles in radio were for the most part limited to singing, being a member of a comedy team, working on a women's show, or working behind the scenes, there continued to be exceptions as the 1930s came to an end. Lisa Sergio was a woman with an international reputation, whose voice had been heard all over Europe via her short-wave broadcasts. She was hired in 1939 to consult, and few if any women in radio were consultants. Miss Sergio's consulting work was for WQXR in New York, where she also did some announcing. Since her expertise was in classical music, she did a classical program and discussed opera.[105]

Sadly, there is considerable evidence that women of color did not benefit from the limited opportunities available to middle-class women. Government programs were often unwilling to give assistance to nonwhites, and while some training programs did provide useful job skills, it was mainly the white trainees who were offered the jobs.[106] This must have been especially frustrating to young black women, since a higher number of them were attending college, and as a result of the Harlem Renaissance, many black authors, poets, and performers appeared to be getting more respect than in previous generations; several were guests on women's shows on New York radio. First Lady Eleanor Roosevelt often expressed her support for the work of the distinguished black educator Mary McLeod Bethune, a founder of the National Council of Negro Women and an influential advisor to the government during the New Deal. And yet, despite the gains some middle-class black women seemed to be making, the vast majority were denied equal opportunity, especially in parts of the country that were segregated; many of the government's programs seemed designed to keep them in traditional roles of maids and house cleaners, no matter what their education.[107] Such inequities probably should have been discussed on the public affairs radio shows, but by and large, those shows concentrated on foreign policy issues or on matters such as politics. As mentioned earlier, an occasional black leader did get on the air to discuss racism; there was also at least one network special that paid tribute to the immigrants of all races and nationalities, discussing how each group had contributed to America. But the networks were nervous about losing their southern affiliates and offending the sponsors; occasionally, a writer might give a character some dialog about a social issue, but with network censors ever vigilant, this did not happen too often. Even radio performers who were opposed to segregation made few public statements.

Over all, it seems that most performers saw themselves first and foremost as entertainers, and while in their private life they did take stands on issues that mattered to them, on the air they seemed to feel they should remain neutral. In this, radio was not unique: Wenzel and Binkowski, in their history of sheet music, have observed that the Tin Pan Alley songwriters turned out mostly encouraging songs during the Depression; yes, there was the pathos of "Brother Can You Spare a Dime," but for the most part, the popular songs were about love, romance, and escape, as if nothing at all was wrong. Protest songs about economic inequality were considered too depressing to become popular. "Fantasy was what people wanted, and a sophisticated, witty, polished song genre that ignored the poor rural white or urban black was the result."[108]

Even those performers who tried to help minorities usually preferred not to discuss it. Benny Goodman was the first major bandleader to integrate his band, for example, but when the "King of Swing" performed with the Benny Goodman Quartet and CBS carried it in October of 1936, there was no conversation about racism in the jazz world or the benefits of integrated bands; Goodman wanted to talk only about music. *Downbeat* magazine did have a discussion about jazz and segregation in several articles during the late 1930s; some of Goodman's contemporaries said they opposed integrated bands, while others commended him for being courageous. Said popular black vocalist Ella Fitzgerald, "I believe the hiring of colored musicians in a white band is really mutually beneficial. Both races have a lot to offer each other. It would be hard to understand the advisability of racial distinction where artistry in musical advancement is concerned." Goodman, who was famous for being taciturn, said only that his intention was to hire the best possible musicians.[109]

Sometimes, of course, mentioning the racial question could not be avoided, as when the popular black contralto Marian Anderson was refused the right to perform at a concert hall in Washington, D.C., because of her race; again, it was Eleanor Roosevelt who took a stand and who arranged for Miss Anderson to perform a concert at the Lincoln Memorial on Easter Sunday 1939. Radio carried it, and the subject of segregation was all too briefly on the minds of average white Americans, many of whom were puzzled at why such a great singer had been denied a place to perform. But this was the era when the most commonly heard representation of the Negro (as they were called back then) was the popular comedy show *Amos 'n' Andy,* wherein the two stars were white men who wore blackface and spoke in dialect.

Since some black performers now had their own shows on the network, perhaps the average white person assumed things were going just fine for black people. The same assumption may also have been made about the status of women: given how many shows had a high-profile female vocalist on them, it would have been easy to decide that women were not being discriminated against at all. So the bandleaders and masters of ceremonies and nearly all of the owners and managers were men, and the women were sometimes treated like inferiors by their male bosses; still the radio women seemed to have exciting and glamorous jobs, far more interesting than the jobs the average working woman held. I doubt that most people thought about whether women working behind the scenes in radio were paid adequately or treated well; chances are, even the women themselves accepted whatever pay they received, just as they accepted being patronized or treated discourteously by certain men in authority.

At the beginning of the 1930s, Emily Newell Blair had written an article wherein she expressed her disappointment that women had not yet made more gains, and that what few career successes they had were in traditionally female occupations (Elizabeth Arden in the cosmetic industry, for example). Said Miss Blair, "The positions that decide policies of any importance are still held by men. Women work only as assistants or secretaries. In the business world today, most women play the part of servants, not equals."[110] And yet, she predicted at the end of the piece that the younger women were ready to reach for real equality, and she believed the next decade would see some very important gains. Little did she know, writing in 1931 during the Depression's darkest period, that only ten years hence, women would suddenly be essential to businesses, and they would even be asked to take jobs that had never before been open to them. World War II was about to dramatically change women's roles again, and that change would be felt in every occupation, including radio.

Timeline: The 1930s

1931	Judith Waller becomes educational and public affairs director for NBC/Midwest
	Kate Smith Show debuts
1932	Frances Perkins becomes first woman Cabinet official
1934	Mutual Broadcasting System is created
	Mary Margaret McBride Show debuts
Late 1930s	Kathryn Cravens and Dorothy Thompson do network news commentary

Chapter 4

The 1940s: Visible for a While

At the 1939 World's Fair in New York, attendees had marveled at the new technologies of the World of Tomorrow, and they saw a demonstration of TV from RCA. Some cities now had experimental FM stations; FM promised to end problems with station reception and advertised itself as "static-free radio." But in 1940, few people had a TV or an FM radio. As the new decade began, AM radio still ruled, and there were now over 800 radio stations in the United States. Comedy shows remained popular; the *New York World-Telegram*'s annual poll of radio editors had Jack Benny at number one and Fred Allen number two. Fanny Brice, with her character "Baby Snooks," was the only women among the top ten comedians, although several of the male winners worked with a female sidekick (Fred Allen performed with his wife, Portland Hoffa, and Jack Benny often included his wife, Mary Livingstone, in the show). There were many popular female vocalists—the editors liked Frances Langford, Kate Smith, and Connie Boswell, but Dinah Shore, Mildred Bailey, and the Andrews Sisters had hits too; popular male vocalists included Bing Crosby, the Ink Spots, Kenny Baker, and an up-and-coming young man named Frank Sinatra. Fan magazines came and went. *Radio Stars* was no longer around; it had become part of the movie magazine *Modern Screen* in 1939. The same thing happened to *Radio Guide*—it was now *Movie and Radio Guide*. Publishers could save money by combining two similar magazines, and it made sense in this case, since many movie stars were heard on radio and many radio stars performed in film. Then, as now, celebrity talk and celebrity gossip were always popular. Syndicated gossip columnist Louella Parsons had her own show in the early 1930s; she would soon return to radio. But her archrival Hedda Hopper was on the air, doing a show for CBS; so was Nellie Revell, or "Neighbor Nell," who also knew every celebrity in New York and was able to get them to appear on her show.

Although a war was going on in Europe and Adolph Hitler had repeatedly shown his desire for conquest, two-thirds of all Americans polled stated that America should not get involved and should continue to remain neutral.[1] In his Fireside Chats, President Roosevelt agreed and said he hoped it would not be necessary to enter the war. But radio coverage continued to increase as events overseas escalated. Edward R. Murrow and H.V. Kaltenborn were two of the contingent of radio journalists who were reporting from Europe, along with countless print journalists; about fifty female newspaper and magazine reporters were credentialed, as well as a smaller group of women radio correspondents—including Kathryn Cravens and Dorothy Thompson. It was probably the first time that broadcast journalists were competing with print journalists for news stories in foreign countries. For a number of reasons, prior to the late 1930s, most radio stations did not have a large news staff and often got their news from an affiliation with a newspaper. But now, radio was in the midst of the action, keeping the public up to date as the situation in Europe worsened. Edward R. Murrow's live broadcasts from London via CBS were compelling, as air raid sirens and the sound of bombs could sometimes be heard in the background as he spoke.

On a happier note, radio was still the home of escapist entertainment, so fans of young movie star Shirley Temple were pleased when they heard her on the air for the first time on Christmas Eve 1939, as she sang a song with Nelson Eddy on the CBS *Screen Guild Theater;* her appearance was for a good cause— a charitable fund that supported former actors, actresses, and behind-the-scenes workers who were now too old or too ill to support themselves. Meanwhile, many Americans were waiting for their phone to ring with the hope that it would be good news from "Pot o' Gold," perhaps the first "big money" giveaway on radio, in which people were called at random and the prize was $1,000—a large sum in those days. Much-loved radio star Gracie Allen decided to launch a comedic run for the presidency in early 1940. Her humorous campaign—she represented the Surprise Party—was not only fun for the audience, but Allen used the skit on a number of other network shows where she appeared as a guest to promote her mythical run for the White House. (While Allen's on-air character was dumb, in real life she was a resourceful businesswoman who knew how to get publicity for herself and her husband, George Burns.)

Women Newsmakers of the Early 1940s

Women in nontraditional occupations were getting some attention from *Time* magazine. In a cover story about French women and their work during the war, the article concluded with discussion of a certain "spinster" (as unmarried women were called) who was also described as "brilliant," Eve Curie. Curie, who was one of the few women to make the cover of *Time* (February 12, 1940), was the daughter of physicists Marie and Pierre. While older sister Irene got most of her parents' attention because she wanted to be a scientist, Eve carved out a career in music and literature and had recently written a biography of her famous mother; the book was getting good reviews and Curie enjoyed being interviewed.

The women flyers were in the news again. Tragically, Amelia Earhart's plane had been lost in 1937 and she was presumed dead, but the rest of the Ninety-Nines were still advocating for more respect for women pilots. The controversy in early 1940 was a ruling by the Civil Aeronautics Authority (CAA) that banned pregnant women from flying airplanes. Numerous women who were private pilots were very upset by this ruling, which purported to be to protect women from harm—the five men on the board believed that a pregnant woman should not fly because she was too weak and subject to fainting spells. Mrs. Betty Huyler Gillies, a pilot and president of the Ninety Nines, did her best to refute this; it was her contention that this ruling was not about protection, but about making sure women did not fly enough hours to be allowed to keep their licenses. If a woman did not fly the required number of hours each year, she could not renew her certification and had to start all over again. But the CAA refused to change their ruling, although they said they would take it under advisement.[2]

The White House Conference on Children issued its annual findings, and the results were mixed. The good news was that infant mortality was down again; it had been reduced by 25 percent since 1930. Fewer children were dying of diseases such as tuberculosis. More communities had built new parks and playgrounds. And child labor had dramatically lessened; there was the hope that soon it would be eliminated. On the other hand, the conferees were surprised to find the birth rate was down considerably. Perhaps this was due to the Margaret Sanger campaign, or perhaps people could not afford to have as many children during the Depression, but there were 2 million fewer children now than there were a decade ago. The bad news was that two-thirds of the children in America did not have a decent standard of living, and about 1 million of them received no schooling at all.[3] Clearly, there was still work to be done in the area of child welfare, a fact that the women's shows often discussed.

A number of the guests (and some of the hosts) came from the Federation of Women's Clubs, and they were accustomed to raising funds for worthwhile causes. In fact, since the dawn of radio, women's clubs were among the most active users of the medium. The stereotype about these clubs was that they held teas and discussed gardening, but the fact was that many clubs were run by women who worked at least part time and often had careers; even in the 1920s and 1930s there were Business and Professional Women's Clubs (BPW), and they knew how to forge alliances with radio. The FCC still wanted stations to do local public service programming, and the women's clubs were often the only organization willing to provide some. Their concern for such issues as equal pay for women or better health care for children was a large part of their use of radio, although in some of the smaller cities, entire women's club meetings got on the air. In Little Rock, Arkansas, during the mid-1940s, the local chapter of the BPW Club decided to sponsor a monthly forum where important local issues could be discussed and possibly resolved; these town meetings were well attended, and they were broadcast over station KXLR.[4]

The literary magazine *Atlantic Monthly* had also entered into a partnership with radio. The magazine's editor, Edward Weeks, had begun doing a Tuesday night educational show on NBC Blue, in which he talked with a variety of interesting guests about books, poems, or other topics related to the literary world. One show, about the style of men writers versus women writers, featured British author Jan Struther, who had written *Mrs. Miniver*. *Atlantic Monthly* began a writing contest with the Federation of Women's Clubs; winners who wrote the best essay would have it published in the magazine and win $100.

And women were not just writing essays. Thanks to a new publishing organization, Broadcast Music Incorporated (BMI), aspiring songwriters were getting their songs published; this was of major importance for women because in BMI's first year, the company had signed over seventy women songwriters, 22 percent of the total number working for them. Their competition, ASCAP, had been in existence for twenty-six years, and in that entire time, only 130 women had ever been signed, never making up more than 12 percent of the roster, according to the editors of the *Big Song Book,* who clearly believed that BMI would bring some talented newcomers the chance that ASCAP had denied them.[5]

Women Radio Characters

In the summer of 1939, *Jane Arden,* a soap opera with a woman protagonist described as a "fearless girl reporter, the most beautiful woman in the newspaper world," ended after a brief run. But, as *Radio Guide* reminded its readers, "Gone are the days when adventure was a man's monopoly. [Today], a woman may be a miner, a soldier, or . . . an ace reporter."[6] So, even though one series with a woman in a somewhat nontraditional role (allowing of course for the fact that she could not just be a good reporter, she also had to be beautiful) ended, it was not long before another began. In October 1940, *Portia Faces Life* made its debut, with Lucille Wall playing the role of Portia Blake, a crusading woman lawyer who battled corruption and endured many trials and tribulations, as every good soap opera heroine must. There was also a popular series called *The Story of Mary Marlin,* which had been on the air since the mid-1930s, undergoing numerous plot twists along the way. Written by a woman (Jane Crusinberry), its plot revolved around the character of Mary, who had inherited her husband's Senate seat after he disappeared and was presumed to be dead. Unfortunately, the series constantly endured network censorship every time Crusinberry tried to insert some realism about life in Washington, D.C., or some political commentary into the story.[7] Despite that, in 1940, the show was still getting good ratings, and Mary the senator was an intelligently written character by soap opera standards.

But realism was not something the networks found easy to deal with, especially when the subject was women's issues, and the fear was that the show would have too much of a feminist slant; it was still believed that the audience wanted female characters who gave it all up for love. There were occasional documentary or educational shows about real-life women who had made a difference, such as *Women in the Making of America*, but by and large, the new decade had begun with the same soap opera dichotomies: women as either good and long-suffering or evil and devious, and men as either unaware of who really loved them or callously ignoring the good woman to pursue the evil woman. Once in a while, a soap opera tried to be somewhat more cerebral: *Against the Storm,* written by Sandra Michael, won a 1941 Peabody Award for being intelligently written and thought-provoking; yet despite critical acclaim and better-than-average ratings, it was taken off the NBC schedule in 1942.

Much has been written about how soap operas demeaned women, and how they portrayed women in stereotypic terms; but the enduring popularity of this genre cannot be ignored. In 1940, over sixty soap operas were on the air, attesting to their popularity. Several critics have suggested that soap operas served as a sort of catharsis for the female audience. The complex plots enabled women fans, most of whom were at home all day, to feel as if they were eavesdropping on the characters' lives and problems, which were then talked about among friends. The characters, even though they were fictional, displayed believable traits like jealousy, compassion, or insecurity, and fans could endlessly analyze their actions in the story.[8] It is also an irony of the 1940s that while soap opera plots had assorted divorces and infidelities (but no bad words, of course), several women's groups were having trouble getting advocacy advertisements about birth control on the radio. Margaret Sanger's campaign to make contraception legal had hit a snag in Massachusetts and Connecticut, and with votes coming up in legislatures, proponents of changing the law wanted to make their voices heard. Afraid to offend their largely Catholic and very conservative audience, certain stations refused to air the advertisements or even mention the controversy.[9]

Constructing the "Good Woman"

Another irony of the time was how soap operas often portrayed strong women (even if some were villains), while many popular magazines of 1940–41 kept telling women that their biology made them too weak and unsuitable for careers; it would be better for them to stop thinking about themselves and start paying more attention to their home and their family. By 1943, the same magazines would have to do a total about-face, praising women for being independent, able to do a man's job, and unselfishly balancing the needs of home with the desire to help America win the war. The happy housewife who might faint if she flew in an airplane while pregnant was suddenly supposed to transform herself into a capable and determined woman who would climb a tower or fix an automobile or show an aptitude for welding. Feminist scholars refer to "hegemony" in this context—the process by which women have been persuaded by the dominant (male) culture to accept and even defend their own oppression. Professor Cynthia Griffin Wolff has suggested that "[w]hen a society gives its sanction, even its praise, to stereotyped images of womanhood, the women who live in that society form their own self-images accordingly. A stereotype may become, by a sort of perversity, an image of reality that even women seek to perpetuate."[10]

Having been told by generations of authors, psychologists, and theologians that women were by nature emotional, dependent, and in need of protection, it is not surprising that some women dismissed feminist ideas about independence and lauded the woman who gave up her job and put her own needs on hold for her husband's and family's sake, as heroines in soap operas and novels usually did. And yet, some women did continue to work, if not for pay then for charitable organizations. It is interesting to read the monthly issues of *Independent Woman,* the magazine of the National Federation of Business and Professional Women's Clubs, and to contrast the women portrayed in that magazine (women achievers in fields like law, diplomacy, or media; women in nontraditional or previously all-male occupations; women winning awards for community service) with the women portrayed in the so-called women's magazines. As they had done during the 1930s, the mainstream women's magazines continued to stress in articles and in advertisements that a woman's primary goal should be keeping her husband happy and keeping herself beautiful. If she used the right shampoo and the right lipstick, if she smiled, did not burden her husband with her problems, and was efficient in stretching the family budget, all would be well. Some of the radio homemakers often gave advice about keeping a husband from straying; that advice seemed to come down to telling the wife to cook excellent meals, keep the home spotless, and wear attractive clothing for him when he came home. That, too, was ironic, given how the advertising community would rally around the character of "Rosie the Riveter" in 1943, after gradually changing the image of women in print ads during 1942. Suddenly, the working woman was portrayed as a heroine, admired not just because she used the sponsor's product, but because she was able to stand on her own two feet, while helping America in its hour of need.

More Women Get on the Air

Radio listeners in 1940 and 1941 probably noticed that there were a few more women in nontraditional (i.e., not homemakers) and "non–soap opera" roles. Several of the symphony orchestras had begun to hire women musicians; by 1943, the Houston Symphony would have twenty-six female members, and the Kansas City Orchestra had sixteen. Some of the new opportunities in symphony orchestras resulted from men getting drafted during the war, but many of the symphonies that were now employing women had simply decided some of them were talented, despite the stereotype that women were not disciplined the way men were. The belief that women lacked the commitment to their careers and were not serious musicians was still prevalent in the jazz and big band world, where an occasional woman was hired by an orchestra, but where, by and large, women were still expected to be only vocalists. *Downbeat* magazine was one of many that published articles opposed to women musicians; one was entitled "Why Women Musicians Are Inferior."[11]

In the world of classical music, one important trendsetter in bringing women into a formerly male orchestra was the famous conductor Leopold Stokowski, whose one-hundred-member All Youth Orchestra broke with precedent in mid-1940 by including twenty young women. Other orchestras followed suit, to the point where when *Newsweek* did a survey of orchestras in major cities in 1943, it could find only three that would not hire women.[12]

A familiar voice on radio, First Lady Eleanor Roosevelt was back on the air again, about to begin a new chat show on NBC Red, which was sponsored by Sweetheart Soap. *Time* magazine mentioned that the First Lady planned to donate the $3,000 she got per show to the American Friends

Service Committee, a charitable organization run by the Quakers.[13] It was good to have her back—a 1942 poll voted her one of the top three most popular women in America.[14]

In some cities, there were more women doing news and commentary; for example, Elizabeth Bemis was commenting on the news for station WLW in Cincinnati, and in 1942, she began reporting the news for KNX in Los Angeles. There was also Sigrid Schultz, who had covered hard news as a print journalist in Chicago and was now the Mutual network's correspondent reporting from Berlin. And the grande dame of women in radio news, Dorothy Thompson, who was named Outstanding Woman Commentator in a *Movie and Radio Guide* poll, was still around. In addition to being a guest speaker on various chat shows, she was now working for NBC Blue. What the listeners probably *did not* know was at least one CBS reporter in Europe was forbidden by the network to read her own reports. To Betty Wason's great frustration, CBS only let her write the scripts, after she had covered the story; they said her voice was "too feminine" for news. And what frustrated her more was that the man who then read her reports was offered a contract, while she was offered only work as a freelancer.[15]

There were also several more women doing sports announcing, most notably popular tennis champion Alice Marble, who was hired by New York's WNEW. In New Orleans, Jill Jackson, a former tennis and golf champion locally, was not only doing sports commentary for station WWL but was even trying her hand at some play-by-play of local events. When not doing that, she produced radio dramas for the station and even did some acting.[16]

Broadcasting had no trouble finding many interesting women to whom they could pay tribute in the early 1940s, and not all of their choices did women's shows. For example, there was Frances "Frankie" Basch, who used the air name Frances Scott. She had been moderator of a quiz show on New England's Yankee Network, a commentator on local news events, and she spent some time working in New York doing special events publicity for station WMCA. Now, she was producing special features such as *It Takes a Woman,* a show on which she did short profiles of interesting and unusual women.[17]

At the Federal Communications Commission, which was still all male (this would change later in the 1940s), there was a woman attorney in its Broadcast Division; Fanney Neyman Litvin was the resident expert on FCC rules and regulations, and her experience with the FCC went all the way back to the agency's formative years in the late 1920s when it was still called the Federal Radio Commission.[18]

At more stations, there was now a full-time director of publicity. This had become an increasingly important job, since without publicity, stations could not attract more listeners. Ever since Nellie Revell, who claimed to be the first woman press agent (her clients had included Al Jolson and Will Rogers), there had been some women publicists at theaters and clubs, so moving into radio was the next logical step. While on paper this was a behind-the-scenes job, the director of publicity often planned station events, bringing him or her in direct contact with the audience.

Other women found a career in advertising. Bertha Bannan, whose radio career had begun at a small station in Vermont, was now running her own ad agency in Boston and had a number of small- and medium-market radio stations as her clients. Numerous woman had worked their way up in the field of advertising, and some time-buyers, like Carolyn Bonnesen of Sherman & Marquette in Chicago, were responsible for accounts that billed millions of dollars in network commercials. In the 1930s, Miss Bonnesen had begun placing commercials for Tums and was now responsible for deciding the advertising budgets of such major brands as Colgate-Palmolive and Quaker Oats.[19] The war also brought some additional opportunities to women already working in radio. Helen Sioussat, who was assistant director of talks and public affairs for CBS, working with her boss, Edward R. Murrow, inherited his job when Mr. Murrow went off to Europe to cover the war. Miss Sioussat was now responsible for arranging the entire CBS network's public affairs programming. She scheduled hundreds of broadcasts, booking the appropriate speakers from diverse fields such as politics, government, education, labor, industry, religion, civil rights, and international affairs. She was also part of the team that formulated policy for all CBS public service programs. In 1941, she created, produced, and hosted one of the first roundtable discussion programs on TV, *Table Talk with Helen Sioussat,* on CBS's experimental TV station W2XAB.[20]

Speaking of Edward R. Murrow, one of his biographers has noted that his wife, Janet, sometimes broadcast shows on CBS about the war as it affected women. Unfortunately, as has also been pointed out, there is little evidence that Murrow encouraged Janet's (or any newswoman's) career. In fact, in 1946, Murrow would tell Pauline Frederick that CBS did not need any women newscasters, and that her voice was just ordinary. Years later, the veteran newswoman still kept a copy of that memo.[21] Murrow, like many men of his era, seemed much more comfortable with the traditional roles, and with his very successful career dominating so much of his time, that left the raising of their family entirely up to his wife. Janet Murrow seemed to accept this as the way it was supposed to be, something many women of her generation did.[22]

As the war allowed some new female voices to get on the air, a few women could still be found managing radio stations. Corinne Jordan, whom you read about in the previous chapter, remained the program director at

KSTP in St. Paul, Minnesota, where she also did a weekly music program. She had at one time been a popular vocalist and still enjoyed singing. (Later in the decade, when she was no longer station program director, she returned to singing one evening a week and became known as the "Stardust Lady.") Another woman in management in the early 1940s was Miriam Louise Dickey of Fairbanks, Alaska; she was treasurer of the company that owned station KFAR, where her job description sounded like what we today would call the operations manager.

And, of course, several women were still very much involved with another area considered appropriate for women: educational and children's programming. In addition to the work of Judith Waller, another notable example was Nila Mack, who won a Peabody Award for Excellence in Children's Programming in 1943 for *Let's Pretend* (the first Peabody Awards were given in 1940, and Miss Waller's educational program, *Chicago Round Table of the Air,* won in 1941). The problem was that while academic committees recognized a good children's show, the broadcasting industry itself still tended to regard the educational and children's shows that women produced as relatively unimportant. It seemed that while the networks talked about their commitment to public service and education, if a show did not generate money for advertisers, it was not considered very useful, no matter how many awards it won. One surprisingly honest program manager admitted this in an interview, stating that a good juvenile program was one that "create[d] a demand among children for merchandise adults are willing to buy."[23] Given that many women who wrote or moderated children's shows opposed excessive commercialism, it is not surprising that the men in the industry looked down on their efforts.

The Importance of Radio Homemakers

Although women producers or managers might be written up in an occasional magazine, the average listener was more familiar with the female performers and the radio homemakers. In Yankton, South Dakota, where a large audience of farmers' wives depended on the radio homemakers, station WNAX had hired a young woman named Wynn Hubler (later Wynn Speece); by the early 1940s, she created the character of the "Neighbor Lady," a friendly woman who dropped by to chat each day with her rural audience. Women waited eagerly for her show, and several generations grew up listening to Wynn and learning from her. When she married and had children, she moved the show to her house and broadcast from there, giving it even more of the homelike touch her audience loved. Mrs. Speece did the show for over thirty years, and thousands of housewives regarded the Neighbor Lady as a true friend of theirs. In a society where women's roles were frequently debated, the Neighbor Lady and other shows like it were a constant in the lives of rural women, giving them a membership in an extended radio family and reinforcing the choices they had made. If Marshall McLuhan's theory of the "Global Village" could be applied to old radio shows, then many of the women's shows certainly were examples of an electronic community. Women traveled great distances to be in the studio audience or to appear on the air with the Neighbor Lady, but most were content to just listen at home, write fan letters, and collect memorabilia from the show; the books of favorite poems Wynn read on the air were especially popular. She also held picnics and special events for her audience, giving them a chance to meet each other. And while like most women's show hostesses, it was her job to be enthusiastic about her sponsors, the audience came to trust her and take her advice to heart.[24]

It was easy to criticize the women's shows, since they broke so many of the rules. Many of the hostesses were not professionals and had never gone to radio school. Some talked too much or lacked a "radio voice." But what they did not have in polish, they made up for with their ability to ease the loneliness of the women in their audience. Motherhood and family may have been held in high esteem by clerics and philosophers, but the reality of life for many women was that they felt isolated and unappreciated in a culture where what men accomplished received most of the attention. The woman who baked the best cake or stretched the family budget and made healthy meals was seldom rewarded with public praise, except on the women's shows, where such achievements did matter. Mary Margaret McBride, Ida Bailey Allen, Caroline Cabot, Wynn Speece, and other radio homemakers took the housewife and her daily problems seriously and tried to help. The homemakers also saw themselves as more than people who dispensed the latest household tips; some became involved in local charities, others inspired good works in the community, and some became well known for their ability to persuade celebrities to be on the show. When the great operatic baritone Lauritz Melchior performed in the Midwest, one show that got him for interviews was *For the Ladies,* a long-running program on WTCN in Minneapolis, moderated by Mary Proal. Proal also had guests like the distinguished painter and illustrator Rockwell Kent and a number of famous women performers like Jessica Dragonette.[25]

In New York City or Hollywood, listeners expected to hear well-known stars on the air, but it was the ingenuity and tenacity of the women's show hosts and their producers in cities of all sizes that enabled them to keep coming up with interesting guests. This dedication may help to explain why the radio homemakers enjoyed such longevity. In Chicago, for example, since the early 1930s, a popular women's show was done by "Martha Crane" (real name Mrs. Martha Caris) on station WLS; it was still successful throughout the 1940s and 1950s. That was typical—many of the women's shows kept the same host for twenty to thirty years.

Since the 1930s, nearly every radio station had a director of women's programming; in May 1942, a number of women's show hostesses and women's directors formed their own organization, under the auspices of the almost entirely male National Association of Broadcasters (NAB). The Association of Women Directors (AWD) was the forerunner of the American Women in Radio and Television (AWRT), and while that may seem like a lot of initials, the members of these organizations were very active in trying to improve broadcasting and in giving stations a voice in the issues that mattered to their community. Clearly, the women of the NAB felt that women's issues were not being adequately represented, and their solution was to form their own group. (Later, they would explain they felt like a "Ladies Auxiliary" of the NAB rather than an actual part of it. When they formed AWRT in 1951, they made an amicable but formal break with the NAB.) The Association of Women Directors had two veteran broadcasters among its founders: Ruth Chilton, women's director of station WSYR in Syracuse (later with WCAU in Philadelphia), served as the AWD's first president and Mildred Bailey, of WTAG in Worcester, Massachusetts, was its first secretary. The organization immediately became involved in public service and in improving the quality of women's shows. By 1945, it had 650 members. Also active in women's issues, especially regarding education, was Dorothy Lewis, vice president of the NAB's Radio Council on Children's Programming, who conducted surveys for the NAB and issued reports about what radio was doing to benefit education. She worked with the women directors in the group's formative years.

Women in the Popular Culture

Although the Depression had ended and some women were finding new opportunities, the popular culture was still portraying women as it always had. As I discussed earlier, prior to United States entry into the war, women in broadcasting generally appeared as singers or as characters in radio's many soap operas, where they usually were cast in very stereotypic roles. Yes, sometimes a woman character was a senator like Mary Marlin, but even on a show that tried to be different, eventually the show's sponsors became concerned over whether the audience really wanted an independent woman senator as the protagonist. This led to plot changes that the show's founder and writer Jane Crusinberry opposed vehemently; she was removed from the series, and Mary's character was made into just another woman obsessing over marital problems. The show soon lost its audience, proving that perhaps a woman Senator was okay after all, except it was too late to resurrect the old plot and save the show.[26]

With only a few exceptions such as *Independent Woman* magazine, prior to World War II, books, magazines, and advertising seldom deviated from the message that women were incurable romantics who would do almost anything to get a husband. Some of the women in broadcasting were a direct contradiction to that belief, of course. They seldom discussed their personal life and dedicated themselves to their work. This was especially true for Judith Waller; if she had any relationships, she never spoke of them in all the interviews she did over the years. And Bertha Brainard waited until she retired before she married.

Women and Freud

Meanwhile, the old myth about women's inherent weakness and their emotional instability was being given new life by the field of psychiatry, where the growing acceptance of many of Sigmund Freud's theories was finding its way into college courses and even into magazine articles. Freud's writings reinforced the traditional concept of "biology is destiny," and while a few psychiatrists, most notably Karen Horney, would challenge his views, Freudian psychology was gaining adherents from many male psychiatrists and medical doctors. Some Freudian concepts were destined to become part of the American vocabulary (*defense mechanisms, subconscious, ego,* and *libido,* just to name a few); on the other hand, Freudian theories about women proved to be more troublesome as time passed. Most problematic were the now discredited beliefs that women spent their lives being jealous of men because men have penises and women do not; that women were by nature passive and masochistic; and that only through having a baby could a woman overcome her ongoing disappointment about not being as good as a man. Much of this had been said in one way or other before, but when the medical community decided there was some truth to it, Freud's theories, which he offered with little if any scientific proof, were embraced by countless therapists.[27]

The publication in the United States of Freud's book *Femininity* in 1933 and the appearance in 1938 of his *Basic Writings* contributed to a resurgence in his popularity well into the 1940s. And although he died in late 1939, he continued to be quoted in numerous popular magazines, where editors, eager for controversial subject matter, gave his views considerable attention. The effect of Freud's most misogynistic teachings would not fully manifest itself until the 1950s, when the therapists trained by his methods would be saying that a truly feminine and "normal" woman derived her happiness (and her identity) from knowing that she was the object of her husband's sexual desire, and that she could bear his children. A woman who wanted more than that was said to be rejecting her femininity.

Considering the myriad depictions in print of happy homemakers, and considering all the energy expended by various authorities on how women ought to be docile and demure or else they were not normal, it is even more amazing how successful the campaign to involve women in the war effort was. Once the United States entered the war in December 1941, on what President Roosevelt called the "day that will live forever in infamy," suddenly the radio and print journalism community united with the sponsors to offer an entirely different message to the American woman. Now, the intention was to show her that she was really courageous, and it was her patriotic duty to work outside the home. Women's studies as an academic discipline is fairly recent, so it is doubtful that any professors studied the female psyche to any great extent during the war years (and the idea of the psyche is, of course, Freud's), but surely it must have confused more than a few women to be told one day that it was selfish and wrong to want a job and then almost the next day to be told it was selfish and wrong *not* to want a job. Historian Glenda Riley, remarking on this phenomenon, wrote:

> [T]he course of American history has made it obvious that women were regarded as a flexible labor supply to be pulled out of the house when needed and pushed back in when not. But the difficulty in 1941 was that women had been lectured for better than a decade on their responsibilities as wives and mothers. . . . Now the government had to recast the image of women as potential workers. To pull women out of their homes and into wartime industries, the War Manpower Commission created the character of Rosie the Riveter.[28]

Rosie Appears on the Scene

Many women have claimed to be the real Rosie, and I have found quite a few newspaper accounts saying the one in their city was in fact the model for the character. There is also some evidence that no actual Rosie existed at first: it was a character that was created by the government's Office of Facts and Figures, which later became the Office of War Information.[29] And there was also a popular song recorded in early 1943 called "Rosie the Riveter," sung by the Four Vagabonds (I have been told by several musicologists that this song was named for a woman named Rosalind Walker); in any event, perhaps the character of Rosie had been decided upon, and then a campaign to promote her began. Some historians believe the woman who was chosen as the first representation of Rosie was Rose Will Monroe, who worked at a factory in Ypsilanti, Michigan, where she riveted military airplanes. The story goes that it was she who became the model for the poster, which was all part of a publicity campaign. She was also asked to appear in a government-sponsored promotional film about the war effort, and she did numerous public speaking engagements to persuade Americans to buy war bonds. The character of Rosie got a big publicity boost when Norman Rockwell's depiction of her appeared on the cover of the Saturday Evening Post on May 29, 1943.

Whether or not she was Rose Will Monroe, the concept of Rosie the Riveter seemed to speak to the American woman. In the four years after the United States entered the war, over 6.5 million women entered the workforce, many in jobs that only a little while ago had been forbidden to them or considered impossible for them to do. Journalist Paula Watson, whose mother had been one of the Rosies, wrote an editorial saying Rosie the Riveter should have been the Woman of the Century.

> Rosie was romanticized in pop tunes and in movies. It was an era of Wonder Woman comics and the All-American Girls' Baseball League . . . But you didn't have to go to the movies to see a Rosie: she was the girl next door . . . [she worked] in shipyards, refineries, aircraft plants, train yards, offices, stores, shops . . . Rosie the Riveter became the symbol of women's ability and willingness to do their part.[30]

It was impressive the way women of the 1940s managed to adapt to work environments with equipment many of them had never seen before, and learned to handle demanding and dangerous jobs for which they had received little training previously. Granted, the news magazines mentioned there were some initial problems: there were women missing work due to painful menstrual cycles, caused by the stress of standing on their feet for hours and doing much heavier lifting than most were accustomed to. Companies began giving the women more frequent breaks and suggesting stretching exercises, which seemed to help.[31] And some work sites had to make tables and work benches lower so women could reach them when doing assembly: men were usually taller, and most plants had placed shelves or drafting tables at a level for the typical man, which presented a problem when suddenly women were taking over those jobs.[32] But while many men who ran the plants undoubtedly expected total disaster, they were pleasantly surprised. Most of the women learned quickly, took pride in what they were doing, and gradually adjusted to the working conditions. *Newsweek* did a special article in the summer of 1943, evaluating the progress of the women war workers. The writer noted that the War Manpower Commission at the beginning of the war had tabulated how many jobs were felt to be suitable for women. But by 1943, it had been found that this practice was unnecessary.

> There are practically no jobs, it has been found, that cannot be adapted for women workers. They are in the shipyards, lumber mills, steel mills, foundries. They are welders, electricians, mechanics, and even boilermakers. They operate streetcars, buses, cranes and tractors. Women engineers are working in the drafting rooms and women physicists and chemists in the great industrial laboratories.[33]

Given all of the experts who had repeatedly told women that working outside the home would make them unfeminine and disliked by men, it is no surprise that the ads meant to encourage the new Rosies stressed how their jobs would help their husbands and boyfriends, and how women who were helping their country would in no way lose male approval, nor would they lose their femininity.[34] As articles had done in the 1920s when a woman achiever was interviewed and the writer quickly mentioned that she was "pretty" or "still a lady," so the ads in which a product like lipstick was linked with women in the workforce always showed attractive women talking about how they were willing to do without makeup until after work, because they just wanted to concentrate on their jobs; after work, of course, it was the sponsor's makeup they would hurry to use so they could feel ladylike again.[35]

Woman in Radio During the War

Few of the news magazines mentioned it, but radio too was experiencing a major change in the roles considered appropriate for women. Suddenly, it was as if radio had returned to the early 1920s, when Eunice Randall repaired equipment and worked side by side with the men at the AMRAD factory. (By the way, Eunice, as an experienced ham radio operator, was one of a number of women during World War II who volunteered in what was called the War Emergency Radio Service, helping to deliver emergency messages and other communications as part of civil defense.) With increasing numbers of men from every occupation being drafted into the service, soon radio began to lose male announcers and engineers, while the networks began to lose pages and messengers. Proving how arbitrary the "men's jobs" and "women's jobs" classifications were, few of us today can figure out why messengers, who mainly delivered mail and carried interoffice correspondence in that era before computers and faxes, were supposed to be young men, or why studio pages, who guarded the door or showed people to their seats during live performances, much like theater ushers, also were supposed to be male. None of this seems like work that would be too difficult for any female.

The engineering dilemma was somewhat more difficult to fill immediately, since few women had been to school for engineering during the 1920s and even fewer in the 1930s. Commissioner Ray C. Wakefield of the FCC observed in early 1942 that the situation was about to become a crisis since ". . . of the 5,500 qualified broadcasting engineers in the United States, 1,000 have already entered the Army or the Navy, and that's just a beginning."[36] Some stations found that female ham radio operators could be trained fairly easily to do some of the work needed; the number of women in ham radio had grown so much since the late 1930s that women amateurs had formed their own national organization (the YLRL—Young Ladies Radio League); some of them were willing to work in commercial radio. Other young women were trained in quickly established courses, often run by the government specifically to give women the background they lacked. And a few got their engineering training in conjunction with learning to fly—Helen Cottrell of WJW in Cleveland was a woman aviator, and while a member of the Civil Air Patrol, she got an engineering license, which helped her to quickly get hired as a radio engineer. But getting hired was only half the battle: certain social changes were not so easily accepted. *Broadcasting* captioned a picture of new female engineers with two words in bold type: "FEMININE INVADERS of the control room have added two more stations to their ranks." It mentioned that one woman had no experience other than a brief course at her college station, while the other held a First Class license.[37]

As the newspapers did in the early 1920s with brief articles about women doing unusual jobs, so each week *Broadcasting* would print more photos of these female engineers. While at times the tone of the captions was slightly incredulous, in other cases the next couple of lines noted that despite the newness of the person, the manager of the station reported she had learned quickly and was doing a fine job. There is no evidence these managers were just being chivalrous, because at a few stations, there was definite—and very vocal—resistance to hiring the women, and this, too, made the news. At one midwestern station, the male engineers walked out rather than work with a woman trainee.[38] And an important technical union, International Brotherhood of Electrical Workers (IBEW), put forth its official war policy, saying that the women would be allowed to work, and allowed to join the union, but only on a temporary basis. Once the war was over, the policy stated, the women had six months to resign from both. The fact that some of the women might like their new jobs or might even be good at them was never considered. These were men's jobs; the women were only allowed to occupy them until the men returned.[39]

Looking at this agreement in light of today's climate of antidiscrimination laws, a modern reader might wonder why the women accepted such limitations. The answer is complicated. Based on my interviews with some women of that era, I believe that many had indeed been persuaded that they were only supposed to work during the war and once the war ended, they should return to their homes; they felt the jobs did not really belong to them, and there was no chance to win them. Others were more concerned about their loved ones overseas than about what they might want after the war. Work provided a sort of catharsis, taking their minds temporarily away from worrying and waiting for news. Few of these working women had a career strategy, and even if they did, the culture did not encourage women to make any demands. More will be said about that later.

Meanwhile, although AM radio was still king in the early 1940s, more than thirty FM stations were now on the air, operating in many large cities. Several had already begun to employ women announcers and engineers: *FM* magazine paid tribute to one of them, Marjorie Eleanor Allen, who was the first woman transmitter and control room engineer at station W47NY in New York. She also reported the news, and, in her spare time, taught radio courses to other women via the American Women's Volunteer Service.[40] Another FM station was run entirely by women: W47B in Boston had a two-person staff, comprised of engineer Muriel Kennedy and announcer Ruth Sherrill, both of whom kept the station on the air during its operating hours of 3:00 to 9:00 P.M. Miss Kennedy had long been interested in matters technical, having worked for a tube manufacturer where she also learned to repair most radio receivers.[41] And several FM stations were now carrying famous commentator Dorothy Thompson. The proponents of FM saw it as a major benefit for women announcers. ." . . FM reception of women's voices is greatly superior to the reception afforded by AM. The contrast is really striking. Listeners say when they hear Dorothy Thompson on FM, [it is] as if she were right in the room."[42] Unfortunately for women's voices, very few FM receivers were available, and with World War II on most people's minds, trying out the new FM technology was not a priority yet. (On the other hand, the limited number of people who did hear FM were very impressed, especially with how beautiful classical music sounded on an FM radio.)

Women Announcers Return

Besides radio engineers, there was a demand for women announcers again, although for reasons other than a sudden return to egalitarianism. Male station executives had decided that a woman with a sexy voice (and if she was young and attractive, so much the better) was somebody the soldiers would enjoy. Many cities had military bases in the vicinity, and the men did indeed seem to get a boost from hearing young women doing request and dedication shows for them. One especially popular show was written up in a number of magazines in 1942: Jean Ruth, better known by her on-air name of "Beverly," entertained the troops with her show *Beverly at Reveille* over station KFEL in Denver, where, said *Life*, ". . . she is the dream girl of four Army posts . . . at KFEL [she] broadcasts records, chatty personal messages, camp bulletins, and Pep . . . [she also] kids [the men] out of their early morning blues, to the delight of morale officers."[43]

Similarly, in Richmond, Virginia, Glenn Graham "the WRNL Reveille Girl" provided "music and pleasant chatter" every morning beginning at 6:30 A.M. Miss Graham, who had already appeared in film, was chosen by WRNL to become "a big sister, girl friend, and pal to the boys at Camp Lee" via her radio show directed to them. Like Beverly, Glenn made appearances, did shows from various military bases, and generally did what she could to keep morale high.[44] The same technique was used on the shortwaves, where an attractive young woman named Kay Turner (real name Kathryn Setzer), who had started as a mail-room messenger at NBC, was now doing her own show aimed at the overseas military personnel. The music she played was jazz and swing, which the men were really glad to hear, in addition to enjoying her voice. She also sent out photos of herself in a "sweater-girl" pose, which were gratefully received by her soldier listeners.[45]

In addition to the influx of young women doing local wake-up shows for the troops, the networks had to make some changes, too. As mentioned before, one change was they hired women as pages and messengers. But they also began to examine their programming. With more women working, the traditional stay-at-home housewife audience was no longer there. Now, for women listening at work, there needed to be more news and information, more music, and more story lines of radio dramas built around the current crisis. Jokes about shortages or the problems of rationing got into the scripts, but, of course, the story lines could not break any new ground; there was government censorship to contend with, and to the dismay of the radio news reporters, even the military was beginning to make strong suggestions about what could or could not be broadcast, so that national security would not be compromised. To make matters worse, the FCC had ruled in the famous Mayflower Decision that radio stations were not allowed to editorialize. This strange ruling was perhaps the last one influenced by the power of the print journalism community, which had tried for years to restrict how much news radio could cover. The Mayflower Decision would not be overturned until mid-1949.

But while all of this was occurring, the networks had a more immediate concern—as was happening at the local affiliates, some of the networks' best male announcers were getting drafted. NBC, CBS, Mutual, and Blue did not necessarily need somebody with a sexy voice to do a wake-up show. But they needed professional and experienced broadcasters who could handle pressure; as the male announcers left, some of the women got a chance to return. Suddenly, the same stations that had removed all the women (except the one radio homemaker) from the air by 1929 were auditioning female announcers.

Judging from the ratings, the public learned to accept this with a minimum of complaint. The women on the air in the 1940s were allowed to break out of the women's show ghetto, and they found all sorts of opportunities. Popular radio actress Arlene Francis was mistress of ceremonies (or "femcee" as *Newsweek* called her) of a show called *Blind Date,* in which servicemen were fixed up with models or actresses, an enjoyable evening sponsored by Maxwell House. The servicemen had two minutes to sell themselves and their good qualities, such that the beautiful starlets listening would want to choose them as their "blind date"—the success of the show went to Francis, whose quick wit and ability to put guests at ease kept the show moving.[46]

Another interesting new program in the mid-1940s featured journalist and gossip columnist Dorothy Kilgallen, who began doing a morning show in 1945 with her husband Dick Kollmar. *Breakfast with Dorothy and Dick* had celebrity gossip, talk about the theater, appearances by their two kids, and interesting conversation. And on a competing New York station, another celebrity, Jinx Falkenburg, who had been an actress and a model, and her husband, Tex McCrary, a former journalist, were doing their own version of morning chat, interviewing plenty of well-known newsmakers and celebrities in the process.

As for the traditional women's shows, they, too, had undergone some modifications as a result of the war—many were providing practical information about how to handle rationing, how to prepare nutritionally sound meals despite food shortages, and offering other tips on day-to-day problems the average woman might encounter. Trying to apply a little humor in difficult times, comedienne Billie Burke did a CBS show on Saturday mornings beginning in mid-1943. Called *Fashions in Rations,* she interviewed experts from the government and industry and answered listener questions about food and nutrition. Her assistant on air was Alice White, a member of the cast of the radio comedy *Blondie.*

In some cities, women both produced and announced their own feature shows with war-related content. There was *Women's Place,* heard on KGW-KEX in Portland, Oregon. Peggy Williams and Vera Kneeland offered a fifteen-minute show about what local women were doing in the war effort, and also provided information for women seeking to volunteer. At another Portland station, KOIN, Miss Clare Hays did a nightly show called *Women in Wartime;* she focused attention on women working in defense, as well as offering advice to women trying to find the right job in that industry. What was interesting about her show was that it was on in the late evening, rather than in the typical midday women's show time. Miss Hays told Judith Waller of NBC that the listeners themselves had asked for an evening time slot, following the 10:00 P.M. news; since most were out working during the day, they enjoyed relaxing at night and catching up on information about the jobs local women were doing, what companies needed workers, and how local women were coping.[47]

While these shows might not sound fascinating to us, keep in mind that this was a time of loneliness, fear, and uncertainty for millions of women whose loved ones were suddenly fighting overseas. The helpful women on the air were like friends to their audiences. They had information, they had facts, they sounded confident, and they could help a listener get her questions answered. Darragh Aldrich, who became women's director at WCCO in Minneapolis in 1942, was remembered even years later by many grateful women for all the interviews she did with government spokespeople, members of the International Red Cross, groups that worked with prisoners of war, and numerous members of the armed forces. Women in Minneapolis-St. Paul counted on Aldrich to reassure them during difficult times. She was perceived as someone who genuinely cared about her listeners, a reputation that would be reinforced in the late 1940s when the polio epidemic struck the Midwest and Aldrich worked long hours to bring accurate information from medical authorities, as well as visiting patients in hospitals and clinics throughout the area.

In our more cynical era, it is harder to imagine that women's directors really wanted to do all the public service and organize all the events they did, but from talking to a number of them, it became very clear that for these women, radio was not just a business or a place where they got a paycheck. They were still idealistic about what they did, sincerely believing that their job comprised much more than just selling their sponsors' products.

The war even brought opportunities to some women who had never expected to be on the air. In what would become a recurring theme of the 1940s, there were stations that lost every one of their male announcers; they became all female until the war ended, with station receptionists and secretaries often pressed into service to fill the openings. NBC's magazine *Tune In* noted that the first entirely female station in a large city was KCKN in Kansas City, run by "four attractive and enterprising local girls who are proving that they can write, sell, announce and spark a program on equal par with any man." The ratings bore this out—the station's Hooper listener survey showed excellent results for the station since it hired the women.[48] Meanwhile, *Radio Mirror* mentioned that radio actress Ona Munson (she had been in the crime drama *Big Town*) was being trained as a director. She had noticed that a number of CBS's men directors were getting drafted, and she offered her services.[49]

In Miami, a popular announcer of the 1940s used her radio show to help her cope with a devastating personal tragedy. Eve Tellegen of WQAM had at one time been a radio and stage actress, but during the mid-1940s, she became known as a fashion expert whose new radio show brought Miami's garment industry much positive attention. The idea for the show occurred after Miss Tellegen learned that her husband had been killed in action during the war, and not long after, her son, who was also fighting overseas, was taken prisoner. Understandably distraught, she did not work for a long while, but when she finally heard from her son, he told her he had been wounded and would soon be coming home. Lacking enough money to provide for him, Eve decided to make use of her fashion expertise and pitch a station on the idea of doing a radio program. On her new show, she also did movie reviews, interviewed celebrities, and, of course, talked about theater. She became so successful that she was soon referred to as "Miami's First Lady of Radio."[50]

There were also other new women's shows. In St. Louis, Kay Morton (real name Ruth Markus) was doing a half-hour women's show on WIL in 1941, and with so much going on both overseas and at home, her intention quickly became to "open up the windows of the kitchen and look out on the rest of the world," she told me in an interview. She recalled that she seldom did any recipes on her show, preferring to talk about current events, local people, and the celebrities who were in town. She was one of the fortunate hosts who had the opportunity to chat with Eleanor Roosevelt, and she also interviewed Duke Ellington and Tyrone Power.

A few women found themselves managing radio stations in place of their husbands when they went off to war. Helen Wylie's husband, Cole, was general manager of KPQ in Wenatchee, Washington. When Cole joined the Air Corps, Helen Wylie became the manager, a job she held until he returned.[51] And, as always, there were women who were writing new series, and, in some cases, even getting the starring role. Peg Lynch had gotten her start doing local radio in Albert Lea, Minnesota, at station KATE, where she created a comedy about a married couple, despite the fact that she was single. The series became *Ethel and Albert,* and it had a very successful run on the Blue Network (later called ABC), beginning in 1944, with Peg herself playing the role of Ethel. And speaking of playing, on many network shows, the background music was performed by organist Rosa Rio, who had been an accompanist on such programs as *The Shadow, My True Story,* and *When a Girl Marries.* There was also another talented network organist who was female—Ann Leaf, who, in addition to being the accompanist for a number of soap operas, had played on Fred Allen's show.

Meanwhile, Hollywood took some of the better-known radio singers and movie stars and combined them in a comedy called *Four Jills in a Jeep,* which was ostensibly based on the real-life experiences of some of the women who performed for the troops. The reviewers thought it was silly and contrived, but during war time, that may have been the kind of escapist fare that made people feel better. As a bonus, they could see as well as hear Jimmy Dorsey, Martha Raye, Betty Grable, Carmen Miranda, and George Jessel. In the days before TV, a chance to watch some of your favorites in the comfort of a theater made up for what a film might lack in a compelling plot.

More Changes on the Air

In addition to more women announcers, the war affected radio in other ways. The music began to change, as more patriotic songs were written. Tin Pan Alley songwriters were put to work turning out war songs as soon as the United States officially entered the conflict, and in 1942, *Your Hit Parade* featured such songs as "Remember Pearl Harbor," "He Wears a Pair of Silver Wings," and "Praise the Lord and Pass the Ammunition." Lyrics of some love songs now included pledges to wait for the soldier or pleas from the soldier to his girl, asking her to wait. Shows about the military began to appear: one NBC series that began in April 1942 was *The Army Hour.* It provided information from locations around the world about what the troops were doing, and it was invaluable to listeners at home who wanted all the news they could get about the boys overseas. Like most shows of this genre, *The Army Hour* was produced by men, and since women were not allowed in combat, there was not a large female presence in the scripts; but each program included musical interludes and sometimes, female vocalists sang patriotic songs, some of which were specially written for that particular episode. The biggest winner in the audience surveys was the president: Franklin Delano Roosevelt received monumental ratings whenever he gave a radio talk. News broadcasts made large gains, too, as the war escalated and people were hungry for as much information as possible. But in amongst the serious programs, the public still wanted escape, and 1942's most listened to program was *Fibber McGee and Molly.* Comedian Bob Hope had begun doing broadcasts for the troops (as did a number of American movie and radio stars), and he won several awards for doing so. There was a new network, or rather an old one with a new owner and a new name: the FCC had ordered NBC to divest of one of its two networks. It sold off NBC Blue, which was now just the "Blue Network" and would ultimately become ABC. The war did nothing to diminish radio advertising, and even with the uncertainties of war, commercial time sales continued to rise.[52]

There was one other interesting new development in broadcasting. Many of the popular female vocalists and comedians, along with some of the most popular men, were now internationally famous, the result of a new program heard overseas. In March 1942, the U.S. War Department began producing a variety show especially for the fighting forces. Called *Command Performance,* the show featured performances by celebrities such as Bing Crosby, Eddie Cantor, The Andrews Sisters, Spike Jones, Count Basie, Dinah Shore, Ethel Waters, and Bob Hope, as well as playing mailed-in requests from the GIs. All the performers on this extremely popular show volunteered their time, and that included even highly paid stars like Judy Garland and George Burns and Gracie Allen. *Command Performance* and *Mail Call,* another celebrity-oriented variety program (with such stars as Ozzie and Harriet and Danny Thomas), were incorporated into the new American Forces Radio Service (AFRS) when it officially took to the air on July 4, 1943. Suddenly, American music was exposed to an entirely new audience, since it was not just the soldiers who listened to AFRS.

Women in the Military

And speaking of the armed forces, in mid-1942, the so-called Petticoat Bill was enacted. Sponsored by Massachusetts Representative Edith Nourse Rogers, it provided for a Women's Army Auxiliary Corps (WAAC—later, the name would be shortened to the Women's Army Corps, or WAC). In June, when the corps announced that it had 450 openings for officers, over 13,000 women applied.[53] The WAC and the similar all-female units created by the Navy and the Marines were not for combat. Rather, they trained women to work in supporting roles such as switchboard operators, cooks, chauffeurs, and clerks, in order to free up men for active duty. Still, the pay was better than in some traditionally female civilian jobs, and many young women had a sincere desire to serve their country during the war. (Among the 440 young women chosen were 40 black women, who although as educated as their white counterparts, had to endure segregated quarters, theaters, and services such as beauty shops. They did, however, attend classes with the white recruits.)

The first director of the WAAC was Mrs. Oveta Culp Hobby, a former executive at Houston's KPRC, whose husband owned the *Houston Post* newspaper, at which Mrs. Hobby had also been an executive. An experienced businesswoman and a fund-raiser for several charities (as well as the mother of two children, as *Broadcasting* pointed out in its tribute to her), it would now be her responsibility to organize and direct the new program, as well as continue to persuade the public that women in the military, even in non-combat positions, was a good idea. She was ultimately given the title of Colonel, and she devoted herself to the task of making the idea of women in the military acceptable.[54] At first, the WAACs were largely expected to do clerical work and menial, repetitive tasks such as sorting mail. However, it did not take long for the duties of the WAACs to expand into some critical areas of defense such as cryptography, weather observation and reporting, radio equipment repair, and control tower operation.[55]

Undoubtedly, Director Hobby's advocacy proved useful in persuading the right people in the military to let the women do more. In addition to the WAACs, the Navy began its own unit, known as the WAVEs. While most female movie and radio stars themselves did not hurry to sign up for either (and some would not have qualified because of their age), a few of their children did, such as the daughter of radio actress (and former star of the silent screen) Irene Rich. Lt. Frances Rich made several tours around the country, encouraging young women to sign up for duty with the WAVEs as she had done.[56] As for her celebrity mom, Irene Rich volunteered with the Women's Ambulance and Defense Corps.

There were many other female performers who volunteered and who were photographed in uniform to encourage others to do their patriotic duty and help the war effort. Singers Dinah Shore and Kate Smith did numerous shows for the soldiers who were in training, signing autographed photos and generally helping to keep morale up, in much the same way the female morning show hostesses like Beverly were doing. Gracie Allen put on the uniform of the American Women's Voluntary Services and spent time visiting the bases to serve coffee and chat with the soldiers. Gracie also was part of the group of entertainers who performed on the show *Stage Door Canteen,* a musical variety show aimed at American servicemen. Each week, the cast, who did the show in New York on CBS, wore patriotic red, white, and blue outfits and sang the national anthem at the close of the show. Stars like Jane Froman, Connie Boswell, and Orson Welles not only performed for the servicemen, but then stayed around and signed autographs for them as well. In fact, many of the celebrities of radio and film, both male and female, helped to sell war bonds (Kate Smith became especially known for her efforts in this regard, and so did Mickey Rooney and numerous others).

While it is probably true that some of the celebrities did their volunteer work only because it brought them good publicity (pictures of stars in uniform performing or signing autographs became a staple of most fan magazines during the war), it is also true that patriotism and wanting to help defeat Hitler were factors for a number of the performers. For some of them, that meant going overseas to entertain, often at great personal sacrifice. In 1943, singer Jane Froman, who was on her way to Europe as part of a USO tour, was so severely injured in a plane crash that she was unable to walk without crutches until 1948; several other performers lost their lives in similar plane crashes while on their way to perform. And, for some male stars, it was not just about posing for pictures; a few enlisted in the military to fight for their country.

Women in the War Effort

As for what women outside of radio were doing during the war years, even in the earliest days of the WAAC, not all women were doing office work for Uncle Sam, nor was every woman a riveter. Peggy Lennox, an advertisement for cigarettes announced proudly, was a female aviator and she was training some of the future pilots.[57] The *Army Times* newspaper was very pleased to find that a few of the new instructors hired by the military were women, including Miss Fran McVey, another of the women flyers, who had been hired to teach a course about the proper use of machine guns.[58] At this time, one of the most prominent woman flyers and member of the Ninety-Nines, Jacqueline Cochran, was trying to persuade the military to put the skills of her aviator colleagues to use in the service of the country. Miss Cochran proposed a new unit, a squadron of women pilots who could ferry supplies and do other important jobs, using their flight skills. She submitted her plan several times but to no avail. Then, Eleanor Roosevelt mentioned it in her newspaper column, giving the impression that she thought the idea had merit. This finally led to a unit of women pilots known as the WASPs (Women's Air Force Service Pilots), whose job it was to ferry supplies, but who also served as test pilots and trainers. Cochran was named director of the WASPs, but for many years after the war, the contributions of these courageous women would scarcely be mentioned; they were not even considered veterans and were awarded no benefits. This would not change until November of 1977, when an act of Congress belatedly rectified the injustice somewhat.

The chances are that the average person did not think much about women in the military, unless there was a base nearby or unless there was a news story about them. There was a period of time when rumors were flying about the allegedly loose morals of the WACS, rumors that were refuted by everyone from Oveta Culp Hobby to the President and Mrs. Roosevelt. The subject got mentioned in the press at the time, and a few of the chat shows probably discussed whether women belonged in the service.

Eunice Randall, one of the first women announcers, is shown circa 1921 in the studio of 1XE/WGI, Medford Hillside, MA. (Author's collection, with thanks to Alan Douglas)

Although she had retired, Eunice Randall Thompson still loved ham radio; she is shown here in the early 1960s. (Author's collection, with thanks to Eunice Stolecki)

Cover of *Radio News*, June 1923. Women were as excited about the radio craze as were men. Note that headphones had to be used to listen. (Author's collection)

A rare 1924 photo of Nellie Revell, press agent to the stars, popular columnist, and radio host. (Author's collection)

In 1927, WASN (All Shopping News) went on the air in Boston. This rare photo shows the staff of what was probably the first all-female station. (Author's collection)

The first woman to own a radio station was Marie (Mrs. Robert) Zimmerman. (Author's collection, with thanks to Dave Ciesielski)

Seen here in a 1936 photo, Kathryn Cravens was one of the few women news commentators of the 1930s. She had a CBS show called "News Through a Woman's Eyes." (Courtesy of Photofest)

The dean of women news commentators, Dorothy Thompson also had a successful career in print journalism. She is shown here in 1938, broadcasting for NBC. (Courtesy of Photofest)

Perhaps the most successful women's show host on radio, Mary Margaret McBride is shown in the late 1930s, when her chat show was heard on CBS. (Courtesy of Photofest)

Shown here in 1940, Bertha Brainard was the first woman executive at NBC radio, in a career that began in the early 1920s. (Courtesy of Photofest)

Among the most popular first ladies, Eleanor Roosevelt constantly made use of the airwaves. She is seen here at the WBZ studios, Boston, in October of 1941. (Author's collection, with thanks to Fred B. Cole)

Shown here in 1941, Kay Morton did a popular chat show for women on KXOK in St. Louis. (Courtesy of Ruth Markus)

A 1942 photo of "Reveille with Beverly," one of the shows put on the air to boost the morale of the servicemen. (Courtesy of Jean Hay, with thanks to Dean Opperman)

Reflecting the gender roles of that time, this late 1945 picture of a Philco factory shows women doing assembly work under the watchful eye of male supervisors. (Author's collection)

A popular interview show on NBC radio in the late 1940s featured Jinx Falkenberg and her husband Tex McCrary. They are shown here with the famous songwriter Irving Berlin. (Courtesy of Photofest)

Martha Rountree, who produced "Meet the Press" and "Leave It to the Girls," is shown in her office, busily booking guests. (Courtesy of Photofest)

Before she became a consumer reporter, Betty Furness had her own talk show and did commercials. This 1953 photo is from her CBS-TV show, "Meet Betty Furness." (Courtesy of Photofest)

Virginia Graham, shown here in 1956, began her career on radio but later became a successful TV chat show host with a syndicated program called "Girl Talk." (Courtesy of Photofest)

Among the most popular women's show hosts in Boston was Louise Morgan, shown here in the studios of WNAC-TV, the Yankee Network. (Author's collection)

The most successful talk show host on Hispanic television, Cristina Saralegui has become a role model for Hispanic women during a career that has spanned three decades. (Courtesy of Cristina Saralegui Enterprises)

The author, Donna Halper, in the studios of Northeastern University's radio station, October 1968, after she became their first female D.J. (Author's collection)

But then there was a network program called *American Women,* which ran for a while on CBS. It paid tribute to women in the war effort, praising their achievements. NBC also aired a short series that praised the work of women in the military—a four-week public service program called "Now Is the Time." Jane Tiffany Wagner, one of NBC's women managers (director of Women's War Activities), gathered up an all-female staff (she even borrowed engineer Muriel Kennedy from the NBC affiliate in Boston, making Kennedy the first woman to ever engineer an NBC network program), and the NBC women produced the entire series. According to *Newsweek,* most of the men around the NBC studios regarded the project with amusement and seemed to be waiting for it to be over, since the women Miss Wagner had assembled for her staff were numerous office assistants, whom she trained as script girls, announcers, and even actresses. Instead of being impressed by what Miss Wagner had accomplished, one man commented that he could hardly wait to get his secretary back.[59] While this comment may have been made partly in jest, it does speak volumes about the commonly held attitude that women who achieved during the war were not trying out for a new career. Rather, their achievements were regarded as temporary; some of what they did was impressive, but everyone knew once the war ended, women would go cheerfully back to their "normal" subordinate position.

These attitudes were expressed in a memo that was published in the July 1943 issue of the magazine *Mass Transportation;* the author instructed male managers in how to handle their new women employees, giving such advice as don't hire older women because they are "cantankerous and fussy," hire women who are slightly overweight because they will be grateful to have a job and are "more even tempered and efficient," and make sure you tell your female workers exactly what you want them to do because ". . . women make excellent workers when they have their jobs cut out for them, but . . . they lack the initiative in finding work themselves."[60] Bosses were also reminded that women would probably need more frequent breaks than men did, and that female workers worked best when supervisors did not yell at them. Some women did in fact redecorate, cleaning up their work environment and making it more aesthetically pleasing, but by and large, most women were there to work, and that is what they did.

Of course, not everybody was happy about all of this social change. Women in some defense jobs wore pants—which, to traditionalists, violated the biblical verse about women wearing a man's garments. But for the women war correspondents especially, wearing skirts just was not practical. One woman even met the pope while she was still dressed in pants. Eleanor Packard, of United Press, had no intention of making a fashion statement; she just had not had a chance to change into a dress before meeting him.

Interestingly, Pope Pius seemed amused rather than offended: "You're an American, I see," he remarked, "And you have been reporting the war?" She replied yes and he smiled understandingly.[61] But not all such encounters went that smoothly, especially when matters of the "proper place" of women and minorities were concerned.

Downplaying Racism and Sexism

Sociologists who try to analyze the ethics and values of people from previous generations are often mystified by what seems like hypocrisy even in the lives of the greatest leaders: how, for example, could a man like Thomas Jefferson write about freedom and yet have slaves? In the 1940s, some social critics were asking how could the networks and the journalism community praise "the American way" and contrast our country's democracy with the fascism of the Axis powers when the president had signed the order placing all Japanese-Americans into euphemistically described "relocation centers" (the people forced to live there called them "concentration camps"), or when the networks allowed their black artists to suffer the humiliation of segregated hotels and restaurants? The issue of racism was especially painful during the war, since many black soldiers were now fighting in a military that was still segregated, yet fighting for the concept of freedom from tyranny.

The black press was incensed and wondered why the mainstream white media had been so timid about discussing racial prejudice. On a number of occasions, distinguished black educators came to both NBC and CBS with proposals for public service shows about discrimination and the unfair treatment of blacks in the military, but the networks were very reticent to air such controversial material, insisting that any shows about black people include mostly popular music by black artists.[62] Yet the executives of the networks would often write articles and give speeches about the large number of public service programs they offered.

When a network on some rare occasion did permit a controversial show to air, no matter how good the show was and how much praise it received, there was seldom any follow-up. Such was the case in 1943 when the National Urban League decided to do a radio tribute to black women. In a culture where symbols were important, the black woman was truly invisible. Although many had a good education and large numbers wanted to do war work, the few that were hired often got the dirtiest and most menial jobs. And while the popular advertisements praised the working woman, it was the working white middle-class woman most frequently shown in illustrations or photographs. In fact, if a person read the news magazines or the women's magazines, it would have been easy to assume only white people wanted jobs, because so few nonwhites were depicted. If a black woman was seen at all, she was portrayed in the background, as a mammy or as a maid.

The Urban League felt it was time for the nation to learn about some of the black women who had made a difference in the history of America. The radio special they created was written by Ann Tanneyhill, a young black woman who had graduated from Simmons College in Boston and who had expertise in publicity as well as vocational counseling. "Heroines in Bronze" was perhaps the first program on a major network (CBS aired it in March of 1943) to focus on black women workers. The first part of the show featured vignettes about three heroines of the past—Phillis Wheatley, Sojourner Truth, and Harriet Tubman. The show then moved into its segment on the black woman today, which included a speech by Mary McLeod Bethune, who was still active in the government. Bethune discussed how black women were doubly discriminated against, and how despite the number of black soldiers risking their lives in the war, many businesses still refused to hire black people. She reminded the audience that black women were loyal to the American ideal, and all they wanted was the opportunity to participate. The show then went into live interviews with black women who had obtained war jobs: a radio technician, a flight-training instructor, a woman working with the Red Cross. Each discussed her work and commented on how her training was the same as a white woman's, yet black women were not given the same opportunities. The show had no singing and dancing, no comedy skits, and the music was limited to inspirational songs. The reenactments of the lives of the famous black women were done by professional black actresses, and the narrator was a well-known black stage actor; all of them had a difficult time getting work on the radio, given how few dramatic roles were considered appropriate for a black person in those days. The program had a serious tone to it, educational and thought provoking, as it asked the white listeners to imagine what life must be like for a black woman in modern society.[63]

Ann Tanneyhill's writing was powerful; her hope was that "Heroines in Bronze" would dispel some of the prevailing myths about the black woman. The black press gave the show excellent reviews, praising not only its representations of black female achievement, but also its unique way of making its point, without falling back on the stereotypic use of dance music and ladies singing the blues. Even white listeners sent fan mail praising the show and calling it informative. But, unfortunately, a single one-hour dramatic documentary, no matter how well done, could not compensate for hundreds of years of myth and prejudice. And as mentioned earlier, the network evidently felt it had done its one controversial show. No follow-up ever aired, despite Tanneyhill's repeated efforts to get more programming about black women produced.[64]

Occasionally, there would be a news show about racial prejudice, especially when race riots broke out in the summer of 1943; now and then, a white commentator spoke in favor of racial tolerance, and sometimes, a public service show would address the subject amidst lots of popular songs meant to show the contribution of black people to the field of entertainment. But if the status of white women did not get much recognition on the air, the status of black women got even less. The role of black women on the networks returned to the occasional singer or the maid in a radio drama. The few public affairs programs that did address current events, such as the well-respected *America's Town Meeting of the Air,* aired several discussions of the "race problem" in the mid-1940s, but not one woman was ever asked to be on the panel of guests. At first, the network public affairs shows that discussed the race question did not even have black men as panelists; it was considered quite controversial the first time a black panelist was included.[65]

Except for an occasional iconoclast, few print or radio journalists spoke out against racism or sexism in any meaningful way, and the injustices that seem so obvious today either were not noticed or were ignored. Perhaps the men at the networks felt they had done their part for working women by having women as heads of educational programming, children's programming, public affairs, and, of course, women's shows. Perhaps they felt that by giving several prominent black musicians their own network shows, that was enough. But suffice it to say that subjects like whether it was fair for women to be arbitrarily fired from jobs even after they had proved their competence, or why black women were so totally underrepresented in broadcasting, somehow never got chosen by the major public affairs shows. And if the women's magazine editors even thought of these issues, they seldom if ever pursued them, evidently convinced that readers preferred makeup tips and romantic stories rather than the realities of job discrimination. As for the fan magazines, they mainly showed how the stars were participating in the war effort, just like ordinary citizens. And radio programming focused on boosting the morale of the troops and keeping anxious families informed; the networks brought out more famous singers and more variety shows and continued to provide war news live from Europe.

One of the very few places where advocacy and serious discussion about women's issues could still be found throughout the 1940s was in the pages of *Independent Woman.* The Business and Professional Women's Clubs (BPW) continued to use radio throughout the war years, even establishing a committee whose job it was to get more discussion about the achievements of business and professional women onto the airwaves. When Maine's newly elected Senator Margaret Chase Smith spoke at the BPW convention in Cleveland, Ohio, in 1946, the talk was carried over WHK and the Mutual network; those who listened heard the Senator encourage women to become more active in politics, to become leaders in their communities, and to work together to expand the opportunities for women who wanted careers. And, whether in the home or in the workplace, she stressed that women must no longer be passive and wait for things to change; they must take on the challenge of improving them.[66] In a media climate permeated with sponsors telling women that their future success depended on the right lipstick, it must have been somewhat surprising to hear a woman Senator telling her female listeners that they could in fact become leaders and change society through their actions.

How Women Coped

Now that women were working at jobs that paid more than the typical "women's work" did, they had more money to spend. Cultural historian John Morton Blum wrote that by 1943, there were 5 million more women employed than in 1941, and despite shortages and rationing of certain items, shopping was a national obsession. In 1942, Americans (large numbers of whom were female consumers) had purchased $20 million more in pharmaceuticals than in 1941; jewelry sales rose between 20 and 100 percent. By December 7, 1944, the third anniversary of Pearl Harbor, Macy's department store had the biggest selling day in its history.[67] And responding creatively to shortages became a way of life, too. When the Office of Price Administration, the agency established to attempt to control inflation by controlling prices and rationing scarce goods, announced that cloth for women's bathing suits needed to be rationed, manufacturers found a perfect way to reduce the use of this cloth by 10 percent, as they had been asked to do. They marketed two-piece bathing suits, thereby making the wearing of a sexier garment seem like a patriotic gesture.[68]

While the women working as Rosies made the news, what often was ignored was the hardship such women endured. The government wanted women in the labor force to keep industry operational, but only a few companies offered their women workers any day care or help with their duties at home. Rather, women were in the familiar double bind, praised in the advertisements for being patriotic and taking on difficult jobs in industry, but often criticized in the popular magazines for neglecting their children. In a climate of so many double messages, women's responses reflected that confusion. A poll taken in 1943 by the Women's Bureau showed that over 70 percent of working women liked their new jobs and hoped to keep on working after the war (the BPW did a survey a year later and found similar results); but another 1943 survey showed that 73 percent of young women planned to become housewives. Only 18 percent said they planned to combine marriage and career.[69]

The uncertainty of war and the many social changes taking place made more people into radio fans: the medium brought listeners comfort, escape, and stability. For women, familiar voices like the Neighbor Lady or Mary Margaret McBride were reassuring—and a research study showed that women listeners did not perceive commercials on women's shows as annoying, but, rather, they found them informative, like shopping news. As for Miss McBride, whom the critics loved to hate, her listeners supported her with enthusiasm. On her tenth anniversary in 1944, over 18,000 fans packed Madison Square Garden to honor her. The critic from *Newsweek* couldn't understand it: "[She] prattles rudderlessly . . . For 45 minutes, she just talks. She interviews a guest or two and tells a story or two . . . she squeezes in a plug [for her twelve sponsors] wherever she can . . ."[70] Yet, Miss McBride was receiving hundreds of letters a week, and her show was as popular in 1944 as it had been in 1934; even with more women in the workforce, she knew how to make her audience feel they belonged, whether they were working outside the home or not.

Meanwhile, Hollywood cranked out over 900 movies during the war. Women in these dramas were the ones waiting patiently at home or doing their part to help the war effort in socially accepted ways, such as in the classic 1942 movie *Casablanca,* where Ingrid Bergman's character Ilsa was there basically to look beautiful (the lighting at times makes her seem angelic) and provide inspiration to both Rick and Victor Laszlo. This was not really a time when the media did any prolonged or serious analysis of the roles of women. Men were still portrayed as the doers, and women as their appreciative audience or their helpful assistants. Even when women were active in some way, it was always placed in the context of what it did for the men, such as when *Time* magazine did a March 1945 cover story on the Women in the Naval Reserve (WAVEs). The cover showed Captain Mildred McAfee in her uniform, but the caption was "Women can still be women," and the article, after praising the many contributions of the highly trained female navy recruits (and mentioning that black and white recruits had been serving together with no problem), pointed out that the addition of these women had "freed more than 70,000 men for combat." The public was also assured that the WAVEs were "models of correct, seamanlike behavior."[71]

Where the WAACs (by now known as the WACs) had tried to attract women by making military life seem glamorous, the WAVEs marketed their service in a much more dignified manner. To her credit, the captain did not see servicewomen as some gimmick. When reporters asked about what kind of underwear and lingerie the women recruits wore, Captain McAfee refused to answer; she responded only to questions about what the WAVEs could do and what they were achieving in the war effort. And she made it very clear that the women under her command deserved to be taken seriously.[72]

The news of the war may have been controlled to some degree, but for radio listeners, the voices of the news commentators were becoming as well known as popular singers, and the networks were providing longer newscasts because people wanted them.[73] Even local announcers got into the act of selling war bonds—WNEW's Martin Block liked a Spike Jones novelty record called "Der Fuehrer's Face," a song that used comedy to insult Hitler and was wildly popular with listeners. Block promised to keep on playing it if listeners would pledge a certain amount to buy war bonds. Within a week, he had raised nearly a quarter of a million dollars, and the song was played at least fifty times.[74]

Of course, soap operas found more ways to insert the war into their plots. "These . . . are the friends you hear daily in the exciting true-to-life story of a girl who changed from the role of backstage wife to war wife," headlined *Radio Mirror* in its February 1944 pictorial tribute to the popular series *Backstage Wife*. In this war plot, our heroine Mary, married to a handsome actor, must now deal with his being sent overseas as a member of the Coast Guard. How will she adjust to life without him? Will he remain faithful to her? And will they be reunited at war's end? During the war years, *Radio Mirror* had become not only a fan magazine, but "the magazine of radio romances," with more pictures of the soap opera stars and more romantic fiction, much of which was inspired by radio shows. In this climate of patriotism and enforced unity (criticism of the war somehow did not make it onto most radio programs), media critics still found plenty they thought radio could do better. But as for the public, surveys continued to show that listenership was rising, and people were, in general, satisfied with the amount of war information they were receiving. The networks had presented about 7 percent news in 1939; by 1944, this had increased to 20 percent.[75] Music, especially the star-studded variety shows, still was the first choice of most listeners; and even though a vocal minority of listeners did express criticism of the soap operas, saying they all sounded alike, people listened to them faithfully, and new ones continued to be produced.

Despite radio's ability to help take people's minds off of their worries, one event of the mid-1940s proved impossible to ignore. The sudden death of the beloved President Roosevelt on April 12, 1945, stunned Americans of all races and economic backgrounds. Even his political enemies stopped what they were doing to pay tribute to him. The networks stopped running commercials for three days, and coverage of his funeral was done by nearly every station.[76] As TV would do years later after President Kennedy was assassinated, so radio helped a grieving nation come to terms with the loss of a popular and influential president. And it goes without saying that when President Truman announced the surrender of Japan and the war's end, the radio networks received some of their highest ratings.

The War Ends

Throughout the war, any time women did something that was considered unique, the story made the news. Women baseball players and women umpires got plenty of print; although there had been both in the 1920s, now that there was a semipro baseball league for women, some of the players developed a following and were guests on the chat shows. Women in a number of unusual occupations were profiled in print, especially some of the Rosies. But while these stories put a human face on women trying to cope with separation from their loved ones, the women themselves did not seem to think their efforts were especially noteworthy. When asked about their newfound skills or their success at a certain thing, the most common response I noticed was "I was just lucky," or "I was glad to help out." Granted, back then it would have been considered arrogant for anyone, male or female, to say "Yes, I'm wonderful," but part of the expectation for women was humility. Women were not accustomed to being in the limelight unless they were movie stars or radio singers. Average women suddenly thrust into unusual situations that got them interviewed may very well have thought they were lucky. Besides, what mattered most was awaiting the day the war officially ended so that families could be reunited. It was difficult to think about achievements on the job when sometimes no letters from their soldier arrived for weeks or even months.

As for the media, when at long last the war did end, what was about to happen to the women workers was not on most reporters' minds. The soldiers were coming home. *That* was the story. There were parades to plan and a hero's welcome to be given. The forces of tyranny had been defeated and now it was time to celebrate.

But although there was euphoria in the streets, and throngs of people who did not even know each other were hugging and cheering the victory, 1945 was also a time when some uncomfortable facts were coming to light. America was finally learning the truth about the Holocaust. The Jewish press had been warning about this for years, but the U.S. government had basically ignored all pleas to intervene. By the time America did get involved, it was too late to save millions of innocent people from destruction in the Nazi death camps. And, as some people were finding out, anti-Semitism was not just something in a faraway country. In 1945, the first Jewish woman to ever be named Miss America, Bess Myerson, was crowned. She endured repeated and virulent examples of anti-Semitism throughout her reign, including being denied admittance to an event that was being held at a club that did not allow Jews.[77] She finally decided to become a spokeswoman for religious and racial tolerance. Meanwhile, returning black veterans found the same conditions and the same segregated facilities they had left behind. Japanese-Americans were no longer shut away in camps, but the experience had been extremely traumatic and would continue to be a source of pain and humiliation for many years.

But none of this was the story the journalists had in mind, either. They wanted to honor the troops, and who could really blame them? This was no time to bring up controversy. As for the returning soldiers, I am told by a number of my relatives who fought in the war that they were so glad to be home that they thought about nothing else. White soldiers, who had sometimes fought side by side with black soldiers overseas, went back to their old neighborhoods, many of which were still segregated; and while there were painful memories of the brutality of the war, these men were proud that they had defended the cause of freedom. Some white veterans undoubtedly noticed that social and racial inequalities still existed in America, but the majority was focused on having a normal life, relaxing, and spending time with their families. In fact, whatever their ethnicity, most of the returning soldiers couldn't wait to see their loved ones. The results were a large number of marriages (in 1946, more than 2.2 million couples said "I do"), and in 1947, the birth of 3.8 million babies, one of whom is the author of this book. By the end of the decade, 32 million babies would be born, and the so-called "Baby Boom" would cause even more social change.[78]

Women Lose Their Jobs

Life magazine explained the first phase of the postwar social changes for women in this way: "As part of the guns-to-butter economic transition, many factories and other businesses had to lay off workers. Women were especially hard hit by the layoffs. In 1947, pink slips were handed out to almost two million working women. Within months, factories had retooled and began churning out consumer goods at a record pace, but almost all the new jobs went to men."[79] It sounds so matter-of-fact. But somehow, I don't think it was. Professor Stephanie Coontz remarked upon the surveys done by the Women's Bureau, which showed that a majority of women wanted to keep their job but were not given any option:

> [I]n the immediate aftermath [of the war], a combination of factors led married women to temporarily pull back from full-time work or at least to down-

grade its centrality in their lives. Following the war, women were laid off from manufacturing jobs in droves. . . . The proportion of women in the labor force fell from 36.5% in 1944 to 30.8% in 1947. *Most women workers did not lose their jobs permanently but were simply downgraded to "women's work," such as clerical and service jobs.* [80] (author's emphasis)

So, rather than the commonly held belief that once their men came home, women just wanted to be housewives again, the reality may be that economics played a large part in the decision. Women with good-paying jobs had lost them, and seeing no way to get them back, perhaps they resigned themselves to being happy for their husbands (who did get those good-paying jobs), and perhaps taking a little part-time job to help out, but only if he said it was okay. Why didn't the women stand up and fight for those good jobs that were being taken away? For one thing, this was an era before the civil rights movement, before the next wave of feminism brought back the discussion about sexism. At this point, women had been taught repeatedly that their role in life was to make whatever sacrifices were needed to keep their home and their family running well. There were few rewards for women who were too different. Yes, there were still some women in positions of authority in the late 1940s, but the popular culture that had been marshaled to get women into the workforce was now working overtime to tell them they would be much better off staying home again. A few women did make an effort to keep their war jobs (Rose Will Monroe was one who tried), and in the pages of *Independent Woman,* the BPW kept up its advocacy and kept doing monthly profiles of women in nontraditional jobs, but this was rapidly becoming a minority viewpoint. By and large, fighting to keep a job just did not seem worth the effort, especially when the government abruptly ended federal support of child-care facilities in 1946. Now, if a woman had children and was not rich, she had fewer options. But, women were assured, now that the men were home, life was going to be fine. After all, on the radio, there were so many happy moms with kids; they had problems, but somehow, things worked out just in time for the commercials.

Blaming the Women

For readers of women's magazines in the late 1940s, it was as if there had never been a Rosie the Riveter. Instead, the doctors and the psychologists wrote lengthy articles warning women that here was their big chance to do things right, and woe to them if they failed. Lest you think I am being melodramatic, here are just a few of many quotes criticizing women who worked— as well as women who stayed at home. It seemed that suddenly postwar women could do nothing right. For example, James Bender, director of the National Institute of Human Relations, said, "Authorities have reached the conclusion that . . . mothers have more and more been shifting their responsibilities of child-rearing to the schools and churches." Further, he said, women who are bosses in the business world are ". . . oversensitive to criticism; too jealous of one another; [do not] work well with other women [or] have a sense of fair play."[81]

The president of a major manufacturing company spoke about how a woman could be an asset to her husband's career if she was supportive, and could destroy his career if she was not. William B. Given Jr. said he would never hire any man without first assessing the man's wife. "Many a home has broken up because a wife has no understanding of her husband's business problems," he said. And continuing to discuss the wife's responsibility, he warned that "a nagging wife with too much ambition makes life miserable for a man who is doing well," and he reminded wives to never complain about how much their husband had to travel or work late because such negative attitudes could "wreck a husband's career." He then gave an example of how the company resolved personnel problems. There was one man who was "something of a hell raiser" and was not showing up for work on time as a result. His supervisor paid a visit to the wife, admonishing her for not "making it more fun for [him] to spend his evenings at home," and telling her to find ways to entertain him, such as inviting his friends over or playing cards with him. She did so, and the employee was a problem no longer.[82]

In addition to devoting herself to understanding her husband's career, the former Rosie was also supposed to strive to become the perfect wife. Said regular columnist Dr. Clifford Adams in the *Ladies' Home Journal,* "A woman can overcome her shortcomings as a wife, once she knows what they are." He then listed the most common complaints of the husbands he had surveyed. These included: "She lets her feelings be hurt too easily . . . [is] nervous or emotional, [t]ries to improve [her husband], and [is] a poor housekeeper." He advised wives to notice their faults and correct them before it was too late.[83] In an earlier column that same year (1948), he advised parents to give their children chores so they would be trained for their future. "Sons and daughters should be taught specific household skills . . . While Johnny helps his father put on the screens or mow the lawn, Jane can bake a cake or set the table for company . . . [This] will help children achieve harmony in their own homes later on."[84] Of course, there was no guarantee any of this would work. I never wanted to learn to bake a cake, and my father ultimately resigned himself to the fact that I was a devoted baseball fan. But until the day they died, I am sure my parents wondered what they had done wrong.

With magazines running ads that showed happy women who used to have careers but who gave them up to raise their families ("It's More Fun Being a Mother than a Model" read one headline in a toothpaste ad), even articles about women who still worked carried the implication that maybe this just was not worth it. The May 3, 1948, cover story in *Life,* for example, was "Career Girl: Her Life and Problems." A long photo-essay, it contained pictures of Gwyned Filling, a young woman who had come to New York to work in an advertising agency. While sometimes she enjoyed her work and had gotten several small raises (although we may safely assume she made far less than men in her agency), the copy also contained lines like "Gwyned's life is interesting . . . but beneath the gaiety lie the problems which confront all career girls. How much of her time and nerves must she sacrifice for success? When should she marry, and will she jeopardize her chance by trying to close her eyes to everything but her career?" Another caption shows her in tears and says that, "Gwyned is under continual strain because she is anxious to make a success of her career." And finally, after a grueling day at the office, "Sometimes she lies awake thinking . . . she has not solved the career girl's problem. It requires only a letter from a happily married friend to make her pause—and wonder . . ."[85]

It could have been the plot of a soap opera, and, in fact, it *was* the plot of numerous stories and soap operas, which persisted in offering to women the choice of a happy marriage or a career, but not both. Career women were frequently depicted as lonely or somehow incomplete; the word *spinster* lacked the complimentary tone that *bachelor* had. The idea that an unmarried woman in business might find companionship with another woman, or might be perfectly content to live alone, did not resonate with many writers in the 1940s. Lesbian relationships were considered abnormal by psychiatrists, and a woman alone was depicted as a potential home wrecker or perhaps as somebody too unpleasant or too ugly to attract a man.

The Experts Speak

That there was already some ambivalence from women about the choices they were being given was hinted at by a 1946 Roper Poll, in which 25 percent of all women surveyed said they would rather have been born male. But the mental health profession knew what women needed, and as mentioned earlier, it came from the ideas of Sigmund Freud. In 1947, a book called *The Modern Woman: The Lost Sex* came out. It was published by a woman known for her traditionalist views, Marynia Farnham, and her colleague, Ferdinand Lundberg. As with Dorothy Thompson, Dr. Farnham was a career woman writing about how wrong it was for women to have careers;

but few if any of the critics of that time asked the Freudian psychoanalyst why she was working if it was such a terrible thing to do.

The reviews show that the book polarized many who read it. Some reviewers said the book was "good humored and shrewd" or "the best book yet to be written about women"; but others were appalled by how "dogmatic and sensational" it was or why the book devolved into "a savage attack on the feminist movement . . . it seems unfair to hit [women] with every verbal missile . . ." One critic said the book was a "frank and complete acknowledgement of the thorough bankruptcy of our age," but another retorted that the book was "hazy sociology, dubious psychiatry; [it] expounds all the old prejudices about women . . . [but] what strikes me most about [this book] is its cruelty."[86] The same polar opposite interpretations still apply to how modern critics have evaluated the book's influence. Some feminist critics like Christine Lunardini say it was very influential and affected society's attitudes toward women from the late 1940s well into the 1950s.[87] But this is disputed by Professor Joanne Meyerowitz, who wrote an article that claimed *The Modern Woman: The Lost Sex* was regarded as very reactionary even in its day and was part of a small body of similar antifemale writing that was not taken very seriously.[88] The truth probably lies somewhere in between, but the attitudes in the book simply reinforced what future doctors and therapists were being taught.

As mentioned earlier, a consistent number of experts had said for years that women should be submissive and traditional if they wanted their marriage to succeed. But as the soldiers returned, these old beliefs suddenly took on a new urgency: men had been in a terrible war and now it was time for the country, especially the women, to make them feel important and not cause them any problems. While Farnham and Lundberg's book may not have been treated like the Bible, it was a big seller and was excerpted or quoted in popular magazines. Among its assertions were that women were not capable of being independent; feminism was a mental illness, or as the authors put it, "a neurotic reaction to natural male dominance";[89] the theory about penis envy was absolutely true, because women who wanted to work outside the home were merely trying to be men; and finally, feminism had produced hatred of fathers and rejection of motherhood. If a woman was not totally satisfied by raising a family, she was in dire need of psychoanalysis to help her become better adjusted. Many experts, who had been writing in a similar manner (although perhaps without the Freudian terminology), defended some of Farnham and Lundberg's assertions.

While it may indeed be true that the average lower- or middle-class woman had little interest in what Freud said, this was still an era when people generally did not question the media. If an expert said women who wanted careers were mentally ill, there must be some truth to it. (I can still hear my late father saying about any number of things, "Why would the newspaper print it if it wasn't true?") Books that reinforced society's need to have women recede into the background came at just the right time. And although a few authors did take issue with Farnham and Lundberg's claims, *The Modern Woman,* with its controversial statements, attracted most of the media attention. Critics of the book were not widely seen or quoted. Margaret Culkin Banning, a BPW national executive, spoke to the National Association of Women Broadcasters in New York in March 1947, and she tried her best to disprove Farnham and Lundberg, using the achievements of women in broadcasting as her framework.[90] Not as many people, however, read *Independent Woman* as read *Reader's Digest* or the other mass appeal magazines, thereby leaving people with the impression that Farnham and Lundberg's views must be valid.

It was not easy being a dissenter in those days, as numerous women in the 1950s would discover. When they expressed dissatisfaction with their lives as homemakers, they would be accused of being neurotic or ungrateful. Even some celebrities appeared to be taking the side of motherhood: a cover story in *Look* showed a smiling Shirley Temple with her adorable baby daughter. The headline said: "I'm Bringing Up My Baby." Inside was a lengthy pictorial essay with the popular actress, her husband John Agar, and little Linda Susan. The pictures showed the happy mom feeding, hugging, and walking her child, and the implication was that this was much more fun than anything else in the world. Buried within one of the paragraphs, however, was the fact that Miss Temple was still working and that a nurse cared for the baby while Mom was making her newest film.[91]

With so many ads and articles saying the same thing, housewives could easily have gotten the impression that motherhood was the unanimous choice among every other woman. The BPW made speakers and scripts on "Jobs for Returning GI Janes" and "Pink Slips or Paychecks?" available to women's show hosts and mounted a concerted effort to get radio to discuss women who wanted (or needed) to work, but again, this was vastly overpowered by what seemed like a concerted effort to show women agreeing with the idea that men work and women stay home. As for why there were few protests by those women who thought it was wrong to be arbitrarily banished from the workforce, as Carolyn Heilbrun has pointed out in *Writing a Woman's Life,* most women of that era were taught never to express negative emotions—especially anger—in a public forum for fear of being called "strident" or "shrill." Women who complained about their situation were accused of being both.[92] It is not surprising that large numbers of women threw themselves into raising their families in the hope that it would provide the magic answer, as they were promised that it would. And it certainly revitalized the women's shows, giving them a new audience of stay-at-home moms in need of advice.

On radio in the remainder of the 1940s, marriage seemed to be everywhere. *Bride and Groom* was a popular new show that featured interviews at the altar after the couple had said "I do." These were human-interest stories about what had brought the two together. Soap opera characters had plenty of weddings, and, of course, no radio fan could fail to notice that many of the most highly rated shows featured husband-and-wife teams. In the spring of 1947, Fred Allen (with his wife Portland Hoffa) was still so popular that he was given a cover story in *Time,* not known for extensive coverage of the stars on a medium still regarded as competition. But suddenly, some critics were accusing the husband-and-wife comedy teams of putting too much emphasis on the woman and making fun of the man. Interestingly, when women were stereotyped as stupid or helpless, there were not many articles from 1930s or 1940s critics that accused the writers of misogyny. When, in 1947, another show about an archetypical "dumb blonde" appeared in a new radio comedy, *My Friend Irma,* the critics said the show was clever. Yet, Vance Packard, writing in 1948, was very upset at how radio comedies insulted manhood, made fathers look like idiots, and participated in a trend in which ". . . American women are increasingly taking over the dominant role in marriage." He was especially concerned that these situation comedies were teaching children it was acceptable to make fun of men.[93]

Women Announcers Who Stayed on the Air

While once again, as had happened in the late 1920s, women announcers found themselves no longer needed after the war (and relegated once again to the women's shows), a few did maintain their jobs on air. In New York, radio actress Margaret Arlen was not only a women's show commentator, but she also did some commercials and public service announcements. During the war, it was noted that after she made some pleas for volunteers for the WAC, over 1,400 women volunteered in only a month.[94] After the war, she remained as an announcer, and she continued to get respectable ratings; on the women's show, her work was not so much about recipes as finding and interviewing interesting people. (Speaking of those respectable ratings, one of the main companies that did the audience surveys, Hooper, called people at home to ask about their radio preferences; only women were used to make those calls, perhaps because of the association the public had with women as telephone operators. Many of the women working for Mr. Hooper were former telephone operators, in fact.)

There were a few other women who were announcers. At WWRL in New

York, a young woman who thought she would be allowed only to do the women's show found to her surprise that the program director wanted her to DJ a new hit-record show aimed at the teen audience. Lucille Small not only played the hits, but she also did a show called *Teen Topics* and produced a three-times-a-week program about show-business news. And then there was a small but very interesting photo in the July 1948 *Radio Best,* showing Count Basie performing live in the studios of WDUK, Durham, North Carolina, as disc jockey Miss Dee Deering watches approvingly. As might be expected, no mention is made that WDUK was not a black station, and the South was still segregated in 1948. Yet there they were, white disc jockey and black musician, brought together by a love of music. Given the heated debate this subject could arouse, perhaps the magazine felt the less said, the better; I am sure Miss Deering was genuinely pleased to get such a big-name star on her show.

In the late 1940s, a few women were now farm broadcasters; that is, they did shows about subjects like agriculture and techniques for raising healthier animals. Sue Bailey Reid did a farm show on WPJB in Providence, Rhode Island, in the late 1940s; she and Louella Engel, farm director of station WMOH in Hamilton, Ohio, were two of a handful of women members of the National Association of Farm Broadcasters.[95] Of the women who remained as announcers on music shows, many were part of a male-female performing team, and they announced their own songs. *Radio Best* (which would soon be *Radio and Television Best*) in 1947–48 ran full-page ads for WMCA radio in New York, where a husband and wife did a radio show together. Known as "Mr. and Mrs. Music," singer Bea Wain and her husband André Baruch entertained the audience with records, musical guests, songs, and interviews. Both shared the announcing duties. This was not just a New York phenomenon; in other cities, too, married couples did their own live shows or had their own segment on a variety program. One of the most popular vocal duos in country music was Lulu Belle and Scotty of WLS in Chicago's *Barn Dance.* Lulu Belle (real name Myrtle Cooper) had become an instant favorite when she joined WLS in 1933. She was voted "Queen of Radio" in a 1936 poll, and her success as a vocalist was only enhanced by her partner Skyland Scotty (Scott Wiseman). The two sang duets and ultimately fell in love and got married. The *National Barn Dance* was aired by NBC, and well into the 1940s, it continued to get good ratings. Lulu Belle and Scotty won over fans even in cities where country music was not that popular.

Radio Best also began a new feature, "Who Is the Nation's Most Glamorous Disc Jockey?" Said the introduction, "Not so long ago, the disc jockeying profession was inhabited exclusively by men. But the war-time shortage of capable record-spinners changed the picture. The so-called weaker sex moved in, and it now looks as though they're here to stay . . ." The magazine invited the audience to nominate women disc jockeys who were both beautiful and talented. First to be profiled was a young woman from WWDC in Washington, D.C., Natalie Towle. Towle, a former music librarian at the station, "chooses her own records and writes her own scripts, in addition to her daily spin session, she and Bill Cox give with the chatter and music on the Hollywood Saturday Night Dance Party once a week at 11 P.M."[96]

Disc jockeying was about to become a career in its own right, having evolved from announcer. In radio's early days, a more formal environment had prevailed, with the expectation that a station would have a live band and a live announcer to introduce everyone. But in the late 1940s, stations moved away from the expense of live bands and toward friendly personalities who either played phonograph records and chatted with the musical guests or did the performing themselves; the old-fashioned and very serious announcers were being replaced by much younger disc jockeys, who mainly played records and took requests. This approach had been tried in a few cities as early as the 1930s (Al Jarvis in Los Angeles, Jack L. Cooper in Chicago, and Martin Block in New York were three of the earliest pioneers of this style), but the late 1940s saw the style flourish. The majority of the new jockeys were male, but there would continue to be a few exceptions. One was a sexy-voiced lady disc jockey who called herself "The Lonesome Gal." *Radio Best* had given her real name and story in September of 1948— she was Jean King, born in Dallas, who had had a rather undistinguished career as a Hollywood actress and a showgirl until she found radio and created her role. In the late 1940s, she was on the air at WING in Dayton, Ohio; soon her show would be syndicated all over the country.

Perhaps the biggest exception to the rule of men in the most important radio positions occurred when Frieda Hennock joined the FCC in 1948, the first woman ever to be appointed to the FCC. Hennock was a lawyer by profession and an immigrant success story (she was one of eight children; her family had come from Poland). It goes without saying that the male columnists who interviewed her for her new job were quick to write that she was "attractive," "glamorous," "blonde," and "a smart dresser." I doubt the men on the FCC were similarly described, although perhaps none of those adjectives applied to them. One writer noted that Miss Hennock was "a feminine feminist, [who] does champion women's rights—their right to be heard and their right to have a hand in . . . matters that directly concern them and their families."[97] And this she would definitely do. Frieda Hennock became a tireless advocate for educational radio and TV and spoke forcefully about the media's obligation to do more than just sell products.

There was at least one more young, attractive, and very important woman in the news in the late 1940s: proving that not every woman had quit her job after the war, there was Ruth M. Leach, one of the few women executives for a major corporation, International Business Machines (IBM). She had been made vice president in 1943, and contrary to the myth that women did not want to help other women, Leach spent much of her time making speeches before professional organizations (including the BPW) about improving the training and the status of women office workers. She was the first woman ever appointed to the level of vice president at IBM, and in addition to her skill in managing her own employees (she was said to have a "pleasing personality"), she advocated for women to receive more training in management. She believed women would make good managers if given the opportunity, because they "can both soften and strengthen human relationship and help bring about better understanding between labor and management."[98] Throughout the 1940s, Miss Leach won numerous awards for her achievements, including being named one of ten outstanding women by the Women's National Press Club. What is especially interesting about her continued presence is that she was never depicted as a tragic figure who had no husband, and somehow all of the pressure on women to leave their jobs did not affect her, just as it did not affect Frieda Hennock.

Novelist Fannie Hurst, who seldom missed a chance to speak out on women's issues, gave a talk while on a book tour, during which she expressed her horror that so many of the daughters of the suffragettes were giving up their jobs and becoming homemakers.[99] She had reason to worry—even the activists at BPW were older women who had won their equality in the 1920s. A new and younger generation had not come along to replace them. As for the fan magazines, they were still preoccupied with such important questions as why Kate Smith had never married; that she truly loved her career evidently mystified the writer, who thought Kate would be a perfect wife because "[s]he cooks, she bakes; she knits, she sews, collects antiques. She loves little children . . . How then can she live alone—and like it?"[100]

But for radio, the 1940s was a transitional era. It marked the changing of the guard, as some of radio's pioneers retired. Bertha Brainard, one of NBC's first women executives, died suddenly of heart disease in June 1946. After many years of single-minded devotion to her work, she had only recently retired and married Curt Peterson, an advertising executive who had been a friend and colleague for years (they had met when he did some announcing for NBC in the 1930s). Several of the male pioneers from radio's formative years also died during the 1940s, notably KDKA Pittsburgh's founder Frank Conrad, and one of the first big-name announcers, Graham McNamee.

As new, younger voices were heard on the air, other changes occurred, most notably in music, as the transition away from live big band music and toward phonograph records began; the music itself was still dance music, but by the early 1950s, listeners would hear the beginnings of rock and roll. In 1949, a young man named Todd Storz became president of Mid-Continent Broadcasting (which he and his father founded). Todd began doing some experiments at one of the stations, KOWH in Omaha, rotating a specific number of hit songs over and over and repeating them frequently. This idea of radio as a juke box would be refined and modified by several other owners and managers; eventually, in the 1950s, it became known as "top 40."

As the 1940s ended, more black music was being played and not just the occasional Duke Ellington or Ella Fitzgerald. The first all-black music station had gone on the air in 1948 (WDIA in Memphis); it featured famous blues stars like B.B. King, and one of its announcers was Willa Monroe, who did a women's show for the black audience. This in itself was groundbreaking, since the common wisdom from white advertisers was that there was no need for such a program—black women were all supposedly servants, and they would not be around to listen. But Miss Monroe's success proved not only that the common wisdom was untrue, but that there was in fact a black middle class that did want to listen and did want to purchase what sponsors were advertising.[101] This was just the beginning of some dramatic social change, both for minorities and for women.

Now that the war was over, there was still a demand for news and information. In 1945, freelance writer Martha Rountree had co-created (with Lawrence Spivak) a radio show where major journalists asked the tough questions of important newsmakers. Sometimes, Miss Rountree served as moderator and received critical praise for her even-handed approach.[102] And in an era where radio news shows were not scripted, the guests actually tried to answer the questions. *Meet the Press* did so well that it went to TV as early as 1947. (The critics at *Radio and Television Best* were not fond of the televised version, saying it had too little action and made a much better radio show.) *Meet the Press* had some women journalists (one frequent invitee was May Craig, a reporter and former war correspondent, who worked for the Guy Gannett newspapers in Maine and was known for being outspoken), but it had very few women as guests, reflecting perhaps that women were seldom perceived as political leaders or newsmakers the way presidents and members of congressional committees were. Martha Rountree also created and produced one other series, which ran on the Mutual radio network—*Leave It to the Girls*. According to historian John Dunning, the show was originally conceived as a serious panel discussion by four career women who would answer questions sent in by listeners. But the show ended up being more comic than serious, and the questions tended to be about male/female relationships. Panelists were expected to think fast and come up with clever repartée. Among the famous women who served on the panel were Ilka Chase, Lucille Ball, Dorothy Kilgallen, and Jinx Falkenburg.[103]

In another note, *Newsweek* magazine observed that print journalism was hiring more women in 1949—not because editors had suddenly realized that talent has no gender, but rather because journalism still did not pay that well, and the experienced men were leaving for more lucrative jobs. Their place was being taken by bright young women who, *Newsweek* reported, were eager, enthusiastic, and willing to work for less money.[104] Still, a few experienced newswomen managed to continue working. In Cleveland, Dorothy Fuldheim, who had been on radio since 1944 doing book reviews and news commentary, decided at the age of fifty-four to try the new medium of TV. She began working at WEWS-TV as early as 1947, certainly making her one of the first women to do news on local TV. People who recall her earliest TV shows have told me that she did not want to be restricted to what was considered women's news; like Dorothy Thompson, she preferred issues and current events, and while she did interview her share of celebrities, she regarded herself first and foremost as a journalist. Dorothy Fuldheim would become well known for her commentaries and her interviews with important newsmakers in a TV career that lasted thirty-seven more years.

The fact that a woman of the stature of Dorothy Fuldheim and a program as respected as *Meet the Press* had both made a commitment to TV was certainly the biggest change that affected radio in the late 1940s. Finally, after years of predictions and technological setbacks, radio had some competition; TV was really here and a number of cities had TV stations operating. There were not twenty-four hours of programming yet, nor would there be for a while; there also were not many channels—most big cities had two. If you have ever seen kinescopes of 1940s TV, you know early TV (and TV reception) was quite primitive by modern standards, just as early radio had been. But the public was fascinated. Of course, many radio stars decided to try their luck with the new medium (just as former vaudeville stars had tried their hand at radio in the early 1920s). Some radio stars would do very well on TV, and their shows made the transition easily; others should have stayed in radio. But any new technology is an adventure, and TV was no exception. Prognosticators said this was the end for radio, and a number of advertisers did, in fact, switch from supporting radio to taking a chance on the new kid in town. But change occurred more slowly because not every city had TV yet; in 1948, the FCC had placed a temporary freeze on new licenses. So, in the cities that did not yet have TV, radio was still of major importance.

Many radio performers worried what would happen when every city got TV. WLW radio had a popular women's show hostess named Ruth Lyons, who was the Mary Margaret McBride of Cincinnati. Lyons was known for her interviewing skills and her ability to make radio listeners feel as if she were talking directly to them. But as several of her colleagues recalled, she

was also somewhat overweight, and she was concerned that this would dis-
qualify her from TV. Kate Smith had no problem, but then, Kate Smith had
an illustrious career of many years' duration, and her picture had been in
countless magazines. Ruth Lyons decided she should go on a diet immediately. Determined to put her best image forward on the company's new TV
station, she lost sixty pounds before her first TV show, and she never gained
it back.[105]

Whether or not the sudden preoccupation with looks was a good thing
(and men, too, worried about how the new medium would affect their appearance, since on radio, whether a man was bald or overweight was of no
consequence), the public reacted to it all with great curiosity. Now they
could see some of the stars they had only been able to hear, but there is no
evidence that the stars who were not handsome or beautiful were despised.

From oral histories I have read, it seems that audiences had a sense of
humor and were very much aware that this was still sort of an experiment.
As early radio once did, TV in its formative years relied on personality and
the ability to make the best of the situation when equipment suddenly broke
or some prop did not work right. While some boomers would later look
back on early TV with fond nostalgia, the critics noticed that much of the
first several years was awkward at best. Stars stood woodenly in front of
cameras that were difficult to move, or they looked in the wrong direction
when saying their lines. The lights were hot, and it took tremendous poise
for celebrities to appear natural when they feared their makeup was melt-
ing. TV was definitely trial and error, except now, millions of people could
watch as the mistakes occurred.

Louise Morgan, who had done a successful women's show on WNAC
radio in Boston during the mid-1940s, went on TV in 1949 and recalled for
a reporter some of the more terrifying moments of her first year doing live
TV, such as when the show started at noon and the guest had not yet arrived
at 11:58, or the time she was cheerfully interviewing a movie star who suddenly began to tilt (one leg of his chair had broken). She also remarked
upon the time she was announcing the next segment of the show, when
suddenly a mouse ran across the studio floor, just as some models were
coming into view to show the newest spring fashions.[106]

But TV was no laughing matter for radio executives, who sat in meetings, worrying about what they should do. Was this really the end for radio?
Would all the big stars jump to TV and leave radio with nothing? Little did
the radio executives realize that the answer was in the hands of the millions
of so-called baby boomers, who at the end of the 1940s were still infants.
But soon enough, they would have a lot to say about the future of TV, as
well as the future of radio.

Timeline: The 1940s

1942	Association of Women Directors is founded, forerunner of American Women in Radio and Television
1942–45	Numerous women working in "men's jobs" during World War II
1943	Character of Rosie the Riveter is created
1947	*Meet the Press,* co-developed and moderated by Martha Rountree, debuts
1948	Pauline Frederick covers political conventions for ABC
	Frieda Hennock named first woman on the FCC

Chapter 5

The 1950s: Forward into the Past

In the late spring of 1949, Mary Margaret McBride had celebrated her fifteenth anniversary. If her tenth required Madison Square Garden, her fifteenth needed Yankee Stadium—she was that popular. In fact, she would be on the cover of the August 1951 *Radio and Television Mirror,* which did a tribute to her. She was fifty-one years old now, expressed no desire to take her show to television, and continued to be the personification of the women's show genre. Said *Radio and Television Mirror* in an extensive look at her career, "McBride admirers are all ages . . . the younger woman sees her as the warm mother-confidante, tolerant, understanding, and brimming with life; to her contemporaries, she is an extension of themselves, the woman who gets around and relates to them the things that chance [prevents them from] doing; to the older woman, she is the good daughter, the one who has gone far in the world but who has never forgotten . . . the training she received at home."[1]

Another woman who had made an impact in the 1940s and was still a presence as the new decade began was champion golfer Babe Didrikson Zaharias. She was named "Woman Athlete of the 20th Century" by the Associated Press in 1949; her years of achievement in sports had elevated the status of women athletes, and in 1948, she had been one of the founders of the Ladies' Professional Golf Association (LPGA). As the new decade began, the idea of women athletes in certain sports was totally acceptable—but up until now, that meant as long as they were white. In 1950, that finally changed, as Althea Gibson became the first black woman to play in the U.S. Open tennis championships; a year later, she was the first to be invited to play at Wimbledon.

But strong and successful women were not often mentioned in the magazines, where male editors persisted in seeing what men did as more newsworthy than what women—even businesswomen—did. Few average Americans were aware of Frieda Hennock, although on college campuses, the fact that she had fought for educational broadcasting was much appreciated.

A new class of 10-watt educational FM stations went on the air, enabling students to learn about broadcasting. Unfortunately, they also learned about sexism, although they probably did not think of it that way back then. Emerson College in Boston was perhaps the first in the East to get one of the 10-watt educational FMs going on the air in the late fall of 1949. But in the Emerson radio station's operations manual, in use throughout the 1950s, it stated that announcers must be male. Women could be on the air, but only doing "programs of interest to women," which were defined as storytelling for children, fashion, and cooking (one show was called *Feminine Fancies,* and another was *The Magic Mirror*). Women also were not allowed to become program directors of the stations, although they could apply to be in charge of the women's program.[2]

In these attitudes, Emerson was reflecting a view that was typical of professional broadcasting; rather than being different, most colleges simply reflected what the instructors (who often worked at local stations) believed. At most college stations of the 1950s, a male professor was in charge of the broadcasting department; few if any women would be in positions of authority until well into the 1960s, which is when some college stations finally began allowing women to be announcers and program directors.

In professional broadcasting in the early 1950s, there were more women station owners than there had ever been, but the number was still comparatively small: twenty-five women now ran their own station. One of them was Gene (short for Imogene) Burke Brophy, who owned and operated KRUX in Phoenix. Her twenty-one-year career in broadcasting included working for CBS as a talent scout in their Hollywood Artists Bureau, where she ultimately became the final say for what talent was hired by the network's entire West Coast operation. Another female station owner was in charge of KING Broadcasting in Seattle: Dorothy Stimson Bullitt owned KING AM, FM, and TV. When her husband had died in 1932, she took over a realty business that her father had originally begun. She became so successful that she was soon managing many large properties she had acquired. In 1947, Mrs. Bullitt was instrumental in acquiring a small AM (KEVR) that she and her company turned into KING.[3] A third was known by her legal name of Claudia Taylor Johnson, but she would become much better known as "Lady Bird" Johnson, wife of soon-to-be president Lyndon Johnson. Mrs. Johnson had owned KTBC in Austin, Texas, since 1943 and put KTBC-TV on the air in late 1952. And in the growing field of television, there was at least one other woman in the executive ranks—Maria Helen Alvarez was the general manager of KOTV in Tulsa. During the war, she had started in radio, learning all phases from typing scripts to reporting news. She ultimately went into sales and became one of the few women account executives (another was sales manager Claire Crawford of the Yankee Network in Boston). When George Cameron Jr., a wealthy businessman in the oil industry, decided to purchase a TV station, he hired her; it did not take long before she was running KOTV.[4]

A Few Women Announcers

There were still a few women (and even some young girls) on the radio in the early 1950s who were not doing women's shows, and a few whose women's programs were not typical of the genre. One of the youngest announcers on the air was Betsy King—she was ten and did her own children's show called *Let's Have Fun* on WCOP in Boston. In Memphis, Willa Monroe was still having great success as "The Tan Town Homemaker," but her health was not good, and WDIA realized they might need a replacement for her. The programming staff had come to believe that women announcers went over well with their audiences, so they auditioned several (that in itself was unusual—the tendency at most stations was to have one female, usually the one who did the women's show).

Throughout the early 1950s, women's voices were on the station regularly doing various features, although men held most of the regular shifts. One particular female announcer did become extremely popular and influential: Martha Jean "the Queen" Steinberg. She was hired to do a show called the *Night Spot,* and if females were the target audience, she did not agree with that strategy. Her style was one that certain women on the air had already found success with—remember the Lonesome Gal? Using a sultry voice and some double entendres, Martha Jean became a major success with the male listeners, and her shift was soon expanded as a result. Sounding sexy was one of two options for women announcers of the early 1950s. The ones who had what their program director felt was a sexy voice usually were given a late-night shift to appeal to the audience of third-shift workers who were presumed to be all male (housewives and children supposedly went to bed early, and many jobs still would not allow women to work the later shifts). An example of where women fit into the radio schedule was the Bea Kalmus show. Miss Kalmus was a popular nightclub singer when she became the late-night disc jockey for WMGM in New York; in addition to interviewing music industry guests and taking song requests from her own club repertoire, sometimes she would sing along with the records. The other option for women was, of course, to sound like a happy homemaker and do the women's show, carving out a niche the way Tina Redmond of WBKB in Chicago was doing with her two programs, *Sewing Is Fun* and *Cooking Is*

Fun. Of course, women who did not fit either archetype would have problems getting hired, and as the decade went on, women would be almost completely excluded from the new format called top 40.

But in the early 1950s, the total elimination of women announcers had not occurred, and there were still roles for women to play. Betty Brady was doing the farm program on WLW in Cincinnati, where she had become the Farm Home program director. WLW's signal had long extended into rural areas of Ohio, and many farmers and farmers' wives found her shows, *Everybody's Choretime* and *Family Fair,* both useful and entertaining. To the female audience, WLW was best known for Ruth Lyons, whose "Fifty Club" (named for the fifty people in the studio audience) was briefly picked up via NBC-TV, giving her national exposure. The show was renamed the "50–50 Club" because it was simulcast on both TV and radio. In late 1952, NBC cancelled the national airing of her show, but it remained on the air in Cincinnati, where it continued to enjoy great success and raise large sums for children's charities.

As the TV era began, more of the women's shows were making an effort to be more polished, more like a radio magazine, rather than like a group of friends chatting. *Variety,* which was not fond of women's shows, had high praise for Olivia Brown of WMC in Memphis. The reviewer felt Miss Brown's program was not like a typical women's show at all; she had interesting guests, asked excellent questions, kept the show moving, did plenty of research, and had a style that was both listenable and smooth.[5] Another professional-sounding women's show was done on WJW in Cleveland by Barbara Reinker, who not only earned the praise of *Variety*'s reviewer,[6] but, in 1954, won the AFTRA Award for "Best Woman's Show." But outside of women's shows, there were fewer and fewer women doing any announcing or disc jockey work and not many doing news as the 1950s continued. Some of the women's shows would be gone by the decade's end, as stations moved away from talk and toward more music.

While some stations did continue to keep one female voice for commercials, if more than one woman announcer remained at a station, there was often a gimmick behind it. In October 1955, record company owner and producer Sam Phillips bought a daytime-only station in Memphis and put it on the air as "WHER—All Girl Radio." Among the "girls," who played light pop and middle-of-the-road music with a heavy dose of love songs, was general manager Dotty Abbott and Sam's wife Becky Phillips. Sam Phillips, who owned Sun Records and had also discovered Elvis Presley, later claimed that WHER was the first "All Girl Radio Station," perhaps unaware that there was at least one all-female station in the 1920s (WASN in Boston) and several more during the war years.

Some of the women who worked behind the scenes in the early 1950s radio were working in the music library. As more stations moved to phonograph records, somebody had to keep the library organized, a skill that was often attributed to women. Since many announcers picked their own music, being able to find a song right away was crucial, and when records became scratched, the music librarian made sure a replacement was available. (Audiotape existed, but most stations still used records; 78 rpm had been the standard, although the switch to the much smaller 45 rpm was already beginning.) And while being the music librarian was often as far as a woman was able to advance, there were always exceptions: Betty Breneman, who became an influential national music director for the RKO Radio Group in the late 1960s, began her radio career as a music librarian at KLAC in Los Angeles in 1954. As for the job that was once called musical director, which involved hiring or auditioning the live bands, it was being eliminated at most stations. While not everyone had done away with live bands, the expense of doing TV encouraged many owners to seek ways to cut costs on the radio side; orchestras were a casualty at an increasing number of stations. By the late 1950s, there would be music directors, and more will be said about them in the next chapter. As for radio performers, not all of them gave up on radio—some, like Gertrude Berg, decided to keep their show on both radio and TV. Others, like Lucille Ball, would make some modifications to their radio show before it went over to TV: Lucy's radio comedy, *My Favorite Husband,* got a new name and a new male co-star (Desi Arnaz, her husband in real life) when it moved to CBS television in 1951.

Keeping Women in Their Place

Even though TV was supposed to be the future, the roles for women were very reminiscent of the roles they had played on radio in the past: scatterbrained wives in comedies, singers (and now, dancers), assistants behind the scenes, and hostesses of women's shows. There were still opportunities for women who wanted to work in radio rather than TV, although not everyone agreed on what those opportunities should be. In the early 1950s, there seemed to be a tendency at all too many stations to put women back in the old traditional jobs, rather than letting them pursue the ones they had trained for during the war. The fan magazines had quickly returned to writing articles about the women behind the men: Bill Slater was the moderator of Mutual's *Twenty Questions.* But how knowledgeable he sounded when responding to the panelists was largely the result of hours of work by his wife Marian. Said *Radio and Television Best,* "Marian Slater [is] the unsung heroine of 'Twenty Questions,' devot[ing] as much as twenty hours to checking facts at museums, at libraries, through home reference books and by telephone." She wrote up all the information on file cards and then prepared her husband before he went on the air. Like most researchers, she received little acknowledgement for her hard work, but she found it very gratifying to help her husband.[7] And despite what some female journalists had achieved during the war, newswoman (or "news hen" as some male critics called her and other female journalists) Pauline Frederick was told by her network that a woman's voice was not authoritative, so she would not be permitted to do any hard news; like many women who wanted to broadcast the news, she was only allowed to do "women's news," that is, interviewing the wives of celebrities and male newsmakers.[8]

Some women made the best of the situation and became experts at doing the so-called women's news. A good example was Betty Adams, whose career began in Providence on WJAR-TV doing a children's show, before she began doing features for women. Ultimately she was hired by WBZ-TV in Boston, and she traveled all over the world doing interviews with women from many countries and cultures. But it took a long time before her role was expanded so that she was not restricted to reporting what the candidates' wives were wearing.[9] Bea Johnson, of KMBC Radio and TV in Kansas City not only won the Golden Mike Award in 1953, but she traveled all over the world doing interviews with interesting women (and some men). Once, she went to the BBC in London to do a report for her audience, and the network wanted to do an interview with her. She discussed how American women's shows were done. In November 1955, she did her 2,500th broadcast.[10] But she, too, despite having press credentials, worked only on women's news.

The old guard, mostly men, had some very definite ideas about women in a newsroom. In their opinion, women should be typing, and men should be reporting. *Time* magazine circa 1950 had only one woman editor; all the reporters were men, while all the researchers were women. The same could be said of other news publications; most radio newsrooms had also returned to being all male. So, it probably came as no surprise when veteran radio newsman and network correspondent H.V. Kaltenborn, in an interview with *Radio and Television Best,* decided to offer his view of women's place. Among his beliefs were that a woman's only career should be helping her husband. He suggested that if a woman ever gets bored with homemaking, she should do some volunteer work, but her first priority should be to love, honor, and obey the man she married. He smiled when using the word *obey,* since his wife was sitting by him during the interview. He explained that what he meant by "obey" was to obey his interests, in other words, make his interests her primary concern. His wife seemed to agree, saying that because her husband was famous, she realized he needed her to be a hostess, a photographer, the one who organizes his schedule, etc., and she was happy to do these things.[11] News legend Walter Cronkite, interviewed several decades later, concurred with the traditional beliefs about women in the newsroom, even though he had seen some very competent women doing news. Admitted Cronkite, he still felt that a woman's voice was too high pitched to be easily understood, the way a male voice was.[12] He recalled only one woman who reported any news on network radio in the early 1950s, the previously mentioned Pauline Frederick, who despite the limitations placed on her by network executives, was covering the United Nations, along with colleague Gordon Fraser, for ABC.

If there was a message being delivered by the media to the early 1950s woman, it was that her goal in life should be to marry somebody famous and devote her life to making him happy; living vicariously through him would get her into newspapers and on radio and TV to talk about what it was like to have a famous husband. And if she could not marry somebody famous, she should devote her life to helping her husband and be an asset to him in whatever ways possible. In and of itself, there is nothing wrong with telling a wife to be devoted to her husband, but the message did seem rather one-sided, with the emphasis on his achievements only. She was supposed to derive her joy vicariously, through seeing him happy, or through bearing his children (preferably sons, of course)—certainly a belief that came from Freudian psychology. Perhaps it did not occur to any of the experts or the writers who promoted this belief that telling women to totally submerge their identity might be harmful to them. Perhaps the women who tried to do it really believed it was the right thing to do. But self-denial was a goal that was difficult, if not impossible, to attain. Betty Friedan and other theorists of that era believed the women's liberation movement of the 1960s was a direct reaction to that imposed self-denial of the 1950s. Still, any woman reading the magazines or listening to the radio in the early 1950s would have heard more about Mamie Eisenhower (wife of Republican presidential candidate Dwight D. Eisenhower) in the context of what it was like to be married to a famous war hero. Her clothes, the kind of hats she preferred, her new hairstyle, and what she did to help her husband were all dutifully reported by the media. Mr. Kaltenborn's dictum about the wife of a famous man certainly was exemplified in the life of Mamie Eisenhower, a much less controversial wife (and soon to be first lady) than Eleanor Roosevelt had been. This belief in letting the man be first even affected some businesswomen. In Boston, in 1950, Mrs. Nona Kirby, who had a long and successful career in advertising and radio sales, was next in line to become president of the Radio Executives Club. She declined, saying she believed a man should hold that post.[13]

Since most people in the early 1950s had started watching television, if we are to accurately analyze the 1950s, we have to examine the representations of women on TV as much as the images expressed in the soap operas or the shows of the radio homemakers. For many of the radio performers, the switch from radio to TV was gradual, and as I said earlier, some radio stars hedged their bets by appearing in both media. (And some, like Fred Allen and Mary Margaret McBride, expressed resistance to going on TV at all.) Until the TV Freeze ended in 1952, and massive numbers of new stations went on the air, it was difficult to measure TV's full impact, since many cities did not yet have access to it. In 1951, the radio industry was still able to say more people preferred radio than TV, but that was the last time. In fact, there were definite signs in 1950 that TV was a force with which to be reckoned: while only about 9 percent of American homes had TV in 1950, that still was over 9 million TV sets. In May of 1950, Baltimore became the first major U.S. city where more people watched evening television than listened to radio.[14]

McCarthyism

It seemed that every time somebody might have analyzed the status of women, another major crisis took attention away from such an analysis. In the 1940s, the emphasis had been on winning the war and then on welcoming the returning soldiers and helping them to get acclimated. In the early 1950s, the big issue was the fear of Communism, as Senator Joe McCarthy was beginning his reign of terror, aided to some degree by the media. The senator was quotable and controversial, and his accusations were given more attention than they probably deserved. Writer Norman Corwin, who was working in the industry and watched the development of McCarthyism, still believes that neither radio nor print asked enough of the hard questions, and they allowed McCarthy to accuse people without any proof whatsoever.[15] But in an era when people were genuinely afraid of a Communist invasion and wanted to protect their families, McCarthy sounded like somebody fighting to expose America's enemies. With the publication of the book *Red Channels,* which claimed that a number of entertainers and media figures were secret members of the Communist Party, suspicion fell on numerous people in broadcasting and film. Suddenly, networks wanted performers to sign loyalty oaths, and anyone who had ever criticized the government could be accused of treason. In such an atmosphere of rumor and innuendo, it did not take long before actual blacklisting began, costing a number of people their jobs. Among those accused, with minimal evidence, was radio's Singing Lady, Ireene Wicker, who was finally successful in proving her innocence, but who lost the TV show she had been doing and was unable to find work for several years while she tried to clear her name. Based solely on accusations in *Red Channels,* TV actress Jean Muir was fired from her job on *The Aldrich Family,* per order of the show's sponsor, General Foods. Character actor Philip Loeb, who played the role of Jake when Gertrude Berg's hit series *The Goldbergs* was rejuvenated and returned to radio in 1949, was another performer whose reputation was ruined by reports that he was a Communist; although Gertrude Berg and others defended him, the unproved accusations still cost him his livelihood. Ultimately, depressed and unable to find work, he committed suicide.[16]

The fear of a Communist threat was made more real to the average American when the Communist government of North Korea invaded South Korea. American soldiers would soon be involved, but unlike World War II, our involvement in the Korean War remained controversial. However, it reinforced in people's minds that communism was expansionary and dangerous: experts were warning that the Russians, no longer our allies as they had been during the war, were building an H-bomb that could destroy us all. In March 1951, Julius and Ethel Rosenberg were found guilty of espionage—of selling U.S. atomic secrets to Russia. After a trial that attracted intense debate and publicity, they were both sentenced to death. Years later, when the Cold War hysteria had passed, grave doubts were cast on that sentence, as newly declassified documents showed that Ethel was most likely innocent and Julius at best a low-level recruiter for the Communists; but in the midst of the McCarthy era, anything seemed possible, and despite pleas for clemency from numerous public figures, the Rosenbergs, still proclaiming their innocence, were both executed in 1953.

Women and Office Work

Meanwhile, in businesses all over America, more workers were needed, and although no call went out for Rosie the Riveter, it was, in fact, an increasing number of women who were going back to work, as the cost of living escalated, and the items every middle-class American was supposed to own became increasingly out of reach on just one salary. Business magazines noted that more women, including married women, were now returning to work, albeit on a part-time basis. Of course, thanks to reruns of 1950s situation comedies, the era would later be recalled as a time when Mom was always at home, but statistics do not bear that out. Historians like David Halberstam have refuted the mythology of 1950s TV programs that show Mom totally devoted to her domestic chores. Halberstam also points out that TV's image of life was a very sanitized and idealized world where ". . . there were no economic crises, no class divisions or resentments, no ethnic tensions . . . no intrusions from other cultures.

[T]he family sitcoms reflected—and reinforced—much of the social conformity of the period."[17] Yet, unlike during World War II, when women were told they were capable of doing any job, now what they were offered was mainly low-paying clerical work (there are magazine ads showing little girls being given typewriters and referred to as "future secretaries"). "Men were taken seriously," wrote David Halberstam. "Women, by contrast, were doomed to serve as support troops. Often, they worked harder and longer for less pay with lesser titles . . . Because young women were well aware of this situation, there was little incentive to commit an entire life to fighting it and becoming what was then perceived of as a hard and brittle career woman."[18] In the TV sitcoms, the woman who wanted to work was usually told no by her husband, and the plot often involved the woman showing her incompetence when she left the safety of the home. How these women who only a few years earlier had built fighter planes and done radio engineering had become so stupid in such a short time was never addressed.

While the political climate of the early 1950s was fixated on communism, in homes all across the country, people were still preoccupied with their children and the right way to raise them. The U.S. Government Printing Office sold over 7 million copies of its pamphlet "Infant Care," and "Pre-Natal Care" sold over 4 million copies.[19] Dr. Benjamin Spock's book about baby and child care, first published in 1946, was highly regarded, too; it had sold over a million copies by 1951.[20] And for every article about why women should be stay-at-home moms (even though in real life, many were not), there were just as many articles about the proper way to bring up baby. The general consensus about this subject was that a mother's life should center around giving her children unconditional love and permission to learn. Said Dr. Spock, "Children raised in loving families *want* to learn, *want* to conform, *want* to grow up."[21] Other experts concurred. They felt that a woman instinctively knew how to raise children, and in a comment that today is rather offensive, one late-1940s expert had suggested that women hire black female servants because "[it] is well known that among the colored race there are many women who are supremely endowed with almost unique emotional equipment which makes their services ideal for infants and young children."[22]

Another thread in the critical discourse of the late 1940s and early 1950s was that education for women should serve only the purpose of making a woman a better mother, and that since motherhood was basically instinctive, women did not really need to go to college (unless it was to find a husband, of course). Thus, women who persisted in wanting a career, even women who wanted to study, were potentially damaging their children by not being there to provide undivided attention and approval. Looking back on the 1950s and the advice offered to women by books and magazines, feminist author Betty Friedan recalled, "It was suddenly discovered that the mother could be blamed for almost everything. In every case history of the troubled child; alcoholic, suicidal, schizophrenic, psychopathic, neurotic adult; impotent homosexual male; frigid promiscuous female . . . could be found a mother . . . A rejecting, overprotecting, dominating mother."[23] And women were also warned to make sure boys saw proper models of manhood or it would affect them when they grew up. A boy who saw a man doing cooking could be damaged for life, said the experts.[24] Now, it must be said here that very quietly, in homes all across America, there were undoubtedly men who helped their wives with housework on some limited basis, and, as far as I can tell, the republic did not fall as a result. (My father was the king of the male traditionalists, and he said all the right things about men's work versus women's work, yet every night he helped my mother with the dishes—not because he was henpecked but because he had memories of his father treating his mother like a servant, and he did not want to treat my mother that way.) Still, the official belief that boys needed to see men acting "manly" was a frequent topic of articles and discussions. Vance Packard's complaint about radio soap operas was carried on in the 1950s by other male critics, who now accused TV shows of making fun of men and diminishing their masculinity. One critic lamented that the father on TV had become ". . . emasculated . . . and domesticated . . . tenderly stupid, and utterly inadequate in every department of his life except his profession."[25]

TV as the Housewife's Escape

For a generation that married young, had babies almost immediately, and moved to the suburbs (assuming the suburbs allowed them to be there—Levittown was restricted to whites only), the new medium of television was a godsend. It took the housewife's mind off her work, it provided the kids with something to do while Mom was busy, and it gave Dad a chance to relax when he got home from work. In the late 1940s and early 1950s, women who had been on radio were a visible presence on TV. Gracie Allen of Burns and Allen was able to adapt to the new medium, after some initial reluctance. The TV version still featured Gracie as a lovable scatterbrain, but critic Michael McCall has noted that the ending to Burns and Allen's TV show each week was extremely clever. Reminiscent of vaudeville, it featured a back-and-forth routine with George as the "straight man" for Gracie's cleverly mixed up wordplay and comic timing.[26]

In addition to the already well known Lucille Ball and Gertrude Berg, there were several other popular female comedy stars on early 1950s TV—one appeared on the variety program *Your Show of Shows* with Sid Caesar; Imogene Coca starred with Caesar in a number of skits. Miss Coca, who had been born into a show business family and had been performing since she was a teenager, was an excellent dancer, actress, and mime, and she seemed totally at home with live TV (it was hard for people watching her animated comic routines to believe that in real life, she was actually very shy). Eve Arden, who had first performed in her own CBS radio series in the late 1940s, took the character of Connie Brooks, a high school English teacher, and brought her to TV in the situation comedy *Our Miss Brooks.* Like Gertrude Berg, Eve Arden used both radio and TV for her show, which revolved around her students (they liked her) and her irascible principal Mr. Conklin (he did not like anyone). Eve Arden's style was one of wisecracks and sarcastic wit, and *Our Miss Brooks* was one of a few 1950s comedies where the woman was not portrayed as an airhead or a fool; it did well on TV from 1952 until 1956. And then, there was the Jackie Gleason Show, which would not have been such a success were it not for the comic skill of its costar Audrey Meadows. Feminist critics have found some of the dialogue in *The Honeymooners* disturbing—although we are to assume Ralph was only joking, he does threaten to hit Alice; she of course is able to use humor and sarcasm to calm him down, and at the end he usually concludes that "Baby, you're the greatest."

In the 1950s, a woman was expected to deal with her husband's moods and cheer him up; conversely, a husband was supposed to deal with his wife's stupidity or her refusal to do things his way and rescue her from the trouble she got herself into.

As mentioned earlier, the sitcom plots were predictable, but excellent comediennes like Lucille Ball and Gracie Allen could bring new life to old stereotypes. Audrey Meadows and Eve Arden portrayed the female role with a more sarcastic edge than Ball and Allen did, but, in general, the women seen on early TV were unable to break new ground in their portrayal of female roles. As much as Meadows's character Alice Kramden held her own against Ralph's bluster, she still put up with it and was still defined mainly as a housewife, whose future was tied to getting along with her husband. One other popular show in early TV stressed a woman in her maternal role: the comedy/drama *Mama* featured Peggy Wood as a warm and loving mother of a Norwegian-American family; it has been a hit movie under the name *I Remember Mama,* and the TV show was loved just as much. First telecast in 1949, the show lasted until 1956, and many critics observed that Peggy Wood, a talented stage actress, really brought the part to life. Sadly, few if any episodes of this hit show (it was in the top ten in the ratings) were ever filmed, and as critics Tim Brooks and Earle Marsh have pointed out, ". . . while [I Love] Lucy will be with us forever, the weekly dramas of life [with Mama] in the big white house on Steiner Street are, for the most part, gone forever . . ."[27]

Women in Educational TV

As I said earlier, many of the roles for women on TV mirrored their roles on radio. Women in early 1950s TV were often involved with children's shows, for example. Miss Frances (Dr. Frances Horwich, an experienced educator from Chicago) helped to create one of early TV's best-known children's programs, *Ding Dong School*. Her concept of using TV for early childhood education impressed NBC's Central Division Director of Public Affairs, Judith Waller, who, during her long career, had always been interested in developing new radio shows to educate kids (even in the college textbook she wrote, *Radio: The Fifth Estate,* she discussed the importance of radio's educational role). Now that many of the little baby boomers were old enough to appreciate TV, Miss Waller sought programs that would teach them something useful. *Ding-Dong School* first aired locally in Chicago and then was picked up by NBC-TV in November of 1952. In its first two years on the air, it won over thirty awards.[28] Another Chicago-based children's show featured two puppets and a talented woman who interacted and did skits with them. *Kukla, Fran and Ollie* starred Fran Allison, a successful radio actress and a former schoolteacher. Fran did the show spontaneously with the show's creator, Burr Tillstrom (it was he who came up with the puppets, as well as many of the other characters on the show). *Kukla, Fran and Ollie* won an Emmy for Best Children's Program in 1954. Women in numerous cities did their own local children's shows as well. One successful example was in Seattle, where Ruth Prins played a story-telling clown named Wunda Wunda. The show received praise from local educators and also won the Peabody Award during its long run on KING-TV.[29]

As radio had made use of a Story Lady, TV too seemed to believe that educational programming was a woman's domain, especially if it involved shows for children; after all, weren't most elementary school teachers women? (Interestingly, there were now more men teaching high school, and men had always predominated as college professors.) Long-time educator Dorothy Gordon had been moderating a radio show called the *New York Times Youth Forum* since the 1940s. On this show, students were the panelists, and they discussed the issues of the day with a weekly guest; Miss Gordon had never avoided subjects that were controversial and allowed her young participants to grapple with issues that ranged from politics to parental rules. In 1951, *McCall's* magazine gave her an award for public service, one of many awards she won during her long career in broadcasting. When she brought the *Youth Forum* to television that year, the critics were quick to praise it as one of the few really intelligent programs for young adults; the show lasted well into the 1960s. There were also some new TV shows for little kids, in addition to the previously mentioned *Ding Dong School*. A show called *Romper Room* made its debut on WBAL-TV in Baltimore in 1953, with Miss Nancy as the teacher/hostess. Preschoolers were invited into the studio to learn and play, along with the kids who were watching at home. Rather than putting the show on a network (CBS wanted it), Nancy Claster and her husband Bert decided that syndication was a better way to keep the local, personal feel of the show. Nancy trained each new teacher (in Boston, we had "Miss Jean") in each city that broadcast the show.

If women were not comics and if they were not telling children stories, some were dancers. Variety shows often had segments where a band played and in-studio dancers demonstrated the steps to the latest dances or did actual routines. *TV Guide* explained how a "girl" (all females of any age were referred to as girls back then; older females were sometimes called "gals") might be considered for one of these opportunities. A female dancer, the article advised, should have "fairly small thighs, straight legs, [weigh] 106 to 125 pounds, [be] of medium height, with well-rounded but not over-developed curves." The average age of a TV dancer was twenty-three, and she was usually unmarried. She went to dancing school and had already been a professional dancer in a club or perhaps in the chorus line of a Broadway show. In other words, if you were not pretty, young, lithe, and experienced, TV was not going to call you.[30] One rather ironic article explained what Ken Murray, the host of his own variety show, was seeking in female dancers: he described in detail how he insisted on youth and beauty and charm for his "glamour-lovelies." Next to the article was his photo, showing him to be an aging, not especially handsome gentleman, smoking a big cigar. The double standard had found a home on TV.

As for the women who did not run a children's show, could not dance, or were not comediennes, they still might get a role in a soap opera, for soap operas were also making the move from radio to television. Irna Phillips, the queen of the radio soaps, brought *The Guiding Light* to TV in 1952; by 1956, she had created another successful TV soap, *As the World Turns*. Roy Winsor, a successful radio director whose credits included *Ma Perkins*, created two soaps for TV in 1951: *Search for Tomorrow* and *Love of Life*. All of these shows were of the same style as had made the radio versions so popular: melodramatic plots about problems in marriage, problems with children, problems in the family. Here again, if a housewife needed any reinforcement to the idea that women were only concerned with romance and relationships, the soaps (or "daytime serials") provided it.

There did seem to be a few locally produced shows that tried to be somewhat different, but they either did not find a sponsor or were not picked up by a network. In the East, a syndicated drama about a woman lawyer ran daily throughout much of 1951. Making it more interesting, Susan Peters, the actress who portrayed "Miss Susan," was disabled and played the role from a wheel chair. A disabled character in a nontraditional occupation was certainly unique for 1950s television; had Peters not died tragically in 1952, I wonder if her show would have gained a wider audience.

Women Sell the Products

The one other place where women were frequently seen on early TV was on women's shows, because while Mary Margaret McBride was in no hurry to do TV, lots of other women's shows jumped right in. Local stations had slots they needed to fill in the daytime, and many of the women's show hostesses had become big enough names on radio that the move to TV was a logical one. In Boston, Louise Morgan had done very well on radio in the 1940s, and when she put her show on TV, under the name *Shopping Vues*, her audience responded very enthusiastically. Morgan was not one to confine herself to recipes and fashion, although these were two important elements of her show. But like other women's show moderators, she had gained considerable experience interviewing celebrities who happened to be in town for a performance. Housewives, many of whom had small children and could not get to the theater, were undoubtedly grateful for being able to see the people they had previously only heard or read about.

In a number of cities, the women's shows were on both radio and TV in the early 1950s. They never got big ratings, but they were successful because they brought in lots of money in advertising dollars. Ironically, as *TV Guide* pointed out in 1954, TV had opened up a new role for women, or perhaps more accurately, created a more obvious extension of their role on the women's shows. Women had become "hucksters"—pitchwomen whose job was to sell products. If the original women's shows had been conceived to be educational and cultural, that vision had long since been replaced by the ability of the hostesses to persuade the female listener or viewer to purchase what the sponsors had to offer. The women's shows had become expert at working in plugs for all sorts of items, and the sincerity of the women themselves really struck a chord with the audience. A male general manager remarked in the *TV Guide* article that his two biggest shows for bringing in advertising dollars were the farm show and the women's show. More than 97 percent of the women's shows on TV had sponsors.[31]

Mary Margaret McBride had become the undisputed queen of radio selling; on TV, the best-known pitchwoman was probably Betty Furness, who became known for her commercials on behalf of Westinghouse refrigerators. Looking back on those days of all-live TV, Betty recalled:

Commercials, which now run from 10 to 30 seconds generally, were a minute and a half to three minutes . . . The teleprompter had not been invented and I wasn't comfortable using cue cards; I wanted to look into the eye of the camera, therefore the eye of the viewer. So I memorized one three minute and two minute and a half commercials each week. Once I opened my mouth, there was no way out. I *had* to know them and say them correctly and promptly.[32]

Women viewers were fascinated by Miss Furness. They did not find her excessively sexy, nor excessively matronly. Rather, she seemed to be credible, warm, and professional in her work. In 1952, she was voted one of the ten best-dressed women on TV, and viewers said they regarded her as very stylish.[33] Although she had had a successful career as an actress prior to TV, her commercials for Westinghouse caused sales of kitchen appliances to soar. CBS-TV even gave her a show of her own to discuss fashion, the home, and show business. A personal life that included having been married three times (again that disconnect—in 1950s society, divorce was still perceived negatively, especially for women, yet Betty Furness was someone the viewers admired) had not prevented Furness from becoming one of the most recognizable and popular women on TV.[34] *TV Guide* remarked that advertising men were scouring the country for women who could do for their products what Betty Furness had done for Westinghouse. The ideal pitchwoman should be ". . . charming [and] glib, with [a] broad smile . . . [she should] look and sound like a housewife, but need not be; must believe in [the] product; [an] actress [is] preferred."[35]

Where in radio's early days, sponsors believed women could not do commercials—a view gradually modified to permit them to do some of the commercials on the women's shows—now, the belief was that anywhere there were women viewers, a female doing the selling would be perceived as more honest and more persuasive. Said one woman who was making a good living doing these commercials on TV, "We dress . . . not in aprons or flimsy little prints like most homemakers, but rather in the clothes a housewife would wear if she only had time." But she also admitted she hoped she would not be doing commercials forever; she wanted to use this as a stepping-stone to serious dramatic roles. Betty Furness had the same comment and was ultimately able to do some serious acting again, but chances are most viewers from the 1950s still saw her as the woman in that beautiful Westinghouse kitchen.

One other well-known woman on early TV was Faye Emerson, who had also been in movies and theater prior to television. She had been on TV as early as 1948, narrating a fashion show for NBC, but she also worked on

CBS throughout 1949 and was a panelist on the previously mentioned radio show *Leave It to the Girls,* which in its TV version had been turned into a comedy battle of the sexes. NBC gave her a show in 1950, a fifteen-minute interview program called *Fifteen with Faye.* The show's name was soon changed to the *Faye Emerson Show,* and like other women's shows of the time, it featured chat about theater, the arts, music, fashions, and whatever else Miss Emerson wanted to discuss. But there was controversy about her TV image because Faye Emerson frequently wore dresses with very low-cut necklines; this was considered scandalous in early 1950s television and generated a lot of discussion. It did not hurt her career, however: in January of 1950, she was named the most pleasing female personality in *Look* magazine's TV awards, and she continued to have her own show for several more years. Throughout the 1950s, she appeared on a number of women's shows, quiz shows, and even an occasional interview program.

One other role for women on early 1950s TV evoked as much controversy as Faye Emerson's clothing. Wrestling, which had always been popular, and had been broadcast on radio even in the 1920s, was now on television. But when the lady wrestlers were on, various church and civic groups protested vehemently. Writing in *New England TV Guide,* wrestling authority Bill Johnston remarked that although the public liked the matches, as did the promoters (who felt the ladies always brought in a large crowd), there was continual pressure to ban them from TV, on the grounds that women's wrestling was obscene and immoral. And one of the male wrestlers was quoted as saying that female wrestlers were an intrusion that degraded the sport of wrestling.[36]

As far as how women felt about TV in the early 1950s, besides the ubiquitous game shows and women's shows, they seemed immediately attracted to shows that involved human interest. Edward R. Murrow did a show that was comprised of interviews with interesting people, some celebrities but some not. He took the viewer into the guest's life and helped the audience get to know the guest better. *Person to Person* did very well in the ratings, but women especially liked to watch it. They also liked Ralph Edwards's biographical show, *This Is Your Life,* which not only told the famous person's life story, but often reunited him or her with people not seen in years.

What women did not like was TV violence, even back in the supposedly tamer 1950s. A 1955 survey done in Philadelphia by the Home and School Council took Jackie Gleason's show to task for excessive battling with his TV wife Audrey Meadows. The group also felt that TV westerns had begun to resort to gratuitous scenes of shooting just to spice up the plot. And in a comment that was surprisingly modern, the women criticized programs that made insulting remarks about stepmothers, since "many children have step-mothers these days," and painting them as villains was considered in "bad taste."[37]

The women who had remained on radio were by no means forgotten, although TV had certainly diminished the size of radio's audience. But still, radio and TV editor Elizabeth Sullivan of the *Boston Globe* reminded her readers at the end of 1953 that reports of radio's death were quite premature. "There are 45,000,000 radio families, with 75,000,000 radio sets. There are 2500 AM stations on the air and 550 FM. Listeners bought 13,500,000 new [radio] sets in 1953 for their homes, their cars, and for gifts."[38] Yet, the majority of the news about broadcasting was only about TV. *Variety* magazine commented that even so-called radio editors at the newspapers were ignoring radio entirely; *Variety*, which many years ago had been totally opposed to radio, now said that radio did not deserve such a brush-off, given its years of providing entertainment and service.[39]

But as early as 1950, even the fan magazines that still had *radio* in their title had decided that TV was what people wanted to read about. And yet, some radio programs, especially the soap operas and the women's shows, still had a following; also, individual performers remained popular whether they were on radio or on TV. Comedienne Minnie Pearl (real name Sarah Ophelia Colley) was a featured performer on country music's long-running *Grand Old Opry* every Saturday night on NBC radio; she also began doing her comedy routines for TV as a guest on the late-night Jack Paar show in the mid-1950s. But as radio became more of a music-oriented medium, it was a few network dramas, such as *One Man's Family,* and the local radio homemakers who continued to hold on to their audience, while the overall ratings showed that more adults had indeed migrated to television.

That women remained devoted to the radio homemakers should not have surprised anyone, since theirs was the perfect programming for an era when being a housewife was glorified. Some of the women's show directors even expanded the programming, hiring new (and often younger) hostesses who could relate to the 1950s housewife because they themselves were of that demographic. In the smaller markets, where TV was still fairly new, the daily women's radio shows provided exactly what they had in the 1930s—companionship. At KMA in Shenandoah, Iowa, most of the women's shows still originated from the hostesses' homes, since they usually had families to take care of, and that was a large part of what they talked about. So popular were these shows with the farmers' wives, that KMA in the early 1950s still had as many as six radio homemakers. But this was the exception. Most stations had one well-known female personality, and as time passed, more of these women moved over to TV. The women's shows probably became more interesting now that they could include visuals—it was especially beneficial for cooking and fashion programs, and guests who had traveled could now show slides and pictures of their trip, instead of just describing what they had seen.

Edythe Fern Melrose, better known as the "Lady of Charm," had done a successful women's show in Detroit on WXYZ radio for a number of years. She moved the show to WXYZ-TV, where it remained on the air throughout the 1950s. Like many women's show hosts, Miss Melrose would not recommend a product or a recipe until she had personally tested it; this was probably one reason why women's show hostesses had such credibility with their audience.

AWRT Is Founded

Meanwhile, in an effort to get more respect for women's show directors, some women who had been instrumental in starting the Association of Women Directors (later the Association of Women Broadcasters) created a new organization, American Women in Radio and Television, in April of 1951. Edythe Meserand, who had worked in news and special features at WOR Radio (and later at WOR-TV) in New York, was the group's first president. Also among AWRT's founders was Ruth Crane Schaefer, who had been a radio homemaker for a number of years at WJR in Detroit (as "Mrs. Page"), before moving to Washington, D.C., to become women's director at WMAL radio in the mid-1940s. Ruth Crane would also do some women's programming on TV in the 1950s. And Edythe Fern Melrose was very active in the new AWRT; by the mid-1950s, she was serving as its president. The women in AWRT used their annual convention to network with each other, as well as to bring in interesting and well-known guest speakers who could advise them on doing women's shows more effectively. They acknowledged that selling was a big part of what they did, and some of the guest speakers at their meetings were from ad agencies or major sponsors. But what they mainly wanted was for their industry to take what they did seriously. For example, when *Broadcasting* magazine published its fifty-year anniversary tribute, neither the founding of the Association of Women Directors nor the founding of AWRT was even mentioned. This might be forgiven as just an oversight, since a lot can be forgotten in fifty years, but when the magazine published its twenty-fifth anniversary issue in 1956, the AWRT had been founded only five years earlier, and it still was not mentioned. This is somewhat ironic because in the introduction to that issue, the editor of the magazine, Sol Taishoff, praised his wife, Betty, and said that it was she who came up with the idea for *Broadcasting*. The introduction also said Betty Taishoff was the treasurer of the company, although she had seldom been mentioned prior to this.

But if Mrs. Betty Taishoff had any influence on the magazine's coverage of women, it was minimal at best. Nearly all of the writers at the magazine (now called *Broadcasting• Telecasting*) were male; women's organizations and their accomplishments, as well as the achievements of pioneering women in broadcast history, were not considered important enough to commemorate in the magazine's otherwise extensive timeline of radio. Given the social scene in Washington, the Taishoffs would certainly have met and spent time with members of the AWRT, several of whom were active in Washington, D.C., media. Thus, the omission of the group's history is even more puzzling.

In 1952, when new ownership took over WOR in New York, Edythe Meserand was fired, despite an impressive career with numerous awards. She went on to found her own advertising agency and continued to work with AWRT. Throughout the 1950s, the organization continued to grow. And while it was never as big or as influential as the National Association of Broadcasters, it advocated for women in the industry at a time when nobody else was doing so. By 1956, AWRT had over 1,400 members. In a survey, president Edythe Fern Melrose found that the vast majority (over 600) were women's show directors, while 126 were station publicity directors. Only 12 were station managers, and only 4 were disc jockeys. (The rest did a variety of clerical and business office work, and a few produced programs, sold advertising, or worked for an ad agency.)

Creating the TV Secretary

Meanwhile, the media were doing some selling of their own. If the 1940s was the era of creating Rosie the Riveter, then the 1950s was about creating Susie the Secretary. In ads, on TV shows, and in magazines, the secretary's job was held up as the perfect job for a woman. It enabled her to meet interesting people—preferably a handsome and single boss—and do the support tasks at which women were supposed to naturally excel. Unlike factory work, which was dirty and potentially dangerous, secretarial work allowed a woman to dress nicely, have her own office space, and be treated as part of a professional team, or so the story went. Where in the 1920s, newspapers were seeking women doing unusual and exciting jobs, in the 1950s, there were many articles about women who worked for famous men. As newspapers and business magazines lamented the lack of good secretaries and told how there were so many openings in offices, guidance counselors led bright young women to believe that they would be better off doing secretarial work rather than pursuing an independent business career. The myth of the unhappy and bitter career woman was strongly entrenched, reinforced by countless magazine articles. Even entertainment magazines like

TV Guide were quick to point out, when interviewing a successful woman on TV, that she did not see herself as a career woman, and that her first priority was her husband and kids.[40]

Where men's success in show business was explained by hard work and persistence, women in the *TV Guide* interviews were said to have become successful by some fortuitous accident. As Carolyn Heilbrun has pointed out, "ambition" in our culture has had a negative connotation when referring to women. In private letters to friends, a famous woman might admit her excitement over having planned or carried out some successful venture, yet in public, she would say it was just luck. Women who were perceived as "too ambitious" were in danger of alienating the public, since ambition was synonymous with being unfeminine.[41]

So, if a woman was not the ideal housewife, she could train for that role by being the ideal secretary, and a number of TV shows of the 1950s promoted that message. In a culture that had encouraged women to marry young and start a family (in the early 1950s, the average age for a woman to marry was twenty; by the late 1950s, it had dropped to nineteen), now there was also encouragement about the right job to have in the event that a girl had not yet found her Prince Charming. The assumption still remained that women did not want to work after marriage (and those who did, as in the TV sitcoms, were simply told no by their husbands, who, of course, knew best), so a selling point in media recruitment for secretaries was the chance to meet lots of eligible men, who would presumably be impressed by an attractive and well-dressed young woman who could type and answer phones. In this, too, consumerism definitely played a part, since the secretary was, of course, supposed to look good, wear the right makeup, and project the right image if she wanted to make a good impression; advertisers jumped at the chance to introduce the female office worker to products that would help her be more attractive to her future husband.

Thus, when women's magazine ads of the 1950s did portray a woman working, she was usually in an office, and the ads encouraged her in how to maintain the right look. Once again, her intelligence and her ability were not nearly so important as whether the men in the office would approve of her appearance. Even the magazines aimed directly at the professional secretary encouraged the belief that professional success was linked to the use of beauty items. On TV sitcoms like *Meet Millie,* which had first begun as a radio comedy in 1951, the plot centered around Millie, who worked as a secretary, and whether her mother would be able to fix her up with the right potential husband.

While young secretaries were mainly biding their time while looking for Mister Right, TV also presented older secretaries, like Ann Sothern's character in *Private Secretary* or actress Barbara Hale's character Della Street, who assisted Perry Mason. On TV, "older" seemed to mean over thirty-five, and whether these women were widows or had grown children, or perhaps never married, was not as essential to the plot as their exciting jobs. Still, as nicely dressed as they were, and as impressive as their offices may have been (although early- to mid-1950s TV was still in black and white, much attention was paid to describing the ideal office and how it should be decorated), secretarial work was still a subordinate position. The emphasis was on assisting the boss, who was always male. Such assistance meant serving coffee, doing his shopping, and making sure his schedule was easy for him to follow. TV secretaries were always being thrust into the middle of exciting events, and their bosses frequently valued their opinions. But while it is doubtful that most real-life secretaries had beautiful and spacious offices or made enough money to buy designer clothes or had a charming boss who appreciated everything they did for him, the image of the TV secretary was a woman who was successful and happy and loved her work. As with the family sitcoms that showed the ideal marriage, the message of the TV secretarial sitcoms was that if good fortune smiles upon a girl, she too can have the ideal job until she gets married. (That the better secretarial jobs were usually reserved for attractive, white, middle-class women was somehow never discussed. Television was not doing many groundbreaking things on social issues yet, and when black women did appear on TV, they were more likely to be singing on a TV variety show or playing the role of a maid like *Beulah*.[42])

Since the early days of radio, doing office work was one entry-level way for women to break into the industry; in the 1950s, however, there was less mobility, and office work became an end unto itself, rather than a stepping-stone to a higher position in the company. As radio dramas were no longer produced (the resources were going mainly to TV, and by decade's end, few radio dramas would remain), the need for radio scriptwriters or producers or sound effects experts no longer existed. Women were excluded from the newsroom, except to type copy for the newsmen, and other than the women's shows, few radio stations offered many jobs to women, aside from front-desk receptionists or secretaries to the station's managers. (The typical picture of a major-market radio station's staff in the 1950s was much like the one of the WCCO Minneapolis newsroom in 1957: out of twenty-two people, only two were women—the news department librarian and the news department secretary.)

As for women who made news, they tended to be wives of politicians or movie and TV stars. Jacqueline Cochrane, whom you may recall as one of the women aviators and founder of the WASPs during World War II, became the first woman to break the sound barrier in 1953; she continued to compile other aviation firsts and even wrote a book, but women aviators were not a big story anymore. Oveta Culp Hobby, whom you may recall from her World War II work with the WACs, was named the first woman Secretary of Health, Education, and Welfare in 1953 by newly elected President Eisenhower. But it is interesting to look back on the important achievements of several women scientists of the early 1950s and contrast the minimal coverage they received with the fascination the media exhibited about Mamie Eisenhower's hairstyle or Faye Emerson's neckline. In 1950, for example, geneticist Barbara McClintock demonstrated that genes could pass from cell to cell, something that was not believed at the time. Her work was generally dismissed and barely reported; it was not until the early 1970s, when other researchers found that McClintock's theory explained such things as how bacteria developed a resistance to antibiotics, that scientists revisited her theories, but she was never accorded the attention her discovery had deserved.[43] In 1951 and 1952, Grace Murray Hopper (who is credited with coming up with the term *bug* for a computer programming error—and yes, it really was a bug: a moth flew into the machine and stopped it from working) was doing groundbreaking work with computers, inventing a compiler that would enable computers to carry out basic functions. While today she is recognized by many as the Mother of Computing (since her research led to the development of the first computer languages), she received no awards and little recognition during the 1950s. It would not be until the late 1960s that she finally began to receive public acclaim for her years of hard work. In 1969, she was named "Man of the Year" (really) by the Data Processing Management Association.[44]

Women scientists just were not perceived as sexy, plus very few people understood the importance of their work. They tended not to be guests on chat shows, which preferred celebrities or women athletes or authors of best-sellers. And if a young woman showed an interest in science in school, she was quickly channeled into teaching, since guidance counselors believed this was a much more appropriate career for someone who was only going to work until she got married (and she could always go back to it when her kids were older). Given such attitudes, it is amazing that there were any women in science at all, especially since the few that overcame the cultural prejudices tended to be offered the lower-paying jobs doing research rather than the higher-paying jobs as professors or heads of college departments.

The educational system, like many other aspects of 1950s society, seemed geared to tracking boys into their future role as breadwinners and girls into their future role as homemakers. Even the textbooks presented this message, as early as first grade. The most commonly used reading book, *Fun with Dick and Jane,* depicted a peaceful suburban world where everyone knew his or her place, and everyone was white and middle class. In this ideal world, Dick was an active, adventuresome boy, who was also polite, well behaved, and reliable. Jane was a pretty little girl who always wore a dress, and she loved to help her mother clean the house. Mother, of course, was a housewife who enjoyed household chores and never had a hair out of place. Father wore a suit and came home each night from his important job. He drove the family car and fixed things when they broke. As David Halberstam wrote, "Not only were women [of the 1950s] now reared in homes where their mothers had no careers, but male siblings were from the start put on a very different track: The boys . . . [learned] the skills critical to supporting a family, while daughters were to be educated to get married."[45] And even schoolbooks reinforced this gender stereotyping.

Women's Limited Roles on TV

The few glamorous jobs that existed for working women in the 1950s were still in the entertainment industry, but these jobs were already limited by the expectations of what women should be doing. For example, few women on TV hosted their own show unless it was a homemaking or women's program; now and then a famous singer, like Dinah Shore, would have her own variety program, but the vast majority of the TV shows had a male host, especially the midday human-interest shows like *Queen for a Day,* hosted by Jack Bailey on both TV and radio. On this show, real women with tragic lives appeared as the guests, each one telling her story with the hope that she would be voted Queen and given prizes that would help her rise above her tragedy. The women contestants vied with each other in telling of the struggles and burdens they bore, and how they hoped that winning on this show could solve their most immediate problem. For example, one woman asked for a photography studio so she could bring in extra income in helping to care for her disabled husband. Another, who had a large family and lived in poverty, asked for the vacation she had never had and new school clothes for all of her kids. At the end of the program, Jack Bailey crowned the winner (the woman voted by the studio audience to be most deserving of sympathy and most in need of help), and he would then give her the prize she had asked for and usually more on top of that. It was certainly a "feel good" show, although it reinforced the stereotype of women as helpless victims awaiting a male rescuer.

A look at prime-time TV revealed that the game show hosts and quiz show hosts were all male. As for the news shows, with one or two exceptions (such as Pauline Frederick, now working for NBC), all of the reporters and commentators on the networks were male. Women were assistants to the host on many shows—they wore beautiful gowns, directed the guests to their chairs, and stood around looking ornamental as they waited for the host to beckon. Some women performers also served as panelists on the game shows—Dorothy Kilgallen was on *What's My Line,* as was Arlene Francis (Francis was so popular that *Newsweek* put her on the cover on July 19, 1954); comedienne and actress Peggy Cass was a panelist on *To Tell the Truth*—but the moderator was always a man. In the mid-1950s, TV stations began hiring pretty young women to read the weather, evidently assuming that sex appeal would make the forecast more interesting to watch in those days before computerized graphics. (In 1953, the National Weather Service began naming hurricanes after women; whether they intended to be misogynistic or whether they just thought they were being clever, this action continued to spread the cultural myth that women were like storms—dangerous and unpredictable.)

A large amount of publicity went into promoting a new NBC-TV "magazine" show for women in early 1954, but closer examination of it showed that *Home* was a more visual version, sometimes even broadcast in color, of what the radio homemakers had been doing. *Home,* starring actress Arlene Francis as the hostess (or in keeping with the magazine metaphor, the "editor in chief"), was advertised as "an electronic magazine for women" with segments on "everything that interests women." These segments were "food, fashion, beauty, child care, family affairs, leisure activities, decorating [and] gardening."[46] Evidently, the man who created the show, Sylvester "Pat" Weaver, assumed women did not like to read and were not interested in current events. Some of the experts on *Home* were published authors such as Dr. Ashley Montague and Dr. Rose Franzblau, and they probably provided good information about family life to the women viewers. Hugh Downs, who years later would co-anchor (with Barbara Walters) the successful ABC magazine show *20/20,* was the show's announcer. Ruth Lyons, the previously mentioned radio homemaker from WLW in Cincinnati, who was now doing her show on TV, had attempted to syndicate it in 1951–52, but the resources of a major network like NBC were more likely to assure big-name guests and more lavish production than even the best local show could do. As for *Home,* despite all the money, the promotion, and the experts, the show only lasted until 1957.

Thinking About Sex

Although the 1950s are often recalled as a decade of sexual repression, there was considerable evidence that sex was on the minds of many people. Dr. Alfred Kinsey, a professor from Indiana University, who had been widely criticized for his study of male sexuality in 1948, released a study of female sexuality in 1953, causing a firestorm of condemnation when his study revealed that 50 percent of women were not virgins when they married. That it also reinforced the belief that women have less sex drive than men and engage in less "forbidden" sex than men was barely noticed by the report's critics, who refused to believe that American women would engage in sex before marriage. In a case of shooting the messenger, Dr. Kinsey was blamed for the report's results, accused by such famous clergymen as the Reverend Billy Graham of contributing to America's deteriorating moral standards.[47] The controversy about the study cost Dr. Kinsey his job, and the stress may also have contributed to his dying only three years later.

America evidently was not ready to honestly acknowledge premarital sex or admit that not just men had sexual needs. But Hugh Hefner believed the time was right for a more open attitude about sex, and in late 1953, he began to publish *Playboy*. In its first issue was a nude pinup photo of Marilyn Monroe. Men loved the magazine; censors hated it and tried repeatedly to have it declared obscene. Meanwhile, women on TV were supposed to look sexy, even if the subject of female sexuality was still taboo. And yet, even in the 1950s, scandal fascinated the media, especially if sex was somehow involved: people were still talking about George Jorgensen, who had gone to Denmark and come back a woman. The scandalous topic of Christine Jorgensen and her sex-change operation was one the talk and interview shows were happy to pursue for months. And as for sex and scandal, nothing could top Grace Metalious and her 1956 novel of small town hypocrisy, *Peyton Place*. Although it became a best-seller (few people wanted to admit they had read such a book, but evidently, lots of people did read it because it would ultimately sell over 10 million copies over the next decade), it, too, was the object of efforts to ban it, and some libraries did refuse to carry it.

Meanwhile, as the 1950s progressed, more and more radio dramas were leaving for TV, as were some well-known features. Even Edward R. Murrow's former radio show *Hear It Now* had become *See It Now* and was instrumental in the downfall of Senator McCarthy. In 1954, there was the first nationally televised Miss America pageant, which was won by a nineteen-year-old Californian named Lee Ann Meriwether, and even the Pope appeared on TV. NBC and CBS were transmitting a few broadcasts in color, which still had technological problems, but not many viewers noticed since only 1 percent of U.S. homes owned a color set. And to make it even easier to watch more TV, 1954 was the first year for frozen TV dinners.

Rock and Roll Saves Radio

It seemed radio was not on the minds of many people at all, despite various surveys showing that daytime listening remained strong. At the end of 1954,

TV's profits had exceeded radio's.[48] But radio was about to find itself a new niche, and the solution to radio's problems came from a rather unlikely place—the music industry. In 1954, for the first time, a new style of pop music that the young people liked was making its presence felt. Originally descending from so-called race music, or rhythm and blues, it came to be known in the early 1950s as rock and roll (or rock 'n' roll). A Cleveland disc jockey, Alan Freed, was said to have coined the term, but more likely, he popularized some terminology already in use: the phrase had been heard in blues lyrics as a euphemism for sex, and although not all rock was sexual (parents would think it was, but that is another matter), it had an energy that appealed to young people. Whoever used the term first isn't really important—what matters most is that Alan Freed turned it into a musical trend. A white disc jockey who played black music at a time when America was still segregated, Freed was considered controversial, as were some of the other white disc jockeys who had begun to play this music. Young audiences were rejecting what they felt was the bland, middle-of-the-road music the Tin Pan Alley songwriters were turning out. These kids did not want big band music. They wanted something with a beat. The previously popular 78 rpm record was declining in sales, and the smaller, easier to carry 45 rpm was gaining the support of young consumers.

In 1954, Bill Haley and the Comets recorded a cover version of "Shake, Rattle, and Roll," a song originally done by the black artist Joe Turner. The song became a pop hit. (Record companies had begun the practice of putting out white versions of hits by black artists, on the theory that white kids would only buy "white music"—a theory soon to be proved very wrong.) Bill Haley's version of the song made the year-end list of the biggest hits of 1954 and signaled a change in America's musical tastes. The kids wanted rock. And they were listening to the increasing number of stations that played "negro" music. Soon, the charts would have more and more hit songs from the rock genre and fewer and fewer from the pop or middle-of-the-road style. While that was good news for black musicians, some of whom for the first time were introduced to a white audience, it looked like bad news for the pop singers, many of whom were women—Patti Page, Kitty Kallen, Teresa Brewer, Peggy Lee, and Jo Stafford. Stafford was one who definitely had a lot to lose—in 1952 alone, her record company estimated that she had made over $300,000 from sales of her hit songs. How would she and other pop vocalists be able to adjust to America's shifting musical preferences? The question also affected shows like *Your Hit Parade,* the radio legend that had moved over to TV briefly in 1950, and then began simulcasting with the radio version in 1951. All was fine as long as the show could adhere to its proven formula of presenting the hits, sung by the Hit Parade Singers. But when rock and roll took over the charts in 1955–56, the teen audience did not want to hear the Hit Parade Singers. They wanted to hear Elvis or Jerry Lee Lewis or Buddy Holly. Conversely, the Hit Parade Singers had for years sung in a particular style, and that style was not aimed at young people—although, ironically, when the show first went on the air in 1935, young people were its target audience. But those young people of 1935 were now older adults, who wanted the show to stay the same as it was twenty-five years ago. *Your Hit Parade* struggled with this dilemma while its ratings began to slip dramatically.

The year 1955 saw a very eclectic mix of hits on the charts: some still reflected the pleasant vocal harmonies of the 1940s, such as "Sincerely" by the McGuire Sisters—the sisters had sung on WLW radio in Cincinnati when they were in their teens, and their career blossomed after they were the winners on the *Arthur Godfrey's Talent Scouts* show in late 1952[49]—other hit songs in 1955 reflected the new rock beat, such as "Rock Around the Clock" by Bill Haley and the Comets. But by 1956, the balance on the charts shifted dramatically: at the end of the year, five of the biggest hits were by Elvis Presley. A couple of the pop artists such as Gogi Grant and film star Doris Day managed to have Top 40 hits, and the genial Perry Como maintained his following as well, helped no doubt by his TV variety show (prior to TV, he had been a radio singer since the late 1930s).

As top-40 music became more and more in demand and the records increased in sales, radio stations that had continued to offer live bands began to replace them with disc jockeys and commit to going after the youthful audience. Such changes did not always go smoothly, and the older listeners protested when their favorite band or singer was replaced by a fast-talking disc jockey. But by the late 1950s, very few radio stations had live music. On the other hand, some new radio formats would begin to emerge, such as news/talk and full-service (called Middle of the Road or M-O-R in those days, it featured the old songs from the big band era, and lots of sports, public affairs, and news features; full-service/M-O-R was aimed at listeners over forty-five years old). The demise of live music also meant the demise of some of the jobs women on radio had held as singers. And although a handful did manage to hang on and persuade their managers to let them play Top 40 records, it would be safe to say that 99 percent of the new Top 40 disc jockeys were young men. Meanwhile, the older male disc jockeys, like Martin Block, who hated rock and roll and only played the phonograph records from the big band era, had to face the fact that radio was changing; in order to stay current, they would have to play the modern hits, like it or not. Many decided this would be a good time to retire. Martin Block was able to find a couple of stations that were going against the trend and still played the older songs; he was able to keep working until the late 1960s.

Dealing with Social Change

Along with the changes in music came changes in society. In 1954, Linda Brown, a black student from Topeka, Kansas, whose family wanted her to attend a good high school that would prepare her for college, ended up as the "Brown" in the famous legal case *Brown* vs. *the Board of Education*. The court's ruling put an end to the doctrine of "separate but equal" (black schools in most cities were far from equal), and the process of ending segregation began in earnest. It would be a time of turbulence, protest, violence, and resistance. TV and radio were there to cover it all.

Although TV might have had the pictures, radio still had some very respected and famous news commentators. In December 1955, a black woman named Rosa Parks was arrested in Montgomery, Alabama, for refusing to give up her seat on a bus to a white person. This injustice led to a bus boycott and brought a new community leader into the headlines—the Reverend Martin Luther King. Interestingly, some of the women's shows, which had avoided current events in the belief that women were not concerned with them, found themselves dragged into the ongoing national controversy, as the audience weighed in with its opinions. In an oral history of WHER in Memphis, several of the announcers recalled that even though their station was supposed to be a light and nonthreatening respite for the housewife, news events were too compelling to ignore, and the staff began reporting on the marches and racial confrontations. One announcer even tried to do a talk show during the 1960s about the tragic death of Martin Luther King, but white listeners called in and verbally attacked her, causing her to stop the program.

It was a difficult time to be talking about only recipes and fashions while out in the streets, the entire society seemed to be changing. In fact, the biggest issue for most of the women's shows of the early 1950s was not racism or even sexism—it was the polio epidemic, which had struck over 50,000 children in 1952 alone.[50] Many women's shows distinguished themselves in their ability to get accurate medical information to the public, as well as arranging visits to children's hospitals and raising funds for research. Another accepted role for women was that of advice giver in matters of the heart. On the women's shows and in the newspapers, there had long been this sort of conversation, with a psychologist or an educator offering the advice. In print journalism, the syndicated columnist Dorothy Dix wrote a daily column of advice to the lovelorn that lasted for many years. Miss Dix died in 1951; the next major syndicated advice giver first appeared in October 1955: Esther Pauline Lederer used her newspaper's house name of "Ann Landers." A year later, Ann Landers would get competition from her twin sister, Pauline Esther Phillips, who wrote under the name of Abigail Van

Buren, or "Dear Abby." Between the two of them, they handled a wide variety of queries, many of which were not about love, and some of which even came from men. (Gossip columns and advice columns fit with traits still ascribed to women—that they could not keep a secret and that they were naturally empathetic.)

Meanwhile, ABC radio saw an opportunity to bring an advice show to radio. Well aware that the women's shows still had a faithful audience, in October 1954, ABC formed a partnership with the *Woman's Home Companion* to produce a feature based on material in the magazine about marital problems—the "can this marriage be saved?" concept was common to many of the women's magazines, where an expert (often male) would listen to both sides and then offer advice for how to rescue the troubled relationship. The working title for the radio show was "Marriage Counselor," and the moderator was going to be a man. NBC tried a radio drama about marital problems during late 1953 and into 1954—the plot of *The Marriage* involved a former businesswoman who was adjusting to her life as "just a housewife" and the various problems she encountered. The gimmick for the show was that each week the point of view alternated—one week the story was told from the wife's point of view, the next week the story was from the husband's.[51] The show did not become a hit, but its stars already were: Hume Cronyn and Jessica Tandy, an award-winning couple with many triumphs on the Broadway stage.

But again, for all of the advice shows and the efforts of the radio homemakers, radio could only do just so much to hold on to what was in many cases an older audience. To the advertisers, older people were not a very attractive market—the myth about them was they would go to the old-age home and not buy anything new or modern. With all the babies born after the war, the society was suddenly oriented toward youth, and it was youth the advertisers wanted to reach.

For many baby boomers, two shows of the 1950s stand out: the *Mickey Mouse Club* and *American Bandstand.* Walt Disney's efforts to reach the youth market paid immediate dividends, as the show, which went on ABC-TV on October 3, 1955, was a huge success with young people all over the United States. It was up beat, and it had talented young performers and a jovial host who genuinely seemed to like what he was doing. It was clean and wholesome entertainment, although a bit sexist. One segment featured a TWA film about choosing a career. Of course, boys were shown how to be pilots, while girls were portrayed as being stewardesses. But overall, it was hard to complain about the show: for every feature that showed the boys doing something interesting, there was another that highlighted the girls. The photogenic cast had both male and female singers and dancers, who all dressed in very nonsexual clothing (although my male friends tell me they recall eagerly watching as Annette matured), and all of whom performed in various skits. And yes, in what had become an archetype of TV, the host (Jimmie Dodd) was male, but the female talent got plenty of time on camera, and female Mousketeers introduced segments just like the male cast members did. The *New York Times* criticized the excessive commercialism of the show (Disney was a master of merchandising, and it would not take long for items related to the show to be on sale everywhere), saying it was basically a vehicle to sell soft drinks and cereals to an impressionable young audience,[52] but that was the only negative review. Every other critic praised the show, and kids (myself among them) began watching it faithfully. As for Annette Funicello, she did more than transform from a cute girl to an attractive young woman during the show's run. She also had several Top 40 hits and became a success in movies for the teen audience.

Some Bright Spots on 1950s TV

What I found interesting even as a kid was that while the boys of the *Mickey Mouse Club* got to star in most of the action serials (such as "Spin and Marty"), there was also an action serial that starred a girl—"Corky and White Shadow," which featured Darlene Gillespie as a young girl with definite tomboy tendencies, who was not afraid to handle a dangerous situation. It was one of the few times I could recall a TV character who was strong, courageous, and female. I was sorry when that segment of the show came to an end, as there were not many shows on TV in which a young woman did something other than sing or dance or wish she had a boyfriend. (There was one series on early TV that also featured a strong female lead—Gail Davis as *Annie Oakley*. The message of this western, as far as I was concerned, was that a woman could be cute and popular and yet defeat the bad guys all by herself. Annie never acted like the "stupid woman" and she never let anyone dominate her. Her friendships with men were very egalitarian. I was about eight when the show went on the air, but already I was being told I was not acting "feminine" and was ordered to stop playing "Cowboys and Indians" with the boys and start playing with dolls like I was supposed to. Watching Gail Davis as Annie gave me hope, although at that young age, I probably did not analyze it all that deeply. She just seemed so in control of her life—I couldn't picture anyone forcing *her* to play with dolls . . . I was even more impressed to learn that Gail Davis did a lot of her own stunts.)

And then there was *American Bandstand*. It first went on the air on ABC in the fall of 1957, having achieved local success in Philadelphia before that; a number of cities had locally produced dance shows, Boston among them. The formula was simple: a male host with a friendly personality played the hits, and teenagers danced in the studio. Sometimes guest performers appeared and mouthed the words to their hit song (lip-synching); sometimes teens from the studio audience would rate a record to predict if it would be a hit. And sometimes there were dance contests. All the teens observed a very safe dress code, with the boys wearing coats and ties and the girls wearing dresses. If there was a message *Bandstand* wanted to convey, it was clearly aimed at parents who feared the effects of rock music. The *Bandstand* dancers looked very wholesome, as did the host, Dick Clark; this was reassuring to the adults who had heard only bad things about rock and roll.

For those of us who were fans of the show, *American Bandstand* became a sort of daily soap opera—we were preoccupied with the kids dancing together. Were they going steady? Those two looked so cute. Didn't he just break up with that other girl? Watching what the kids on *Bandstand* wore, how they did the latest dances, and how confident they seemed made me wish I could be on the show, too. Of course, I never was; the show's success transformed some ordinary Philadelphia teenagers into instant celebrities, and those of us at home admired and envied them. Years later, it was amusing to read the story of who in fact ended up getting married, who got divorced, who never were a couple at all—even if they seemed like it—and what happened when the kids who danced on that show grew up and were no longer celebrities.[53] As I write this, Dick Clark is billed as "the World's Oldest Teenager" and still moderating various programs.

Years later, I can still remember hurrying home from school to watch *Bandstand.* I did not know about the payola scandals, I did not know about Alan Freed, and I did not know why there were no women hosting any of the teen dance shows. Like many of the kids my age, I truly loved rock music. I loved the beat, and even when I could not understand the words, the enthusiasm of the singers appealed to me. The lyrics expressed common teen frustration about going to school and obeying teachers, or talked about being young and wanting to break free from all the rules. As Susan Douglas wrote, "The reason [this music] spoke to us so powerfully was that it gave voice to all the warring selves inside us, struggling . . . with a crushing sense of insecurity to forge something resembling a coherent identity . . . Pop music became the one area of popular culture in which adolescent female voices could be clearly heard."[54]

Professor Douglas was also referring to the early 1960s "girl group sound"—but although most of the big Top 40 hits of the late 1950s were by guys, the lyrics expressed universal emotions like wanting to find somebody to love, somebody who would accept you and not try to change you. To me, the hits had no particular gender; they just made me feel better when

I was having a depressing day. And I loved listening to the various Top 40 stations, even if they did play the same songs over and over; I thought that disc jockeys had the best job in the world—they were playing the hits and making people happy. And suddenly, I knew that I wanted to be on the radio, too. I could not decide between being a sportscaster (I loved baseball) or a disc jockey, but I knew I had found my career path. I had no idea that this goal would seem so radical to so many people. And while I heard no females on the air in Top 40, I just assumed in my naiveté that none had applied recently. But I was going to apply as soon as I was old enough. I did not realize what a problem that would be.

Criticism of Sponsors

Meanwhile, Vance Packard, a sociologist who received no respect from the academic community but was widely read by the average person, published a scathing critique of the advertising community in 1957. *The Hidden Persuaders* was quite sexist, as Packard's style of writing often was. But this book was not an attack on women. It was an attack on how advertisers used techniques from Freud and from other psychologists to manipulate and control the public. At a time when TV was still fairly new and not many people were seriously thinking about what effect those cute advertising jingles had on viewers, Packard's book raised some very important points about the need for media literacy. He showed how marketers appealed to the audience's fear or hope or anxiety. He showed how Marlboro cigarettes had been repositioned to make them "masculine"; he showed how easy it was to trick the public into thinking they needed a particular product.

Today, we know much of this (yet some of those same techniques are still effective), but in 1957, what he was saying about the dangers of rampant consumerism was very much ahead of its time. The women's shows were a good example. Many had made a sort of devil's bargain with sponsors. Some hostesses tried to remain in control by only allowing certain products on the show or refusing those that did not pass some test. But by and large, it was that sales function that kept the women's shows on the air. That is what made them their money and enabled them to do good for the community. It was their job to persuade the audience to buy what the sponsors were selling. Yet we know that most of these women saw themselves as much more than shills or hucksters. But the fact remains that even on the best and most cerebral women's shows, a large part of the program was about consumerism. And as Stephanie Koontz explained, the very same advertising executives who created the idea of the housewife as a marketing strategy were about to go after kids in a way that had never been done before. "It was the marketing strategists of the 1950s, not the 'permissive' child-care ideologues or political subversives of the 1960s, who first attempted to bypass parental authority and pander to American youth. As one marketing consultant pointed out: 'An advertiser who touches a responsive chord in youth can generally count on the parents to succumb finally to purchasing the product.' . . . Although the 1950s introduced new levels of hedonism and materialism into American culture, the decade 'contained' the radical implications of these values by attaching them to family togetherness."[55]

But with the all-out approach of going after the kids, on *Mickey Mouse Club* as well as on many other children's programs, it was harder for Mom to just say no. There were so many things kids wanted, so many things they were sure they had to have. A new market had indeed been created, and it would have a profound effect on popular culture.

So the women's shows struggled to maintain their radio audience even though radio listening was down. The TV audience was growing somewhat more sophisticated as the decade ended. Rock music would be attacked by psychologists and social critics who said it caused delinquency (no scientific link was ever established, but lots of hearings were held in Washington). The fan magazines tried to mediate. Articles in *TV-Radio Mirror* reminded parents that when they were young, they screamed for Frank Sinatra, they had fads their parents felt were bizarre, and they did strange dances, too.[56] Some of the middle-of-the-road vocalists who could not get played on a Top 40 station found that TV enabled them to reach that older audience: Dinah Shore was a prime example—even the way she sang the theme song for her sponsor, Chevrolet, was appreciated by her many fans. Where radio had chosen to appeal to youth, TV could still put on programming the grown-ups enjoyed, and many of the variety shows of the 1950s still featured performers who did music from the "good old days," such as Lawrence Welk, Patti Page, and Frankie Laine.

Popular Culture and Women's Place

The youth culture contributed to a number of fads in the 1950s (remember Play-Doh?), and people of all ages had fun with Frisbees and hula-hoops. Loose-fitting dresses for women (called chemises or sack dresses) were a fad, too, although many people, men especially, disliked how they hid a woman's curves. Adults were beginning to use credit cards (Diner's Club had been first in the early 1950s, but now there were several more major cards); a Diner's Club executive predicted in 1959 that ". . . some day you will be able to charge everything and cash will be virtually obsolete."[57] The small, portable transistorized radio (often called just the "transistor") changed the way kids listened, allowing them to take their favorite songs and their favorite station wherever they went. In the celebrity world, rock star Jerry Lee Lewis (already controversial for his explosive on-stage performances, complete with high-intensity gyrations and pounding on the piano) scandalized the entire country by marrying his thirteen-year-old cousin. The record industry created an award ceremony known as the Grammy Awards; the first ones were handed out in May of 1959, and among the winners was Ella Fitzgerald. TV had lots of Westerns, but by 1957, none with a woman as the lead character: the men were the doers; the women were prizes to be won or ladies in need of protection.

And while a few women did have hit records (Brenda Lee was one notable example, as was Connie Francis), the biggest star was Elvis, and nobody, male or female, came close. The rest of the 1950s was about male disc jockeys with deep voices playing Top 40 hit songs repeatedly and doing record hops where kids could do the latest dances and possibly win prizes. Women in suburbia joined the Parent-Teacher Association (PTA) or did volunteer work; some became active in women's service organizations. The Federation of Women's Clubs, like the PTA, was worried about pop culture and its effect on young people, so some women's clubs issued a set of standards for TV stations to follow, such as fewer commercials and less violence. It is doubtful that station executives took any of the recommendations to heart.

By and large, women were excluded from the major decision-making roles of the 1950s, and other than their roles as consumers, it was easy to marginalize and ignore them. But every company wondered how best to reach them in order to tell them about new products. One survey conducted by NBC-TV in the summer of 1955 showed that women got 36 percent of the information they wanted from magazines, 24.6 percent from newspapers, 23.9 percent from television, and only 4.7 percent from radio.[58]

As for the girls, they were encouraged to be passive and deferential and do whatever it took to get a boyfriend. In one advice column in *TV Guide,* girls were advised never to beat a boy at bowling, to talk only about things that interested him, and to always let him make the decisions.[59]

With little fanfare, Marlene Sanders had become a TV news producer in New York in the mid-1950s, and by decade's end, she would be doing some reporting; but there were few if any openings for women in Top 40 radio and not many in the other kinds either. In the Top 40 world of the 1950s, most of the singers were men, their managers were men, the record companies for which they worked were nearly all run by men, the magazines that wrote about them were owned and/or edited by men, and the records were promoted by men. There were occasional exceptions, but not too many. One came from the popular style of rock known as doo-wop, which was just about entirely comprised of male groups (although, in one way some of the groups were noteworthy because they were integrated, at a time when this still was unusual).

In the summer of 1957, five girls from PS 109 in Harlem had a Top 40 hit with a song originally written about a teacher of theirs, "Mister Lee." The Bobbettes were the first female group to have a top ten hit on the pop charts, as well as a number one record on the rhythm and blues charts. Unfortunately, it was their only big hit. There were a couple of other Top 40 records by female groups like the Teen Queens or the Poni-Tails, or by male groups that had a lead vocalist who was female: the Tune Weavers' one hit, "Happy Happy Birthday Baby," had Margo Sylvia singing lead. But the girls who were seeking a role model and not finding one on TV did not find one in Top 40, either. In fact, about the only way girls could participate in Top 40 was with their purchasing power: by some estimates, they bought as much as 90 percent of the hit singles.[60]

Most girls of the late 1950s did not have many opportunities to become directly involved with radio, however. Some started fan clubs for their favorite stars, and some became regulars at every event their favorite station sponsored. And for a very few, if they were photogenic, they might be chosen to participate in a station promotion. One rather egregious example of the belief that a sexy girl would attract male listeners was a 1957 promotion for an announcer, in which two pretty young models paraded down the street carrying portable radios. They were wearing barrels and nothing else; on the barrels was the slogan "We've got nothing on but the Herb Oscar Anderson show." Needless to say, this got attention from the businessmen who stared at them, but there is no guarantee that it got Mr. Anderson more listeners.

Of course, there were a few women who held important jobs in TV (in addition to those who performed), but those jobs were the behind-the-scenes positions that did not get much attention from the media. The executive producer of the very popular *Perry Mason* series was a woman who had a legal background, Gail Patrick Jackson. She was not the only woman to produce or direct on TV, and many successful shows were still being written by women as well; but very seldom were any of these women mentioned. There was a woman journalist, Denise McCluggage of the *New York Herald Tribune,* who wrote about sports—*Time* found this amusing, referring to her as a "tomboy with a typewriter"; she had been told at first to write women's features, but she loved the human drama of professional sports and persuaded her editor to let her cover some of the athletes and their exploits.[61]

But as always, it was not the lone female sportswriter or the women who wrote the radio dramas who were famous—it was the performers. In that, there was nothing new—the women who appeared on camera seemed so much more glamorous and exciting than the women producers; most fans had no idea what a producer did anyway. So, in the TV universe, the singers sang, the dancers danced, the TV moms baked brownies and looked lovely while vacuuming the house, and the TV dads had the final say on all important matters, unless, like Lucy, a woman caused so much trouble that her husband finally gave in to her.

Meanwhile, middle-of-the-road vocalists like Jo Stafford had resigned themselves to the changes in musical trends. But Miss Stafford made a very interesting observation when asked why rock was so different. "Rock and Roll is an economic thing," she told *Billboard* magazine in 1958. "Today's nine- to fourteen-year-old group is the first generation with enough money given to them by their parents to buy records in sufficient quantities to influence the market. In my youth if I asked my father for 45 cents to buy a record, he'd have thought seriously about having me committed."[62] The advertisers who had envisioned a youth market were seeing their dream come true, as sales of "singles" (45 rpm vinyl records with a hit song on the A side, and a song that was often filler on the other, or B side) continued to skyrocket. Kids could now make a song a hit whether their parents liked it or not. Stations began to tabulate the number of phoned-in requests, as the young listeners were surprisingly active about their favorite songs.

In 1957, Judith Waller finally retired, after a long and distinguished career in educational radio and public affairs. She had originated several highly acclaimed radio series, such as the *University of Chicago Round Table,* a discussion show in which well-respected educators talked about the issues of the day, and had written several books and scholarly articles about the importance of educational broadcasting. In an era when most people were poor and educational opportunities were scarce, these shows had a vital function, and the heads of the departments that created these shows were nearly always women.

But when the foremothers of broadcasting retired, their jobs seemed to retire, too. There was not as great a demand for educational radio now. Despite Frieda Hennock's vocal advocacy, educational TV was limited to a few stations (KUHT in Houston was the first, in 1953) and a few programs; most children's shows were sponsored and concerned with pitching products. Somehow, it was not how Judith Waller had envisioned the future of her industry. But Ida McNeill was proving local radio could still be ageless; she won the Golden Mike from *McCall's* magazine in 1957 for her many years of service to her radio audience. She was still very visible, with a career that encompassed three decades. Her story was unusual though; most of the other women pioneers had faded from the public eye. In 1958, Nellie Revell died. She was perhaps the first woman publicist, a syndicated columnist, a former stage actress, a radio announcer, a woman who had come back from a bout with paralysis to walk again, a feminist, an independent-yet-popular woman whose friends were some of the rich and famous, the author of three books, and a hostess of a successful network interview show, yet today few people have any idea who she was. This was a pattern that would be repeated frequently, as the women who achieved in radio during the 1920s and 1930s were no longer important to the industry they had helped to create, and most were forgotten. (Nila Mack died in 1953, and so did the kind of children's programming on which she prided herself.)

And while millions of sports fans still know who Babe Ruth was, Babe Didrickson (Mildred Didrickson Zaharias) has become a footnote in sports history, although she was regarded even by male sportswriters as the best all-around female athlete of the century. An articulate woman who knew how to give a good interview, she passed away much too young, from cancer, in 1956.

At the 1958 AWRT convention, the men who were the heads of the major broadcasting companies, the same men who refused to hire women for anything except women's shows or as weather girls, gave speeches about how important women in broadcasting were. Said one executive, "[Radio] has outgrown the limited concept of women's participation [only through] stereotyped cookery, fashion and homemaking shows . . . our industry must give more cognizance to the contributions women can make to commercial success." He then encouraged women to become better at selling and find new ways to market to the woman listener.[63] And, admitted one male general manager, women need to "face the fact that opportunities [for them] are quite limited in radio today." He then blamed Top 40 and said that when the era of the Top 40 disc jockey passed, there would be room for women's shows again.[64] But the owners who had hired the Top 40 disc jockeys, replacing live orchestras, radio dramas, and all sorts of educational and public service programming, did not address why women could not be disc jockeys or Top 40 program directors. And while there were more women owners at the convention and some excellent women speakers (including the FCC's Frieda Hennock and advice columnist Abigail Van Buren), the prevailing sentiment stayed the same. Women were supposed to do women's shows on radio. If they could not do those shows any longer, radio had no room for them. And if they were not young and pretty, TV did not seem to have room for them, either. And I was only eleven, and I truly believed that by the time I was ready, the industry would be ready for me.

Timeline: The 1950s

1951   American Women in Radio and Television founded
1952   *McCall's* Golden Mike Awards begun

1953   KUHT, first noncommercial TV station, debuts
Betty Furness does her first Westinghouse commercials
I Love Lucy wins an Emmy; Lucy and Desi sign $8 million contract
Oveta Culp Hobby named first woman secretary of Department
of Health, Education, and Welfare
1956   The ponytail becomes a fad for girls; boys start growing side-
burns like Elvis
1957   *American Bandstand* debuts on ABC-TV

Chapter 6

The 1960s and 1970s:
And When It Changed

For broadcasting, the new decade began with scandals—first the quiz show scandals in 1958 (who knew these shows were rigged? Even *Time* magazine had been fooled); and then in 1959–60 came the payola scandals—accusations that the Top 40 charts were rigged and that disc jockeys took money from record companies to play certain songs. Soon, the quiz shows were gone from TV, and one winning contestant who had been perceived as a hero, Professor Charles Van Doren, was shown to have been part of the fraud. Rock and roll was getting assaulted by members of Congress, out-of-work musicians (playing the hits had meant the official end of live orchestras on most stations), and assorted media critics who preferred the music of the big band era. Parents became concerned—was the music their kids liked really as dangerous as some legislators claimed? There had been controversy about so-called suggestive lyrics in rock since the mid-1950s; *Variety* published an editorial about how the double entendres had to stop (most kids, myself among them, could not understand many rock lyrics, so we had no clue what the critics were complaining about), and, just like the 1920s, there were parent-teacher groups and politicians who accused rock music of causing everything from pregnancy to delinquency.

Radio stations, worried about controversy, immediately overreacted. Control of the music was taken away from the disc jockeys (the majority of whom had never taken bribes from anyone) and put into the hands of the station's program director and music director; playlists became more restrictive. Record companies, too, worked on repairing their image, putting out songs that were not as hard-edged or raw as some early rock, with no suggestive lyrics to offend the mass audience. Pop hits of the early 1960s often featured a light, fun, nonthreatening sound and catchy lyrics that nearly anyone could understand. (There was one notable exception, of course: the Kingsmen, a garage band from Portland, Oregon, had an unlikely hit with the song "Louie Louie" in 1963, and since absolutely nobody could understand the words, rumors spread that the lyrics were obscene. The FBI actually investigated the song and came to no definite conclusion, but some politicians still demanded that "Louie Louie" be banned.) The "surf sound" of groups like the Beach Boys was in marked contrast to the high energy of Elvis's "Hound Dog" or Little Richard's "Good Golly Miss Molly." Surfing music celebrated the carefree, good life of the young and the affluent. Songs about fast cars, leisurely days, and summer romance became popular; as Professor Reebee Garafolo pointed out, this period of time following the payola scandal was about toning rock music down and making it safer, which was a euphemism for making it whiter and more middle class.[1]

With the congressional hearings on payola in 1959–60, the culture wars had begun; the young people's musical preferences were clashing with what the older people thought they ought to like. It would be the first of many such clashes, and as the 1960s progressed, those clashes would be about issues much more serious than Top 40 hits.

A Woman-Owned Record Company

In Passaic, New Jersey, in the late 1950s, a housewife was considering her options. Florence Greenberg probably did not think of herself as especially unique at this point in her life: she was in her mid-thirties and had done what society told her to do, raising her children and staying home. But now that her kids were in school, she really wanted to go back to work. As the story goes, a friend of her husband's worked for a music publisher in New York City, and Florence was invited to hang around the office. But office work did not appeal to her—the music business did. She had always been interested in popular music, and now she had a chance to really learn about what went on behind the scenes; she even met some of the songwriters and began to familiarize herself with the names of the important disc jockeys. Then, she started a small record label, but although it had one promising female vocal group, it did not have any hits. Florence Greenberg was not one to give up, however. The second time she started a record label, she had learned from the mistakes of the first venture, and she decided to do more promotion and publicity for her artists, to make sure the right people knew them. Her new label, Scepter Records, was begun in 1959. She released a number of songs, but Scepter did not get its first hit until the fall of 1960, when the Shirelles rocketed to number one with "Will You Still Love Me Tomorrow." For one of the few women in the record business, having a number one group and running a label was quite an accomplishment, but it would be only the start of her success in the music industry. The early 1960s was about to bring a new sound to the forefront—the so-called girl group sound. Florence Greenberg would be involved with it, as would a young songwriter named Carole King, and another named Ellie Greenwich.

Looking back on the beginning of the 1960s, there was no reason to assume much was going to change for women. *Time* had a cover story about the suburban housewife, although later in 1960, there was also a cover story about the unusual Senate race in Maine—unusual because both candidates were female, for the first time in U.S. history (incumbent Margaret Chase Smith versus challenger Lucia Marie Cormier). But female celebrities were still being portrayed as vapid and shallow, concerned only with shopping or beauty parlors.[2] And speaking of stereotypes, the decade began with a long article in the syndicated magazine *Parade* about why women bosses were so unpopular. Since there were not many women bosses in 1960, the magazine, which had always expressed a very traditional view of women's role, may have had its own agenda: perhaps women were getting tired of being part-time secretaries and were trying to move up, and this article tried to discourage them from doing so. The author told us that most people think "lady bosses" are two-faced and cannot be trusted. "Call it prejudice or truth—the cold fact is that most men, and most women too, do NOT like [women as bosses]." The author then listed all the alleged sins women bosses commit, including being too nosy, too controlling, oversensitive, vain, unreliable, and impatient. And worst of all, some women bosses overdressed, wore too much makeup, or let themselves get fat. And, rehashing one of the most enduring stereotypes, the author said that women could never be good bosses because the qualities that make a boss effective make a woman seem "mannish" or "bossy."[3]

It should not have been a surprise that women were more critical of women bosses than men were. Since most women of that time were stuck in subordinate, low-paying jobs, they probably resented the few women who did move into supervisory jobs. Further, women had heard endless negative myths about the female gender for years and might have come to believe some of them were true. And also, women had long been socialized to be tolerant and deferential toward men, but they were never taught to be that way to women; as a result, traits like impatience, which male bosses certainly might display, were seen in a much harsher light when a woman displayed them. Still, this article, and several others like it, was making the rounds in 1960. Even *TV Guide* had weighed in at the end of 1959; in the midst of a profile of a successful TV actress, who, of course, said that what really mattered most to her was that she had a husband, the author paused to remind female readers that "You can't work constantly and still be a good wife and mother."[4] The irony was that, once again, the woman being interviewed (Diana Lynn) was, in fact, a hard-working performer who had no plan to give up her TV career for her husband and family.

Signs of Change

And yet, there were a few small indications that things might change after all. In Washington, D.C., a woman had been hired to be a TV news reporter for WTOP-TV, and while the article had to mention that she was "attractive" and "pretty," Morna Campbell reported national and local news, wrote her own scripts, and edited her own news film. The article also stressed that she did not do so-called women's news, but, rather, the hard news that any serious reporter would do. Still, having a woman on camera doing news was so unusual in 1960 that when Morna Campbell appeared as a guest on *What's My Line* (a game show where guests in unique occupations stood in a lineup with several imposters; the panel had to guess, by asking yes-or-no questions, which of the three was the real tree surgeon, beekeeper, perfume tester, or whatever), she stumped the panel with ease. Nobody guessed that her occupation was TV news reporter.[5]

And then, there were the only women network correspondents—Nancy Dickerson at CBS and Pauline Frederick at NBC; both were always professional, yet they still received some of the lighter assignments rather than the hard news they preferred to do. Still, they were on the air, and if radio was using even fewer women as announcers or news reporters, at least network TV now had several in good shifts. As if a harbinger of things to come, in November 1960, Pauline Frederick narrated a special called "The Trapped Housewife," about how housewives had become disenchanted with the role society had assigned to them. By the decade's end, a newly emerging movement called women's liberation would be a topic of discussion, but in 1960, it was not yet in the spotlight.

One topic, however, that was about to dominate the media's attention was a newly available form of contraception. In 1960, the Food and Drug Administration approved the birth control pill; it was a first step in the gradual process of giving women more control over their own bodies, but it would continue to be controversial. Critics would accuse the pill of causing American's sexual mores to decline, clergy and some magazine columnists worried that it would lead to promiscuity, and talk shows thought it was a wonderful discussion topic. On the other hand, some stations proved to be a bit squeamish about discussing controversial subjects. Here in Boston, which was still a religiously conservative city, one station refused to air a 1962 episode of the TV legal drama *The Defenders* because it expressed a pro-choice view about abortion.

Women's Show Hosts Get Little Respect

Society in late 1960 had become preoccupied with the Kennedys. After the television debates (John F. Kennedy was considered much more photogenic than Richard M. Nixon), when Kennedy was elected president, the spotlight shone on his wife, Jacqueline. Jackie was young and equally photogenic, and the media, already trained to cover the candidates' wives, found her very charming. Said one reporter, "If Jacqueline Kennedy was beautiful before, you should have seen her today. Her skin was translucent, like mother of pearl, as she walked by her husband's side . . . [she] was the picture of calm contentment and admiration [for her husband] . . . she stood a trifle back of her husband, a habit that always brings to mind her saying 'the main thing for me is to do whatever my husband wants. He couldn't—and wouldn't—be married to a woman who tried to share the spotlight with him.' "[6] Jackie was a woman of her generation; she knew her role, and she accepted it with dignity and grace. She was expecting another child, her husband was now the president, she was elegant and wealthy, and so many women wished they could be like her.

And yet, there were a few women carving out their own niche, whether they had a husband or not. One 1961 winner of *McCall's* magazine's Golden Mike Award for excellence in broadcasting was Betty Adams, who, you may recall, had come from Providence's WJAR-TV to Boston's WBZ-TV in the spring of 1959. Adams had just returned from filming in Africa, one of many countries she had visited to explore how women lived and how their culture regarded them. In her own personal life, she was a young widow raising two children and had gotten into broadcasting originally to do children's shows. When she was also assigned a daily women's show, she began coming up with interesting ways to approach it. She won a number of awards in her three years with WBZ-TV (she moved to New York in 1962), and she proved that a women's show could have a news and human interest component and still get good ratings.[7]

She was not the only woman trying to expand the formula of the TV women's shows. Like newswomen Pauline Frederick and Nancy Dickerson, many women's show hosts had journalism credentials and were increasingly frustrated at covering only what women were supposed to wear this year. True, for some, fashion and food were of genuine interest, but for others, the best part of their show was the opportunity to interview celebrities. And for others, the opportunity to create understanding about social issues was of great importance. Kitty Broman, on her WWLP (Springfield, Massachusetts) show, *At Home with Kitty,* produced a report on the misconceptions and myths about epilepsy; Nancy Clark of KTVB-TV in Boise, Idaho, did a feature about children with mental retardation and what their prognosis might be. Both women won Golden Mike Awards in 1962, as did Valena Minor Williams of WABQ radio in Cleveland, Ohio, for her series on race relations in her city. These awards, begun by *McCall's* in 1952, honored women broadcasters who had gone above and beyond in public and community service.

Unfortunately, one thing that had not changed at all was the level of respect accorded to the women of broadcasting. There was still a hierarchy, with singers and performers at the top, and women's show hosts at the bottom. No matter how many awards a women's show host earned, no matter how many celebrities she interviewed, she was seldom considered as management, even though she had a title that looked important: director of women's programming. And although there were a few female megastars who received big salaries (in the 1950s, Betty Furness was very well paid, as were Gertrude Berg and Arlene Francis), anecdotal evidence still showed that it was the men who made the big money, since it was the men who hosted the major shows and did the news anchoring.

Some of the women who were on the air during the 1930s and 1940s were still broadcasting in the early 1960s, but pay inequity was something they never mentioned. Working conditions was a taboo subject, too. Only when some of these women did oral histories during the 1970s and 1980s did they finally discuss how they were harassed in the workplace, often treated contemptuously, and denied the raises they deserved. The articles and books these same people wrote in their own day were all very positive: Judith Waller and Bertha Brainard especially said that they suffered no discrimination and that broadcasting was a wonderful career for a woman; articles by women's show hostesses agreed. Some of this is understandable: nobody wanted to be perceived as a whiner, and women historically had been trained to make the best of things. All of the popular psychological theories, as we have seen, stressed that a neurotic woman complained, while a good (normal) woman accepted her lot in life with a smile. Anger was not an emotion a woman was supposed to display if she ever wanted to be seen as feminine. Further, since most stations had only one woman on the staff back then, and she often worked on her own (the women's department was usually an end unto itself), there may have been nobody to ask about the station's pay structure, and nobody from whom to get much sympathy when things were going wrong. The expectation was that women would entertain the female audience and give a lot of plugs to the sponsors. And while most did so, even the bigger names like Betty Furness eventually began to tire of doing endless commercials. In an interview with the *New York Times,* Miss Furness gently reminded people that she had been a dramatic actress at one time and would like to do more than sell refrigerators.[8]

The print reports of AWRT conventions (which tended to be noticeably shorter than the reports about the male conventions like the NAB) always stressed the great speakers and panels—most of which reinforced the importance of keeping the sponsors happy; if there were any problems behind the scenes, few women back then felt they could talk about such things in public. (In the 1970s and early 1980s, when some women, myself among them, spoke out about how radio conventions were like fraternity parties, complete with scantily dressed females handing out products to the mostly male attendees, the response was to have at least one "women's panel," so that women could discuss whatever they wanted to discuss. Men showed no interest in attending and seemed to feel such a panel was unimportant compared to the numerous male experts on the rest of the panels.) AWRT conventions probably became the one opportunity for women to compare notes and get advice from other female colleagues. Ruth Crane Schaefer, a founder of AWRT, in a 1975 interview, recalled that the women's director at a station was considered almost a separate entity, rather than a member of the team. ". . . [O]ddly, the lowest branch of the organizational tree was usually that of the woman who did foods, children's programs, women's activities, and so on, no matter how well sponsored [her show was], and notwithstanding [that she] was also her own complete staff—writer, program director, producer, public relations . . . [even] saleswoman for her own sponsors, radio or TV, and sometimes both."[9] She went on to relate how male technicians and announcers would make fun of the women's shows and often try to play tricks on the women while they were on the air to see if they would lose their cool. It must have been incredibly frustrating for these women, who were putting in so many hours, bringing money into the station, and yet getting so little respect for what they did. And although they were famous within their own universe, Ruth Crane Shaefer acknowledged they were not really considered professional broadcasters by their male peers.

In the early 1960s, it was still possible to read an entire issue of a trade publication like *Broadcasting* and not see one woman's name, except for the occasional obituary of a broadcasting pioneer, such as when controversial journalist and network commentator Dorothy Thompson died in late January 1961. Although hundreds of women worked in radio and TV, nearly all of the officers and district managers of the National Association of Broadcasters, as well as the executives of the other important broadcasting organizations and the executives at the publishing companies, were men. At the networks, the decision makers were all male, too. It was no wonder that organizations like AWRT worked so hard to get recognition for the women of the industry, women whose work was often marginalized. And with time, the focus of AWRT began to branch out from just an organization of women's show directors—in 1960, the president-elect was Esther Van Wagoner Tufty, a no-nonsense journalist who had been on radio, TV, and in print, and who was determined to elevate the level of respect women in broadcasting received. By 1963, AWRT's description in the *Radio/TV Annual* read: "AWRT is a professional organization of women working as broadcasters, executives, administrators, and in a creative capacity in broadcasting and broadcast advertising."

And yet, at some time, perhaps as far back as the late 1920s, the way men did the news or the way men announced the music became the norm; women had shown they could do the job time and again, but once more, in the Top 40 era, they were excluded. This comes as no surprise to social psychologists like Carol Tavris, who has observed that "[i]n almost every domain of life, men are considered the normal human being, and women are . . . considered deficient because they are different from men. [W]omen . . . worry about being abnormal because male behavior, male heroes, male psychology, and even male physiology continue to be the standard . . . against which women are measured and found wanting. Despite women's gains in many fields in the past twenty years, the fundamental belief in the normalcy of men, and the corresponding abnormality of women has remained virtually untouched."[10]

So while male program directors stated that it was the public that preferred male voices or male hosts or male reporters, women who struggled to break into the industry in the 1950s and 1960s found that logic puzzling, since few of them had been permitted a fair chance at building a following. Pauline Frederick, the pioneer network newswoman, was told repeatedly by her male bosses that "when [a woman] broadcasts news, listeners are going to tune out, because a woman's voice does not carry authority."[11] I, too, was told that women do not sound credible discussing serious subjects: one program director told me that when a woman does the news, it sounds like gossip. Again, I have never seen any statistics that back up these beliefs, but they seemed to be truisms for most of the men who ran both radio and TV in the 1960s.

New Trends in Music

For the baby boomers in the early 1960s, radio meant neither talk shows nor women's shows; it was where we heard the hits. TV had become somewhat predictable, and even the critics were writing about the sameness in the programs. In 1961, when he was appointed as head of the FCC, Newton Minow gave the famous speech in which he called television a "vast waste-land," and many viewers were inclined to agree. Like Frieda Hennock, Mr. Minow advocated for more and better educational TV, which would later be renamed "public broadcasting."

But if TV was not too exciting, the early 1960s did bring several new musical trends. One was a sudden interest on college campuses in folk music. Playing guitar and singing old folk songs became a popular way to pass the time, and it was not long before some talented songwriters became part of the scene and started using their songs to call attention to problems they felt that society ignored. A number of young men (and a few young women) began to put their feelings about racism, consumerism, conformity, and other social issues into music, and sing on campuses, in clubs, and in coffee houses. Bob Dylan, Joan Baez, Phil Ochs, and Peter, Paul, and Mary were among the best known. Miss Baez puzzled the news magazines, which had evidently never seen a woman who did not like to wear makeup. In June 1962, *Time* wrote about her and a few of the other "Folk-Girls" (as *Time* put it); the article noted that Baez had already sold more albums than any other female folksinger in history, yet she seemed to have no interest in playing the lucrative concert tours or making large sums of money.[12] A couple of the fan magazines even tried to create a rivalry between Joan Baez and one of her competitors, Judy Collins. In a 1985 interview, Baez recalled how strange that seemed to her. "There was no rivalry between us. We were [both] working hard . . . and . . . doing different things. We weren't trying to outdo each other; we were trying to do the best we could for ourselves and our audience. People could appreciate what [all the female folk singers] were doing; they didn't have to select one [of us] . . . I guess that kind of controversy sells records."[13]

Record companies, which did not object to having a number of male folk singers on their label, seemed reticent to have more than one female. There was even a rule on the radio—never play two female vocalists in a row. It was another of those truisms for which no good explanation was offered, and the rule persisted well into the 1980s.

The folk music fad, which then led to a hybrid called folk-rock, was eventually replaced by the "British Invasion" and the Beatles, but the desire to change society through music did not go away entirely; it would reemerge on a very underused medium, FM. In 1964, the FCC issued a ruling that changed what had been broadcast on FM up to that point. While modern audiences take FM for granted, in the early 1960s, only audiophiles listened to it. Mostly, FM stations broadcast either classical music or educational programs. If FM owners also had an AM, they would simulcast what was on that station, enabling them to reach two audiences at no additional cost. But now the FCC said this had to stop; FM stations had to have their own separate programming. In 1964, few owners had any plan about what to put on their FMs other than classical music. But that, too, would begin to change as more and more baby boomers went to college; the changes on FM would ultimately affect women announcers.

Females on the Pop Charts

The other musical trend of the early 1960s was the "girl group" sound, a rare time in Top 40 when female singers were heard on the airwaves frequently. Some of these groups were black, like the Crystals, the Chiffons, and Motown's big hit makers, the Supremes. What the Shirelles had begun with "Will You Still Love Me Tomorrow" (and subsequent hits like "Dedicated to the One I Love" and "Soldier Boy"), other girl groups would continue. The Angels and the Shangri-Las were the most popular white girl groups, but again, color was not what most baby boomers were thinking about—the songs spoke about emotions that teenagers understood all too well. Phil Spector, the man who produced a number of the hits for groups like the Crystals and the Ronettes, has been described as a controlling, obsessed individual who, while certainly a genius, wanted to totally dominate every aspect of the recording process. His success could not be questioned—from 1961 to 1965, he had seventeen Top 40 hits. But his way of dealing with people has been described as "Svengali-like," "eccentric," or "rude."[14] Some of the female artists who worked with him recalled how he bullied them and did not pay them the royalties they felt they deserved, while he was able to get wealthy from their efforts.[15] Spector was not the only one accused of doing this: unfortunately, early rock had all too many record company executives who cheated inexperienced young musicians out of what they had earned. But back then, the media said little about this issue, so the average listener had no idea that many of the young vocalists heard on the radio would never get paid for their work. To the fans who saw them on TV, the girl groups did not look oppressed (if such a concept existed in 1960); they seemed to have a glamorous and exciting life.

Most of the hit songs performed by the girl groups were written by songwriting teams. In the early 1960s, among the most successful were the husband-and-wife teams of Barry Mann and Cynthia Weil, Jeff Barry and Ellie Greenwich, and Gerry Goffin and Carole King. The music these teams produced was often lyrical and upbeat; most of them worked at a New York locale called the Brill Building. As we saw in previous decades, songwriting was one aspect of the music business where women could get involved; some of the songwriters were also singers, doing their own demonstration versions, called demos, of prospective songs—popular vocalist Dionne Warwick would be discovered through a demo song she recorded and signed to a recording deal with Florence Greenberg's label. Some of the Brill Building songwriters eventually branched out on their own; the best-known woman to do this was Carole King, who would have a giant hit of her own in 1971 with her album *Tapestry,* and its number one hit single "It's Too Late."

Conflicting Messages in the Music

As mentioned earlier, the music on radio in the early 1960s was not as harsh or as raucous as before the payola scandal. Lyrical and upbeat songs were welcome, whether sung by guys or by girls. But a couple of the girl group songs had a darker sound to them—one big hit, "Leader of the Pack" by the Shangri-Las, became a sort of anthem for guys who rode motorcycles and for girls who loved a "bad boy." Except in this song, the bad boy was killed, complete with screeching tires and realistic sound effects at the end. And then there was a rather disturbing song that came from the usually pleasant Goffin and King ("Will You Still Love Me Tomorrow" and "The Loco-Motion" were written by them)—the song was called "He Hit Me (And It Felt Like a Kiss)," and was about a girl whose boyfriend thought she was unfaithful, so he got angry and hit her; but she saw this as proof he loved her. Even in the unenlightened prefeminist era when nobody discussed battered women, that song really bothered some people, including the Crystals, who recorded it. Perhaps the song just reflected the belief that women were supposed to be masochistic, or perhaps Goffin and King were assuming somebody else's persona (they claimed it was inspired by the black eye their babysitter had gotten from her boyfriend). The song still seemed to accept battering as normal behavior. But just to demonstrate what a strange era it was, and how confusing were the messages young women got from the music on the radio, in addition to "He Hit Me," there was a big hit by Lesley Gore called "You Don't Own Me," in which she told her boyfriend that she was not his property and did not intend to let him boss her around.

News/Talk Radio

More AM radio stations were switching to Top 40 in the early 1960s, leaving those that did not to do some serious thinking about finding a new direction. The networks had one by one moved their successful soap operas to TV; by 1961, there were no more radio soaps, unless a radio station wanted to put forth the time and expense of producing one. The networks did continue to send out news however, and lots of it. Many adults had come to rely on the network commentators, and while TV was slowly improving its news gathering, the technology still made the process much more complicated, whereas radio news sounded professional and offered familiar and well-known reporters. Some radio stations had talk shows by 1960, but most talk was still one-way. A radio homemaker, a sportscaster, or an expert talked, and people listened—or the studio audience asked questions. The popular KDKA Pittsburgh team of Ed and Wendy King found ways to work around this problem on their late-night show *Partyline;* when listeners would call in, either Ed or Wendy would restate their question, since there was no technology in the 1950s that made the actual call sound good on the air.

Meanwhile, in St. Louis at CBS-affiliate KMOX, vice president and general manager Robert (Bob) Hyland and his staff created a format that was unique for its time, revolving around talk, features, and information—and no music. In late February 1960, a program called *At Your Service* made its debut, gradually expanding to become KMOX's format. This was one of the earliest departures from playing music of any major radio station—and it helped KMOX to maintain number one ratings with adults for over twenty-five years. From the format's inception, station personnel were able to get famous and outspoken guests, including Eleanor Roosevelt, Margaret Mead, Governor George Wallace, and Reverend Billy Graham, as well as local people who had done interesting things—such as two nuns who had gone down south to participate in a Freedom March for civil rights.[16] Critics said the concept would fail—after all, adults, especially housewives, were supposed to like soothing music and soap operas. Not only was talk and information successful for KMOX, but stations all over the United States began to imitate it; to this day, news/talk remains popular on AM radio. Yet, for many years, it was another format that tried to reach women but was run only by men. Given that many elements of the new format had been successfully done by women's shows for years, it seems strange that women hosts were not involved right from the beginning. But while KMOX often had women on the air as guests and as experts, there was no female talk show host on the station until 1975.

Tragedies in the News

While Top 40 passed through numerous musical fads, the country was beginning to experience something far different from the prosperity and the family-oriented emphasis of the 1950s. The 1960s brought crisis, protest, and even violence. To this day, many baby boomers can recall exactly where they were when President Kennedy was shot in November 1963. The next few days were traumatic for everyone, but especially for young people: when we had lost three of our young music heroes in a plane crash (Buddy Holly, Richie Valens, and the Big Bopper on February 3, 1959), that was the first time many of us had thought seriously about death. Now, only a few short years later, a young president had been shot down.

Much has been written about how TV held the nation together; it was the first time that television news really had an opportunity to show what it could do, and the coverage of the president's funeral was watched by millions. Polls would soon indicate that more people got their news from TV than from newspapers. Meanwhile, there were other tragedies that year. Country music star Patsy Cline, one of the first country performers to have a pop hit, and *Billboard* magazine's Female Artist of 1962, was killed in a plane crash in March 1963; she was only thirty-one. Dinah Washington, a popular black vocalist of the 1950s, also died young, from substance abuse, in December 1963. In late August, over 200,000 people, blacks and whites, had marched in Washington, D.C., to dramatize the need for civil rights legislation. But only weeks later, a tragedy occurred that would be the subject of several folk songs (and later, a movie) as well as the cause of riots and protests: four young black girls were killed when racists exploded a bomb in their church in Birmingham, Alabama. Lest you wonder what that has to do with the topic of women in broadcasting, read on.

The Report of the Women's Commission

Several years before he was assassinated, President Kennedy had established (at the behest of Eleanor Roosevelt, who was still active in women's causes) a commission on the status of women. For a long time, only the Women's Bureau and the League of Women Voters advocated with any consistency for women's role in society to be improved or expanded. This committee was going to provide some research and take a close look at whether women's rights were being protected. Professor Christine Lunardini has pointed out that President Kennedy was by no means interested in women's rights, nor had the presidents who came before him wanted to do such a study. But Kennedy was being criticized for having appointed so few women to his Cabinet since he became president, and when he was approached by Women's Bureau head Esther Peterson with the suggestion that he establish a committee to do the study, he agreed, figuring that it would help restore his credibility with women voters.[17] Eleanor Roosevelt chaired the committee, but unfortunately, she never lived to see the results of its work—she died in November 1962. For many years, she had been among the most admired women in America, even if some of her stands on issues created controversy—America still was uncomfortable with strong women who spoke their mind. To remember and honor Eleanor Roosevelt, the committee issued its final report on October 11, 1963, the anniversary of her birth. Its long list of recommendations included permitting women to serve on juries, promoting more women to high-level government jobs, providing day care for working mothers, and passing an equal pay act. One addenda to the report criticized the media for portraying women as only wives and mothers and for promoting stereotypes; another criticized the government for not moving faster to assure blacks of equal rights and especially stressed the problems of black women.

When some of the best-known feminists in the United States gathered to form the National Organization for Women (NOW) in November 1966, the *New York Times* put the story on page 44, on what would be considered the women's page. This was actually rather typical thinking in the journalism world: any story about a group of women went on the women's page, whether it was a serious story with hard-news implications or a light story about the garden club. The assumption was that men would not be very interested in what women were doing, even if the women in question were ambassadors or scientists, so the stories got blended in with the cooking and fashion news.[18]

One of the members of NOW's board of directors was also one of the few women involved with hard news in the early 1960s: Lucy Jarvis of NBC News, a producer and coordinator of specials for the network. She won a Golden Mike for her five months of research in Moscow, which led to a series called *The Kremlin*. During her time in Russia, Nikita Khruschev gave Mrs. Jarvis unprecedented access. (Five years later, she was horrified to learn that NBC had not even bothered to keep copies of her rare footage; she found out it had been thrown away because there was allegedly no room in the warehouse to store it.)

Broadcasting Meets *The Feminine Mystique*

At first, radio and TV were mostly oblivious to the newly emerging conversation about "the feminine mystique." True, some women's shows had discussed certain aspects of feminism, but the majority concentrated on household tips, fashion news, relationship advice, and celebrity gossip, with an occasional newsmaker. Betty Friedan had written several magazine articles about the profound depression and frustration affecting so many housewives, and while prior to this, an occasional column (some even by male writers) lamented the waste of women's talents by society's insistence that they remain only in the home, it was the publication of her 1963 book *The*

Feminine Mystique that really got people seriously thinking about how women in America were treated. As often happens when authors write controversial books, Ms. Friedan eventually found herself on several women's shows, where her beliefs undoubtedly made some of the hosts uncomfortable; after all, many of these women had invested much time and energy in defending the traditional gender roles. Newswoman Liz Trotta recalls a meeting with Betty Friedan in 1967, wherein she did a radio interview with the outspoken feminist. Trotta was by her own admission very opposed to the women's movement, yet she was unable to answer when Friedan asked her if things were just fine for women, why hadn't a highly qualified journalist like Trotta ever been asked to become a news anchor?[19]

Meanwhile, as a result of the work of the President's Commission on the Status of Women, the Equal Pay Act of 1963 was passed; finally it was illegal to pay women less than men for doing the same job. Of course, nothing changed right away. The newspapers had long since decided, somewhat arbitrarily, to list certain jobs in their classified ad section as "Help Wanted—male" and "Help Wanted—female." The male jobs included all managerial and upper-echelon jobs, while the female jobs were mainly clerical or domestic jobs.

In July 1964, the Civil Rights Act finally became law, and it prohibited employment discrimination based on race or gender—it almost did not include gender, but some proactive work by several of the women in Congress, including Maine's respected Senator Margaret Chase Smith, got it passed after lengthy debate. The act established an Equal Employment Opportunity Commission (EEOC) and gave it the power to enforce the new law. Now, the newspapers were in a quandary: were they discriminating by the way they set up their classified section? Rather than change, most, the *New York Times* and *Boston Globe* among them, simply continued separating the ads, but on the top of each page, they put a disclaimer saying they were continuing to do this for the convenience of the readers. It would not be until the 1970s that newspapers changed this policy. And it would take even longer for the rest of society to catch up. Throughout the 1960s, despite the new law, I know a number of women (myself among them) who applied for jobs in broadcasting and were told, "we don't hire women." But soon, stations would no longer be allowed to say that, as the FCC was about to issue its own ruling about equal employment opportunities.

And that brings us back to women in the industry. In the fall of 1964, I began college, and I could not wait to try out for the campus radio station. The Beatles had come to America, music was fun, and I wanted to play the hits. To my great surprise, the program director told me the station did not put "girls" on the air. I asked him why not, and he told me "because they don't sound good." I asked him how many he had put on the air, and he said,

"None; they don't sound good." It would take me four long, frustrating years before I was finally allowed to be on the air at Northeastern University. I had no idea that what I was encountering was what other women of the mid-1960s also encountered. Jessica Savitch, who would eventually have a career in TV news, went to her college station at Ithaca College about the same time I did; the professor who was the advisor told her she was wasting her time because "[t]here's no place for broads in broadcasting."[20]

Barbara Walters, who became a famous anchorwoman and interviewer by the 1980s, was working behind the scenes at the *Today* show in the early 1960s, mainly as a writer. Marlene Sanders was working in the news department of WNEW radio in New York, having been a producer and writer for some Dumont Network TV shows prior to that. Ida McNeil, who had done it all at her little station in South Dakota for so many years, was now seventy-four, and she decided it was time to retire; she sold KGFX in 1962, marking the end of an era for one of the oldest of radio's women pioneers. Former FCC commissioner Frieda Hennock, now Frieda Hennock Simons, was only fifty-five when she died suddenly of a brain tumor in June 1960.

Women as TV Witches

Meanwhile, neither radio nor TV felt the urgent need to take on any more women or minorities than it had to. The status quo was just fine with most of the decision makers. Betty Friedan could write all the articles she wanted: there was no reason for radio or TV to change, and besides, the public was supposedly content with what was being provided. ABC-TV even put out a new series in 1964 starring Elizabeth Montgomery as a witch who gives up her identity to be a wife and mother; in this very popular series, Miss Montgomery's character, Samantha, totally submitted herself to the desire of her husband that she be just an ordinary housewife. Of course, sometimes she could not help doing a little magic, but Susan Douglas and other media critics have noted that the appearance of this series right after the best-selling *The Feminine Mystique* and the equal pay act is no coincidence. The danger of a woman having too much freedom is obvious: her powers must be channeled and contained. Says Professor Douglas:

> In [TV] shows like "Bewitched" [and] "I Dream of Jeannie . . ." [s]eemingly normal-looking female characters possessed magical powers, which men begged them not to use; if women did use them, their powers had to be confined to the private sphere. Whenever women used these powers outside the home, in the public sphere, the male world was turned completely upside down . . . Men were made impotent by these powers, and the hus-

bands . . . were stripped of their male authority and made to look foolish and incompetent in front of their male superiors . . . Although the men insisted (usually unsuccessfully) that the women not use these powers, there were three exceptions the shows' narrative systems permitted: to complete domestic chores, to compete over men, and to help men out of embarrassing situations, which usually had been caused by the woman's unauthorized use of her magic powers in the first place.[21]

So, even a witch would rather be a housewife, and giving up her powers was a small price to pay. The mid-1960s was a time of conflicting messages, as young women began to attend college (still being told to seek a husband rather than a career) and their mothers, who had immersed themselves in being housewives, were hearing Betty Friedan and others telling them that there really was more to life than housework. Some of the older radio home-makers, such as Ruth Lyons on WLW Radio and TV in Cincinnati, were still very relevent to the 1950s housewives—Ruth won a 1963 Golden Mike Award in recognition of her fund-raising for children's charities, and she was one of the most visible hosts in her area. But there was an unspoken question about how radio homemaking shows would change: would younger women, raised on the hits, want to listen?

Vice President Lyndon Johnson's wife, Lady Bird, predicted in May 1963 that there would soon be changes in women's role in radio and TV, changes she said were long overdue. Mrs. Johnson, whose twenty years of experi- ence as a broadcaster was seldom mentioned by the media, was the keynote speaker at the 12th Annual AWRT convention, attended by over 1,000 women in broadcasting. In that speech, she stated that doors were opening wider for women in broadcasting, and while she acknowledged women's skill at sell- ing products on the women's shows, she also said that in such a rapidly changing world, the media needed to make fuller use of women's brain power in the ongoing effort to keep the public well informed. She predicted that the old traditional way of presenting the news would soon change, and she called upon the women delegates to make their presence felt in news. She also challenged both the men and the women in the industry to seek out the stories that went beyond scandal and celebrity gossip.[22]

But the old traditional way of defining women's jobs on TV did not change overnight. Some of the early 1960s shows that featured women remained stereotypic. The female audience supposedly loved gossip (hence the popu- larity of Louella Parsons, Hedda Hopper, and even Nellie Revell in the 1930s and 1940s), so a TV show aimed at women should have celebrity gossip. In 1963, one woman made the most of this belief. Virginia Graham, who had already been seen on TV doing commercials as early as 1951, began hosting *Girl Talk,* a syndicated program that as Professor Jane Shattuc wrote, set the stage for shows like *Geraldo* and *Oprah.* On this show, female guests with strong but opposing points of view were invited on, with the hope that a clash, or as it was known back then, a "cat fight" would erupt. When not moderating between battling celebrities and guests, Miss Graham discussed issues that affected women, but the show's staged confrontations made it very unusual for 1960s TV.[23] The audience liked it almost immediately and *Girl Talk* developed a large audience.

TV had a new advice giver in the 1960s, an author and psychologist who had once been a successful (and, she insisted, honest) quiz show contestant: Dr. Joyce Brothers. Dr. Brothers continued doing a New York radio show, but she began to syndicate her advice on television in 1961; she received large amounts of mail asking her for guidance, mostly about relationship problems.

1964—A Year of Social Change

1964 was another year of contradictions. On the one hand, the Beatles were making the term *Beatlemania* a part of the American vocabulary: when they arrived in New York to begin their U.S. tour, about 5,000 screaming fans (mostly girls) were waiting for them at the airport. Ed Sullivan, never a fan of rock music but always able to spot a trend, put the Beatles on his TV show and got some of his highest ratings ever. By April, the "Fab Four" (as the media nicknamed them) would have five hits on the Top 40 charts. Dance crazes like the frug, the watusi, and the swim were popular, along with an old favorite that became popular several years ago, the twist. Mary Tyler Moore won an Emmy as Best Actress for her work on CBS's *Dick Van Dyke Show.* The TV game show *Jeopardy* made its debut, and the novel that had once scandalized millions, *Peyton Place,* was a successful movie and then a TV soap opera. However, its author, Grace Metalious, died of liver disease, exacerbated by alcoholism, early in 1964. She was only thirty-nine and had been subjected to relentless criticism over a book that by today's standards seems rather tame. Legendary radio and TV comedienne Gracie Allen passed away in 1964. So did former president Herbert Hoover: while many people blamed him for the Depression, media historians remember him from when he was secretary of the Department of Commerce, the agency that supervised radio during its formative years. He spoke out against commercialization of broadcasting and believed that radio should not have any advertising at all (needless to say, his advice went unheeded). And KSTP's Corinne Jordan, who had been a program director when few women were, died in December 1964; she had finally retired due to poor health but had been a radio vocalist until the late 1950s.

While more people were going to dances, overseas the war in Vietnam was escalating and more young men were worried about being drafted. A number of strikes, marches, and protests over civil rights took place, and not all of them were peaceful. In July, a demonstration in Harlem against police brutality exploded into rioting; in Mississippi, three Northern civil rights workers, who had been sent to Mississippi to help black people register to vote, were found murdered. And in a case that stunned nearly everyone who heard about it, in March, a twenty-eight-year-old woman named Kitty Genovese was assaulted and brutally murdered as she screamed and pleaded for help—over thirty of her neighbors watched from their windows, yet nobody responded, not even to call police. This shocking indifference would be discussed on numerous talk shows as the details of the murder emerged, and journalists wrote columns decrying how detached city dwellers had become.

Album Rock and Women

On some college campuses, young women were starting to express dissatisfaction with the status quo. While they did not stage any protest marches yet (the demonstrations held by feminists in 1968 to protest the Miss America pageant would be reported with both inaccuracy and disdain by the mainstream media), by the mid-1960s, an increasing number of female high school and college students were speaking out, demanding respect and equal treatment, and criticizing the way women were depicted in the media. It was the era of the miniskirt and the minidress, and some women were offended at being depicted as little girls or as sex objects. But at the college I attended, it was not media sexism but dress codes that came under attack: men could now wear what they wanted, but women students still had to come to class in dresses or skirts and blouses. That changed, and I helped to change it. At other colleges, the male dorms had no curfew, but the female dorms did; that, too, changed after some protests. Emerson College's WERS-FM (and numerous other college stations) decided women program directors were not such a bad thing after all; in 1967, they got one, and they also had a woman engineer. But something else was taking place in radio as a result of the turbulent times. In a decade of marches and protests for civil rights, an increasingly heated debate was also taking place about America's growing involvement in Vietnam. Students were becoming politically active on some campuses, especially on the West Coast, where the Free Speech movement at San Francisco State University made the news. None of this affected Top 40, which kept on playing the hits (no song was supposed to be more than three minutes in length) and playing lots of commercials.

But on FM, the FCC ruling that owners had to create actual programming or give up their license forced some owners to consider new ideas for programming. In San Francisco, Larry Miller, Tim Powell, Tom Donahue, and others created what would become album rock—or free-form progressive rock, as it was called back then. KSAN became one of the pioneers in this new format, which played long versions of songs (as opposed to the short version the Top 40 stations played) and also mixed in poetry, commentary about politics, album cuts by obscure bands, and whatever else the announcer wanted to share with the audience. Among the air staff at just about every album rock station was one female disc jockey. Granted, album rock created a new archetype for women—the "hippie chick," usually with long hair and a sexy voice. Album rock was a male format, although it had plenty of female fans. The rock was usually hard rock, but the songs the stations played often had lyrics that protested the war or spoke out against racism. It is interesting to note that sexism was seldom in the conversation; perhaps station personnel felt they had addressed this issue sufficiently by having female announcers, which AM did not. KSAN had Dusty Street as its first woman on the air; Bonnie Simmons began in the music library and rose to become a program director as well as an announcer (FM personalities did not think of themselves as disc jockeys).

Looking back on those days for an interviewer, Dusty Street recalled that the first board operators and engineers at KSAN were young women, but they were not allowed on the air until a group of them insisted that they should be given a chance. They were finally allowed a show on Sundays.[24] In New York, WNEW-FM's first female announcer was the legendary "Night Bird," Alison Steele. Steele had originally been on the previous incarnation of the station, a gimmicky all-girl format of softer music. When that failed, the station switched to progressive rock in October 1967, and she was kept on. Alison Steele was no stranger to radio—she had been on the air with her then-husband, bandleader Ted Steele, doing the kind of show that was still popular on AM in the 1950s, before stations took all the live music off the air (their show was called *Ted and the Redhead*). In the 1960s, with the advent of FM progressive, she became one of New York's most popular announcers and remained with WNEW-FM until 1979.

Sexism in 1960s Radio

I would like to tell you that I, too, was a legendary FM broadcaster, but I was still in college at the time; and to be honest, in the mid-1960s, I still preferred the music of Top 40, although by the late 1960s, it was getting very stale, and the disc jockeys were trying way too hard to pretend all the social issues were not happening, which drove many listeners to investigate FM. Gradually, even Top 40 was forced to play some shorter versions of the protest songs, as contentious social issues were brought into the mainstream through music. I finally got my first radio show in late October 1968, and by that time, our college station had decided to switch to progressive rock, too, something many college stations were doing.

But while FM had its sexy-sounding hippie-chick announcers, and while a growing number of FM progressive stations featured programming that talked about issues like the war in Vietnam and, of course, the use of drugs, AM Top 40 basically ignored all of this and continued its own set of stereo-types. I was one of many young women trying to get a radio job in Top 40, even as an intern. I was told that women only answered the request line (the "Hitline"); and so it was that I became a Hitline operator at WRKO in Boston. Gradually, it became obvious to the staff that I could write, and I knew a lot about music. I ended up helping the music director and the disc jockeys with all sorts of projects, none of which I got credit (or pay) for doing. My experience was not unusual.

FM progressive, for all of its talk about civil rights and war protests, still maintained many of the old stereotypes about women, except in a new form. Since I know a number of the founders of the format, and I truly applaud what they did to bring something new to radio and shake up the status quo, I must also say that I always was puzzled by how modern their ideas were about equality for people of color and their passion for pacifism, yet how old-fashioned their ideas were about women. The FM progressive founders were men who were 100 percent in favor of women having freedom of choice sexually. They liked the idea of women being liberated from having to be virginal. But when it came to promoting women to positions of author-ity in radio or giving them more to do than appear at station promotions looking attractive, they were opposed. Raechel Donahue, wife of one of FM progressive's legends, Tom Donahue, acknowledged that she carried out Tom's ideas,[25] but there is little evidence he carried out (or even considered) many of hers. In FM progressive, men led and women followed, except the women had long hair and played album cuts rather than on AM where they had short hair and did women's shows. Even years later, the founders of FM progressive defended their beliefs about women. They repeated that women's voices were perceived as less persuasive and claimed that only men applied for most of the jobs,[26] which, of course, contradicted the experiences of all the women I knew who applied and were told the station did not hire women. In interviews, the founders of FM progressive and Top 40 admitted that only when the federal laws changed and equal opportunity policies were put into place did they begin seriously trying to find women, or, better still, black women (often referred to in private as "two-fers," since stations got credit with the FCC for having fulfilled two requirements—hiring more women and more minorities), to put in visible positions.

Misconceptions About Feminism

Meanwhile, just as radio was changing, on college campuses and in the workplace, society had its own set of adjustment problems. The mid- to late 1960s was a time of transition, as people gradually examined and reconsidered the beliefs of the 1950s regarding women's place. The media did not help: men commentators were often snide or sarcastic in coverage about the new women's liberation movement.[27] The women demanding equality were regularly framed as man-hating, bra-burning lesbians, which is especially interesting since the first major demonstration, the 1968 protest of the Miss America pageant, was done by using visual symbols that the protesters felt oppressed women—such as large-size bras to represent the fact that the Playboy Bunny archetype implied that women were only as good as the size of their breasts. Women protesters did *not* rip off their bras and burn them; they tossed bras, hair curlers, high heels, and other symbols that represented the male standard of female beauty, into a large trashcan labeled a "Freedom Trash Can."[28] Yet the mainstream media would persist for years in making the women's movement synonymous with angry women who burned their bras. And while it was easy to trivialize women who claimed the media representations of them led to oppression (what was the problem with consumerism—wasn't America built on it?), it was not so easy to ignore the concerns they kept raising. But many people were confused about exactly what changes the women in this movement wanted to see. Did they want to become soldiers? Were they rejecting marriage entirely? Did they feel that having children was out of the question? Some of the women in broadcasting, including Liz Trotta, even expressed total dislike of the women's movement. Professor Joyce Hoffman found this negative attitude somewhat ironic. She wrote:

> Although the inroads achieved by the women's movement in the 1960s helped to compel editors to assign women [reporters] to Vietnam, . . . many of these women appear to have been at the very least indifferent to, if not downright contemptuous of, feminism. Few would credit feminism with any part of their success. They believed instead that they had made it on their own . . . NBC correspondent Liz Trotta challenged the movement's philosophy . . . [I]n Trotta's view, the "excessively liberal demands" made by leaders of the women's movement "smacked of special-interest crankiness masquerading as the people's will."[29]

But on the other hand, even traditionalists like Vance Packard had begun to examine the prejudices against women in society, as he noted in *The Pyramid Climbers* that just being female still arbitrarily excluded women from most good jobs. Said Packard, "Although nearly 4 out of 10 job-holders in the United States are female, women rarely obtain the executive suites . . . except in secretarial capacities. They are perhaps the most discriminated of all minority groups in industry."[30] One businesswoman noted in a 1966 article that there was now a sort of schism among women: the women who worked in a professional or career-oriented track were often looked upon with suspicion by those women who did not work outside the home. Having heard via the media for years about women who were gold diggers and husband stealers, and that working mothers contributed to children becoming delinquents, this attitude is not surprising, but the woman who wrote the article found it depressing. She noted that she, too, was a wife and mother, and she was not working to steal anybody's husband. Rather, she loved her job and was happy her company was giving her the chance to move into an executive position. Yet the women in her neighborhood treated her like a pariah for showing devotion to a career rather than staying home with her children.[31] *Newsweek* noted that a survey done by Harvard Business School that year also showed that out of 1,000 businessmen, 41 percent viewed businesswomen as less competent. One executive, asked why more women were not hired offered the reasoning that building more ladies rooms would be impractical. And reinforcing the fear of many women about what a career would do to their personal life, *Newsweek* mentioned that most of the women they interviewed for their article were either single or divorced.[32]

In early 1966, Barbara Walters, by now a reporter for the *Today* show, wrote about how being a woman helped her get certain stories, because women were able to bring empathy and human interest to a story. She said that women were finally being hired for their intelligence rather than just for their plunging necklines or good looks, and she praised both NBC's current correspondent in Vietnam, Aline Saarinen, and veteran UN correspondent Pauline Frederick, two women with two different styles, yet two examples of the changing face of network news. And as might be expected, Walters said that being a woman had never hindered her in doing her job.[33] Also, contrary to the myth that successful women are "Queen Bees" who would never help other women, Cokie Roberts, today a news anchor with ABC, recalled that CBS's first woman correspondent, Nancy Dickerson, could not have been kinder and more supportive when she was just starting out; Cokie was quite in awe of Dickerson, who was "one of the most powerful people in Washington."[34]

But while the 1960s would see a few more women in nontraditional positions, including NBC-TV anchor Andrea Mitchell, whose broadcasting career began in 1967 at KYW radio in Philadelphia where she was a reporter, most of the changes in women's status would not become noticeable until the 1970s.

Meanwhile, one woman was transforming children's programming on TV, the way the late Nila Mack had done for radio several decades earlier. Joan Ganz Cooney had long been upset at the poor quality of what children could watch. Like Frieda Hennock and Newton Minow, she felt TV could do better, and she was determined to make it happen. She first worked in media as a publicist before becoming a producer for a public television station in New York. But children's programming stayed on her mind, and in 1967, she secured grant money to research how preschoolers learned, and how TV could best teach them. Out of her research, Joan Ganz Cooney created the Children's Television Workshop, and her concept was a show that took place on a city street, with a diverse cast and realistic scenery. The result was the award-winning *Sesame Street,* which went on the air on public television stations in November 1969 and taught countless numbers of children to count, to know their letters, and to sing along with the characters on the show. Interestingly, although some of the characters were of undetermined gender, and some were certainly male, none of them were female.

Women as Music Directors

It was during the early to mid-1970s that FM radio, including the supposedly avant-garde progressive format, slowly became more corporate, as companies like ABC instituted stricter controls and took the freedom to pick the music away from the announcers. The roles of the program director and music director became more important as a result. At Top 40, the procedure since the 1960s had been that the music was chosen in a meeting that involved the music director (who screened the songs, saw the record promoters, and chose the records most likely to become hits) and the program director (who was the final say on which songs would be added that week). At some stations, the most popular announcer was in the meeting, too, since he (and it was usually a he) knew what was being requested and what fans at station promotions wanted to hear.

An interesting hierarchy had developed at many Top 40 stations, and it was repeated on FM as well. Music directing became a female job, while program directing remained male. Some of the best known of the Top 40 music directors had quite a bit of power, even though their importance would be understated when histories of Top 40 were written. Rosalie Trombley of CKLW in Detroit/Windsor, Ontario, was directly responsible for the success of numerous artists, including Bob Seger. She told me in an interview that when she first got into radio, she had no career aspirations. She was divorced, had kids to support, and needed a job. But she quickly moved up from station receptionist into the position of music director for CKLW's program director, Ted Atkins. Unlike the music librarians of the 1940s, who basically filed records and replaced what was scratchy, the music directors of Top 40 and album rock often served as musical advisors to the program director, finding the best songs to bring into the meeting. Ted Atkins of CKLW quickly saw that Rosalie had an innate ability to choose hits; she knew what the public wanted. This ability is not specifically male or female —some people can hear a hit, while others cannot. Rosalie could, and it earned her the respect of her program director, as well as the appreciation of all the musicians whose careers she helped.

Another woman who made her name as a music director in Top 40 was Marge Bush of WIXY in Cleveland. She, too, was originally hired for secretarial work, but she soon proved she could do much more than type letters. In the 1960s and early 1970s, AM Top 40 still ruled, and Mrs. Bush (as she preferred to be called) was in charge of doing music research, keeping the library organized, seeing all the record promoters, and bringing the songs she felt would be hits into the music meeting for her boss to hear.

One of the mothers of the modern music director was probably Bertha Porter, who worked for WDRC in Hartford, Connecticut. During the 1940s, when most women in radio saw their jobs vanish after the war, Bertha kept hers and wielded considerable power. Her boss, Charlie Parker, told me that her knowledge of big band and Middle-of-the-Road music was encyclopedic: a listener could ask for a request knowing only a few words of the song, and Bertha would identify it immediately. "She planned out every announcer's show," Mr. Parker told me. "She wrote it out on a yellow legal pad. Every day she would plot out every show—how many male vocalists, how many females, how many instrumentals; nothing got played at WDRC unless Bertha Porter said so."[35] And this was long before computers, so one can only imagine how long it took her to plan each show, yet the announcers respected her judgment. Mr. Parker also told me that artists, too, respected her ear; they would come to Hartford to sit with her and ask her opinion about what song they should release next. And even into the Top 40 era, Bertha Porter was there, doing her job, choosing the music, predicting the hits. When she finally retired in 1969, a testimonial was held in her honor, and *Billboard*'s radio editor Claude Hall said that all music directors owed her more than they realized.

Also an influential music director was Betty Breneman, who first held this position in Los Angeles for KHJ; she worked with consultant Bill Drake and then with program director Ron Jacobs. Like other women music directors, she had a good ear for a hit song; when KHJ added a record, many other stations followed. In 1967, she was named national music director for the RKO radio group and for all of the stations that Bill Drake consulted. Later in the 1970s, she began producing her own "tip sheet," in which she predicted the hits and helped music directors to decide what songs had potential.

But as if to reinforce that women in the industry were invisible, the radio editor for *Billboard* magazine, Claude Hall, wrote a very well reviewed book in 1977, assisted by his wife Barbara; it was called *This Business of Radio*. In its 353 pages, the women of radio were given only two pages. One was about radio wives. The radio wife, said Mr. Hall, must learn to accept that radio will always come first in her husband's life. A woman who marries a disk jockey must have compassion and understanding; he cited as a good example Bonnie Campbell, wife of Tom. Bonnie evidently had great talent in production, but that was not her focus any more. "Her whole life is devoted to his career." Most of the radio wives he praised gave up their own radio careers to concentrate on helping their husbands. "You'll find a countless number of radio wives . . . they may be working as secretaries while their husbands fortify their careers . . . they emotionally support their husbands . . . Enough praises couldn't be sung about them."[36] Now, don't misunderstand me: I agree 100 percent that a wife should be supportive of her husband's interests and his job. But nowhere in the equation did Hall even mention the wife's needs or suggest that consideration should go both ways. For a 1977 book, this could have been written in the 1950s, since it seemed to be advocating a return to the wife as suffering servant. To Mr. Hall's credit (or perhaps to his wife Barbara's credit), the book did go on to acknowledge that a few women actually had radio jobs of their own. There was a far too brief mention of Rochelle Staab, who had risen from music directing to become the program director of KIIS in Los Angeles, one of the few women in such a job at that time. It also mentioned album rock legend Mary Turner of KMET; she had started at KSAN, where she had been one of the women who did engineering. Mary ended up on the air when the overnight guy frequently failed to show up for his shift, and she found she loved being an announcer. In 1972, she had joined KMET, having fallen in love with album rock as a format, and had made a name for herself during the 1970s. And that was all—two women from Los Angeles and nobody else. When the book came out, I was on the air in a top-ten market, and I recall wanting to call him up to give Claude a long list of women he could have mentioned, but I figured it would not do any good, since the book was already published.

As if being ignored, underpaid, or left out of Claude's book was not bad enough, there was one other problem for the women in radio during this time. In addition to the women music directors I mentioned before, there were many others, on the FM side as well as on AM. Most of my music directing was done on FM during my radio career, in Cleveland, New York, and Washington, D.C. And I found that I shared something in common with all of the women music directors who came before me: no matter how influential we were, no matter how many hits we picked, or how many albums were dedicated to us, we were seldom if ever promoted to program director, or even considered for the job. That is why I wish more were written about Rochelle Staab, one of the very few who did get the big promotion. (There was also Joyce Monroe, national program director for Rounsaville Radio in Miami.)

As for the rest of us, we were often asked to train the next program director but never asked to be one. As I told Professor Michael Keith when he interviewed me for one of his books, there was an interesting catch-22 for women in radio in the late 1960s and throughout the 1970s. If we wanted to move up, we were told we lacked the experience because we had been "only" music directors. But if a guy wanted to move up, the press release often spoke of all his great experience when he was a music director. As we will soon discuss, the FCC in 1970 told radio stations they had to hire women, but the attitudes about how far women could advance could not be legislated, and the change was painfully slow.

A Turbulent Era

No book about broadcasting can ignore the turbulence and chaos of the 1960s and early 1970s, which affected the news and the music of the era, as well as even polarizing some of the broadcasters. There were many tragedies to report: in 1968, both Martin Luther King (in April) and Robert Kennedy (in June) were assassinated. War protests became more dramatic and more ugly: in August of 1968, TV was there in Chicago for the Democratic Convention, and anti-Vietnam War demonstrators gathered outside the hall to protest. As several thousand of them chanted "The whole world is watching," police and the National Guard, under orders from Chicago's mayor, dispersed them with nightsticks. Over 1,000 protesters were injured. And with increasing numbers of baby boomers now in college, it is not surprising that college campuses became fertile ground for a wide range of protest groups. In early May of 1970, two college demonstrations ended with tragic consequences. At Kent State in Ohio, the National Guard fired on the protesters and killed four of them (which became the subject of a hit song by Crosby, Stills, Nash, and Young), and not long after, at Jackson State in Mississippi, police fired on the protesters (who were protesting both the war and racism), killing several and injuring twelve.

It has been noted by media critics that the Kent State killings of white

students received far greater press coverage than the equally horrific killings of the students at the black college in Mississippi, but both cases showed
how the emerging generation gap about the war was widening. Most of the
men who had fought in World War II looked with contempt upon the protesters who refused to go to Vietnam. While generation gaps were common
throughout the century, with kids thinking parents were old-fashioned, and
parents worrying that kids were on the road to delinquency, now the differences of opinion about the war played out much more vehemently in all too
many families. On album rock radio, many young announcers began to editorialize against the war, both with musical selections and with the way
newscasts were done. A generation gap even emerged at some radio stations; management was often older and more conservative, and the air staff
was young and eager to speak out about the issues. As mentioned in previous chapters, controversy was considered bad for business, so management
and air staffs found themselves in a number of clashes.

Women Cover Hard News

Meanwhile, for the first time, the visual medium of television was able to
bring images from the war right into people's living rooms. As mentioned
earlier, among the war correspondents was Liz Trotta, sent by NBC to report from Vietnam. It was a far cry from what executives had previously
asked her to do—covering President Johnson's daughter Lynda Bird at her
wedding and discussing her wedding gown, an assignment she refused because she felt it was not a news assignment. Liz Trotta offended some of the
men she worked with when she insisted that she would not do stories that
she felt were trivial. She did not have anything against weddings, wedding
gowns, or Lynda Bird Johnson; she just felt that celebrity news was not
news at all, and she did not want to be excluded from doing hard news just
because her producer believed his female reporter should concentrate on
what famous women were wearing.[37]

   At ABC, Marlene Sanders had the same dilemma. She, too, was an experienced correspondent, winner of a Golden Mike Award, and yet she, too,
was often given only soft news assignments; she was told to cover the wedding, and she did so, because she believed there were just so many times she
could complain that the men get all the hard news assignments. She felt she
had to balance her complaints with proof that she was a team player. As-
signing women to report the serious stories was still new territory for the
networks, and the handful of women correspondents only sometimes were
given good assignments (Marlene anchored some ABC newscasts and did a
brief stint in Vietnam in 1966; she produced a number of feature pieces

about the country and its people); all too often, the men for whom they worked still had preconceived notions about what women reporters were capable of doing. Liz Trotta had little patience for any of that. She was regarded as a tough and talented reporter with an abrasive personality, according to a former colleague, Jon Katz. She was considered too volatile, too ambitious.[38] Because she had a strong radio and print journalism background and was a capable reporter, she had finally won the assignment to report from Vietnam in 1968; she was one of the first woman correspondents to report from the scene. NBC would have the most female reporters by the end of the 1960s—Aline Saarinen, who became the first woman bureau chief when NBC made her head of their Paris news bureau; the two mothers of modern TV news, Pauline Frederick and Nancy Dickerson (Dickerson had come over from CBS in 1963); and Liz Trotta—a total of four women. And that was better than it had ever been in TV news. CBS still had only one female correspondent, and ABC had two.

A woman who continued to succeed even under the old rules was NBC's documentarian Lucy Jarvis, who did critically acclaimed presentations about drug abuse, mental illness, and other social issues throughout the late 1960s. But she also did harder news, as when, in 1973, she did an award-winning production about the People's Republic of China, receiving unprecedented access to the people and places in that Communist country.

Negative Reports About "Women's Lib"

The antiwar movement continued into the 1970s and justifiably garnered a large amount of media attention. So did Earth Day; the first one was held in April 1970, and millions of young people and adults united to call attention to pollution and damage to our environment. But the women's movement refused to disappear, as feminist leaders from NOW, as well as campus activists, persisted in speaking out about inequality until the news magazines finally got around to doing a story on "women's lib" in 1970. And while some of the coverage was patronizing (did it really matter whether or not feminist author Kate Millett's hair was not neat enough?), at least some of the issues were being brought to the mainstream. Male journalists, especially news anchors (who tended to be older men), seemed mystified by feminism. They expressed their puzzlement in their news reports, using phrases like "bra-less bubbleheads," reminding viewers that women could not get along with other women, so how could they be expected to get along with men, and stating that since American women were so well off, what was there for them to be upset about.[39] In fact, both *Time* and *Newsweek* seemed truly puzzled that these feminists were so angry. *Newsweek* framed its article in these opening words: "A new specter is haunting America—the specter of militant feminism."[40]

And, of course, out came the usual male experts to say that equal pay was certainly okay in some circumstances, but that these "women's libbers" were just self-hating, abrasive, and unfeminine. They were also fed up, evidently, since at *Newsweek*, forty-six women researchers, frustrated at never getting promoted no matter how qualified they were and not getting equal pay, filed suit in 1970, charging *Newsweek* with violating the Civil Rights Act. The Equal Employment Opportunity Commission agreed with the women, and their suit was eventually upheld. At Time Inc., the women who filed a complaint and won worked out an agreement that led to more women being promoted and an end to the practice of arbitrarily reserving certain jobs for men and others—lower-paying ones—for women.[41]

Yet in spite of this, the mainstream news magazines still seemed incredulous that American women, who supposedly had the best of everything, were complaining. The news magazines seldom mentioned their own treatment of women employees (nor did the radio and TV networks) and ignored the growing frustration the women stuck in the research or secretarial ghetto felt. Rather, the coverage of the women's movement frequently used terminology like "extreme women's libbers" and "radical feminists"; it implied that certain angry women were manipulating impressionable younger women (after all, a common myth was how easily led women were) and imposing rage and hostility where none needed to be, since after all, most women did not really want to be "liberated."[42] The decision by some feminists to wear no makeup and not shave their legs was held up as proof that these women were possibly neurotic and certainly odd. When outspoken feminist Bella Abzug got elected to the House of Representatives in 1970 (her slogan was that a woman's place was in the house—the House of Representatives), male reporters concentrated more on her assortment of hats, and, of course, called her strident. Veteran TV commentator Howard K. Smith announced that while he was sympathetic toward "Indians and Negroes" who had truly been the objects of discrimination, he was quite unsympathetic toward women's libbers who were already more than equal and could easily live off of their husbands.[43] Walter Cronkite, normally a reliable journalist, cited Sigmund Freud as an example of an expert on women and repeated Freud's famous quote wherein he had said in all of his research, he still could not answer the question "What do women want?"[44] Some women might have suggested that what they wanted was not to be patronized by either Freud or Mr. Cronkite, but that was typical of the debate on "women's lib," with older men saying women had it easy, and women themselves feeling torn between agreeing with some things the feminists were saying (even

Newsweek's correspondent had to admit she came away with much greater understanding and sympathy for the women's movement after doing her article) and not wanting to be perceived as a militant or a radical. And of course, some women totally disagreed with everything the women's movement was saying; in their opinion, being a housewife was in fact the best of all possible worlds. One *Time* expert suggested the problem had started when women were encouraged to go to college. "Until very recently, wives were simply supplementary to their husbands, and not expected to be full human beings . . . [When women go] to liberal arts colleges, . . . the professors take them seriously, and this gives them big ideas. The unhappiest wives are the liberal arts [college] graduates. The trouble comes from the fact that . . . marriage can't hold two full human beings; it was only designed for one and a half."[45] Such rhetoric made great fodder for talk shows, where it mainly rehashed all the old stereotypes, even as some women appeared on radio and TV to try to disprove them. And where in the early 1960s, the decidedly unphotogenic but very articulate Betty Friedan had often been asked to discuss her book, by the early 1970s, some women in the movement were upset that Gloria Steinem was getting most of the requests from TV stations. Granted, she was the cofounder of *Ms.* magazine and an articulate speaker on women's liberation, but it seemed she was being requested not because of what she had to say, but because male reporters enjoyed looking at her. The belief that women who were not pretty would be ignored seemed to be coming true even when the subject was feminism.

Women's pages in newspapers were also confronted with the problem of how to deal with the women's movement. By the end of the 1960s, many women's pages had shifted away from food and fashion and more toward issues that affected women's lives, such as child care or working part time and still raising the kids the right way. Several of the women reporters who did have kids were dismayed that male assignment editors did not think "women's issues" were particularly newsworthy; Susan Stamberg and Nina Totenberg of National Public Radio would each remark in the early 1970s that one thing they liked about the new network was the freedom to do stories about these very real problems and discuss how women were coping with them. But because the mainstream media offered such a negative portrayal of feminism, some of the women who had founded NOW and a few other young feminists decided to do something that would ensure fair and accurate coverage of the emerging women's movement—remember, there was *no* bra-burning at the first Miss America protest, and no, not all the "women's libbers" were angry man haters. Feeling that issues important to women were too often trivialized or misstated by male journalists, they decided to create a new magazine, different from the so-called women's magazines, to express very clearly what women wanted. The magazine was called *Ms.*, in protest of the fact that all men, married or single, were called Mister, whereas women were defined by whether they had a husband (Mrs.) or did not (Miss). Believing this should not matter, they created the word *Ms.* (It was a word the *New York Times* refused to recognize until the mid-1980s.)

Co-founder Gloria Steinem, who, as mentioned earlier, was the antithesis of the myth about feminists being ugly man haters, continued making the rounds of the talk shows in the early 1970s. But all too often, Ms. Steinem found herself either addressing the fact that she was pretty yet she believed in feminism or being placed on a talk show where her views were treated with condescension. She tried to explain the need for a magazine like *Ms.*, saying that most women's magazines were really vehicles of consumerism, persuading women to look a certain way and maintain an identity the advertisers had constructed for them. As might be expected, the mainstream media did not seem eager to embrace her point of view. But whether people agreed with the views expressed in *Ms.* (not everyone did—one common complaint about the women's movement was that it looked down on women who had chosen to stay home and be housewives), at least it provided one more forum for women's issues to be discussed.

I was working in album rock during the early to mid-1970s, and I do not recall many stations that discussed feminism. Despite the revolutionary pose, and the anti-establishment rhetoric, at album rock stations, the "chicks" were still paid less than the men (I was music directing at a major station when I discovered that my male assistant made more than I did; when I asked about it, I was told I was making excellent money for a woman). The prevailing attitude still seemed to be that since the station had a female announcer (usually doing late nights and usually expected to sound sexy—I was told I did not sound sexy enough), and some females even had the title of music director, there was nothing for us to complain about. But many of the women in radio, while happy to have a job, still felt that they were not being taken seriously. In the 1960s, however, there were not enough of us for our concerns to be noticed. However, that, too, was about to change.

New Laws Help Women Get Hired

In broadcasting, the early 1970s were an especially important time for women—a time when for the first time, stations were under government and FCC mandate to hire more women and minorities. It was not accidental that from 1970 through 1973, more women, myself among them, were suddenly hired. In fact, many of today's best-known TV reporters found jobs during that period of time: Connie Chung, one of the first Chinese-American reporters (1971); producer and correspondent Sylvia Chase (also 1971); *60 Minutes* correspondent Lesley Stahl, another former woman researcher who had been denied the chance to become a reporter for far too long (1972); CNN's Judy Woodruff (1970). But not every woman found instant success on TV—at least one was the subject of what proved to be a disastrous experiment, which may have set back the cause of giving women prime-time anchor slots. To be fair, Sally Quinn had no TV experience; she was a writer (she became famous writing for the "Style" section of the *Washington Post,* and for giving parties that the biggest names wanted to attend). Yet in 1973, in a decision that seemed to be largely based on her being attractive, CBS put her on the air as a coanchor for their morning TV news show. She lasted only three months, as the critics ridiculed how ill at ease she was on camera, even though she showed flashes of cleverness and wit. Why CBS did not choose one of the many experienced women journalists to coanchor is a mystery, but suffice it to say that the failure of this experiment was used as an excuse for not letting other women anchor in prime time for a few more years.

Meanwhile, some of the same AM stations that had previously refused to have women on the air decided that they really needed to find a woman announcer after all. Their reasons were not totally altruistic: it was fairly obvious that the laws were about to change some more. President Johnson had issued an executive order in 1967 making it illegal to discriminate against women in the hiring process (discrimination against a person because of race, religion, or national origin had already been made illegal in 1964, and now a person's gender could not be used as an excuse to discriminate); by 1970, the FCC decided to institute Equal Employment Opportunity (EEO) regulations for broadcasting. Stations were now required to fill out annual paperwork to show what they had done to foster diversity or run the risk of their license not getting renewed. For that reason, many stations quickly hired a token female, usually putting her on overnights or weekends, day parts the management felt would not hurt the ratings (back then, overnights were not rated; in fairness to doing things that way, most of the new announcers, both male and female, got their start on that shift). Some of the newly hired women also were asked to be music director, as I previously discussed; but what was different now was how we were classified: our title was upgraded to an executive position so it would appear that women were in decision-making positions at more stations. In reality, while the title was upgraded and so were the hours, the pay was not, nor was the attitude the men at most stations had about women who wanted to be managers. Few music directors that I know were treated like executives. When I was at WMMS-FM, a major album rocker in Cleveland, the general manager told me I would be responsible not only for music directing, but for typing the daily logs and doing office work for him; my male predecessor had never been asked to perform any secretarial functions. Another female music director I knew was expected to get her boss coffee, run errands for him, and do his typing in addition to music directing. But on the EEO paperwork, we were both listed as "management." And yet, while I was being underpaid and treated like a glorified secretary, WMMS-FM did something very ahead of its time—the station hired a woman announcer for the morning time slot. Women were seldom, if ever, given this shift. The woman they hired was an experienced album rock announcer named Debbie Ullman; for a number of reasons, she did not stay at WMMS much longer than I did. When she left, the shift went back to being done by a male. To this day, few women are put into the morning show except as sidekicks, whose job it is to laugh at the male host's jokes. More will be said in the next chapter about women as morning show sidekicks.

Women and Sports

One other important legal milestone for women of the early 1970s, and not just for women in radio or TV, occurred when Congress passed Title IX (The Education Amendments of 1972). Suddenly, discrimination against women in athletics was no longer permitted; schools and colleges could no longer put all of their resources into boys' sports and do virtually nothing for girls. This would, of course, lead to stronger programs in women's college sports and ultimately to the founding of some women's professional leagues so that talented college players would have a future in sports after they graduated. But in 1967, women were still forbidden from certain events, such as the Boston Marathon. In an embarrassing scene, a male marathon official who noticed that it was a woman running as number 261 tried to forcibly push her off the course. (Her coach, Arnie Briggs, who objected to women runners being excluded, had entered her as K. Switzer, and not knowing the "K." was for "Kathy," officials had given Briggs the number 261 for his presumably male runner. Another woman, Roberta Gibb, had run and completed the race for two years but without getting an official number or any recognition.) Women would not be officially allowed to run the Boston Marathon until 1972.

Meanwhile, also in 1967, Bernice Gera went to Umpire School, and embarked upon the attempt to become baseball's first female professional umpire—evidently those who keep track of "firsts" did not know about or consider the efforts of women who umpired men's games in the 1920s, or perhaps because these women were not part of the major league baseball scheme of things, what they did was not considered "professional." In any event, after legal battles over being denied equal opportunity, Bernice Gera finally won the right to umpire minor league games in 1972, but her career lasted only one game; the hostility she encountered made her rethink her plan, and she quit baseball. Later in the 1970s, another woman, Pam Postema, also became a minor league umpire, and by the early 1980s, she had moved up to the Triple A level; but despite good evaluations, she was never chosen to be a major league umpire, and she finally gave up her fight, retiring after thirteen frustrating years of umpiring in the minors, with nowhere else to go.

Sports-talk radio stations were slow to champion the idea of equality in athletics; the audience at such stations tended to be mostly male, and evidently they believed women should not be umpires, because Ms. Postema received little support. It would not be until the late 1990s before any of the men's professional sports accepted women as referees or umpires—in 1997, two women (Dee Kantner and Violet Palmer) were hired to referee some games in the National Basketball Association. But in the 1970s, women were mainly trying to gain acceptance doing hard news; women's acceptance as sportswriters or sports reporters would be a few years away.

The Audience Moves to FM

While the Watergate scandal dominated the headlines and culminated in Richard Nixon resigning in disgrace after it was shown that he knew about and orchestrated break-ins at the offices of his political enemies, another change was occurring in broadcasting. It was not as dramatic as a presidential scandal, but it was certainly a major transition in listening habits: AM radio was gradually being replaced as a music vehicle by FM. The AM audience got older (people who had listened to AM during the big band era were accustomed to AM, so they stayed with it), while the young people, who did not have years of history with AM, migrated to the FM dial when they felt AM no longer met their needs. Big Band Nostalgia formats (called "Music of Your Life") found a home on AM because of the older listeners who had remained loyal; talk formats would find a new home on AM, too.

As music moved to FM, that included Top 40, which joined the album rock stations that were already there. Suddenly, the women announcers at the FM album stations, who previously had only a cult following among the fans of album rock, began to gain a much wider and more mass appeal audience, and became better known. A number of other music formats were developed and put on FM in the 1970s: one of the most successful combined black Top 40 hits with key album tracks (it was called Urban Contemporary). Later in the 1970s, a dance music permutation of Urban Contemporary targeted young adults who went to the clubs; it was at first known as Disco. A new format that tried to attract young women listening at work was Adult Contemporary, which featured hits that were softer and more melodic. FM radio—which had once been perceived as radio for hippies—was trying to reach a wider audience by becoming more commercial and more acceptable to sponsors. FM owners wanted to make money like AM owners did, and even album rock was forced to become more hit oriented to attract a wider audience. But no matter what the format, following the FCC's ruling, managers made sure there was at least one woman on the air, even on a part-time basis.

One other change occurred during this time: the music at FM rock stations became increasingly more male. Where in the early days of progressive and free-form, there were some female vocalists and songwriters whose work received airplay, rock groups were more and more often ". . . male bands who . . . had their own legends to build. A rock band was a male team. They were also the boys the [girl groups] sang about, supposedly tough, rebellious, lonely, indifferent to the future. They liked girls, but they could take or leave them. One part of the rock genre formula was disrespect for women not only in the dearth of women in the bands but in the lyrics of popular rock songs . . ."[46] I can certainly remember songs like "[Look At That] Stupid Girl" and "[She's] Under My Thumb"; frequently played songs like Led Zeppelin's "Stairway to Heaven" or the Eagles' "Lyin' Eyes" portrayed women as vain, mercenary, and unfaithful. If there was a musical backlash to the women's movement, it showed up in some of the lyrics of rock songs, where once more, women were villains who could not be trusted and who only caused men endless trouble.

And just like when the books that espoused Freud's theories received more publicity than they deserved because few women were in positions of authority to refute them, rock, too, had become a world where few women were front and center; a woman could occasionally be the lead singer of a male band if her sound was tough enough (like the late Janis Joplin, who had several hits before dying of a drug overdose in 1970, when she was only twenty-seven); but 1970s rock was a world where the point of view was usually male, and there were very few women to refute what the songs accused them of doing.

The Women of NPR

As Top 40 and album rock became more and more male, the one bright spot in radio for many women during the 1970s was National Public Radio (NPR). NPR was incorporated in February 1970 and began broadcasting in the spring of 1971 (and speaking of 1971, that was the year when women journalists were finally admitted as members of the National Press Club, showing that change really does happen slowly—there had been women journalists in America since the time of the colonies). NPR established itself as a base for a number of outstanding women journalists, as well as a network where social issues that the mainstream media often ignored were discussed in much greater depth than the commercial stations allowed. One of NPR's first women journalists was Linda Wertheimer, who joined the new radio network during its initial year. She recalled watching, while growing up, Pauline Frederick on TV and wanting to do what Pauline was doing, but when she applied for news jobs, one executive at NBC told her she would be much happier as a researcher, which was still considered a more "suitable" job for women than on-air news reporting.[47]

The arrival of NPR was a blessing for Wertheimer and for other young women journalists like Susan Stamberg, who also joined NPR during its early days. Stamberg anchored a nightly news magazine show called *All Things Considered*. She looked back on the history of NPR in a 1993 book called *Talk;* there were excerpts from some of her best interviews of the 1970s and 1980s, conversations with both celebrities and newsmakers, from jazz great Dave Brubeck and ballerina Dame Margot Fonteyn to civil rights pioneer Rosa Parks and former Watergate coconspirator John Ehrlichman. When Susan Stamberg and Linda Wertheimer first worked at NPR in 1971, the entire staff was 65 people; by 1993, the network had 437 employees, with affiliate radio stations all over the United States.

But more important than the number of people who worked there was the fact that National Public Radio launched numerous careers. The new network was able to offer women good opportunities to get experience, not only because of NPR's mission to foster diversity, but because compared to the established networks, NPR did not pay that well yet, so experienced male journalists did not want to work there. NPR also offered the benefit of creativity: local affiliates were able to create programs about sexism, gay and lesbian rights, racism, and various other subjects the traditional networks tended to consider too contentious.

Another important woman reporter joined NPR in 1975—Nina Totenberg had come from a print journalism background. As the Washington editor for *New Times* magazine, her expertise in legal issues would later prove invaluable to NPR when it was she who first broke the story in 1991 about Anita Hill's accusations of sexual harassment against Supreme Court nominee Clarence Thomas. The mid-1970s was also when Cokie Roberts joined the NPR news staff: it was Nina Totenberg and Linda Wertheimer who helped her get hired. As mentioned earlier, one of Cokie's mentors and heroes had been Nancy Dickerson, the first woman correspondent for CBS-TV. And in contrast to the myths about female jealousy and ego, these three NPR newswomen became close friends; they still remained so over thirty years and several networks later.

Looking Good for TV News

In TV news, things were getting better, as some of the new breed of news reporters of the 1970s were given more opportunities to do the kind of reporting that Nancy Dickerson or Pauline Frederick had to fight for. Radio news, by and large still on AM, had a few women reporters, but opportunities were limited there because the radio networks still relied on many of the male commentators they used on TV. But at the local level, a few more women were getting hired, and the number of women at all-news radio stations would slowly but surely expand in the 1980s. But TV was where most young journalists wanted to be, even if they did get a radio job to start. And if a woman was attractive, she could move up quickly. The down side to TV, of course, was still the emphasis on looks—an emphasis still imposed more on women than on men in the 1970s. As Judith Marlane commented in her book about TV news, "The double standard for appearance and age communicates itself daily in the media and reinforces the secondary status of women who are striving to compete with men on an equal footing. Since beauty is subjective, the male-dominant culture sets the standard of acceptance. In television, a visual medium, the bar is set higher for women."[48] Veteran TV anchor Andrea Mitchell agreed. "These are old boys networks in many ways. The people making the decisions are all male . . . and when they choose women [to be on the air], they often choose women who represent their own fantasy lives, not necessarily the best journalists."[49] A good example of this was Jessica Savitch, who began her TV career in 1971. She had previously been one of radio's few female disc jockeys, at an AM Top 40 station, WBBF in Rochester. But soon, she was moving up quickly through the TV ranks: Houston, Philadelphia, and then, in 1977, an NBC network slot, where she would be groomed as an anchor. Many of her detractors said she had progressed too quickly and felt that she had never really learned how to do quality reporting; they said she was being rewarded for looking lovely on camera. While a certain amount of sniping at the latest boy or girl wonder can be expected, analysis of her career (she died young, in a car accident; prior to that, she was on the verge of being fired, as allegations of drug use and rumors of emotionally unstable behavior swirled around her) shows a woman promoted to anchor long before she was capable of handling the pressure; there seemed to be some truth to the fact that she was promoted because of her good looks and because viewers seemed to like her.

Women Take Legal Action

Women in the 1970s who had strong radio journalism credentials but were not considered lovely were not given a chance on network TV, although they could and did continue to work behind the scenes as writers, researchers, and producers. But as a 1973 article by Sue Cameron (based on research done by the Writers Guild of America) demonstrated, women's opportunities as writers for TV were severely limited: only 2 percent of all series television scripts were written by women. This led Ms. Cameron and several other women to start an advocacy group called "Women in Film."[50] Meanwhile, at NBC, a lawsuit had been simmering since 1971; it began in Washington as female employees of WRC AM-FM and TV accused the network of denying them equal pay and equal opportunity. Where the other networks acknowledged a problem and promised to change, NBC was hostile and refused to address the concerns of the women, according to news anchor Marlene Sanders. Ultimately, a legal battle ensued, and in 1977, after intervention by the EEOC, a settlement was finally reached, but it had been a long and very costly fight that had no real winners.[51]

Also benefiting from the FCC ruling were minority women, quite a few of whom were now doing TV news: *Ebony* did an article as far back as 1966 about three successful black female reporters, whom they referred to by a term still found in broadcasting magazines—*news hens*. Evidently the two men who were the editors of *Ebony* did not stop to consider that calling an adult woman, black or white, a *hen* was somewhat patronizing (it was derived from the slang term for young women, *chicks,* thus making older women *hens*). But the point of the article was that on some levels, things were improving—racism was still a daily reality for most African-Americans, but now they could look on the news and see some reporters who looked like them working at important stations. One of the women in the article, Trudy Haynes, had started her career as a weather girl in Detroit at WXYZ-TV, having been an announcer at a suburban black radio station prior to that. Now, she was reporting for KYW-TV in Philadelphia, where she did both news and human-interest stories.[52]

Other black women were also able to persevere and find jobs in news. In Chicago, in the early 1970s, Carole Simpson was a radio news reporter for WCFL and then WBBM. By 1974, she had moved into doing local TV news at NBC affiliate WMAQ-TV; she then was promoted to reporter for NBC's Midwestern Bureau and next, the network relocated her to Washington, D.C., to work at affiliate WRC-TV. In 1982, she was hired away by ABC news and became an award-winning anchor and correspondent. Andrea Roane first worked as an education reporter for public television's WYES-TV in New

Orleans in 1975. Her career path took her to CBS affiliate WWL-TV in New Orleans, and ultimately she was hired by WETA-TV in Washington, D.C., where in the late 1970s she was host and chief correspondent of *Metro Week in Review.* In 1981, she was hired as an anchor and reporter for WUSA-TV in Washington, where she went on to win several local Emmy awards. It is doubtful that these success stories would have occurred for a woman of color until the 1960s or 1970s. And in a note of irony, when Carole Simpson first applied to Northwestern University to attend journalism school, the admissions counselor refused to admit her, telling her basically that she was wasting her time, since neither TV nor radio news would ever hire a black woman; it was suggested that she become an English teacher instead. Determined to prove the counselor wrong, she attended the University of Michigan, where she was the only black women in the journalism department; despite the prejudices of some people she encountered while searching for work in the late 1960s, she not only ended up with a successful career as a broadcast journalist, but Northwestern ultimately hired her to teach journalism courses.[53] Meanwhile, in radio news, a young woman of color was reporting for WVOL in Nashville circa 1973; she was then hired by WTVF-TV as its first black anchor, beginning a career that few could predict would become so influential: her name was Oprah Winfrey.

TV Makes Some Changes

A comedy and satirical show, *Laugh-in* had begun in 1968, and it changed the style of TV comedy with its quick pace, one-liners, and sly humor. Hosted by Dan Rowan and Dick Martin, it featured several comediennes, including Goldie Hawn and Lily Tomlin; while Hawn's characters were often in the "dumb blonde" mold, Tomlin's humor was much more topical and sarcastic. After the show ended in 1973, Hawn went on to many successful movie comedy roles, while Tomlin became an Emmy Award–winning writer and producer as well as a solo comic; she was also a vocal proponent of feminist causes. By the late 1960s and early 1970s, it appeared that the programming was showing a few signs of positive change in its depictions of women. *That Girl,* starring Marlo Thomas, has been a precursor to the concept of independent working women; the show began in 1966 and ran until the early 1970s. Also showing working women as intelligent people was the *Mary Tyler Moore Show,* although it always bothered me that the men on the staff called the boss Lou, whereas Mary called him Mr. Grant. On *All in the Family,* the character of Gloria often expressed a mildly feminist point of view, and one episode was even entitled "Gloria Discovers Women's Lib."

Marcy Carsey, who after college began her career as a tour guide for NBC, worked her way up the ladder, learning advertising, programming, and TV production, as well as helping to choose scripts. By 1974, she was working for ABC TV, where she ultimately was promoted to senior vice president of prime time series; among the shows she helped to create or develop at ABC were *Mork and Mindy* and *Taxi.* However, her success was the exception rather than the rule. In Sue Cameron's 1973 study, she had found that in two seasons' worth of *All in the Family* episodes, sixty-nine of them were written by men, and only 4 by women. And for every show that portrayed a woman who was intelligent, there were many more shows that featured "male fantasy" women, the type that Andrea Mitchell mentioned—one popular TV show was *Charlie's Angels,* which featured gorgeous women who often went bra-less, who worked for a male boss named Charlie at a detective agency. There was also a show featuring the beautiful yet tough Angie Dickinson as "Police Woman." Follow-up research found slight improvement in the late 1970s, but it was not substantial.

Talking About Sex on Radio

The 1970s also brought their share of contentious social issues. The most notable occurred in 1973 when *Roe vs. Wade* legalized abortion, but another was in 1976 when Congress, after much heated debate, passed legislation to make the military academies like West Point admit women. And on the radio, the programming was beginning to become somewhat more contentious, too. A far cry from the days when the FCC had a list of words that could not be said on the radio, now in Los Angeles, on station KGBS, there was a controversial program called *Feminine Forum.* It featured announcer Bill Ballance getting his mostly female listeners to talk intimately about their sex lives. He insisted to the news magazines that he was not trying to scandalize anyone and that he saw himself as a counselor, helping women with their personal problems. His critics, however, found his show vulgar and patronizing and felt he only talked about sex for the shock value. The FCC would be called upon to pass judgment on the show in 1973, and while it was not banned, it also was not looked upon favorably. The FCC had a difficult time trying to establish a standard for what was "obscene," but the increasing tastelessness and so-called trash talk on radio would come under fire numerous times. Unfortunately for its detractors, it also received good ratings, making station owners willing to endure the controversy. As for Bill Ballance, he would also be responsible for helping one woman launch her own radio career: the story goes that a woman named Laura Schlessinger was listening to his show one day in the mid-1970s and called in to respond to a question about whether women would rather be widows or divorcées if they had to choose between those two options. Ballance found her especially articulate and invited her to visit his show; soon, she began to appear on the air as his sidekick. She insisted their relationship was always that of mentor/student, but years later, he would claim they had a sexual relationship, and controversy erupted, because she was now "Dr. Laura," the popular advice giver, whose message was based on biblical morality.

The Year of the Woman

In 1975, the International Women's Year, numerous magazines discussed the progress women had been making. *Time* named as its Man of the Year a number of important women who had been newsmakers. Among the changes mentioned were the importance of tennis star Billie Jean King (who even defeated male chauvinist Bobby Riggs in a match) in raising the pay of women athletes; Judge Susie Sharp was serving with distinction on the North Carolina State Supreme Court and had been elected her state's first woman chief justice; Carol Sutton was the first woman managing editor of a major news daily, the *Louisville Courier-Journal;* Charlotte Curtis was the editor of the *New York Times'* editorial page; and Barbara Walters was now cohost of the *Today* show. At the end of 1975, Walters commented on the progress women in TV had made, saying she could not understand why her detractors still called her "aggressive" and "ambitious" (which in those days meant "ruthless," reminiscent of Lady Macbeth) when all she had done throughout her career was try to do her job well. (Walters's celebrity had even affected the popular culture: a new TV show called *Saturday Night Live* came on the air in 1975, and among its cast was comedienne Gilda Radner, who did an amazingly accurate, and very amusing, imitation of her.) Sally Quinn, now a journalist for the *Washington Post,* remarked on the sexist hiring practices that permeated TV. "[The men who hired me] wanted a little blonde with some newspaper experience. They thought I was a cute, little flashy thing." And all of the women in the article commented that although more women were getting hired, they were under immense pressure to succeed immediately, and there was little margin for error.[54]

The Women's Movement Affects Social Change

But like it or not, the women's movement was having an affect on the culture, as the radio craze had in the early 1920s. The language was changing to reflect changes in society—as more young women had decided to pursue higher education, a growing number were attending medical school or law school, and now the terms *woman doctor* and *woman lawyer* (as if a normal doctor was a man and a woman was somehow an exception) were becoming passé, as more doctors and lawyers in training were in fact women. But the drive to pass the Equal Rights Amendment had fallen short; most major businesses still had no women in positions of authority, and years of contradictory messages had taught many young women to fear success, because they had been told for so long that men did not want women to be too smart or too successful. And as they did in 1970, the magazines continued to juxtapose feminist concerns about equal pay or equal treatment with comments from women who said that they were very happy being homemakers and felt the women's movement did not speak to their needs at all. In 1979, *Playboy* magazine, which feminists loved to criticize for depicting women as sex objects, was now twenty-five years old, and, ironically, its new CEO would be founder Hugh Hefner's daughter, Christie, who promised the magazine would change with the times. Sexual harassment was becoming more of a news story, as instead of acquiescing in silence, women began to sue male bosses who had demanded sex in return for a job. In February 1979, *Newsweek* did a cover story about barriers still affecting women. In that article, columnist Jane Bryant Quinn could have been talking about music directors when she observed that while women had indeed made a few modest gains, "many of today's female 'executives' are functionally low-level personnel with good titles. Only a minority earn men's salaries and are involved in real corporate decision-making."[55]

Seeking Women's Music

In music, the disco craze kept growing throughout the mid-1970s, with dance music and dance clubs multiplying; some of the most successful performers in this genre were women—often called disco divas—such as Gloria Gaynor and Thelma Houston. In 1975, a new record company, Olivia Records, was founded. It was owned and operated by women and was committed to giving talented female artists a chance to make records. The idea that there was an audience for "women's music" persisted, but this, too, was a concept not easily defined: did it mean music only written and sung by women, music that was feminist in its lyrics, music that spoke about the life of the average woman? Olivia's founders wanted to include all kinds of women, whether identified as feminists or not.

Meanwhile, in radio during the late 1970s, another experiment with an all-female format took place. In 1978, a small station in Hamden, Connecticut, took the call letters WOMN. Owned by two men, the station decided to target the woman listener, and chose two veteran album rock announcers,

Cindy Bailen and Debbie Ullman, to help program it. But despite being an all-female station, the reporter who covered the story quickly reassured the readers that the station had no intention of maintaining a "stridently feminist tone." Rather, the emphasis would be on music by women, including music from the smaller labels (like Olivia, undoubtedly) and some women artists who had a strong following but never received play on Top 40 stations (and were considered too folksy for album rock stations). The sound of the station's music would be mainly soft rock, with songs that the staff believed were positive in their message about women. WOMN also produced features and public service about current events and issues related to the female listener. It was a good concept, and it did attract a loyal group of fans, but the station was not a financial success. Perhaps it was the lack of wattage (only 1000 watts on AM), or the fact that the owners lacked the big budget needed to compete with the 50,000 watt AM and FM stations, but WOMN only lasted for several years. Still, efforts such as this showed that experienced women broadcasters could create a certain sound, and that some male owners realized the female audience was not being adequately served by present options.

Assessing the Changes

In April 1976, one of the last of the women pioneers, who had probably reached the women of her day better than anyone, Mary Margaret McBride, died. Also in April 1976, a midwestern legend in women's shows, Bea Johnson, lost her battle with cancer. Mrs. Johnson had won numerous awards in her long career at KMBC in Kansas City, Missouri. Ironically, at the time when these two women, who were the epitome of what programming for women was in the 1940s and 1950s, passed away, the traditional radio women's show was also dying. Today, most of its better elements have been absorbed by TV chat shows; the kind of program that Bea Johnson or Mary Margaret McBride did so well is seldom if ever heard on radio anymore. Several more of broadcasting's pioneers passed away in the 1970s, among them Ida Bailey Allen, perhaps the best known of the nationally syndicated radio homemakers; she died in July 1973. Judith Waller, who championed educational programming during her years with NBC radio and TV, died in October 1973; and pioneer station owner Ida McNeil died in August 1974. We can only wonder how these women, who had made the most of the limited options for women in the 1940s and 1950s, felt about the dramatic changes in broadcasting, changes that in many ways spelled the end of the kinds of programs they brought to radio.

By 1978, musical trends were shifting, and women artists again were making their presence felt. *Billboard* magazine did a lengthy salute to the women in music in late February 1978: among the important hit makers were Barbra Streisand, Rita Coolidge, Linda Ronstadt, Donna Summer, Aretha Franklin, Carly Simon, and Helen Reddy, whose 1973 hit "I Am Woman" had become a sort of anthem for feminists. Ms. Reddy stated that she believed the women's movement was responsible for women performers once again being noticed.[56]

Groups like Fleetwood Mac, with its two female vocalists (Christine McVie and Stevie Nicks), were also big on the charts, being played on stations in a variety of formats. Some of the older (nonrock) vocalists like Eydie Gormé now agreed that thanks to the issues raised by the feminists, it had become more acceptable for women musicians to assert themselves; even the men were not being as chauvinistic as in the past.[57] Billboard also noted that where in 1967, only nine female singers had major Top 40 hits, in 1977 that number had risen to twenty-five women with best-selling records. In fact, in the late 1970s, the biggest format on FM was Adult Contemporary, softer hit songs for baby boomers in their twenties and thirties.

Women Newsmakers

After the Vietnam War ended and the Nixon era came to a close, President Gerald Ford's wife, Betty, became widely admired for her courage in dealing with breast cancer, as well as for her willingness to speak frankly about it. Betty Ford was very supportive of the Equal Rights Amendment (ERA) and was disappointed when it failed to become law. She became known for her no-nonsense approach to controversial issues and her willingness to discuss them with reporters. She was also very public about her past problems with alcohol and did not shy away from discussing such things during interviews. A well-respected treatment facility for substance abuse, the Betty Ford Center, not only bears her name, but she was one of its founders.

The fact that the ERA failed to win the necessary number of states to become law did not disappoint just Betty Ford. A number of feminists, who had worked hard for its passage, were equally disappointed. But it would be unfair to say every woman shared that view. The one woman widely credited with stopping ERA was Phyllis Schlafly, an educated and articulate conservative who believed that women would lose the protections she felt they already had if ERA passed. Capitalizing on the public's uncertainty about what an Equal Right Amendment would really do (would there no longer be men's and ladies' rooms?) and the mainstream media's ambivalence about women's issues, she was able to lead a successful battle against the amendment; some feminist critics felt the mainstream media tacitly endorsed her views and framed discussions on women's issues so that Schlafly came away looking very reasonable while the feminists looked impractical and extreme.[58]

Of course, the debate about women's role did not end with the failure of the ERA. In the 1970s, more talk shows came to TV, and more AM radio stations began to put talk programming into their schedule. Once again, although the genre was supposed to appeal to women, the major talk shows were hosted by men. Perhaps the best known of the 1970s TV talk shows featured Phil Donahue. This show had begun in Dayton, Ohio, in the late 1960s but was picked up for syndication by the early 1970s and, having moved its base to Chicago, went national in November 1977. Like Virginia Graham's *Girl Talk,* debate was a feature of this show. Donahue liked to schedule guests with views that were polar opposites, such as having ERA opponent Phyllis Schlafly on the same show with ERA proponent and president of NOW Eleanor Smeal. But he also became known for controversial programs about sex, including homosexuality, abortion, and vasectomy. He even did a segment about whether lesbians should be allowed to adopt children.[59] These shows, which were unusually graphic in the precable TV era, caused boycotts and protests, but Donahue continued to tackle hot button subjects. By 1979, his show was reaching over 9 million viewers and would lead to other equally controversial (and even more graphic) shows in the 1980s.

Also, a few women on TV were winning awards for their accomplishments: consumer advocate Betty Furness of NBC won a Peabody Award in 1977 for her feature *Buyline,* which pointed out fraud and showed how consumers were being deceived. The *Mary Tyler Moore Show* won a Peabody that year as well, for its "sympathetic portrayal of a career woman in today's changing society."

Women Astronauts—Almost

In 1978, after many years of women aviators fighting to be taken seriously, NASA finally chose some women to train as astronauts. Russia had already sent a woman, Valentina Tereshkova, into space as early as 1963, but years of resistance from conservatives slowed the process of accepting even highly qualified women to the U.S. space program until the late 1970s. One highly qualified woman, Jerrie Cobb, had actually been part of a planned program to put a woman into space (the so-called Apollo 13 program) in the early 1960s; but the program was quietly disbanded by NASA, even though Jerrie had passed every test that an astronaut was supposed to pass. In the pre–women's movement era, it was evidently felt that society was not ready for an American woman in space. In fact, when Congress called for hearings in 1962 to determine if the program should be revived, the most influential person to speak against it was astronaut John Glenn, who had just orbited the earth a few months earlier. He testified that men were the ones who fought the wars and designed the planes (evidently Mr. Glenn was not around during World War II when women were army nurses in combat areas, and thousands of Rosie the Riveters helped to build and test many planes). Glenn further stated that it was not part of the social order for women to be astronauts and that it might even be "undesirable" for them to do so. The program was not revived, and women like Jerrie Cobb were denied the opportunity to go into space.[60] Years later, ironically, Mr. Glenn earned the right to be the first elder American in space; competing for the honor was Jerrie Cobb, and once again, Mr. Glenn, by now a Senator, made sure he was the only one who was chosen. This time, Ms. Cobb's plight received just slightly more media attention than it had the first time around (when it barely received any).

In 1978, Jo Foxworth, president of an ad agency, wrote in her book *Boss Lady* that more women were moving into radio sales. This was an interesting trend, since women who did women's shows had always been expected to sell advertising for their own program; but now there were women who were part of the radio sales team and making more money as a result. She noted that women had yet to break into the lucrative field of TV sales but saw the advent of women in radio sales as a hopeful sign.[61] Still, as the 1970s ended, many women in broadcasting felt that advancement was still very slow. True, a handful of women had been promoted to important positions in both TV and radio: Marion Stephenson, for one example, began as a clerk in the NBC accounting department in 1944. In 1948, she was named business manager, and by 1962, she became the network's first female vice president of administration. In 1975, Marion Stephenson was named vice president and general manager of the NBC Radio Network. Yet, in an interview in 1981, she acknowledged that few women in her industry received equal pay.[62] In 1979, veteran journalist Pauline Frederick earned the Silver Satellite award from AWRT for her outstanding contributions to broadcasting, but it had taken her until the 1970s to get some of the assignments she had always deserved (including moderating the presidential campaign debates in 1976, the first woman to do so).

More women vocalists were being heard, but women announcers were still limited to the one or two token females most stations had. Beverly Magid, the radio editor for *Record World* magazine, had written a column circa 1972, musing that there were all too few radio women in upper management; at the end of the decade, that was still true. The major talk show hosts were still men. Commercials still showed women as sexual objects, and, with a very few exceptions, the protagonists on major series were male.

Still, on looking back, no one could deny that major changes to broadcasting had occurred during the 1960s and 1970s. Agree with it or not, the women's movement (and the FCC ruling) had placed the role of women back into the public discourse. If the 1950s had been an era when women were confined to a very limited set of expectations, by the end of the 1970s, it seemed that there were many more possibilities for women in broadcasting than at any time since the 1920s.

Timeline: The 1960s and 1970s

1961	Dorothy Thompson, former network commentator, dies
1963	Congress passes the Equal Pay Act
	Betty Friedan's *The Feminine Mystique* is published
	The Civil Rights Act of 1964 protects against discrimination
1964	The Equal Opportunities Commission is established
1966	National Organization for Women is founded
Late 1960s	Album/progressive rock begins to flourish on FM
1970	FCC rules that radio stations must follow EEOC laws
	Feminist Bella Abzug elected to House of Representatives
1971	*Ms.* magazine is founded
1976	Barbara Walters joins ABC, signs million-dollar contract
	Lucy Jarvis becomes producer of Barbara Walters's specials
	Pauline Frederick moderates presidential debates

Chapter 7

And Now What?
The Rest of the Story

In the early 1980s, the mass media still tended to portray feminism in a negative light, such that women who agreed with causes like equal pay would quickly point out "but I'm not a feminist." *Newsweek*, the *New York Times* magazine, and even ABC-TV all did special reports that purported to show that feminism was dead and that it had only brought women unhappiness.[1] Fortunately, there were now a few more women who had come to the forefront in both radio and TV; the presence of these successful women not only provided some positive role models for girls considering careers in broadcasting, but, more importantly, it helped to contradict some of the frequently negative reporting by men about the dangers of being a career woman. And when the major networks seemed to lack objectivity about a women's issue, there was now a new option: women could turn to the growing number of cable channels. At some of the new channels, there were mainly reruns of old TV shows and even older movies. But some of the channels were committed to doing special features and documentaries, and some hired women right from the start: Cable News Network (CNN) made its debut on June 1, 1980, and a number of women were hired as reporters and anchors; it was not unusual to see women coanchoring with men before many of the networks felt comfortable with that. In 1981, a collaboration between Home Box Office (HBO) and *Ms.* magazine resulted in a documentary called "She's Nobody's Baby: A History of Women in the 20th Century," which was honored with a Peabody, perhaps the first such award for a cable presentation. But not everyone had access to cable TV yet, and documentaries about women's issues were still far fewer than the magazine articles and TV shows that cast women in a negative light. For example, there was a 1986 cover story in *Newsweek* that proclaimed a "man shortage" and warned women with careers that they ran the risk of never finding a husband and never having children. That same year, ABC-TV did a special about the same subject; Peter Jennings and several reporters kept driving home the point that feminism came at a great cost and that cost was having a home and a family.[2] It is unfortunate that this program aired in 1986 because NPR's Cokie Roberts did not join ABC until 1988; she might have had a somewhat different viewpoint, given that she was a happily married woman with children and a successful career.

The laws may have changed to make sure that women (and minorities) were hired, but the majority of the programming was still written and produced by men, some of whom clearly were not happy about the more diverse workplace. (One notable exception, as mentioned in the previous chapter, was Marcy Carsey, who in 1980 had started her own production company. In 1981, she was joined by a former ABC colleague, Tom Werner. Their company was responsible for the highly successful comedy about an upscale black family, *The Cosby Show*. Starring Bill Cosby, the show debuted in 1984 and was the first of many hits from Carsey-Werner.) But much of the progress women made in the late 1970s and early 1980s was slow, and it seldom seemed to occur spontaneously. A few lawsuits by women frustrated over lack of opportunity had sent a message to employers that they could no longer tell women to keep waiting for equal pay or for a chance to be promoted. The late 1970s and early 1980s saw a series of these legal actions—women at publications such as *Reader's Digest* and the *New York Times* won settlements in suits about discrimination in pay and hiring, as the women of NBC had done. Marlene Sanders wrote in *Waiting for Prime Time* that for a while it seemed the networks understood the need to promote women; and yet at ABC News in 1983, of nearly one hundred correspondents for the news department, only fifteen were women, and they still did not get good assignments. It took a concerted effort, led by one of the few African-American correspondents at ABC, Carole Simpson, which resulted in improvements, but those improvements were not implemented until 1986.[3]

While some women finally got their concerns addressed, others had no happy ending to their stories: in Kansas City, KMBC-TV anchorwoman Christine Craft sued for gender discrimination because she felt she had been unjustly fired. The case, which went to court in August of 1983, revolved around the fact that before firing her, the news director told her she was too old (she was thirty-six), too ugly (in a focus group, ostensibly convened to see what "typical viewers" thought of her performance, the male running the group called her a "mutt" and encouraged the people in the group to "destroy" her career), and not "deferential" to the men at the station (she was told she acted too much like an expert and interrupted the men on the staff). Although she won the case in court, the judge (whose comments later seemed quite misogynistic) threw it out and ordered a new trial. She again convinced a jury, but again the judge refused to award her any damages, and Metromedia, the parent company of KMBC, appealed the verdict to the Superior Court, which ruled against her.[4]

But although two favorable jury verdicts were overturned, and Ms. Craft ended up working in a much smaller market, the issues raised in that case attracted national attention. Once again, questions about how women in media should look and act were topics for the talk shows to discuss; increasingly, TV talk shows decided to frame discussions about women's proper role as an argument, with a "pro" spokeswoman and an "anti," making use of the old archetype of the cat fight. Certain hot button issues did lend themselves to very heated debate, but on TV talk shows like *Geraldo* (hosted by Geraldo Rivera) and *Sally* (hosted by Sally Jessy Raphael), the hosts were becoming more adept at raising ratings by raising the level of anger of the guests. The issues were seldom clarified by this sort of pseudo-discourse; guests and even the studio audience were encouraged to shout at each other, drowning out points of view that did not please them.[5] But there were some real issues to consider, although the most popular TV talk shows did not often address them: Professor Jane Shattuc noted in her study of daytime TV talk that when she analyzed the content and subject matter of every network and syndicated show for over three months in 1994, she found only six shows that addressed serious feminist themes such as sexual harassment at work, domestic violence, sexism in the classroom, and low self-esteem in girls.[6]

Ageism on TV

As daytime TV was moving farther away from discourse and more toward shock talk, it was also attempting to attract a younger audience. This naturally concerned a growing number of media women, especially those in TV news. As many of them approached middle age, they knew the issues at the heart of the Christine Craft trial could easily apply to them; even though they were successful reporters and correspondents, would they soon be arbitrarily forced out when somebody decided they no longer looked young enough? Would they have to act "deferential" in order to keep their jobs? Women on TV had worked long and hard to change the perception of their role; they no longer wanted to be seen as just attractive adornments to a male host. Where in the 1960s and 1970s stations hired a weather girl (Christine Craft, in one of her early TV jobs, had been asked by her boss to do the weather in a bathing suit), and the *Today* show had the "Today Girl," women were adamant about being seen as adult professionals and as personalities in their own right.

But old habits died hard, and there was still a persistent tendency of all too many male executives to hire beautiful women with no journalism experience, such as when CBS hired a former Miss America, Phyllis George, to be an anchorwoman, even though she had never reported news. Media critic Jack Hilton in 1980 remarked on what he called "the profusion of pretty blonde females" on TV. He wished these women were better interviewers and asked tougher questions; he compared them to "Barbie doll[s]."[7] It was easy to criticize, but in some cases, these inexperienced but pretty young reporters were set up to fail. Managers could then say they had tried to hire women, but the women just could not do the job.

Meanwhile, experienced women journalists were still being passed over for these great opportunities, and the reason was all too obvious. In late March 1994, local New York news anchor Pat Harper died, and a colleague with strong credentials of her own, Linda Ellerbee, wrote a tribute to her. Ms. Ellerbee told how in the late 1970s, despite excellent ratings and many awards, Betty Furness lost her job on the *Today* show. Miss Furness was sixty at the time and would continue to remain active in journalism; years later, she was still mystified by why she had been replaced by a twenty-six-year-old with far less experience than she had. In 1984, the same thing happened to Pat Harper, a woman with the number one rated local newscast. At WNBC in New York, she was the first woman ever to coanchor in the important 6:00 P.M. slot; throughout the 1970s and even into the 1980s, despite the gains they made, few women were anchoring in prime time. But despite Pat Harper's popularity and her credibility with the audience, management decided that a female anchor over fifty was just too old, causing Linda Ellerbee to comment:

> It is ironic—is it not?—that the business which told women not to expect promotion until they were old enough to have the same experience as the guys, later told them they could not keep their jobs because they were too "experienced" . . . I will be 50 this summer. I am still working, still on the air, but I don't kid myself. The news program I anchor is aimed at children . . . I already look old to my audience. But then, so does anyone over 20. And so it goes.[8]

Some of the veteran journalists finally did get better assignments, but as mentioned earlier, the upward move often took years: it took two decades of achievement before Marlene Sanders received her big promotion in 1976, when she was named a vice president in charge of documentaries at ABC. She was the only female news vice president at any of the networks at that time. After corporate politics at the network diminished her position, she eventually left for CBS, where she worked as a producer and correspondent. But by the late 1980s, Sanders, too, was forced out, allegedly due to budget cuts. To most media critics, her departure was one more example of the lingering belief among male executives that older women did not look good on TV; whereas older men were considered "distinguished," an older woman, no matter how much talent and experience she had, was not considered photogenic as soon as she stopped having a youthful appearance. It is not surprising that for many years, women were reticent to reveal their age, for fear they might be dismissed as "too old." Veteran broadcast journalist Judy Muller, whose extensive career in both radio and TV news began in the late 1970s, explained to a reporter why she had plastic surgery to make her face look younger. "Men can still get bald and portly. Women cannot turn grey and wrinkled . . . If I were still in radio, I don't think I would have had it done . . . But I'm in this business of a visual medium."[9] Like Judy Muller, Barbara Walters, too, was aware of the double standard of aging; despite being in her sixties, she has managed to maintain a very youthful appearance. ". . . [Y]ou have somebody like Mike Wallace who at the age of seventy-seven is still on the air and looks great . . . [but] I think different things are expected of a man. A man can look craggy, a man can have bags under his eyes, and if he's fairly trim, he can stay on . . . But a woman is different. It's reflective of . . . our whole society. It's not just television."[10]

Persistence of Sexism

Society as a whole was aging; the baby boomers, the largest demographic group, were now turning fifty and redefining what chronological age meant. Many boomers still enjoyed rock music, for example, and some of the musicians of the 1960s were still performing. A number of older men and women were still in the labor force, many in very responsible positions. As consumers, this group did not fit the myth that at a certain age, people were considered "elderly"; now the euphemism in marketing was the "mature audience." The baby boomers did not seem inclined to retire, they were interested in the new technologies, they pursued relationships, and some even returned to college to embark upon career changes that would have been unthinkable a generation ago. But society's amused tolerance of the boomers' desire to stay young did not mean that everyone was now getting equal treatment. Another entire book could be written about the lingering racism in the culture, and despite several decades of legal protections, sexism had not gone away either, although in many cases, it had gone underground. A company could no longer say to a potential candidate, "We don't hire women." But it could make a woman's life sufficiently unhappy so that she would leave. In 1989, for example, Ruth Spencer, a TV anchorwoman in St. Paul, Minnesota, sued for discrimination after she was removed from her job as coanchor, despite having been promised she would be given a large promotional campaign and status equal to her male counterpart. In trial testimony, Ms. Spencer stated that when she asked why her role had been reduced, she was told by the station's consultant that men, not women, were supposed to be the lead anchor; she was also criticized for spending too much time on her hair and makeup, despite the fact that she had frequently been told her success on TV depended on her looking good at all times (and despite the fact that all the on-air reporters, including the men, spent considerable time making sure they looked just right). While Ms. Spencer won a judgment in court, she never got her job back and ended up finding work in another city, for far less money.[11]

The downside to complaining was that a woman who did so was then perceived as a troublemaker and might never be able to get another job in broadcasting. And, as Marlene Sanders has suggested, "Women tend, by and large, not to be fighters . . . [They] would rather stay in their mid-level positions than risk being shot down on their way up the ladder . . ."[12] It is not surprising that some women, myself among them, got the message that it was advisable to silently endure a certain amount of hostility from male coworkers; this was the price we paid for being able to keep our jobs.

During the 1980s, there was still the same recurrent sexism in Hollywood, too; while there were now a handful of women in important jobs at the major studios, it was men who still had the final say in which movies were made, as Sherry Lansing found out. Ms. Lansing, a successful producer, one of the few women studio executives, was trying to get a feature film made, based on a story line in which a supposedly happily married man commits adultery with a career woman who is single. In the script, there were consequences for both of them, but she wanted to show that the man should be held more responsible for his actions because he had caused his wife so much pain when she discovered the affair. However, the man who was president of Paramount Pictures insisted that the story be rewritten, claiming the male character was too unsympathetic, and the audience would not be able to empathize with him. Only when the script was changed to the point where blame for the adultery was placed almost entirely on the career woman, making her progressively more evil and devious and the man the innocent victim of her treachery, was Paramount willing to make the film; this was a huge disappointment to both Ms. Lansing and to screenwriter James Dearden, both of whom had wanted a film that avoided the stereotypical predatory female.[13] In the ideal universe, Ms. Lansing and Mr. Dearden would have stood on their principles and refused to make such a sexist film. But both chose to remain involved, which turned out to be lucrative—proving that sexism is still popular, the movie *Fatal Attraction* made millions of dollars, and the scene where the female character is brutally killed was often greeted with cheers from the men in the theater.[14]

When Esther Shapiro, vice president of miniseries production for ABC-TV, tried to get a program done about a housewife who got fed up with her marriage and left, she found to her surprise that, although the script was based on a best-selling novel, the men at the network all refused to see its potential: their most common complaint about it was it would alienate sponsors because it was too feminist, and besides, nobody would watch it because it cast aspersions on traditional marriage. A very much watered down version of the script (with some of its allegedly feminist concerns still intact) eventually did run, and even in that form, it got huge ratings, and won an Emmy.[15] Over at CBS, one of the 1980s TV dramas that most women loved almost got cancelled several times, not for low ratings, but due to the objections of the men who ran the network. *Cagney & Lacey* was a cop show with a twist—the two cops were women, and they were friends. One was married, the other single, and neither was a brainless bimbo who was there to provide sex appeal for the male members of the cast. In fact, the show's scripts were quite realistic for early 1980s TV—as Brooks and Marsh put it, "[Cagney and Lacey] fought criminals, the chauvinism of their male fellow officers, the ignorance of their friends regarding their unusual careers, and sometimes each other—with shouting sessions in the ladies room." And although their cases did not always work out, and despite the stresses of police work, their friendship endured.[16] The show won numerous awards, including an Emmy. And yet, from day one, there were those at CBS who hated the concept and hated the show. CBS even tried to cancel it entirely, but a letter-writing campaign saved it. "The offscreen troubles of the series were almost as dramatic as the onscreen problems of its stars," wrote Brooks and Marsh. Or, as Susan Faludi explained, CBS executives like Senior Vice President of Programming Harvey Shephard believed the public would never accept a show about women police officers; he insisted that the writers "soften" the characters to make them more "feminine" and more "vulnerable" because "that's the way most Americans feel women should be."[17] CBS executives regularly meddled with scripts, toning down the parts they felt were too overtly feminist. They even forbade Gloria Steinem from making a cameo appearance on one episode, allegedly because a plot line about women's rights might be considered extreme and could offend female viewers. The two lead actresses, Sharon Gless and Tyne Daly, were told not to mention feminism, even if they appeared on talk shows. An anonymous executive explained to *TV Guide* that this was all being done for the show's own good because, otherwise, people would perceive the two women cops as militant lesbians.[18] Despite all of the behind-the-scenes problems, the show had many loyal fans; it ran until 1988.

Women Achievers in TV News

But not everything for women in media was bleak; there were definite signs of improvement in a number of places. Even the books about careers in broadcasting had changed to reflect the new reality of more women and minorities being hired. Unlike the career guides of earlier decades, which only portrayed white men, *Opportunities in Broadcasting,* written by Elmo Ellis in 1981, included illustrations of women and minorities in a variety of radio and TV jobs and stated that while most executives were still white males, women and minorities were making their presence felt at every level.[19] And as the 1980s became the 1990s, in more and more cases, talent and determination (and perhaps the threat of class action lawsuits) finally paid off, enabling experienced women journalists to get the promotions, the raises, and the respect they deserved. Barbara Walters became a coanchor of ABC's successful newsmagazine *20/20* in 1984; in the 1990s, her interviews of famous people continually garnered huge ratings, and she was one of the creators of a women's talk show called *The View.* She was also among the highest paid women on TV, and the fact that she was in her sixties seemed to be a nonissue. Jackie Judd, who had begun her career anchoring for National Public Radio, went to CBS radio in 1982 as a news anchor and was a member of the press corps that covered the presidential primaries; unlike what Pauline Frederick had endured in the 1940s and 1950s, Judd covered the candidates and their policies, rather than what their wives were wearing. By the 1990s, she was a special correspondent for ABC News and was the first reporter to break the story about the scandal involving President Bill Clinton and his intern Monica Lewinsky in 1998. Other NPR alumnae, Nina Totenberg and Cokie Roberts, were also working with ABC; Ms. Totenberg reported on legal issues, and Roberts did some anchoring, including filling in for Ted Koppel on *Nightline,* as well as coanchoring *This Week with Sam Donaldson and Cokie Roberts.* Diane Sawyer was named coanchor of the CBS morning news in 1981, and in 1984, she became the first woman correspondent on CBS's top-rated news magazine *60 Minutes;* in the 1990s, she became an anchor for ABC's *Prime Time Live.* Lesley Stahl, another award-winning journalist who had been CBS's White House correspondent during the 1980s, became a coeditor of *60 Minutes* in 1991. In 1999, one of the best known African-American journalists in Washington, D.C., J.C. Hayward, was beginning her twenty-sixth year at WUSA-TV, where she had won several local Emmy Awards and the Board of Governors Award for outstanding achievement. Ms. Hayward was not only a news anchor and a producer of documentaries, but in her long career she had interviewed such luminaries as former First Lady Nancy Reagan and opera singer Luciano Pavarotti. She also covered major news events such as the arrival of South Africa's Nelson Mandela for his first visit to the United States. In June 2000, the Society of Professional Journalists inducted her into their Journalism Hall of Fame, along with Ann Compton of ABC News. Ms. Compton had been promoted from ABC's Chief House of Representatives Correspondent (a position she attained in 1987) to become the first woman on any major network to cover the White House full time. In 1988 and 1992, she had also been a member of the panel during the presidential campaign debates. Ms. Compton was another female journalist who had managed to balance her career with a happy marriage and a family. As the 1990s ended, she had been chosen as a correspondent on ABC's daily Internet newscast.

In 1983, the Cable News Network (CNN) hired a young woman who had been working for WJAR-TV in Providence as a graphics designer. But it did not take long for CNN to recognize her talent as a reporter and her knowledge of international politics; as the decade progressed, so did the career of Christiane Amanpour, who became one of the decade's rising stars and CNN's Senior International Correspondent. Throughout the 1980s and 1990s, she reported from all the world's trouble spots, including Bosnia, Somalia, Northern Ireland, and the Persian Gulf, winning numerous awards along the way and proving in no uncertain terms that a female reporter could get the story even in a war zone. Ms. Amanpour also became a correspondent for CBS's long-running news show *60 Minutes.*

Speaking of international politics, CNN's correspondent in South Africa was hired in 1999, but she was not a novice in journalism. Charlayne Hunter-Gault had a distinguished career, including twenty years with PBS. In 1997, she left for a position as chief correspondent in Africa for National Public Radio, based in Johannesburg, South Africa, and remained with NPR until CNN hired her. Ms. Hunter-Gault was the first black woman to ever attend the University of Georgia, and after she graduated, she first went into print journalism before becoming an award-winning TV correspondent. And there was also Katie Couric, who at one time had been told she looked too young to do news. She advanced from working as a CNN producer and correspondent to joining NBC in 1989, and then being promoted to anchor of the *Today* show in 1991.

More Positive Roles for Woman on TV

The 1980s and 1990s were a time when women's roles were redefined yet again. In addition to the previously mentioned women police officers on *Cagney & Lacey* in the 1980s, the 1990s brought a female commanding officer in the Star Trek series *Voyager:* Starship Captain Kathryn Janeway was able to do in science fiction what Jerrie Cobb had not been allowed to do in real life. But there was an all too real tragedy in space in January 1986, when the *Challenger* exploded not long after liftoff. Among the multicultural seven-member crew on board were two women: teacher-in-space Christa McAuliffe and astronaut Judith Resnick. President Reagan immediately appointed a committee to study what went wrong, and among its thirteen members was the first American woman to go into space, astronaut and astrophysicist Sally Ride. The committee's report pinpointed real problems in the space program. Ms. Ride, who had never enjoyed being in the media spotlight, reiterated the committee's concerns during one of her rare TV interviews; she stated that she was not yet ready to go back into space until the shuttle's safety flaws were corrected.[20]

By the early 1990s, women characters on TV were showing up in a number of more positive and inspirational ways. One series that began in 1993, *Dr. Quinn, Medicine Woman,* featured a character who was strong yet compassionate, a female physician in the old West (played by Jane Seymour); she won over the skeptics, became mother to three orphans, and solved various of the townspeople's problems. Another well-received TV show of the 1990s was *Touched by an Angel,* which featured three angelic messengers, sent to earth to help human beings who had difficult problems. The concept was not new—there had even been a somewhat similar program from the 1980s, *Highway to Heaven,* which featured two male angels; but on this equally popular 1990s version, the lead character was female—the older and wiser angel known as Tess, portrayed by Della Reese. She was accompanied by two younger angels, Monica and Andrew—the three angels always imparted a moral lesson in each week's story, while teaching about drawing closer to God. (Della Reese had been a successful pop music vocalist in the 1950s; in addition, she served as an ordained minister and a gospel singer.) Certainly women as God's representatives was a step up from women as domesticated witches, even if we allow for the superb acting and comic skill of Elizabeth Montgomery in the 1960s. In comedy during the early 1990s, Fran Drescher's character on *The Nanny* proved to be a very polarizing one—male critics found her whiny and annoying, while female viewers regarded her as a woman who knew how to get what she wanted.[21]

And then, along came *Ellen,* an entertaining series about a bookstore manager and her assorted friends. This comedy, which first went on the air in 1994, turned into a controversy when comedienne and star Ellen DeGeneris came out as a lesbian during one memorable episode. It was the subject of a 1997 cover story in *Time* magazine and a topic of conversation on numerous talk shows. Sexual orientation was still taboo on most networks, unless it was being played for shock value on one of the outrageous talk shows. *Ellen* attempted to handle the subject with taste and humor, but the controversial subject matter made advertisers and many viewers uncomfortable. The show was cancelled in 1998, amidst accusations from fans that it had been cancelled because of prejudice against gay people. The network insisted it had been cancelled simply because, like all too many comedies, it had ceased to be funny. Still, some critics praised the show for its courage in tackling a contentious issue and for using humor that was neither patronizing nor vulgar.

Another show that the critics praised was *Murphy Brown,* which began in 1988. It, too, began its life as a comedy, with little indication of anything controversial. *Murphy Brown* starred Candace Bergen as a female reporter for a TV newsmagazine, and the series probably would have remained pleasant but unremarkable had Bergen's character not decided in a 1991 episode to have a child out of wedlock. (Murphy had gotten pregnant after briefly getting back together with her ex-husband.) When this plot line surfaced, it was attacked in a May 1992 speech by Republican Vice President Dan Quayle, who saw this as one more example of how America had lost its morality and how TV was encouraging what he called a "poverty of values."[22] The sudden controversy actually helped the show—it went to the top of the ratings later that year. And while there were certainly the usual amount of soap opera roles where women were either long-suffering wives or treacherous whores, it was no longer unusual to see women portrayed in many diverse roles, including detectives, corrections officers, nurses, doctors, lawyers, and journalists. There were working moms, too, and in some of the plot lines, men even helped around the house. With roles as wide-ranging as starship captains and guardian angels, TV's female characters in the 1980s and 1990s were a far cry from some of the brainless but beautiful girls of the 1950s and 1960s, whose main occupation seemed to be husband hunting. Even many comedies of the 1980s and 1990s showed women as much more independent, most notably in *Roseanne*, in which the lead character, a working-class female, was sarcastic, outspoken, and unwilling to be pushed around. Some of these character developments led feminist critics to hope that perhaps TV had begun to show a more positive attitude about women. But all was not perfect yet: even shows that had successful and attractive career women often maintained the old plot line in which their personal life was a disaster, as if to continue putting forth the message that a woman could have one but not the other.[23]

The cultural archetypes of women had not really changed that much, as a number of movies of the 1980s and 1990s show. All too often, women were still portrayed as either helpless victims or treacherous villains. The previously mentioned 1987 thriller *Fatal Attraction* maintained the tradition of making the career woman a symbol of evil, depicting her as neurotic and dangerous, while the stay-at-home wife, the long-suffering woman whose husband had cheated on her, was treated much more sympathetically in the plot. And although an occasional film like *Thelma and Louise* depicted strong women (even if they were criminals), the subplot of many films of the 1980s and 1990s was still that all a woman really needed was the right man, and a woman who loved her career was somehow not to be trusted. The mixed messages about women's place had not gone away either. For every positive working woman in a TV show (*LA Law,* which ran from 1986 through 1994, even featured a successful women lawyer who had a happy, and remarkably egalitarian, relationship; the show's popularity may have contributed to the surge in applications to law school), for every female heroine who could do it all (*Xena: Warrior Princess,* a late-1990s syndicated show, featured an attractive woman who lived in ancient times; played by Lucy Lawless, Xena was athletic, courageous, adventuresome, and eager to help the oppressed), there were characters and plots that showed women making foolish decisions and needing to be rescued from their foolishness, especially on the various soap operas (which featured every stereotypic representation of women from bitches to goddesses).

Women Announcers in Some Formats

On the radio, Top 40 still remained male dominated, with an occasional exception. Women in Top 40 were mainly sidekicks, whose role was to laugh at the jokes of the male host. This had been going on since the 1960s: Judy Dibble, who worked in Top 40 in Minneapolis at station WDGY during the 1970s, told me she was always offered the role of morning-show sidekick but never once offered her own morning show.[24] On the other hand, Judy was the first woman in the Twin Cities to do Top 40 in any capacity; prior to her, women on the air were still doing the traditional women's shows, like the one at station WCCO, where Joyce Lamont was the housewife's best friend from the 1950s through the 1970s.

Top 40 was never especially friendly to women announcers; the legendary WABC in New York, a number one station for several decades, had only one woman disc jockey in its entire history, Liz Kiley, who was not hired until late 1979, and she was put on the overnight shift. The legendary Chicago disc jockey Yvonne Daniels was the first black female announcer ever hired by Top 40 WLS in Chicago; when she was hired in 1973, she, too, was put on overnights, where she remained during her entire time with the station. (Daniels, a jazz expert and mentor to numerous women in broadcasting in Chicago, worked at several other stations, mostly on FM; she died of breast cancer in June 1991.) Even when Top 40 moved over to FM, the belief that male voices sounded best in that format moved too. Women were being hired as disc jockeys in most other formats, but in Top 40, they were sidekicks on the morning show if they were on the air at all.

Judy Dibble made the best of her situation, carving out a name for herself as part of the WDGY morning team, inventing several popular morning show characters. She also created WDGY's first promotion department and was later named promotion director. As of this writing, she is publicity director for KSTP in St. Paul, Minnesota. Like Judy, there were other women in Top 40 during the 1980s and 1990s who were witty, creative, and articulate, yet it never seemed to lead to anything more than the sidekick job. At KKBT-FM, an urban/black station in Los Angeles, Shirley Clark spent much of the 1990s as part of the morning team; she did the news, interviewed celebrities, and acted as sidekick, the way women did in other formats. (During her career, she worked in Chicago for a while, where she had the privilege of meeting Yvonne Daniels, who encouraged her and helped her.) In 1994, Ms. Clark told a reporter that she was feeling some frustration about her status. Despite nearly twenty years of radio experience and a large following, ". . . this male-dominated, male run industry does not see a woman in a position of having her own morning show."[25]

Of course, being a sidekick had its advantages, too—such as not having the pressure that was always on the host of the show. And also, at some stations, the sidekick job became quite lucrative once the morning show made a name for itself. Much like the secretary to a famous person, a sidekick who was part of a successful morning show derived the benefits along with the host; the best example of this in the 1980s and 1990s was Robin Quivers, whose role as a member of the highly rated and very controversial Howard Stern show made her famous, too. But whether on a high-profile show or not, the female sidekick's main job was to serve as an appreciative audience and interact with the host; once in that role, there seemed to be no getting out. Media critic Frank Ahrens wrote about this phenomenon, "By and large, radio program directors . . . tend to be men, and many have set-in-stone ideas about what women ought to do on the radio . . . Program directors are used to hearing women give traffic and read news, so that's something . . . they hire them to do. And when the morning-show 'zoo' concept took off a couple of decades ago, one of the necessary ingredients, market studies showed, was a female voice, whose role would often be limited to laughing at the male deejay's jokes . . . The male host is known as the 'actor'; the female sidekick is the 'reactor.'[26]

But if Top 40 remained stuck in old patterns, formats like Urban/dance featured women announcers in all dayparts. Despite a backlash against so-called disco, a number of dance-oriented radio stations had continued to do well in the 1980s and 1990s: at one New York station of the late 1980s, WQHT-FM ("Hot 103"), Mary Thomas was among the most popular members of the air staff. Ms. Thomas, who died of cancer in 1999 at age fifty-five, was among the best-known dance music announcers in New York during the 1980s, working at Kiss-FM, WBLS, as well as Hot 103, and making an excellent salary for doing so. But even with the urban/dance format, the morning shift was still usually done by a male at the majority of stations; morning newscasters, however, were often female.

There were a few exceptions to the dearth of women in morning drive. One woman who ran the morning show on and off throughout the 1990s was Barbara "Babs" Carlson, morning show host on talk station KSTP-AM, St. Paul, Minnesota. An outspoken and controversial personality, to her fans she was seen as a courageous nonconformist with a biting sense of humor, who was not afraid to take a stand on a contentious issue. To her detractors, she was seen as gossipy, flamboyant, and vulgar, a woman who would do anything to get attention (she once did her show from a hot tub). Like her or hate her, Babs Carlson had the ability to generate discussion (and get herself talked about), an essential part of a good morning show. But whereas a male host like Howard Stern could be vulgar, and the audience did not seem to mind, there was considerable discomfort when a female announcer veered into that territory; society did not seem quite ready to accept women who wanted to talk about sex, unless they were doctors or counselors like Dr. Ruth Westheimer, whose syndicated shows and frequent guest appearances were well received. There were a few other women who did morning radio shows during the 1980s and 1990s, but they were very much in the minority. One woman who had done a morning chat show during the 1970s found that it led to a career on TV in the 1980s. Popular *CNN Headline News* anchor Lynne Russell began her radio career at a small station in Ft. Collins, Colorado (she had been in college studying nursing); her next job took her to Florida, where she hosted a news and interview morning show on WKAT, a talk station in Miami. She worked there from 1971 to 1978, even becoming program director. In 1978, she left radio and became a reporter and anchor at WTLV-TV in Jacksonville, Florida; she was anchoring at KENS-TV in San Antonio, Texas, when she was hired by CNN in 1983. (According to her biographical sketch on the network's website, she also had one of the most varied backgrounds in broadcasting—in addition to having been a talk show host and working as a news anchor, she was a licensed private investigator and had served as a deputy sheriff; she also had a martial arts black belt. Needless to say, she must have done some interesting talk shows.)

Controversial Talk Show Hosts

While a few women were talk hosts, they were still a distinct minority; in 1999, *Talkers* magazine noted that out of the top one hundred most successful radio shows, only sixteen were done by women, and of those, the majority were in the advice-giving genre, as opposed to politics or sports or current events. Historically, radio's women have not done the kind of confrontational and controversial shows that became so popular on TV. But the men who began doing them found a niche on radio with an increasingly angry and often conservative audience. Talk shows had not been so hostile in the previous generation; there were still rules about what you could and could not say on the air. Then the FCC proceeded with deregulation of broadcasting, and among the rules that was abandoned was the so-called Fairness Doctrine. After 1981, radio no longer had to present both sides of an issue, which opened the door for talk shows that were much more one-sided. Radio's women's shows had nearly all vanished, victims to the changing lifestyles of Americans, many of whom were working longer hours to pay the bills and did not have hours to spend cooking or sewing. The number of stay-at-home moms had also declined, which became another subject for talk shows to debate. (There were a few cooking shows still on the air on TV and to a lesser degree on radio; the TV shows were most often done by male chefs, although Julia Child did make a name for herself on the cooking show she hosted for many years. TV cooking shows became sufficiently popular in the 1990s to have a cable channel, the Food Network, feature them. (Interestingly, though food is supposed to be a female area of expertise, the majority of the chefs on the Food Network as of late 1999 were men.)

The style of the talk show on radio was still informational and erudite at some stations (David Brudnoy of WBZ in Boston was frequently praised by critics as one of a very few talk hosts who still engaged in dialogue rather than shouting matches; several of the NPR talk hosts were similarly praised), but an increasing number of shows had gone to the confrontational mode. Perhaps the best known and highest rated of the male hosts in this genre was Rush Limbaugh, who frequently used feminists (whom he sometimes called "femi-nazis") as the object of his criticism and his scorn. He made statements that feminism had actually made things worse for women and also accused women who wanted to pursue careers of being antifamily. In one of his most frequently quoted remarks, he said, "Feminism was established so that unattractive women could have easier access to the mainstream of society." He later claimed during a TV interview that he was only speaking in jest, although he made similar remarks on his radio show quite often.[27]

In a culture where the roles of women had continued to change, it is not surprising that once again, as we saw in previous decades, there were people (often men) who articulated a wish to return to the days when more traditional roles were maintained, and who attacked those they perceived as having caused problems (among Limbaugh's other targets were gay people, "Big Government," and Democrats). But, during the 1990s, there was one controversial talk show done by a woman that took working mothers to task as often as the shows done by conservative men did. Dr. Laura Schlessinger's show became a lightning rod for controversy; it was not the kind of talk show women had traditionally done. Although the role of advice giver was nothing new for women, Dr. Laura's critics said she scolded her callers rather than giving them advice. Where many of the women doing syndicated shows played the role of the compassionate and caring professional, listening to callers' problem and helping to find a solution, Dr. Laura's style was no-nonsense, tough talk, often based on a religious framework; unlike the gentle, grandmotherly Dr. Ruth, Dr. Laura did not hide her disapproval of callers who had behaved in a way she considered immoral. In fact, on her website, she stated that the purpose of her show was to dispense morals, values, principles, and ethics. Although some of her comments were hurtful to certain groups (she made negative remarks about homosexuality, to cite one example), she also won numerous awards, especially from religious groups who felt she was making a much-needed stand for traditional values. The author of many self-help books, Dr. Laura became one of the best known of all the women on the air in the 1990s. In some markets, her syndicated advice show was number one in its daypart, something unheard of for a woman in talk radio.

Women's Status Improves

In the 1990s, it was no longer unusual to see and hear women doing TV and radio news in every daypart, including anchoring in prime time. And if women of the 1960s and 1970s had been restricted to doing human-interest stories, this was no longer the case by the 1990s. At all-news stations such as WBZ in Boston or KCBS in San Francisco, women held down the same reporting, producing, and anchoring jobs as men: there were male/female anchor teams in morning drive and often in afternoon drive, too. Numerous stations had a woman in charge of publicity, which had become an even more essential job in a competitive multimedia world where making an impression and getting noticed were increasingly more difficult. And while at most news/talk stations, the program director and general manager still tended to be men, stations now sent their female reporters out to cover as much hard news as the male reporters did.

At nearly every major radio station in the 1990s, more women than ever were in sales, and an increasing number had risen to general manager. At KMOX in St. Louis, the general manager in the late 1990s was Karen Carroll. Ms. Carroll's long career in radio sales included having been a senior vice president at American Radio Systems; in 1999, the *St. Louis Business Journal* named her one of the 25 Most Influential Businesswomen, and in 2000, she was named a Media Person of the Year by the Press Club of St. Louis.

Another woman decision maker, Cathy Hughes of Washington, D.C., became a successful owner of a growing chain of black radio stations. Hughes, one of the few African-American women owners, stated on her company's website, "I don't attempt to change the world of radio, but I attempt to create my own world where racism and sexism do not prevail, and to do that, you must be the owner."[28] As of September 1999, her company, Radio One, owned twenty-six stations, and *Forbes* magazine paid tribute to her business acumen. She was also well known for her commitment to the black community; she consistently encouraged her stations to present issues-oriented programming as well as music and has even moderated her own talk show. When the broadcasting industry magazine *Radio Ink* named the twenty most influential women in radio in August 1999, Ms. Hughes was in the top five. Her rise to such prominence had not been easy—early in her career, she was almost a one-person staff, much like Ida McNeil had been; in 1980, she had to sleep at WOL (Washington, D.C.), the first station she operated, since she could not afford to hire more help. In an interview with *Ebony*, she recalled, "I had to wash up in the public bathroom at the station," Hughes recalls. "Later I put a prefab shower in one of the offices. I cooked on a hot plate. I eventually made me an apartment in one of the offices. Though now it may sound like a terrible hardship, I loved being in the station for 24 hours. It was like a mother hen sitting on her egg waiting for it to hatch. Radio energized me. For 24 hours a day, I was available." In May 2000, her personal wealth was estimated at about $300 million.[29]

Also high up on the list of influential women in radio was Erica Farber, whose successful career in broadcasting began in radio sales; by 1992, she was named executive vice president of sales and marketing at the industry publication *Radio & Records,* and by 1994, she had been promoted to publisher and chief executive officer. Another successful and influential woman of the 1980s and 1990s was Mary Quass, whose career began in sales at

KHAK in Cedar Rapids, Iowa. By the end of the 1980s, she owned her own company and ran three stations. By the end of the 1990s, her company had merged with Capstar (later known as AM/FM Broadcasting), for whom she continued to work, overseeing many of their midwestern stations. Her tireless advocacy for local broadcasting earned her the 1999 Broadcaster of the Year Award from *Radio Ink*, and the Iowa Broadcasters Association inducted her into their Hall of Fame.

Other Influential Women

But since most sales executives and owners of radio and TV stations usually worked out of the spotlight, it was the people on the air and on camera who were much more familiar to the general public and who were usually perceived as celebrities. While Cathy Hughes was one of the most influential African-American women in broadcasting, she was nowhere nearly as well known to the average person as another woman of color, Oprah Winfrey. Oprah's career may have begun on radio, but most of her success came from her work on TV. Her amazing rise to fame as a TV talk show host was one of the most impressive stories of the 1980s and 1990s.

Oprah Winfrey's first TV success occurred in Chicago, when in 1984 she rescued a failing talk show by eliminating the food and fashion and switching over to discussions about hot button issues. The ratings went up, and that led to the show being syndicated; as I write this, Oprah has become one of the most influential and wealthiest women in media, as well as cofounder of a new cable network and Internet website called Oxygen, and her own magazine for women.

The 1990s seemed to be a time when women could become successful as TV talk hosts, without having to do the traditional women's show. Rikki Lake often took on shocking and bizarre subjects, much like her equally outrageous male competitor, Jerry Springer. Lake was one of the few women who was able to host a show that featured guests who were outside the mainstream, such as cross-dressers or angry spurned lovers ready for a verbal confrontation. If Oprah Winfrey was Everywoman, discussing real problems, bringing experts to shed light on them, and then allowing the studio audience to join in the conversation, Rikki Lake ran a carnival sideshow, keeping order amidst all sorts of outrageous topics and participants whose emotions might explode at any moment. And despite the critics accusing her show of being one of the most tasteless on TV (second only to Jerry Springer—both were often criticized in the same sentence), advertisers could not disapprove of the fact that these shows dramatically increased the number of young viewers, a demographic that had previously ignored daytime talk shows, but that now seemed fascinated by shock talk.

One other interesting show that is somewhat confrontational but often more amusing than shocking debuted in September 1996, when "Judge Judy" went on the air in syndication. An actual judge, Hon. Judy Sheindlin decided real cases during the show and showed her reputation as tough but fair was well deserved. This show was yet one more step away from the gentle and compassionate advice-giver model; while Judge Judy could indeed be caring, she was a no-nonsense type and did not like to hear excuses.

On a kinder, gentler level, there was the type of show done by Rosie O'Donnell; *Newsweek* referred to her as the "Queen of Nice" and suggested that she was the antidote to trash TV. The reporter who wrote the cover story about her praised her for not resorting to mayhem and nastiness like other talk shows did; he noted that she even gave milk and Drake's cakes to her studio audience.[30] O'Donnell, a former comedienne, became host of a syndicated daytime talk and variety show in 1996. She also attracted controversy because of her crusade for gun control and her debates about it with some of the guests on her show.

Deaths of Pioneer Broadcasters

In March 1982, Eunice Randall (who, in the late 1940s, had married Ken Thompson, a former colleague at AMRAD and fellow devotee of ham radio) died, at the age of eighty-four. Although she had been the first woman announcer in New England and a founding member of greater Boston's first station, WGI, the Boston newspapers did not run her obituary. (In fairness, when WGI's owner, Harold Power, died in the late 1960s, the Boston newspapers did not run his obituary, either.) Eunice had a lifetime involvement with amateur radio, setting up a network for the blind and teaching many young people how to build and operate ham radio equipment. Another important woman in both print journalism and radio news died in October 1982. Esther Van Wagoner Tufty, former president of American Women in Radio and Television and a respected journalist (at one time, she ran a news bureau that distributed stories to hundreds of newspapers), was eighty-nine.

The 1980s and 1990s saw the passing of a number of memorable women in broadcasting and the entertainment industry. Among them was one of early TV's most popular women, Faye Emerson. Miss Emerson, who did a TV chat show as early as 1950 and had frequently hosted women's shows during TV's first decade, died in March 1983 at age sixty-five. Another of TV's early stars, even if she first became famous for doing commercials, Betty Furness, died in April 1994 at age seventy-eight. She had moved from being a spokeswoman for Westinghouse into a career as a consumer advocate; she also did many public service features on NBC's *Today* show from the late 1970s throughout the 1980s.

Veteran newswoman Pauline Frederick died in May 1990 at age eighty-four, having come a long way from the first show she was asked to do, when her boss on radio suggested that she do a feature on how to get a husband. She was a UN correspondent for twenty-one years and a role model for many young women who wanted to be journalists. One of the high points of her career had been in 1976 when she moderated one of the presidential debates, the first network newswoman to do so. Her counterpart, Nancy Dickerson, died in October 1997, after an equally illustrious career, during which she won a Peabody Award in 1982 for her study of the Nixon White House. And an early radio newswoman, Kathryn Cravens, who did so much traveling in search of stories during the late 1930s that she was known as the "flying commentator," died in August 1991 at age ninety-two. In the 1940s, she filed reports from twenty-two countries, and her work was heard on the Mutual Network. Martha Rountree, the woman who had co-created "Meet the Press" and was its first female moderator, died in August 1999, at the age of 87.

One of TV talk's earliest female success stories was that of Virginia Graham, who left a career writing radio soap operas to become host of a syndicated TV chat show called *Girl Talk*. During the 1960s, the show often drew as many as 2 million viewers a day. Miss Graham died in late December 1998 at age eighty-six. Album rock pioneer Allison Steele, one of the first important women announcers in that format, succumbed to cancer in late September 1995; she was only fifty-eight. Among the most respected performers in the music industry was the famous African-American contralto Marian Anderson, whose struggle against segregation was championed by First Lady Eleanor Roosevelt. She died at age ninety-six in April 1993. Florence Greenberg, who started Scepter Records and signed such hit groups as the Shirelles and Dionne Warwick, died in November 1995 at age eighty-two. Kate Smith, the popular vocalist who challenged stereotypes about women having to be thin in order to succeed, died in June 1986 at age seventy-nine. And Dinah Shore, who had been a successful network radio singer in the 1940s, host of a long-running TV variety show in the 1950s and 1960s, and a chat show hostess in the 1970s, as well as a popular recording star and the sponsor of a celebrity golf tournament (the Dinah Shore Classic), died in February 1994 at seventy-eight. And speaking of women in sports, one of the first female athletes to become so famous that radio stations wanted to interview her, tennis great Helen Wills Moody, died in December 1997 at age ninety-two. She had won eight Wimbledon singles titles during the 1920s and 1930s and helped gain more acceptance for women athletes.

Advances for Women in Sports

Women and sports was certainly one area where some positive changes had occurred, and Helen Wills Moody lived to see many of them. She was undoubtedly pleased to see the growing popularity of women's athletics, and the number of sports that had women participants. More women were involved with broadcasting sports, too. In New York, one trendsetting announcer of the 1990s was Suzyn Waldman. One of the major breakthroughs in acceptance of women doing men's sports came first with Hannah Storm, who joined CNN in the late 1980s and began anchoring one of their sports shows, as well as doing interviews with various athletes. She was knowledgeable and credible, and she gradually won over even those who doubted a woman could intelligently discuss men's sports. In 1992, NBC hired her away, and she has covered everything from the All Star baseball game to NBA action to the Olympics. What Hannah Storm did on TV, Suzyn Waldman has been doing in radio, where despite the growth of the sports-talk format, few women have ever been hosts or even guests. She had to overcome prejudice and hostility against women doing play-by-play or commentary; like Hannah Storm, her knowledge of sports and a love of athletic competition slowly won over her detractors among the station's predominantly male audience. Waldman, who had a theatrical background but always loved sports, was hired by WFAN in New York City, where she frequently commented on all kinds of sports and also did some work as a correspondent for other stations. She was also very open about being a cancer survivor and did considerable outreach to other women (and to men, especially athletes), providing encouragement to those who were battling the disease. In 1999, the American Women in Radio and Television gave her the Star Award, in recognition of her tireless efforts to promote breast cancer awareness.

Suzyn Waldman had to walk the fine line that many women sports commentators walk: one of the complaints against Christine Craft in the early 1980s was that she interrupted her male colleagues and acted like a know-it-all. It may be unfair, but for Suzyn Waldman and other women sports commentators, they still had to show expertise without making their male cohosts look bad in the process. In several markets where women sports hosts were tried (including Boston), the male audience refused to accept them, so the women who chose to work at a sports-talk station knew they would have an uphill battle. However, a few, like Suzyn Waldman and Hannah Storm, finally seemed to be winning. Another dedicated and somewhat more controversial sports fan, Nanci Donellan, created a persona called "The Fabulous Sports Babe," a brash and tough-talking fan with very strong views; she syndicated the show, making her perhaps the first woman with a nationally syndicated sports-talk show. Meanwhile, the 1990s saw the growing popularity of women's professional sports; for the first time, society was willing to accommodate the idea of women professional athletes in team sports like basketball or soccer, rather than just in noncontact sports like tennis or golf. Even women's hockey was beginning to gain in acceptance. And while some members of the media still concentrated on the physical appearance of women athletes, more was also being written about their skill. Newspapers that had seldom, if ever, mentioned women's sports began following the Women's National Basketball Association (WNBA). The Lifetime cable channel even began airing a regular schedule of WNBA games, with Michele Tafoya, who formerly worked at ESPN, doing the play-by-play, along with former WNBA player (and author of a book about the league) Fran Harris. The performance of the U.S. Women's hockey team in the Winter Olympics received coverage, as did women's college basketball, although the women's collegiate championship games had not yet received the ratings that the men's championships did. And as late as 1999, Mia Hamm and Brandi Chastain, two stars of the U.S. Women's soccer team, which won the World Cup, were still being described in some newspapers by how attractive they were, as if loving sports and being a "normal female" were mutually exclusive. The ambivalence of earlier decades had not gone away entirely, although acceptance of women in sports was definitely greater than at any other time in history.

Meanwhile, some of the women from the "good old days" were still around and still contributing. While TV newswomen wondered if they had finally overcome the stigma of being in their forties and fifties and possibly being considered too old for on-air work, in March 2000, reporter Jane Scott was celebrating her fortieth year as a rock music columnist for the *Cleveland* (Ohio) *Plain Dealer.* Jane had joined the paper in 1952 and began covering pop music in the 1960s. At the age of eighty, she was still doing that job and had just won an Achievement Award from the local Women's City Club. Wynn Speece, the Neighbor Lady at WNAX in Yankton, South Dakota, was still broadcasting on a part-time basis, despite being close to ninety; she was also still active in her community, and several generations of South Dakota women had grown up listening to her shows. And Helen Choat, who had worked at WBIS (what Boston's first all-woman radio station became in mid-1927—her air name was "Nancy Howe"), had spent many years as a radio actress in New York, and now, at the age of ninety-two, was a valuable resource for memorabilia about radio in the 1920s and 1930s.

Assessing Women's Progress—Some Positive News

On the surface, it certainly appeared that things for women in broadcasting had improved dramatically in the 1980s and 1990s. There was one network that marketed itself as "Television for women"—Lifetime, a cable network, had been created in 1984 and had begun marketing exclusively toward the female audience a decade later. But there was a question about how exactly to do that marketing—and what did it mean to gender an entire network? Even for some of Lifetime's female executives, it seemed to mean exhibiting the same ambivalence as in generations past. Said Senior Vice President Marge Sandwick in 1989, "We feared people would see us as 'The Feminism Channel' or the 'Betty Crocker Channel.'"[31] Lifetime chose to make a distinction between being "feminine" and "feminist"; some of its critics accused it of lacking a clear vision and mainly trying to deliver an audience that advertisers coveted (eighteen- through forty-nine-year-old women). But despite that, Lifetime's ratings went steadily up; by the beginning of the year 2000, the network ranked sixth in prime time out of all the basic cable channels, and being owned by the Walt Disney Company and the Hearst Corporation helped get it onto a larger number of cable systems.

In addition to offering dramatic programs and comedies (including reruns of popular comedies like *Golden Girls* and *Designing Women*) that had female appeal, Lifetime produced some award-winning documentaries on women's health issues, dramas about social issues (such as *The Truth About Jane*, the story of a fifteen-year-old who realizes she is a lesbian, and her struggle with whether or not to tell her parents), and biographies of women who made a difference in society. One example was a documentary profile of Houston, Texas, news anchor Sydney Seaward. Ms. Seaward had worked for the Monitor Channel's KNWS-TV, and when she was stricken with breast cancer, instead of hiding her condition, she went public with her treatment and with the story of her attempts to cope. She hoped to demystify the disease and encourage women not to give up. Many women empathized with her, but her honesty also made some viewers uncomfortable: at one point, she took off her wig on camera to show the effects of chemotherapy. Although Ms. Seaward lost her battle with cancer in September 1998 (she was only in her early forties), her courage made her a worthwhile subject in Lifetime's ongoing efforts to raise awareness about breast cancer; the documentary won the network a 1999 Gracie Award—named for the late Gracie Allen and given annually by the American Women in Radio and Television to programs that offer "positive, realistic, and creative portrayals of women."

Cable TV proved beneficial for several women executives, among them Geraldine Laybourne, who helped to build the kids' channel Nickelodeon into an $8 billion success story during her sixteen years with the network.[32] Having made good use of her master's degree in elementary education, Ms. Laybourne next became involved with Marcy Carsey and Oprah Winfrey in the creation of the new Oxygen cable channel, which planned to compete with Lifetime for the female demographic.

Meanwhile, at PBS, the year 2000 saw the network appointing a woman as president and CEO: Pat Mitchell came over from CNN, where she had been the president of CNN Productions and had developed or supervised many award-winning programs. In music, American Society of Composers, Authors and Publishers (ASCAP) elected its first woman president, songwriter Marilyn Bergman. In Bergman's long and successful career, she had earned three Academy Awards, three Emmy Awards, and two Grammy Awards, and with her husband and songwriting partner Alan, had created a number of hits. She was also the first woman elected to ASCAP's board of directors. And one of the biggest success stories for Hispanic women in the 1980s and 1990s was the distinguished career of TV chat show hostess Cristina Saralegui. Saralegui and her family arrived in the United States from Cuba in 1960; she learned English, attended college, and ultimately rose to a position of importance with several women's magazines (including editor in chief of the Spanish-language version of *Cosmopolitan*) before becoming executive producer and host of her own show on the Hispanic network Univision in 1989. Throughout the 1990s, *El Show de Cristina* was the number one talk show on Spanish-language TV; Saralegui herself was voted the most trusted person on TV, ahead of Oprah Winfrey and Tom Brokaw, in a 1999 *People en Español* readers' poll. Like Winfrey, Saralegui started her own magazine (*Cristina La Revista*), and she also has done a daily talk show for ABC Radio International. An excellent interviewer and a tireless advocate for social causes that benefit the Hispanic community, Saralegui broke a major barrier for women on Hispanic television: in an industry where historically females were restricted to singing, acting in soap operas (where the suffering servant, the devious home wrecker, and other traditional stereotypes still ruled), or looking sexy while assisting the male host, she maintained her popularity without compromising her credibility. As of this writing, she is now in her fifties; her show is the longest-running talk show on Univision, and Cristina Saralegui continues to be a role model for Hispanic women.

Problems Still Remain

Yet despite these and other gains, looking back on the previous decade, some things had not changed that much, and others had changed for the worse. In the mid-1980s, a report from the Women's Media Project showed that during a month's worth of TV viewing, of 576 stories filed by network correspondents, 517 were done by men and only 59 by women. In 1992, syndicated columnist Ellen Goodman did the same survey at her own newspaper and found a similar disparity in how many stories were by or about women; she also quoted from a 1992 study of front pages of major newspapers, which showed that stories about women only showed up 13 percent of the time.[33] And while there were more women reporters, a study of TV news found that in 1992, men still reported over 80 percent of the broadcast news stories. When the study was done several years later, the results did not change.[34] Then, in 1997, the Media Awareness Project, in cooperation with the Screen Actors Guild, did a study of the characters on prime-time TV from 1994 to 1997 and found that men still outnumbered women two to one; older women characters were more often portrayed as evil than older men characters; women consistently played only one out of three roles on prime-time TV; and while more African-American males were seen on TV, there was not a similar rise in the amount of African-American females.[35]

Professor Martha M. Lauzen did a study for the organization Women in Film, in which she examined the top-rated prime-time shows on TV during the 1998–99 season and found that:

> Women's employment [was] at a virtual standstill. While the number of female executive producers working on top-rated programs increased . . . the numbers of women directors and creators declined slightly, and the numbers of female writers, producers, and editors remained stable. Women comprised 31% of producers, 24% of executive producers, 21% of writers, 16% of editors, 15% of creators, and 3% of directors. There wasn't a single female director of photography working on any of the programs considered in the 1998–99 season. Overall, women accounted for only 21.5% of all individuals in these key roles. This figure is unchanged from . . . last season. On screen, the story is much the same. Women accounted for only 38% of all characters in the 1998–99 season.

And, she noted with surprise that when the study was done in 1990–91, the results were exactly the same; there had been no progress in these areas in nearly a decade.[36] And the Screen Actors Guild study done during the 1997–98 prime-time television season showed a dramatic decline in roles for women over forty: only 12 percent of the roles were of women over forty; a year earlier, it had been 26 percent. In fact, they found that two of every three jobs went to performers under forty, and older men had higher employment rates than older women. So while some of the women in news were holding on to their jobs, characters on TV were getting younger, and there were fewer roles for older women. With the population aging, this was not a good sign for experienced women actresses. (In film, the same held true, and Academy Award–winning actress Meryl Streep spoke out about it in numerous interviews in 1998.)

Because of the Telecommunications Act of 1996, there had been enormous changes in the structure of who owned radio stations, and as fewer and fewer individual owners could afford to operate a station, a handful of large companies dominated radio. Every one of these companies was run by men, and a number of the smaller owners who had to sell their stations because they lacked the money to compete were women (while others were minorities). President and general manager Edie Hilliard of Broadcast Programming, a major provider of syndicated programming for radio, discussed how the Telecom Act had impacted women managers and owners, saying, "If success is defined as having the most stations or the most money and, therefore, the most power, the answer is no, women do not have as fair a chance to be successful in our business as men do. With consolidation, management opportunities for women are shrinking."[37] Ms. Hilliard was one of the few women presidents or vice presidents in broadcasting at the time of that interview. (It was not much better in the rest of the business world: in 1999, Carly Fiorina became the CEO of Hewlett-Packard, making her only the third woman to head a Fortune 500 Company.)

Despite the achievements of women like Cathy Hughes, Mary Quass, Oprah Winfrey, and Barbara Walters (the latter two were named by *People* magazine in a retrospective book, *The Unforgettable Women of the Century*[38]); despite more female artists having hits and winning Grammy Awards; despite more women than ever on the air in news and in announcing; a 1999 American Federation of Television and Radio Artists (AFTRA) survey showed that women in broadcasting still did not get equal pay, even after all this time.[39] The equal pay issue was egregious in some formats because the man who did the morning show got a huge salary, while sidekicks and other announcers received far less. In 1991, Shannon Dell (Karen Grace Jones) was working for WGCI-FM, a popular urban station in Chicago. Despite high ratings, her salary was only $48,000 while the male host of the morning show, Tom Joyner, made over $600,000. When she complained about the inequity and asked why women were kept out of the lucrative shifts, she was fired. She sued and lost in 1993; she was never able to get another radio job.[40] Her complaint had some validity, as attitudes of male program directors still kept many talented women locked into certain roles, unable to move up and unable to make the money their male colleagues did.

"Thin" Is Still In

Although some high-profile network anchorwomen in their fifties were still employed, as their male colleagues always were, at the local level, older men continued to anchor, while older women saw their opportunities diminish. All those survey results indicated that even in the 1990s, managers (and many writers) still had a preference for hiring or casting only females who were slim and cute. However, a few women were working to change this. TV actress Camryn Manheim, who won an Emmy for her work on the dramatic series *The Practice,* was one of the few larger-sized women on TV who was not in comedy. She was named one of *People* magazine's "25 Most Intriguing People of 1998," and when she accepted her Emmy, she said, "This is for all the fat girls." Yet despite her success and popularity, one of her complaints has been that the writers do not let her character have a successful romance or a sex life, even though every other character on the show has had some love interest. In an interview in 1998, she stated that TV's prejudice against large women had not diminished, even in our more tolerant times; few shows ever portrayed fat women as self-assured or happy. "[In real life], handsome, thin, sophisticated men often fall madly in love with larger women; we just never see it on TV. If we did, perhaps it would give men permission to follow their hearts and do it more often."[41]

Another full-figured woman doing well on TV as the decade ended was Star Jones. Jones had been a prosecutor in New York City and then had become a correspondent with NBC news. She was chosen to become a cohost on Barbara Walters's chat show, *The View,* and in 1998, she issued her autobiography, *You Have to Stand for Something or You'll Fall for Anything.* But reporters often seemed puzzled by Jones's insistence on the need for more stylish and fashionable clothes for larger women and her refusal to hide her figure. Like Camryn Manheim, Star Jones remained very outspoken about how women of size (and women of color, since she is African-American) continued to be underrepresented on TV.

The persistent images in commercials and on TV of slender models, and the stars who endlessly discussed their latest diet on chat shows, did not help. Where Betty Friedan had remarked that in the 1950s, the only way for a woman to be considered a heroine was to have lots of babies, Naomi Wolf observed that in the 1980s and 1990s, for a woman to be a heroine she had to stay beautiful and slim.[42] While TV had found a place for a few larger women (and as mentioned earlier, that place was often in comedy), there was endless media preoccupation with Oprah Winfrey's ongoing battle to keep her weight down, and she received much praise every time one of her diets succeeded. The message to fans certainly seemed to be that a "good woman" diets until she reaches the ideal TV weight, no matter how difficult this may be to maintain.

There were no longer as many commercials that showed airhead females in pearls and high heels enthusing over the latest brand of soap, but on many TV quiz shows, women still served as the sex symbol who assisted the host, and as mentioned previously, commercials still abounded that showed anorexic-looking women or put forth the message that having wrinkles was a national tragedy. A number of media critics commented that in a country of immigrants, Asian and Hispanic women were still barely seen at all on TV—in 1997, for example, Hispanic female characters made up less than 2 percent of all characters on prime-time shows.[43] And although more African-Americans were being hired, and in some cases were given roles as middle- and upper-class professionals (doctors, nurses, teachers, lawyers, etc.), they, too, were quite underrepresented.

While more women served in positions of authority at local radio stations and advertising agencies, as I write this, the president of the NAB, the presidents of all the major networks, and the owners of the five biggest broadcast groups, in other words, all the important decision makers in broadcasting, are still men, just as they were in the 1930s. There are women vice presidents, women who own stations, women who win awards and have the respect of their peers, women who are extremely wealthy and can start their own company. But the broadcasting conventions are still overwhelmingly male, and the decisions that are made that affect women are still made by a small group of men who have that influence and power. Radio and TV have been very slow to change, and, through the years, they have been equally slow to speak out on issues like racism and sexism: fear of offending advertisers often took precedence over doing the right thing. These issues were raised in the 1920s; in some cases, they still have not been resolved.

And yet, the world of broadcasting today is a world that Eunice Randall could not possibly have imagined, a world where a woman could start a cable TV network or be the president of one; a world where women could be seen in a number of roles they had never played even in the free-wheeling days of early radio; a world where a woman, Margaret Bryant, was director of engineering for the ABC radio stations in Dallas (in an interview, she told me that while there were still very few women in radio engineering, she noticed many more joining the technical side of TV); a world where, on several occasions, TV shows had entirely female camera crews; and a world where senior correspondents covering major political issues were women. And yet . . . and yet few media history books mention the achievements of the women of broadcasting.

The newspapers still treat what women have done as less important than what men have done, and while the attitudes of the print media regarding women's issues have improved, the vast majority of editors and owners are still men. There may be more equal opportunity in media than ever before, but authority and power are still regarded as male, and by and large, women are still on the periphery. Some managers still believe that if they have one woman anchor, that is enough; having two women anchoring the news is rare, while having two men anchoring is a common occurrence. More women are now college-trained meteorologists and are no longer inexperienced models hired to be weather girls, but at most stations, the program director is still a man, and women are still held to a higher standard. That standard, as Dr. Carol Tavris has pointed out, is still defined with men as the norm, and women or minorities as the "other," so women are still criticized for exhibiting behaviors that, when men exhibit them, are considered positive. Many historians still follow the "great man" school of thought, concentrating on what the heads of corporations or the great inventors did and passing over the many other people whose ideas and energy have advanced the broadcasting industry.

When I researched this book, I found that in all too many libraries, there was not even a clippings file on award-winning women broadcasters who had worked on radio and TV in that city for over thirty years; there usually was a general file about broadcasting, but the articles it contained tended toward the men who bought and sold the stations or about technological advances the station had made. Seldom if ever did it include profiles of the women whose presence influenced so many people. At the end of the century, women in broadcasting were not completely invisible anymore, but they were also not as visible as they deserved to be, and they still were not welcomed in certain sectors of the industry. The lucrative voice-over market was still largely male territory, as the belief persisted that men sounded more authoritative when doing commercials, station liners, and other recorded announcements. More women were being heard as voice talent on commercials, but the majority of production directors were still men, so the majority of the commercials still featured a male voice. When Phyllis Stark of *Billboard* magazine did some research in 1991, she found that only about 3 percent of the prerecorded station identifications and liners were done by women.[44] As of this writing, nearly a decade later, the percentage is only slightly higher.

Women continue to receive double messages: they are told to be assertive yet not too assertive, and the traditional belief that women are by nature kinder, gentler, and more helpful than men remains at odds with the qualities deemed necessary to succeed as a company president. Barbara Walters recalled a time when saying a woman was "ambitious" was an insult, but to this day, a woman who seems too focused on her career is perceived negatively, while a man who puts his career first is praised. Of course, not every woman wants to be a company president, but many wish they could have a chance to be a decision maker, or even an expert—on all too many network news shows, the experts called upon for comment are still men, unless the issue involves child care or the family.[45] And while more women have found success in radio and TV sales, and more women are sales managers, few have the money to buy their own radio or TV station or move into the upper echelons of management, where the glass ceiling still exists.

Perhaps the next few years will bring society to a place where women are no longer regarded with suspicion; where they are given the chance to prove their competence, rather than having to fight the assumption that they were hired because the EEOC laws required it. Perhaps some of the old myths about women's unreliability and inability to handle pressure will finally be put to rest, and women will no longer be perceived as "too aggressive" if they express the desire for career advancement. Perhaps in the near future, women will no longer have to choose between marriage and career—in spite of many gains and changes in men's attitudes about helping around the house, most of the successful men in broadcasting tend to be married, while many of the successful women are either single or divorced. Perhaps women who want to work in the industry but are not fashion-model beautiful will find that radio and TV do want to hire them for their intelligence, enthusiasm, and solid work ethic. And most important of all, perhaps there will soon be a time when women who had long and distinguished careers, be they in traditional or nontraditional areas, are no longer forgotten or marginalized as Mary Margaret McBride, Bertha Brainard, and Judith Waller were.

As media historians, we should remember that in many cities, only the women's shows addressed social issues like the need for better health care or the need to improve public education; and women's show hostesses were passionate advocates for worthy causes. Rather than remembering only the criticism about women's shows, we should reevaluate their meaning to the generation who relied upon them and give these broadcasters the credit they deserve. We should also revisit how some women broadcasters managed to succeed against overwhelming odds: many of the women of radio and TV's formative decades endured harassment, low pay, and lack of respect, yet they persisted and became role models for their young fans.

Throughout her book *We Are Our Mothers' Daughters,* Cokie Roberts discussed how her women friends sustained her many times during her career. This is not something we associate with career-oriented women—the common wisdom is that they are scheming backstabbers who hate each other. It only shows yet again how much misinformation about women still exists, and how it still needs to be refuted. And in a society that studies the media ad infinitum, too little attention has been paid to how the presence of women has affected both the media and the audience. Issues that men had ignored, those so-called human-interest stories, are today an accepted part of reporting, and it was women who often did the in-depth interviews that helped the audience get to know the newsmakers better. Perhaps one day soon, the pioneering women of radio and television will be given the same respect for their achievements that society has accorded their male counterparts. I hope this book will contribute to that process and keep the woman of broadcasting from remaining invisible stars.

Timeline: The 1980s and 1990s

1980	Cable News Network is founded
1983	Sally Jessy Raphael show debuts in syndication
	Christine Craft sues for sex discrimination
1984	Lifetime cable channel is founded
	Geraldine Laybourne new president of Nickelodeon
	Diane Sawyer is first female cohost on *60 Minutes*
1986	*Oprah Winfrey Show* debuts in syndication
1989	*El Show de Cristina* debuts on Univision
1994	Capt. Kathryn Janeway is first female *Star Trek* captain
1996	*Judge Judy* debuts in syndication
	Telecommunications Act of 1996 allows major media consolidation
Late 1990s	Dr. Laura is most influential female radio talk host

Appendix

Some of the women mentioned in *Invisible Stars:*

Bertha Brainard (Peterson): Her friends called her "Betty," and her colleagues spoke of her with admiration. During more than twenty years in broadcasting, she was one of only a few female executives. Beginning in radio as a theater critic in 1922, she worked her way up to assistant program manager at WJZ in Newark (later New York) and then to eastern program manager for the newly formed NBC radio network; she was later promoted to commercial program manager for the entire network. Miss Brainard held a series of managerial jobs at NBC, where she remained until her retirement in 1946.

Kathryn Cravens: She was ahead of her time—male critics dismissed "News Through a Woman's Eyes," but her many fans found her human interest stories fascinating. She began as a radio actress in St. Louis, but, ultimately, her news program was picked up by the CBS radio network in 1936. She was one of the few female news reporters in the 1930s and 1940s, and she received credentials to cover World War II. After her time with CBS, she worked for Mutual Broadcasting Company and wrote for several newspapers. She was also active in the League of Women Voters.

Nancy Dickerson: A former teacher, she worked in Washington, D.C., as a government researcher before pursuing a career in news in the early 1950s. Her interests were politics and foreign affairs, two areas where only men were hired; however, CBS radio offered her a job as an associate producer of "Face the Nation." She then became a full producer, and, finally, in 1960, she was named CBS news's first female correspondent, paving the way for other newswomen in the 1960s. She moved over to NBC in 1963, where she mainly covered Washington politics and Capitol Hill. In the early 1970s, her commentary was syndicated, and during the 1980s, she produced documentaries for PBS—including one that examined the women's movement and another about the status of women in the Arab world, as well as a documentary about the Nixon presidency, which won her a Peabody Award in 1982.

Pauline Frederick: She began in print journalism but went on to a distinguished career in radio and then TV news. First hired in 1939 by Margaret "Maggie" Cuthbert to do so-called women's news (interviews with the wives of famous men), she persisted in attempts to gain the opportunity to do hard news, but it was a long battle. While freelancing for ABC radio, Miss Frederick was assigned to cover the United Nations; her expertise led to an assignment covering the 1948 political conventions for ABC-TV, the first woman to do network news. She became one of TV's most respected newswomen, winning many awards during a long career that included work with ABC, then NBC, and finally National Public Radio. In 1976, she became the first newswoman ever to moderate a presidential debate.

Dorothy Fuldheim: A former educator and a compelling public speaker, she began her broadcasting career in 1944 when she first went on the air at WJW in Cleveland, Ohio. By 1947, she was a commentator for a weekly show on ABC radio; later that year, she first appeared on TV. A news anchor, a book reviewer, a well-respected interviewer of celebrities, Mrs. Fuldheim became a legend in Cleveland broadcasting, taking stands on controversial issues and speaking out on causes in which she believed. Her career lasted into the early 1980s.

Betty Furness: A former movie actress, she became famous as the TV spokeswoman for Westinghouse refrigerators in the early 1950s. Gradually, she moved away from commercials into public affairs and consumer advocacy features; she was a contributor to the "Today" Show on NBC from 1974 to 1992. She was highly respected for her TV consumer reports, in which she uncovered fraud and defended the rights of the public.

Dorothy Gordon: A specialist in children's programming on radio, Mrs. Gordon's radio career began in New York in 1924; she later developed and directed educational shows for the CBS radio network, including the critically acclaimed "Yesterday's Children." Author of seven children's books, she was a strong advocate for programs that children would find both interesting and informative: she began moderating the "*New York Times* Youth Forum" on radio in 1945, and on TV in 1953; the show, and Mrs. Gordon, won several awards.

Frieda Hennock: The first woman to serve on the Federal Communications Commission (FCC), she had been a lawyer prior to her 1948 appointment. A determined advocate for educational programming on TV, she worked to have a certain number of channels set aside for noncommercial, educational use. KUHT-TV in Houston became the first educational TV station in 1953, and others followed, but Miss Hennock's opposition to broadcast corporations becoming too large—she feared such expansion would allow the more powerful companies to dominate, and possibly eliminate, smaller ones—led to her not being re-appointed to the FCC after her first term expired.

Corinne Jordan: In an era when women program directors were nearly all replaced, Miss Jordan enjoyed a long career programming KSTP radio in St. Paul, Minnesota. She came to KSTP in 1928, and for over fifteen years, she hired and often trained the on-air performers, chose material for the KSTP Players (who performed radio drama), and still found time to do commercials for several local sponsors, as well as to perform on a show of her own. A talented vocalist whose 10:15 P.M. program was especially popular, she was known to her fans as the "Stardust Lady."

Ruth Lyons: She was a mother-figure to the millions of women who watched her "Fifty-Fifty Club" on Cincinnati TV. Her broadcasting career began as a musical accompanist for radio station WKRC in 1929, but when she filled in one day on the women's show, listeners liked what they heard; by 1932, Miss Lyons had made the show one of Cincinnati's most popular. In the early 1940s, she was hired by WLW, and by the end of the decade, she had moved her popular chat show to TV, while also continuing it on radio. Her fans came to know about her ongoing struggles with her weight, and they met her family (she often brought her young daughter to the studio); there were always long waiting lists to be in her studio audience. She was also tireless in raising money for children's charities. Ruth Lyons finally retired in 1967, after being on the air for nearly four decades.

Mary Margaret McBride: From her first days on the air at New York City's WOR radio in 1934, she had a natural, conversational style that made listeners feel they knew her; they certainly trusted her, taking her endorsements of products very seriously. She was originally a print journalist but had carved out a unique niche for herself in radio; her women's show was ultimately picked up by the CBS radio network. Male critics found her excessively chatty and made fun of her, but her millions of fans remained loyal: in 1944, her tenth anniversary celebration was held at New York's Madison Square Garden, and in 1949, for her fifteenth, the size of the audience required Yankee Stadium.

Ida McNeil: Known to her South Dakota listeners as "Mrs. Pierre," Ida McNeil first went on the air to help her husband with his amateur station, which became KGFX in 1927. From that day on, she was a one-woman staff (with occasional help from family members and an engineer). Her specialty was local information and community service, and over the years, she won numerous awards. Her largely rural audience relied on her for the latest gossip, as well as news of changing weather patterns and friendly conversation about what was happening in town. She finally sold KGFX in 1962, when she was 74.

Edythe J. Meserand: One of the founding members of American Women in Radio and Television, and its first national president, Miss Meserand had a long career in radio, beginning in 1926 when she joined the newly formed NBC to work in the publicity department. During her career in New York radio, she was a publicist, a producer, and a writer of educational and public affairs programs. She also worked in news during World War II; while at station WOR (New York City), she not only produced award-winning documentaries, but she also won awards for her community service and charitable work. She worked in early television as well and was a director of special features. When *McCall's* magazine began awarding the "Golden Mike" in 1951, Miss Meserand was one of the first winners.

Eunice Randall (Thompson): She grew up on a farm that didn't even have electricity, but the radio bug bit her, and she became the first woman announcer in Massachusetts, and probably one of the first in the eastern United States. She was on the air at 1XE (later WGI), owned and operated by AMRAD, which manufactured radios, as early as 1920. Miss Randall became a devoted fan of amateur radio, helped by her mentor, Irving Vermilya. During the early 1920s at 1XE/WGI, she played phonograph records and announced them, read the police reports of stolen cars, helped novices to learn Morse code, and did some of the engineering and drafting work; in addition, she sometimes served as the "Story Lady," who read bedtime stories to children. Her own story is one of the more unusual ones in early broadcasting, since she not only sang and announced, but she was also trained in building and repairing broadcasting equipment, something few women of the early 1920s accomplished.

Nellie Revell: Press agent to the stars, Miss Revell wrote for the *New York World*, and later for *Variety* and *Radio Digest*. She was a publicist for the Keith-Orpheum theaters and also did publicity for such celebrities as Al Jolson and Will Rogers. Not only did she seem to know everyone, but she also enjoyed doing interviews: she had her own show on NBC beginning in 1930, and until her retirement in the late 1940s, she continued to do celebrity talk shows on radio, using the name "Neighbor Nell."

Dinah Shore: She started as a popular vocalist during the Big Band era, who sang on the radio many times and had a number of hit records. But it was on early TV that Dinah Shore became especially popular, becoming one of the few women to host her own variety show. Sponsored by Chevrolet (she helped to make their theme song famous), the "Dinah Shore Show" won several Emmys during the mid-1950s, and lasted until 1962. Always able to adapt to the times, in the 1970s, she began doing a syndicated talk show, and it, too, won an Emmy.

Judith Waller: Another of radio's first female pioneers, her career began as station manager of WGU in Chicago (later WMAQ). Her passion was educational programming, and she wrote numerous articles about how radio could be a valuable asset to education. She is credited with launching the popular show "Amos 'n' Andy," and she also created several successful public affairs shows. In 1931, NBC named her public affairs and educational director for the Midwest. Seeing the educational possibilities of TV, she created "Ding Dong School," one of early TV's most successful programs for pre-schoolers; the show, along with its host, Dr. Frances Horwich, was given a Peabody Award for excellence in 1952, and Miss Waller received a Golden Mike in 1954. She retired from broadcasting in 1957, after a thirty-five-year career.

Notes

Introduction

1. Lynn Wenzel and Carol J. Binkowski, *I Hear America Singing* (New York: Crown, 1989), p. 39.

Chapter 1

1. Carroll Pursell, "The Long Summer of Boy Engineering," in *Possible Dreams: Enthusiasm for Technology in America*, John L. Wright, ed. (Dearborn, MI: Henry Ford Museum, 1992), p. 36.

2. Mission Statement, U.S. Department of Labor Women's Bureau, June 1920. Quoted on Internet at www.dol.gov/dol/wb/public/info_about_wb/main.htm.

3. Sarah Jane Deutsch, *From Ballots to Breadlines: American Women 1920–1940* (New York: Oxford, 1994), p. 44.

4. "Women Have Two Squads on Duty," *Boston Sunday Globe*, April 1, 1917, p. 55. Also on same page, "Women for Naval Radio Officers." See also "Wireless Operators: Women Becoming Very Proficient," *Quincy* (MA) *Patriot*, April 17, 1917, p. 3.

5. Dorothy Dix, "Must a Wife Obey?" *Boston Globe*, March 27, 1916, p. 11. Also, "What Is Equality in Matrimony?" *Boston Globe*, October 30, 1928, p. 23. Also, changing fashion and its impact on young women is discussed in an essay by Kenneth Yellis, "Prosperity's Child: Some Thoughts on the Flapper," *American Quarterly*, Spring 1969, pp. 44–64.

6. "Why Women Change Jobs," *Literary Digest*, vol. 79, November 24, 1923, p. 27.

7. Sarah Jane Deutsch, *From Ballads to Breadlines*, p. 18.

8. Ibid., p. 37.

9. Numerous articles in *School and Society* addressed this. See especially "Need for Better Teachers' Salaries," vol. 11, April 17, 1920, p. 462; or "Underpaid Teachers," vol. 10, September 27, 1919, p. 388, in which teachers' salaries are called a "national scandal."

10. Eunice Randall, "Hair Ribbon on a Radio Tower," *Yankee,* April 1964, pp. 111–112. Further recollections of her early on-air experience at 1XE/WGI are contained on an August 29, 1964, cassette of the AMRAD reunion. This tape can be heard at the Library of American Broadcasting, College Park, Md.

11. Christopher Sterling and J. Michael Kittross, *Stay Tuned,* 2d ed. (Belmont, CA: Wadsworth, 1990), p. 66.

12. Gwen Wagner, "A Girl Reporter Speaks Up," *Radio Age,* September 1925, pp. 30, 65, 69. Additional information from Special Collections, Memphis (TN) Public Library.

13. Nearly every newspaper from mid-1922 through 1924 contained stories of how a local station was heard in a faraway place; there were even contests to see who could receive the most distant station, and a surprising number of women participated. (Rena Jane Frew, "Miss Radio of 1925," received stations from as far away as Cuba, Puerto Rico, and nearly every state in the United States.) One dramatic example of how far signals traveled was when WGY (Schenectady, NY) was received in Liverpool, England, on December 24, 1922.

14. Vera Brady Shipman, "KPO—the Voice of the Golden Gate," *Radio Digest,* November 22, 1924, p. 5.

15. Jennie Irene Mix, author, educator, and music critic, wrote monthly columns for *Radio Broadcast* magazine from April 1924 until her death in mid-1925. Her love of classical music was reflected in these columns. See, for example, "The Radio Pianists Play Good Music," September 1924, pp. 396–397.

16. Eleanor Poehler, "My Happy Radio Career," *Wireless Age,* vol. 12, no. 3, December 1924, p. 30.

17. Personal interviews with Dorothy, Dave, and Lorraine Ciesielski, October–November 1996.

18. "Throngs Attend Fine Radio Show," *Boston Globe,* May 4, 1922, p. 6. The author (who gave no by-line, but was probably radio editor Lloyd Greene) noted that instead of an audience of mostly men who loved technology, attendees included "all walks of life: old men, housewives, flappers, businessmen and [little children]." Similar comments were made about the radio show in New York—see, for example, *Literary Digest,* December 15, 1923, p. 25, where the author observed a "surprisingly large number of women in attendance."

19. "Women and Wireless," *Literary Digest,* December 15, 1923, p. 25.

20. Mentioned in Guy R. Entwistle's "Citizen Wireless" column regarding Eunice Randall (see, e.g., *Boston Traveler,* May 31, 1921, p. 10); similar comments can be found in Lewis Whitcomb's article about Jessie Koewing (*Boston Post,* May 6, 1923, p. 27, in which he reprints some of her fan mail) and in Golda M. Goldman's article "His Mistress' Voice" in the December 1922 issue of *Radio News,* in which she discussed the popularity of a number of women announcers of the early 1920s.

Chapter 2

1. Eric Barnouw, *A Tower in Babel* (New York: Oxford University Press, 1966), pp. 162–163.

2. Lewis Whitcomb, "Who's Who in Broadcasting," *Boston Post,* January 21, 1923, p. 26.

3. Lewis Whitcomb, "JEK of Station WOR," *Boston Post,* March 25, 1923, p. 27.

4. Lewis Whitcomb, "JEK to Marry Gloucesterite," *Boston Post,* May 6, 1923, p. 27.

5. Robert Birkby, *KMA Radio: The First Sixty Years* (Shenandoah, IA: May Publishing, 1985), p. 8.

6. Ibid., p. 133.

7. Mrs. G.W. Fitch, Letters to the Editor, *Radio World*, vol. 6, no. 18, January 24, 1925.

8. "What the Farmer Listens to," *Radio Broadcast*, vol. 9, no. 4, August 1926, p. 315. For more about what farmers and farmers' wives wanted from radio, see "No Sleep, Much Company, Farmers' Radio Lament," *Radio World*, July 24, 1926, p. 28; and also "Radio in the Small Town," *The Radio Record*, March 1924, p. 21.

9. Golda M. Goldman, "The Women's Hour," *Wireless Age*, vol. 12, no. 6, March 1925, pp. 34–35.

10. Ibid., p. 34.

11. Susan Strasser, *Satisfaction Guaranteed* (Washington, DC: Smithsonian, 1989), p. 268.

12. See, for example, her article "Radio for Women," *Literary Digest*, November 28, 1925, p. 20.

13. "What Women Spend for Their Clothes," *Literary Digest*, August 25, 1923, p. 57.

14. In the mid-1920s, radio manufacturers began making sets more simple to operate, ostensibly to benefit the female consumer (see, e.g., radio manufacturer Powel Crosley Jr.'s syndicated newspaper column, "Radio Chats," November 13, 1926; or "Women and Radio," a similar article in *The Radio Record*, May 1927, p. 13). But there was evidence at the retail stores that many men could not comprehend how to build a radio set and were pleased to buy one already assembled.

15. Bertha Brainard, "Women Listeners Are Good Critics," *New York Times,* September 18, 1927, section X, p. 16.

16. "Chicago Link of Mid-Continent Chain," *Radio Digest,* October 31, 1925, p. 7.

17. "WHT Makes Scoop: Gets Jean Sargent," *Radio Digest,* July 4, 1925, p. 7.

18. "At the Ball," *Time,* March 10, 1923, p. 22, tells about "Margery Rex."

19. "Method in Kindness," *Time,* January 21, 1924, p. 22, tells about the original "Prudence Penny" of New York, Mrs. Mabelle Burbridge. The home economics department of newspapers often provided a start to women who wanted to be on the radio. Successful announcer Halloween Martin began her career working as a "Prudence Penny" for the *Chicago Herald-Examiner* (see *Radio Digest*, November 1929, p. 57). Another alumna of the Prudence Penny department was KING-TV Seattle, Washington, women's show host, Bea Donovan, whose cooking program aired for an amazing twenty-seven years; she first worked as a Prudence at the *Seattle Post-Intelligencer.* Just like "Betty Crocker," a woman who portrayed Prudence Penny did a women's show on San Francisco radio in the mid-1920s.

20. Susan Smulyan, *Selling Radio: The Commercialization of American Broadcasting* (Washington, DC: Smithsonian, 1994), pp. 88–89. Betty Crocker became a national phenomenon (it had begun on WCCO in Minneapolis) after it was picked up by NBC in late 1926. Local newspapers reported promotional contests that centered around using the sponsor's (General Mills) products, and prizes were awarded at local bake-offs.

21. Christine Lunardini, *What Every American Should Know About Women's History* (Holbrook, MA: Bob Adams, 1994), p. 206.

22. Michele Hilmes, *Radio Voices: American Broadcastding 1922–1952* (Minneapolis: University of Minnesota Press, 1997), p. 137.

23. Perhaps the most incisive media critic of that era was former *Chicago Tribune*

correspondent George Seldes, who wrote books such as *You Can't Print That,* in which he assailed the "prostitution of the press" and gave examples of how commercialization had made the media timid—worried only about keeping advertisers happy and not concerned about investigating the health risks of certain products (he was among the first to print articles on the dangers of cigarette smoking). Another critic of the probusiness bias of the media was Ruth Brindze, whose book *Not to Be Broadcast* (New York: Vanguard Press, 1937) covered some of the same issues as Seldes did; while he assailed print journalism and the "lords of the press," she concentrated mainly on the hegemony of radio networks and how powerful sponsors slanted the programming.

24. "Meet Miss Murphy, 1B," *Boston Globe,* May 24, 1922, p. 11. Also, the *Providence Journal* and other New England newspapers reported on the August 14, 1922, game in which she played on an All-Star team against the Boston Red Sox.

25. "Enter First Official Woman Umps," *Boston Post,* May 27, 1923.

26. "Latest in World Sport—A Woman Umpire," *Centralia* (IL) *Evening Sentinel,* May 3, 1922.

27. "Here's a Girl Farmer Who Is in Real Earnest," *Worcester Telegram,* January 18, 1922, p. 4C.

28. "Women in the News: Engineer and Hockey Star," *Boston Traveler,* September 9, 1925, p. 23.

29. Gail Savage, "Fair Sex Inventor," *Radio News,* May 1925, pp. 2089, 2116.

30. Edith M. Borkgren, "Sister Aimee," *Radio Doings,* vol. 19, no. 7, June 1931, pp. 24–25. Also various articles in the Los Angeles newspapers in early February 1924 when KFSG first went on the air: for example, *Los Angeles Times* of February 5, 1924, section 2, p. 16, "Angelus Station Is Ready."

31. Associated Press, "Cardinal Logue Hits 'Daring Dress'; Girls' Clothing Is Scandal, as Is Dancing," *Boston Globe,* March 1, 1924, p. 16. Also, in a similar vein, "Says Mannishness Cheapens Women," in which Dr. Arthur Holmes, a University of Pennsylvania psychology professor, criticized women for wanting to play sports, have short hair, and "imitate men"—*Boston Herald,* March 17, 1923. A syndicated article, written by Frank Crane of the McClure newspapers, "Women Who Want to Be Men" (*Boston American,* April 22, 1925, p. 8), covered some of the same ground, except the focus was on why women were destined to fail in business. As early as 1919, wives were also being accused of neglecting their family to attend club meetings or find employment: see, for example, "Modern Mothers Rapped by Hub Social Worker: Women Don't Really Love Their Children," the *Boston Herald,* October 12, 1919, special section, p. 33. And historian Frederick Allen devoted a chapter to the 1920s "revolt in manners and morals" in his 1931 book *Only Yesterday* (New York: Blue Ribbon, 1931).

32. United Press sent around a story on Nellie Twardzik, a fifteen-year-old from Webster, MA, who was so talented at athletics that she tried out for the boys' baseball team and impressed even the coach. "To Let Girl Play School Baseball: Coach Says She Will Be Given Position If She Can Make the Grade," *Boston Post,* March 28, 1935. Another was about Betty Schenkel: "World's Greatest Athlete Excels in 17 Sports," *Fitchburg* (MA) *Sentinel,* May 8, 1922, p. 10. Stories of the "amazing girl doing unusual things" genre frequently appeared in wire service items during the 1920s and early 1930s.

33. A typical article, about women and music, expressed it thusly: "In spite of emancipation, woman will always remain what nature has intended her to be . . . Woman is by nature refined and has a stronger sense of beauty than a man . . . a certain

retiring disposition will always be part of a real refined woman, and her sympathy and emotion will continue to get the best of her brain. . . ." Hans Schneider, "Women Composers," *Providence Journal,* June 4, 1922, p. 9.

34. "Women Are Subject Class, Says Alice Paul Bitterly," *New Bedford* (MA) *Standard,* November 10, 1922, p. 3.

35. "What Have Women Done with the Vote?" *Literary Digest,* September 22, 1923, p. 52.

36. Ibid., pp. 50, 52.

37. Frederick Lewis Allen, *Only Yesterday,* pp. 95–96.

38. Emily Newell Blair, "Are Women a Failure in Politics?" excerpted in *Review of Reviews,* November 1925, pp. 545–546.

39. "Texas for Ma," *Time,* September 1, 1924, pp. 5–6. See also Frederick D. Schwarz, "Mrs. Governor," *American Heritage,* November 1999, pp. 104–105.

40. "Northwest's Only Lady Mayor Broadcasts," *The Radio Record,* vol. 6, no. 5, February 1926, p. 35. In June 1925, Wyoming's governor, Mrs. Nellie Tayloe Ross, gave several talks over KOA in Denver, CO; *Radio World* was not sure what to call her, suggesting perhaps "Governoress" (*Radio World,* June 13, 1925, p. 30).

41. The incident, which was a front-page story in the Boston newspapers (see, e.g., *Boston Post,* November 5, 1929), is recounted in a book by Jack Beatty, *The Rascal King: The Life and Times of James Michael Curley* (Boston: Addison-Wesley, 1992), pp. 266–267.

42. "Granted Passport in her Maiden Name," *Boston Herald,* December 14, 1924. (When a British married woman won the right to use her maiden name, Miss Hale, who had lost her own case, now vowed to try again.) See also another similar case—No author given, "Fights to Be Listed as 'Miss,'" *Boston Post,* April 19, 1925.

43. "To Revise Book of Prayer: Word 'Obey' to Come Out of Episcopal Service," *Boston Post,* October 5, 1919, p. 13; and "Episcopal Change in Marriage Ritual Three Years Away," *New York Herald-Tribune,* April 7, 1922, p. 3.

44. Frederick Lewis Allen, *Only Yesterday,* p. 80.

45. Photo caption: "Miss America Is a Radio Girl," *Boston Post,* September 15, 1925, p. B-5.

46. "Beaver, Pa., Girl Is Named 'Miss Radio of 1925,'" *Radio Digest,* September 26, 1925, p. 7. Miss Frew was also advisor to the high school's ham radio club; in a number of other cities (including Boston, Chicago, and Milwaukee), there were women teachers who served in this capacity.

47. Ibid.

48. It was also popular on women's shows, where authors and "experts" were often guests. Lawyer, author, and educator Gleason Archer wrote syndicated columns for newspapers and magazines in the 1920s and early 1930s; he blamed women for the majority of the problems in marriage, which he attributed to their desire to work rather than to see the nobility of domesticity, a view he most probably expressed when he spoke as a guest on Boston and New York radio programs. Among the better magazine articles on married women and work was "Can a Woman Run a Home and Have a Job, Too?" in the November 11, 1922, issue of *Literary Digest,* pp. 40–63. A group of married women, some professionally employed and others not, debated the pros and cons; while most of them said staying home was preferable, a few of the working wives made an excellent case for having both a career and a family. The women who frequently appeared on radio to defend the working wife were members

of the Federation of Women's Clubs. Betty McGee, writing for *Radio Digest* in September 1930 (pp. 90–91) observed that the clubwomen in Pittsburgh were an invaluable resource for KDKA since the station's earliest days; they helped bring in politicians and educators to discuss the important issues, and they kept the housewife informed.

49. "Should Wives Take Jobs?" *Literary Digest,* January 24, 1925, p. 23.

50. Miss Lowell was not the only poet to appear on Boston radio—the station on which she read her poetry in early September 1922 was WGI, which offered college courses by radio, including courses about literature. An interesting portrait of Amy Lowell appeared in *Literary Digest,* May 30, 1925, pp. 27–28.

51. John O'Brien, for United Press International, "Speeds to Discard Her Tomboy Garb," *New Bedford* (MA) *Times,* October 29, 1927, p. 1.

52. When a newspaper owned a station, the radio editor tended to be enthusiastic rather than critical. WMC in Memphis, owned by the *Commercial Appeal,* took to the air in late January 1923, and the front page described the programming as "the highest class of entertainment ever broadcast from a southern radio station." *Memphis Commercial Appeal,* January 21, 1923, p. 1.

53. John Wallace, "Why Is It Difficult to Be Funny over the Radio?" *Radio Broadcast,* vol. 9, no. 2, June 1926, pp. 133–134. Also, "Kind and Unkind Words About Our Friends the Announcers," *Radio Broadcast,* vol. 10, no. 2, December 1926, p. 159.

54. Kingsley Welles, "Do Women Know What They Want in Radio Programs?" *Radio Broadcast,* vol. 8, no. 1, November 1925, p. 34.

55. Jennie Irene Mix, "For and Against the Woman Radio Speaker," *Radio Broadcast,* September 1924, p. 393.

56. Doris E. Fleischman, ed., *Careers for Women* (New York: Garden City Publishing, 1939), p. 401.

57. Ibid. Also, Bertha Brainard, "Sex No Longer a Factor in Business," *Boston Globe,* December 18, 1927, section 2, p. 7.

58. Jennie Irene Mix, "For and Against the Woman Radio Speaker," pp. 391–392.

59. Ibid., p. 395.

60. John Wallace, "Why Is It Difficult to Be Funny over the Radio?" pp. 133–134.

61. Michele Hilmes, *Radio Voices,* pp. 142–143.

62. Kingsley Welles, "Meet Mr. Average Radio Enthusiast," *Radio Broadcast,* vol. 9, no. 6, October 1926, p. 531.

63. "Men Prefer Organ Music but Women Crave the Orchestra," *The Radio Record,* May 1927, p. 24.

64. John Wallace, "Men versus Women Announcers," *Radio Broadcast,* vol. 10, no.1, November 1926, pp. 44–45.

65. A monthly series of engineering articles ran in *Radio Broadcast* during 1926; in January, the issue of microphone placement and distortion was discussed.

66. John F. Rider, "Why Is a Radio Soprano Unpopular?" *Scientific American,* October 1928, pp. 334–335.

67. Interestingly, despite printing quotes from station managers and at least one letter from a female listener who advocated for more women announcers—see Katharine W. Fisher's comments, *New York Times,* May 24, 1926, p. 18—the editors of the *Times* still insisted that only men should do the announcing ("Men's Voices Are Better," *New York Times,* May 25, 1926, p. 26).

68. "WJZ Reserving Certain Hours—Women Announcers in Demand," and also "Overflow of Announcers." Both from *Variety,* December 15, 1926, p. 44.

69. "Musical Clock Girl," *Radio Digest,* November 1929, p. 57. See also "Yank

Taylor at the Mike," *Chicago Daily Times,* December 28, 1929, p. 26.

70. Michele Hilmes, *Radio Voices,* pp. 311–312.

71. Dorothy Thompson, "On Women Correspondents and Other New Ideas," *The Nation,* January 6, 1926, pp. 11–12.

72. "Man Replaces Woman for Household Talk," *Radio World,* April 9, 1927, p. 17.

73. Madonna M. Todd, "Women of West Coast Have Own Magazine of Air," *Radio Digest,* May 1930, p. 15.

74. Susan Smulyan, *Selling Radio,* pp. 88–89.

75. "Corinne Jordan to Program KSTP," *St. Paul* (MN) *Pioneer Press,* February 19, 1928, p. 10.

76. "Station WASN Will Broadcast the Latest Shopping News," *Boston Globe,* January 29, 1927, p. 18.

77. Arthur M. Hyde, "Farmer Is No Longer Imprisoned on His Acres," *New York Times,* September 22, 1929, p. 2R.

Chapter 3

1. Miriam S. Leuck, "Women in Odd and Unusual Fields of Work," *Annals of the American Academy,* vol. 143, May 1929, p. 177.

2. "Higher Education, Lower Wages," *The Survey,* December 15, 1930, p. 309.

3. For more about working conditions and wages for white, black, and Hispanic women, see Sara Jane Deutsch, *From Ballots to Breadlines*, pp. 37–47.

4. Rex Beach, "She Tried the Impossible," *Boston Post,* April 21, 1929, Features, p. 6.

5. Ian Gordon, *Comic Strips and Consumer Culture* (Washington, DC: Smithsonian, 1998), pp. 123–124.

6. Among the jokes was an extended gag about Winnie's crush on a radio announcer—she falls in love with his voice, and then finds out he is really ugly and loses interest immediately. Winnie's superficiality and vanity are discussed by Gordon on pp. 118–122.

7. See, for example, Mrs. Ralph Borsoli, "The New Woman Goes Home," in *Scribner's,* February 1937, pp. 52–53 and numerous other similar essays in women's magazines like *Good Housekeeping* and *Ladies' Home Journal* during the early 1930s. Also common were radio fan magazine articles about wives of famous male performers: the story told how the wife was content to stay in the background and only wanted to devote herself to helping her husband, as in "Can a Wife Help a Man Make a Career?" by Earle Ferris in *Radio Digest,* October 1932, pp. 12–13.

8. "Employment of Married Women," from Edison employees' manual, reprinted in *Edison Life,* May–June 1938, p. 22.

9. "Married Women's Jobs in Danger, Women Voters' League Declares," *Boston Evening Transcript,* May 26, 1936, p. 5.

10. John Dunning, *On The Air: Encyclopedia of Old-Time Radio* (New York: Oxford, 1998), pp. 474–475.

11. See, for example, "Subject: Frances Langford; Object: Matrimony . . . Frances Langford Wants a Husband," *Radio Mirror,* January 1935, pp. 14, 15, 66; or "Take Time For Love . . . Rosa Ponselle Didn't—Is Her Fame Worth the Sacrifice?" *Radio Stars,* August 1934, pp. 20–22. But on the other hand, there were a few stories in which the star said she planned to keep on working after marriage, or even after

having a baby—see for example "How Martha Mears Is Facing Motherhood," *Radio Mirror,* December 1935, pp. 26, 76–77, in which the vocalist stated that she and her husband saw nothing wrong with her continuing to work, and they would sometimes bring their baby on the road with them.

12. In *Radio Stars,* March 1933, pp. 10–13, 44.

13. In *Radio Stars,* March 1934, pp. 44–45.

14. In short stories such as "Why Can't I Marry?" (*Radio Mirror,* April 1939), the young woman realized that being a successful radio star was an empty life. "If Dennis loved me, I didn't really care about my career . . . I knew that giving up my . . . hope of sudden fame was a small enough price to pay . . ." (p. 57). Or, the wife of a popular radio comedian, who now preferred to be known only as "Mrs. Phil Baker," explained to *Radio Stars* her secret for a happy marriage. The former Peggy Cartwright, she had been a promising dancer and actress when she met Phil, and she soon knew she had a choice to make. "On one side was my career, with perhaps fame, glory and success. The other road led to a home with children . . . liv[ing] in the glory of [my] husband . . . I don't see how a woman can be a wife and mother and a careerist besides. I am entirely content to let Phil be the breadwinner and the shining light of the family" (*Radio Stars,* April 1936, pp. 48, 74).

15. See, for example, "She Holds Her Man" (*Radio Stars,* March 1935, pp. 36, 62), in which singer Loretta Lee is separated from the struggling young trumpet player she loves, and until he makes enough money so that she can marry him and give up radio, she sings every song for him, and he listens from whatever city in which he happens to be working.

16. In addition to encouraging women to "play dumb," some magazine articles spoke about women as if they were cute children. While stating that Gracie Allen was really very intelligent in real life, Hilda Cole, writing in *Radioland,* remarked that Gracie was sometimes "an adorably helpless little girl who should be cuddled and tucked into to bed." Her husband and her friends found this quality charming, according to Miss Cole (*Radioland,* March 1934, p. 39). And the success of comedienne Fanny Brice's character "Baby Snooks" was another example of a woman who achieved radio popularity by being a little girl.

17. Herbert Polesie, "She Plays 1,000 Roles," *Radio Digest,* January 1933, p. 31.

18. Christine Lunardini, *What Every American Should Know About Women's History,* pp. 246–248.

19. John Dunning, *On The Air,* p. 301.

20. Ruth Jeffrey, "Radio—Interesting Field for Dramatic Writing," *The Author & Journalist,* September 1930, pp. 3–4.

21. Grace Davidson, "Prefer Jobs in the Spotlight: Women Especially Influenced by Lure of Publicity," *Boston Post,* February 26, 1933, pp. 1, 4. See also Lucille Singleton, "But 1 in 500 Succeed Who Covet Radio Fame," *Boston Globe,* April 5, 1936, p. E-6.

22. "Women Fall Down on the Air," *Variety,* March 11, 1931, p. 67.

23. John B. Kennedy, "Ladies of the Airwaves," *Collier's,* July 9, 1932, pp. 14.

24. Ibid., p. 44.

25. Wilson Brown, "She Cries for a Living," *Radio Stars,* June 1933, pp. 10, 45.

26. Bland Mulholland, "The Girl Behind the Men Behind the Mike," *Radio Stars,* January 1935, p. 68. Even Bertha Brainard had said that women's voices often lacked training. In the June 1927 issue of *McCall's,* she said that ". . . it is difficult to make a woman's voice sound natural on the air. When we're under tension or nervous strain,

our voices show it immediately . . . only the trained actress, or the exceptional woman whose voice is beautifully under control can keep it firm and even . . ." (quoted in *Radio World,* May 21, 1927, p. 16).

27. In addition to "The Nine Greatest Women in Radio" from the December 1934 *Radio Stars,* she was also mentioned in Ruth Arell's "Silent Voices in Radio" (*Independent Woman,* November 1937, pp. 342–343, 367–368).

28. Ibid. The *Radio Stars* article was concerned about Miss Brainard's femininity, while the *Independent Woman* article, in which she was also mentioned, dealt much more with her achievements.

29. "The First Lady's Week," *Time,* April 15, 1940, p. 17.

30. Harold Brown, "Twists and Turns," *Radio Digest,* October 1932, p. 4.

31. Mary Margaret McBride, *Out of the Air* (New York: Doubleday, 1960), pp. 32–36.

32. Edythe Meserand oral history, transcribed by the Washington Press Club Foundation as part of their "Women in Journalism" project. (Available at many college libraries; author used the copy at Radcliffe College, Cambridge, MA)

33. Alice Keliher, ed., *Radio Workers* (New York: Harper & Brothers, 1940), p. 34.

34. *The Radio Record,* March 1930, p. 37.

35. Grace Baker, "Price Cutting Under Fire," *The Radio Record,* February 1930, p. 9.

36. Mary Adamick, "Heavy Problems for a Little Girl," *Radio Digest,* May 1930, pp. 67–68. See also "Name Newswriter for Program Position," *Radio Digest,* February 1930, p. 63.

37. Betty Sheldon, "To the Ladies," *Radio Doings,* September 1931, pp. 12–14.

38. Ida Bailey Allen, "Home-Makers Club Is a Magnet," *Radio Digest,* January 1930, pp. 74, 126. Also, Florence Roberts, "Radio Reminiscences: Ida Bailey Allen Recalls Days of Swinging Mikes and Tiny Stuffy Studios," *Radio Digest,* January 1930, pp. 52–53.

39. "Nellie Revell, The Voice of Radio Digest," *Radio Digest,* March 1931, p. 63. Miss Revell wrote columns for *Variety, Radio Digest,* and various other publications during the 1920s and 1930s. Her recovery from a near-fatal illness is detailed in "The Woman Who Laughed at Death," *Radio Stars,* January 1935. An interesting retrospective on her life, "A Springfield Century: Nellie Revell Tells of Childhood Days," by Doug Pokorski can be found in the *Springfield* (IL) *Journal-Register,* September 28, 1999.

40. Mary Margaret McBride, *Out of the Air,* pp. 28, 29, 69, 111. Also, Nanette Kuther, "Does Radio Rule Women Voters?" in *Radio Stars,* July 1936, pp. 20–21.

41. Michele Hilmes, *Radio Voices,* pp. 280–281. Also, Mary Margaret McBride, *Out of the Air,* pp. 74–75.

42. Ibid.

43. George Kent, "Programs for Forgotten Women," *Radio Stars,* May 1935, pp. 48, 60. Another woman, journalist Catherine Mackenzie, author of a biography of Alexander Graham Bell, did a similar kind of interview and chat show on WABC in New York. *Radio Digest* said approvingly, "One of the most captivating speaking voices on radio belongs to her" (*Radio Digest,* November 1932, p. 21).

44. John Dunning, *On the Air,* p. 501. While Dunning seems dismissive of her "human interest" style, her sponsor, Pontiac, reported in Broadcasting that her audience was incredibly loyal and responsive: she did a merchandise giveaway—a "polishing cloth for the automobile"—and over 225,000 women wrote in to ask for one (*Broadcasting,* March 15, 1937, p. 7).

45. *Medford* (OR) *Mail Tribune,* November 1, 1978.

46. Eddie Cantor, *As I Remember Them* (New York: Duell, Sloan and Pearce, 1963), p. 83.

47. She also seldom used her name, saying she was too shy to do so! To the day she retired, people knew her as "Mrs. Pierre." Of the many tributes written about her, see *McCall's,* May 1957, p. 100. The South Dakota State Historical Society in Pierre, South Dakota, has a sizeable clipping file about her long career; their journal, *South Dakota History,* did a profile of her early achievements with KGFX: "Radio in the 1920s—A Social Force in South Dakota" (Spring 1981).

48. Picture section, *Minneapolis Star-Tribune,* May 4, 1952, pp. 6–7.

49. *The First 50 Years of Broadcasting* (Washington, DC: Broadcasting Publications, 1982), p. 1.

50. *Where the Melody Lingers On: WNEW 1934–1984* (New York: Nightingale Gordon, 1985), pp. 5–6.

51. *Broadcasting,* April 15, 1939, p. 46. Prior to that, the magazine had done a small pictorial tribute to seven women managers and owners on July 1, 1936, p. 82. The wording was somewhat odd for a tribute, however: the opening sentence read "Deadlier than the male is the female of the species—but they do make good radio station managers, we are told on competent authority."

52. *Where the Melody Lingers On,* pp. 5–6.

53. Phyllis Read and Bernard Witlieb, *The Book of Women's Firsts* (New York: Random House, 1992), p. 34.

54. This publicity stunt, reported in *Radio Spotlight,* August 14, 1932, p. 25, was one of her last; after swimming the English Channel in 1926, she then spent the next few years touring and performing; by the early 1930s, she had lost most of her hearing from spending so much time underwater.

55. Joseph Conn, "Making Flying 'Thinkable,'" *American Quarterly,* Autumn 1979, p. 560.

56. Anne B. Lazar, "Ladies Must Fly," *Radio Digest,* February 1931, pp. 80–81.

57. Doris Blake, "Airline Hostess Alluring Job for Adventurous Women," *Boston Herald,* June 18, 1933, Magazine section, p. 7B. See also *Reader's Digest,* May 1933, pp. 20–22.

58. Amelia Earhart quoted in "How Women Take to the Air," *Literary Digest,* October 26, 1929, pp. 55–56.

59. From the website of the Ninety-Nines, found at http://ninety-nines.org.

60. Ann P. Harris, "Hers: A Forum for Women," *New York Times,* June 14, 1984, p. 2C.

61. "The Woman 'Pin Money' Worker," *Literary Digest,* March 1, 1930, p. 12.

62. Quoted in *Boston Globe,* April 5, 1936, p. E6.

63. Jack Burton, *Blue Book of Tin Pan Alley,* 2d ed. (New York: Century House, 1965), pp. 393–394.

64. Barbara Dianne Savage, *Broadcasting Freedom* (Chapel Hill: University of North Carolina Press, 1999), pp. 14, 37. In fact, when one 1938 educational program about racism was being written, CBS refused to have any black people on the committee; the entire show was written and produced by whites.

65. *Broadcasting* magazine during the early 1930s stressed the importance of radio as an advertising tool and praised sponsors for developing popular soap operas and radio dramas: sales of toothpaste and cosmetics rose as a result. See *The First 50 Years of Broadcasting,* p. 7. See also Michele Hilmes, *Radio Voices,* pp. 144–146. In fan magazines, articles by the Radio Homemakers seldom mentioned the Depression, other than as a reason for being more creative with meal planning. And in Ida Bailey

Allen's weekly newsletter, "Radio Home-Makers," the May 26, 1930 issue discussed how to treat one's servants.

66. Helen Law, "A New Job For the College Girl," *Review of Reviews,* June 1930, pp. 74, 76.

67. Mabel Barbee Lee, "The Dilemma of the Educated Woman," *Atlantic Monthly,* November 1930, quoted in *Review of Reviews,* December 1930, pp. 71–72.

68. Lois Scharf, *To Work and to Wed* (Westport, CT: Greenwood Press, 1980), especially chaps. 4 and 5.

69. Sarah Jane Deutsch, *From Ballots to Breadlines*, p. 113.

70. Ibid.

71. Lilya Wagner, *Women War Correspondents of World War II* (Westport, CT: Greenwood Press, 1989), p. 33.

72. Ibid., p. 3. See also Nancy Caldwell Sorel, *The Women Who Wrote the War* (New York: Arcade, 1999), p. 95.

73. Robert T. Elson, *Time Inc.* (New York: Atheneum, 1968), p. 146.

74. Cari Beauchamp, "Even for Talkies, the Women Who Wrote Worked Silently," *New York Times,* June 22, 1997.

75. Dorothy Thompson, quoted in the *Boston Post,* March 22, 1936, pp. 1, 8.

76. Several anecdotes about this are recounted in Nancy Caldwell Sorel's book; see, for example, p. 32.

77. See also Hally Pomeroy, "Housewives Are Happier," *Radio Guide,* May 29, 1937, pp. 11, 18, in which Dorothy Thompson said she would no longer focus on her career and was going to concentrate on being a wife only. (After this article, she continued being a writer and a commentator for a few more years, before finally retiring.)

78. John Bantry, "Men Souring on Feminism," *Boston Post,* March 22, 1936, pp. 1, 8.

79. Peter Stearns and Mark Knapp, "Men and Romantic Love," *Journal of Social History,* Summer 1993, pp. 769–795.

80. Ibid., p. 779.

81. Ibid., pp. 780–781.

82. Evelyn Edwards, "Fighting It Out on the Air," *Radio Stars,* May 1936, pp. 42–43. 91. See also John Dunning, *On the Air,* p. 335.

83. Ibid., pp. 30–31.

84. Ruth Brindze, *Not to Be Broadcast* (New York: Vanguard, 1937), pp. 181–182, wherein the news department at the two Crosley stations in Cincinnati were told in May 1935 not to report on any strikes; and pp. 186–187, wherein the head of the NAACP was forbidden from using words like "lynching" or "race riot" or even "segregation."

85. "Not Even Bronx Cheer Left After Hays-ites Nix Naughty Lingo," *Variety,* October 2, 1935, p. 3.

86. Robert Eichberg, "Too Hot to Broadcast," *Radio Stars,* January 1935, pp. 22–23, 76.

87. Ruth Brindze, *Not to Be Broadcast*, pp. 187–188.

88. Lewis A. Erenberg, *Swingin' the Dream: Big Band Jazz and the Birth of American Culture* (Chicago: University of Chicago Press, 1999), pp. 83–84.

89. Ibid., p. 85.

90. Ibid.

91. "West Coast Chatter," *Radio Stars,* May 1938, p. 100.

92. John Dunning, *On the Air,* p. 332. See also "32 Girls and a Man," in *Radio Stars,* July 1936, pp. 48–49, 88.

93. This sentiment was common to most reporting on the "All Girl Orchestra." Phil was portrayed as the hero, taking a chance on the "girls" and fighting for their rights. His total domination of their every move was portrayed as for their own good. "I had to be convinced," he said to *Radio Stars,* "that these were the sort of girls who wouldn't make trouble, who'd cooperate with the other girls, [and] not permit jealousy to disrupt the organization . . ."

94. Nanette Kutner, "Does Radio Rule Women Voters?" *Radio Stars,* July 1936, pp. 20–21.

95. Mrs. Roosevelt published numerous magazine articles, as well as writing a daily syndicated column, "My Day." As for Margaret Sanger, an interesting article about her use of radio to spread her cause can be found in the Margaret Sanger Papers Project, from New York University: "Radio Sanger" appeared in the *MSPP Newsletter,* no. 6, Winter 1993–94.

96. Mary Biddle, "Keep Young and Beautiful," *Radio Stars,* February 1935, pp. 6, 78.

97. "Keep Young and Beautiful," *Radio Stars,* January 1936, pp. 6–7.

98. Pearl Buck, "Why Shouldn't Women Seek Men in Marriage?" *Radio Mirror,* April 1939, pp. 13, 91.

99. Vic Knight, "First Lady in Radio Sports," *Broadcasting,* May 1, 1934, p. 14.

100. Bob Hughes, "Feminine Sports Editor Runs into Difficulty," *Miami Herald,* March 6, 1941.

101. *The First 50 Years of Broadcasting*, pp. 38, 41.

102. John Dunning, *On The Air*, p. 403.

103. Ibid., p. 207.

104. "Women's Place Is in the Studio," *Broadcasting,* February 1, 1939, p. 55.

105. "A Guest of NBC: Famous European Announcer to Broadcast Here," *Broadcasting,* August 1, 1937.

106. Sarah Jane Deutsch, *From Ballots to Breadlines*, pp. 107–108, 114–115.

107. Ibid.

108. Lynn Wenzel and Carol J. Binkowski, *I Hear America Singing*, pp. 104–105.

109. Quoted in *Downbeat,* October 15, 1939.

110. Emily Newell Blair, "Discouraged Feminists," *Outlook,* July 8, 1931, pp. 302–303, 318.

Chapter 4

1. "The Gathering Storm," in *Decade of Triumph: The 40s* (Richmond, VA: Time-Life Books, 1999), p. 31.

2. Quoted in *Time,* February 26, 1940, p. 20.

3. *Time,* January 29, 1940, p. 46.

4. "Little Rock, Take a Bow!," *Independent Woman,* September 1947, p. 272. In addition to KXLR, *Independent Woman* reported that local stations in a number of cities were airing BPW-written features or using BPW speakers. To help local clubs use radio more effectively, the national organization created a Radio Committee in 1945; M. Margariete Ralls was its first chairman, coordinating the efforts of more than 600 chapters that had established local radio committees (*Independent Woman,* July 1946, p. 226).

5. *Big Song Magazine,* vol. 1, no. 3, May 1941, p. 2.

6. "The Radio Playbill—Jane Arden," *Radio Guide,* January 21, 1939, p. 6.

7. Michele Hilmes, *Radio Voices,* p. 177.

8. See, for example, Mary Ellen Brown in *Soap Opera and Women's Talk* (Newbury Park, CA: Sage, 1994), especially chaps. 2 and 3.

9. "Birth Control Issue Worries Local Stations," *Variety,* September 23, 1942, p. 30.

10. Cynthia Griffin Wolff, "A Mirror for Men: Stereotypes of Women in Literature," *The Massachusetts Review,* vol. 13, nos. 1–2, Winter–Spring 1972, p. 207.

11. Quoted in Lewis Erenberg, *Swingin' the Dream,* p. 285.
But this view was not unique—in 1934, Dr. Louis E. Bisch, writing in *Radioland,* basically denigrated every achievement of women in broadcasting. He said, for example, that female vocalists like Kate Smith were nowhere nearly as popular as the male vocalists, which explained the lack of equal pay for women performers—since women were not as popular, men deserved more money (*Radioland,* February 1934, pp. 29, 65).

12. "Women in Symphonies," *Newsweek,* December 6, 1943, p. 88. (One of those three was Boston, which, well into the 1960s, still refused to hire women for the Boston Symphony Orchestra; legendary conductor Arthur Fiedler was very much opposed to doing so.)

13. "The First Lady's Week," *Time,* April 15, 1940, p. 17.

14. More than fifty years later, she still did well in the polls: in December 1999, when *Time* named its 100 Most Influential People of the Twentieth Century, Eleanor Roosevelt was among them.

15. Nancy Caldwell Sorel, *The Women Who Wrote the War,* pp. 74–76.

16. "Meet the Ladies," *Broadcasting,* December 14, 1942, p. 34.

17. "Meet the Ladies," *Broadcasting,* May 4, 1942, p. 45.

18. "We Pay Our Respects," *Broadcasting,* January 31, 1944, p. 42.

19. "Buyers of Time," *Broadcasting,* April 6, 1942, p. 39.

20. Her career is discussed in *Women in Broadcast Journalism* by David H. Hosley and Gayle K. Yamada (Westport, CT: Greenwood Press, 1987); her collected papers are held at the Library of American Broadcasting and segments are available via the Internet at: http://www.lib.umd.edu/UMCP/LAB/COLLECTIONS/sioussat.html.

21. Cary O'Dell, *Women Pioneers in Television* (Jefferson, NC: McFarland, 1997), p. 96.

22. Norman Finkelstein, *With Heroic Truth: The Life of Edward R. Murrow* (New York: Clarion, 1993), pp. 105–106, 158.

23. Charles Burton, "A Juvenile Program That Pleases Parents," *Broadcasting,* December 15, 1931, p. 13.

24. Wynn Speece and M. Jill Karolevitz, *The Best of the Neighbor Lady* (Mission Hill, SD: Dakota Homestead, 1987), various pages.

25. "Meet the Ladies," *Broadcasting,* January 26, 1942, p. 27.

26. Michele Hilmes, *Radio Voices,* pp. 266–268.

27. Franz Alexander, "Wider Fields for Freud's Techniques," *New York Times,* May 15, 1949, sect. 6, p. 15. See also Ruth Herschberger, *Adam's Rib* (New York: Harper & Row, 1948), pp. 29–46; and Betty and Theodore Roszak's collection of essays, *Masculine/Feminine* (New York: Harper & Row, 1969), pp. 201–208.

28. Glenda Riley, *Inventing the American Woman* (Arlington Heights, IL: Harlan Davidson, 1986), p. 113.

29. Ibid.

30. Paula Watson, "All Guts for Old Glory: Rosie the Riveter," *Dallas Morning News,* December 29, 1999, p. 5C.

31. "Cure for Cramps," *Newsweek,* October 4, 1943, p. 88. And advertisers saw an opportunity—Kotex, maker of sanitary napkins for women, offered new booklets about women and menstruation to factory managers and nurses.

32. The dress code also required some changes—at first, women were expected to wear skirts and blouses, but when the women airport control tower operators had to climb ladders to get to the tower, this was difficult in a skirt. They were permitted to wear slacks (*Time,* June 21, 1943, p. 68).

33. "Post-War Horizons," *Newsweek,* August 23, 1943, pp. 52–53.

34. See, for example, "When Someone You Love Goes to War," in the October 1943 issue of *Good Housekeeping,* p. 99; the ad, for Westinghouse (maker of home appliances), tells women that it is their patriotic duty to get a job: "You have a job to do *for him.* For in this War, women who want their men home again won't just sit and wait. They'll step right into the shoes of the men who have gone—fill the jobs those men have left behind!"

35. See, for example, the ad for Pond's Cold Cream in *Radio Mirror,* February 1943, p. 49—it showed Anne Nissen, an attractive, smiling woman, who, we were told, was engaged to a soldier; she had taken a job that helped the war effort. The caption under her picture read: "She Handles High Explosives!" Miss Anne Nissen explained that working in a munitions plant was tough on a young woman's skin. "[Pond's cold cream] helps keep my skin feeling so soft and smooth, and it's a grand grime remover when I get home." Or, see the article in the December 1942 *Radio Mirror,* p. 10, "Look Pretty for Uncle Sam," which told women it was patriotic to buy cosmetics, since a woman wearing the right makeup boosted the "morale, hope and courage" of our fighting men; also, women who knew they looked good would be more productive on the job.

36. "Women's Place on the Air," *Broadcasting,* March 30, 1942, p. 59; the article first examined how in England, women were already announcing, engineering, and doing other more visible jobs. The discussion was about whether this would also occur in the United States. Also, see "Women in Demand as Radio Operators," *Broadcasting,* November 9, 1942, p. 28.

37. "Feminine Invaders of the Control Room," *Broadcasting,* May 4, 1942, p. 45.

38. "KMOX Silenced Five Hours Over Employment of Women," *Broadcasting,* June 22, 1942, p. 41.

39. "IBEW Plans to Adopt Policy to Cover Women Technicians," *Broadcasting,* December 14, 1942, p. 58.

40. Photo and caption in *FM Magazine,* April 1942, p. 21.

41. Elizabeth Sullivan, "Radio Station Run Entirely by Women," *Boston Globe,* January 10, 1943. This was more common on the new FM stations, where sometimes one woman ran all of the programming: in Fort Wayne, Indiana, Rosemary Stanger was the entire staff of W49FW, where she did the announcing, engineering, and managing during the six hours the station was on the air daily (*Movie-Radio Guide,* March 1943, p. 45).

42. "No. 1 Columnist," *FM Magazine,* December 1940, p. 2.

43. "Army Sweethearts," *Life,* February 16,1942, pp. 33, 41.

44. "Richmond's Reveille Girl," *Broadcasting,* April 6, 1942, p. 42.

45. "Chumsy Sweater Girl," *Newsweek,* July 12, 1943, p. 83.

46. "Targets for Tonight," *Newsweek,* July 26, 1943, p. 85.

47. Judith Waller, *Radio: The Fifth Estate* (Boston: Houghton Mifflin, 1946), pp. 148–149.

48. "All Girl Station," *Tune In,* May 1943, p. 58. The same issue also noted that station WHYN in Northampton, MA, was among the first to give the WAVES (women serving in the Navy during the war) their own show: nearby Smith College was training young women to serve in various jobs, freeing men for combat duty, and WHYN gave trainees and officers an opportunity to keep the public informed (p. 39). For more on all-girl stations, see "Orchids to the Capper Stations' Girl Operators" in the RCA publication *Broadcast News—AM/FM/Television,* January 1945; reporter Judy Alessi discusses WIBW in Topeka, KS, as well as KCKN in Kansas City, MO.

49. *Radio Mirror,* January 1943, p. 76. Unfortunately, it doesn't seem that Miss Munson was able to fulfill her dream of becoming a director either in radio or film, although she did help to direct a few radio programs for CBS. A couple of women did make the transition from performing to directing during the 1940s, mostly in film. The best known was Ida Lupino; Joan Harrison, formerly the assistant to Alfred Hitchcock, became one of the few women producers: see *Time,* February 28, 1944, pp. 93–94.

50. Belle Krasne, "Miami's First Lady of Radio," *Independent Woman,* April 1949, pp. 115–116.

51. Bob Doll, *Sparks Out of the Plowed Ground: The History of America's Small Town Radio Stations* (West Palm Beach, FL: Streamline, 1996), p. 66.

52. For example, "Gross Time Sales $237,600,000 in 1941; 14.2% Gain Over Previous Year," *Broadcasting,* February 2, 1942, p. 7.

53. "WAAC's First Muster," *Time,* June 8, 1942, p. 71.

54. "We Pay Our Respects," *Broadcasting,* May 25, 1942, p. 33.

55. Elizabeth Sullivan, "Daughter of Irene Rich to Be a WAVE," *Boston Globe,* May 29, 1944.

56. *Newsweek* did a long article about what a day in the life of a WAAC was like, as well as what they learned in the classroom: July 5, 1943, pp. 44–48.

57. *Time,* March 16, 1942, Camel cigarette ad: "What! A *Girl* Training Men to Fly for Uncle Sam?"

58. "Oh Boy! Women Instructors," *The Army Times,* September 19, 1942, p. 7.

59. "She-Bang," *Newsweek,* March 27, 1944, p. 106.

60. "Eleven Tips on Getting More Out of Women Employees," *Mass Transportation*, July 1943.

61. Nancy Caldwell Sorel, *The Women Who Wrote the War,* p. 236; also recounted by United Press in various newspapers, June 8, 1944.

62. Barbara Dianne Savage, *Broadcasting Freedom,* pp. 158–161.

63. Ibid., pp. 168–176.

64. Ibid., pp. 186–192.

65. Ibid., pp. 195–199.

66. "We've Come A Long Way, and in a Hurry, but . . . ," *Independent Woman,* August 1946.

67. Professor Blum discusses this in his critically acclaimed book, *V Was For Victory* (New York: Harcourt Brace Jovanovich, 1976); but ads in the popular magazines of the early 1940s seemed quite aware that women were now in higher-paying "men's" jobs and had more money to spend.

68. James Kirby Martin et. al, *America and Its People* (San Francisco: HarperCollins, 1989), p. 821.

69. Glenda Riley, *Inventing the American Woman,* p. 116.

70. "Blushing McBride," *Newsweek,* June 5, 1944, p. 81.

71. "Captain McAfee of the WAVES," *Time,* March 12, 1945, pp. 20–21.

72. Ibid., p. 73.

73. Program listings from this time period show a dramatic increase in news and commentary: *Movie-Radio Guide* for a typical week in September 1943, for example, listed daily commentary by Boake Carter, H.R. Baukhage, Lowell Thomas, Fulton Lewis Jr., H.V. Kaltenborn, Raymond Gram Swing, Carey Longmire, Gabriel Heatter, Edward R. Murrow, and Cedric Foster, just to name some of the men on the networks. Local news was provided by a number of other men and some women.

74. *Where the Melody Lingers On: WNEW, 1934–1984,* p. 26.

75. William C. Ackerman notes that in 1938, stations typically ran about 8 percent news a week; by 1943, NBC was running an average of 19 percent. ("The Dimensions of American Broadcasting," *Public Opinion Quarterly,* Autumn 1945, p. 295.) Christopher Sterling and J. Michael Kittross also note that "more homes had radio than electricity, bathtubs, telephones, or car." Radio had become essential, since it was able to bring the news first, right from the battlefields (*Stay Tuned,* 2d ed., pp. 223, 226).

76. William C. Ackerman, "The Dimensions of American Broadcasting," p. 298.

77. Susan Dworkin, *Miss America, 1945* (New York: Newmarket, 1987), pp. 147, 179–180.

78. See Sandra Opdycke, *The Routledge Historical Atlas of Women in America* (New York: Routledge, 2000), pp. 104–105. Also, Glenda Riley, *Inventing the American Woman,* p. 122. And Loretta Britten and Paul Mathless, eds., *Our American Century: The 40s* (Richmond, VA: Time-Life Books, 1999), p. 168.

79. Loretta Britten and Paul Mathless, *Our American Century,* p. 164.

80. Stephanie Coontz, *The Way We Never Were* (New York: Basic Books, 1992), pp. 159–160.

81. See *Reader's Digest,* July 1947, p. 128, where it also stated that women were far less moral than they used to be. And in *Time,* male experts held forth on what makes a happy marriage and decided that the more children a woman has, the happier she will be ("The Vanishing Family," *Time,* February 17, 1947, p. 56).

82. Greta Palmer, "What Kind of a Wife Has He?" *Reader's Digest,* March 1948, pp. 37–39.

83. Clifford Adams, "Making Marriage Work," *Ladies' Home Journal,* July 1948, p. 26.

84. Clifford Adams, "Making Marriage Work," July 1948, p. 26.

85. "The Private Life of Gwyned Filling," *Life,* May 3, 1948, pp. 103–114.

86. *Book Review Digest,* 1947 ed., pp. 573–574.

87. Christine Lunardini, *What Everyone Should Know About Women's History,* pp. 272–273.

88. Joanne Meyrowitz, "Beyond the Feminine Mystique: A Reassessment of Postwar Mass Culture," *Journal of American History,* March 1993, pp. 1456, 1475–1476.

89. Quoted in Christine Lunardini, *What Every American Should Know About Women's History,* p. 273.

90. Margaret Culkin Banning, "Looking Ahead with the Woman Broadcaster," *Independent Woman,* May 1947, pp. 127, 147.

91. "I'm Bringing Up My Baby," *Look,* February 15, 1949, pp. 14, 16–17.

92. Carolyn G. Heilbrun, *Writing a Woman's Life* (New York: Ballantine, 1988), pp. 15–16.

93. Vance Packard, "Married Life in a Goldfish Bowl," *Reader's Digest,* April 1948, pp. 23–25.

94. Joe Koehler, "Radio's Dames as Names," *The Billboard,* July 26, 1946, pp. 3, 10.

95. John C. Baker, *Farm Broadcasting: The First 60 Years* (Ames: Iowa State Press, 1981), pp. 303–304.

96. "Who's the Nation's Most Glamorous Disc Jockey?" *Radio Best,* November 1947, p. 60.

97. Mark Hatch, "FCC Lady Member Gives Her Views," *Boston Post,* October 22, 1950, p. A-4.

98. *Current Biography,* 1948 ed., pp. 373–374.

99. "Hearth and Home," *Time,* March 22, 1948, p. 48.

100. Leslie Towner, "Why Kate Smith Never Married," *Radio Album,* July/September 1949, pp. 4, 6.

101. Louis Cantor, *Wheelin' on Beale* (New York: Pharos, 1992), pp. 89, 117.

102. Anthony Slide, *Selected Radio and Television Criticism* (Metuchen, NJ: Scarecrow Press, 1987), p. 144.

103. John Dunning, *On The Air*, p. 390.

104. Women journalists had long felt they did not get the respect they deserved; in 1944, for example, at the annual White House Correspondents' Dinner, the President of the Women's National Press Club, May Craig—a woman who had covered hard news for many years—was denied admittance, as were thirty-six of her colleagues; no women were allowed at the dinner (*Newsweek,* March 13, 1944, p. 83). In 1959, *Newsweek* revisited women's salaries and found that editors still felt it was acceptable to pay less to female reporters.

105. Dick Perry, *Not Just a Sound: The Story of WLW* (Englewood Cliffs, NJ: Prentice Hall, 1971), pp. 149–150.

106. Milly McLean, "TV's Early Days—A Fond Memory," *Gloucester* (MA) *Times,* July 14, 1977, p. 2.

Chapter 5

1. Jo Pearson, "Here's Mary Margaret," *Radio and Television Mirror,* August 1951, pp. 28, 30–31, 85.

2. Information from the archives of Emerson College, Boston, MA, including catalogs and course descriptions, as well as a 1957 master's degree thesis by Joseph Buerry on the programming of WERS since its inception.

3. "Our Respects to . . ." *Broadcasting,* May 15, 1950, pp. 38, 40.

4. She was first profiled in "Helen of Tulsa," *Time,* December 12, 1949, pp. 60–61.

5. *Variety,* October 8, 1952, p. 34. *Variety*'s weekly "Disk Jockey Review" also had nice things to say about KNBC San Francisco's Barbara Lee, who earned praises for her "voice and diction," as well as for her "charm and authenticity," and her ability to keep the show interesting (*Variety,* March 8, 1950, p. 42).

6. *Variety,* March 31, 1954, p. 34. In that same issue, *Variety* also noted the talents of Alma Dettinger, veteran announcer/producer at WQXR in New York, who served as moderator for some of the station's educational programs.

7. Also, the issue of marriage versus career recurred in all the fan magazines around this time. The majority of the stars said their husband and children came first, despite the fact that each was still working. Host of her own TV show, Faye Emerson stated in *TV Star Parade* (Fall 1951, p. 16) that "[m]arriage is the very finest career for

any woman, and any woman who would prefer a career to marriage and children is out of her mind."

8. Miss Frederick, whose news career went back to 1938 when she wrote scripts for a famous commentator, had been told by her first boss in radio not to even try to get on the air; he believed women could not be successful doing news (*Current Biography,* 1954 ed., p. 291).

9. Miss Adams, referred to in an April 21, 1958 *Newsweek* profile as "a good-looking, 38-year-old widow," was praised for her show on WJAR-TV in Providence, *The World Around Us*, which the writer said "fill[s] some of day-time TV's intellectual vacuum" (p. 90). And *Boston Globe* critic Elizabeth Sullivan added, "Betty has traveled all over Europe with her microphone and film crew, interviewing leaders of the countries she visited" (*Boston Globe,* June 21, 1959). But because Betty Adams was doing a women's show, no matter how many leaders she interviewed, it was still not considered "news."

10. *Broadcasting* did not write much about women's shows, so her station, KMBC-TV, took out a full-page ad to praise her for two decades of achievements (*Broadcasting,* back page, December 12, 1955).

11. Jan Forsythe, "40 Years of Love, Honor and Analysis with H.V. Kaltenborn," *Radio and Television Best,* April 1950, pp. 32, 34, 61.

12. Judith Marlane, *Women in Television News* (Austin: University of Texas Press, 1999), pp. 16–17.

13. See *Variety*, May 10, 1950, p. 23. I have talked to Mrs. Kirby's relatives about this anecdote, and they find it puzzling, since she was in their recollection, always a very strong woman; perhaps she felt she should defer to some of the more experienced men because women in her generation were not expected to run all-male organizations.

14. *You Must Remember This: 1950* (New York: Warner Treasure Books, 1995), pp. 8–9.

15. Norman Corwin, *Trivializing America* (Secaucus, NJ: Lyle Stuart, 1986), pp. 170–171.

16. Tim Brooks and Earl Marsh, *The Complete Directory to Prime Time TV Shows, 1946–Present*, 6th ed. (New York: Ballantine, 1999), pp. 394–395. As might be expected, the fan magazines mentioned that Loeb was being replaced but did not discuss why.

17. David Halberstam, *The Fifties* (New York: Fawcett, 1993), pp. 508–509.

18. Ibid., pp. 589–590.

19. Vincent DePaul Lupiano and Ken W. Sayers, *It Was a Very Good Year* (Holbrook, MA: Bob Adams, 1994), p. 360. See also Glenda Riley, *Inventing the American Woman,* pp. 122–123.

20. Rita Lang Kleinfelder, *When We Were Young* (New York: Prentice Hall, 1993), p. 14. See also Loretta Britten and Sarah Brash, *Our American Century: The Fifties* (Richmond, Va.: Time-Life Books, 1998) pp. 28–30.

21. Barbara Ehrenreich and Deidre English, *For Her Own Good* (New York: Anchor, 1978), p. 198.

22. Ibid.

23. Ibid., p. 212.

24. As mentioned earlier, this belief had been expressed by various male "experts" (and the radio homemaker Ida Bailey Allen, too) for decades. In fan magazines, male stars now espoused the importance of women returning to their traditional gender

role—see for example, "I Like Old-Fashioned Wives" by Mutual Network announcer Bob Poole, who extolled the woman who makes good hearty meals for her husband, gets up early to make sure she looks nice before her husband awakens, and always puts her family's well-being first (*Radio and Television Mirror,* February 1950, pp. 29, 76).

25. Lynn Spigel, *Make Room for TV* (Chicago: University of Chicago Press, 1992), pp. 60–61.

26. Michael McCall, *The Best of 50s TV* (New York: Mallard Press, 1992), p. 18.

27. Tim Brooks and Earle Marsh, *The Complete Directory to Prime Time Network TV Shows,* pp. 618–619.

28. "Seven Women in Radio and TV Win the McCall's Mike," *McCall's,* January 1954, pp. 9, 58. In awarding a Golden Mike for educational programming to Judith Waller, the editors wrote that she was "one of the few people in the world who thought that [*Ding Dong School*] had any chance of succeeding." The show, with its host "Miss Frances," became one of the best-known educational shows for preschoolers in the early 1950s.

29. David Richardson, *Puget Sounds* (Seattle, WA: Superior, 1981), p. 106.

30. "Video's Dancing Daughters," *New England TV Guide,* March 28, 1952, p. 4.

31. "They've Got Sales Appeal," *TV Guide,* November 27, 1953, pp. 10–11.

32. "Kitchen Riches," *Newsweek,* January 12, 1953, p. 70.

33. J.P. Shanley, "Out of the Kitchen: Betty Furness Welcomes Dramatic Role on TV," *New York Times,* May 12, 1957, section 2, p. 11.

34. Her obituary gives a good summary of her many accomplishments: Richard Severo, "Betty Furness, TV Reporter and Consumer Advocate, Dies," *New York Times,* April 4, 1994, p. B-16.

35. "They've Got Sales Appeal," *TV Guide,* November 27, 1953, pp. 10–11.

36. Jimmy Powers, "Lady Wrestlers—Are They Taboo?" *New England TV Guide,* November 14, 1952, p. 5.

37. "Philly Mamas Fed Up with Soapers; Too Much Battling on Gleason Show," *Variety,* September 7, 1955, p. 25.

38. Elizabeth Sullivan, "What Happened in TV and Radio," *Boston Globe,* January 1, 1954.

39. "Radio Editors Ignore Radio: TeeVee Getting All the Play," *Variety,* October 29, 1952, p. 31.

40. See Glenn C. Altschuler and David I. Grossvogel, *Changing Channels: America in TV Guide* (Urbana, IL: University of Chicago Press, 1992), pp. 129–136, 140–141.

41. Carolyn G. Heilbrun, *Writing a Woman's Life,* pp. 23–25.

42. Glenn Altschuler and David Grossvogel, *Changing Channels,* pp. 98–99.

43. Rita Lang Kleinfelder, *When We Were Young,* p. 69.

44. Ibid., pp. 11–12, 106, 246.

45. David Halberstam, *The Fifties,* p. 589.

46. Alex McNeil, *Total Television* (New York: Penguin, 1996), p. 385. See also, "'Home' Nears Top as Idea Source," *Broadcasting,* August 15, 1955, p. 74.

47. David Halberstam, *The Fifties,* p. 280.

48. *The First 50 Years of Broadcasting,* p. 119.

49. Arthur J. Singer, *Arthur Godfrey: The Adventures of an American Broadcaster* (Jefferson, NC: McFarland, 2000), pp. 90–92.

50. Bob Williams and Chuck Hartley, *Good Neighbors to the North: WCCO Radio, 1924–74* (Minneapolis, MN: WCCO Publishing, 1974), p. 27. Darragh Aldrich

of WCCO was one of a number of women's show hosts who won community service awards for their efforts during the epidemic.

51. John Dunning, *On The Air*, p. 438.

52. Lorraine Santoli, *The Official Mickey Mouse Club Book* (New York: Hyperion, 1995), p. 56.

53. See, for example, Michael Shore with Dick Clark, *The History of American Bandstand* (New York: Ballantine, 1985).

54. Susan Douglas, *Where the Girls Are* (New York: Times Books, 1994), p. 87.

55. Stephanie Coontz, *The Way We Never Were*, pp. 170–171.

56. Helen Bolstad, "Rock and Roll: An Evil Influence?" *TV Radio Mirror,* September 1956, pp. 28–30, 85–87.

57. Actually, it took a while for credit cards to catch on—the first ones, Diner's Club, appeared in 1950 in New York (Rita Kleinfelder, *When We Were Young*, pp. 66–67).

58. And while radio advertising revenues remained strong, the radio networks were in trouble, and according to *Broadcasting* (December 12, 1955, pp. 27–32), most of the major agencies were moving the majority of their commercials to TV. For example, J. Walter Thompson spent $53 million on TV, and only $5 million on radio in 1955.

59. Enid A. Haupt, "How to Win Dates and Influence the Dobie Gillis Type," *TV Guide,* December 5, 1959, pp. 20–23.

60. *Scholastic Magazine* found that baby boomer teens had become quite a market —in 1956, there were 13 million of them, and they had money to spend on records. By the late 1950s, 10 million portable record players were sold (David Halberstam, *The Fifties*, pp. 473–474).

61. "Tomboy with a Typewriter," *Time,* April 8, 1957, p. 68.

62. Ren Grevatt, "On the Beat," *Billboard,* October 13, 1958, p. 8.

63. "Ladies Listen to a Man—NAB Prez," *Variety,* April 30, 1958, p. 37.

64. "Femcasters as Missionaries in McGannon's Eye," *Variety*, April 30, 1958, p. 37.

Chapter 6

1. Reebee Garafolo, *Rockin' Out: Popular Music in the USA* (Boston: Allyn & Bacon, 1997), pp. 154–155.

2. A *TV Radio Mirror* story about hit vocalist Connie Francis in June 1960 was typical—it depicted her as only interested in buying more clothes, as if this was what girls naturally cared most about: "Connie's Having a Whirl Being a Girl." Or there was a *TV Guide* article from September 17, 1960, "A Woman's Woes in Television," which rather than being about sexism and the lack of equal pay, was about a bad day actress June Allyson had when she found her dressing room was locked, the dress she was supposed to wear on camera was wrinkled, and she couldn't remember her lines.

3. Opal Ginn, "Lady Bosses—How Tough?" *Parade,* July 10, 1960, pp. 26–28.

4. Altschuler and Grossvogel, *Changing Channels,* p. 135.

5. "Dateline Washington DC," *TV Radio Mirror,* July 1960, p. 12.

6. Mary Cremmen, "Jackie Walks Alone, Then Faces Spotlight," *Boston Globe,* November 10, 1960, p. 4.

7. Unfortunately, she was not able to break out of the "women's show" ghetto and be taken seriously as a newsperson, a fate that befell many of the women's show hosts, whose programs were more news, interviews, and information than recipes.

One of the few who did make the transition was Cleveland's Dorothy Fuldheim; she did commentary and celebrity interviews but seemed to be perceived more as a newscaster—and an outspoken, controversial one at that (Cary O'Dell, *Women Pioneers in Television,* pp. 109–111).

8. J.P. Shanley, "Out of the Kitchen: Betty Furness Welcomes Dramatic Role on TV," *New York Times,* May 12, 1957, section 2, p. 11.

9. Catherine Heinz, "Women Radio Pioneers," *Journal of Popular Culture* (Fall 1978).

10. Carol Tavris, *The Mismeasure of Woman* (New York: Touchstone, 1992), p. 17, also p. 300.

11. Judith Marlane, *Women in Television News Revisited*, p. 17.

12. "Folk Girls," *Time,* June 1, 1962, pp. 39–40.

13. Robbie Woliver, *Bringing It All Back Home* (New York: Pantheon, 1986), pp. 92–93, 95.

14. Gillian G. Garr, *She's a Rebel* (Seattle, WA: Seal Press, 1992), pp. 46–49.

15. Ibid., p. 50.

16. Sandra Hardy Chinn, *At Your Service: KMOX and Bob Hardy* (St. Louis, MO: Virginia Publishing, 1997), pp. 89–90.

17. Christine Lunardini, *What Every American Should Know About Women's History*, pp. 303–304.

18. Lisa Hammel, "They Meet in Victorian Parlor to Demand True Equality—NOW," *New York Times,* November 22, 1966, p. 44.

19. Liz Trotta, *Fighting for Air* (New York: Simon and Schuster, 1991), p. 196.

20. Jessica Savitch, *Anchorwoman* (New York: Berkley, 1983), p. 26.

21. Susan Douglas, *Where the Girls Are*, pp. 126–127.

22. "Doors Are Finally Opening For Women," *Broadcasting,* May 6, 1963, p. 88. There was an interesting tribute to Johnson in *Broadcasting* on September 12, 1955, p. 26, wherein her broadcasting career, as owner of a station in Austin, Texas, and another in Waco was detailed.

23. Jane Shattuc, *The Talking Cure* (New York: Routledge, 1997), p. 36.

24. Michael Keith, *Talking Radio* (Armonk, NY: M.E. Sharpe, 2000), p. 124.

25. Michael Keith, *Voices in the Purple Haze* (Westport, CT: Praeger, 1997), p. 51.

26. Michael Keith, *Talking Radio*, pp. 122, 125.

27. Susan Douglas, *Where the Girls Are*, pp. 163–164, 179.

28. Ibid., pp. 139–140.

29. Joyce Hoffman, "On Their Own: Female Correspondents in Vietnam," *Quest* (*The Research Journal of Old Dominion University*), vol. 2, no. 1 (Fall 1998).

30. He was not the only one to change his views; as equal pay laws were passed, suddenly newspaper editorials began to appear saying what a good thing it was for women to be paid what they deserve. See, for example, *Boston Globe,* May 27, 1963, "The 'Weaker' Sex?" *Newsweek* did an article about women executives in their June 27, 1966 issue (pp. 76–78), in which the usual myths were explored, and in some cases challenged. And many other publications began to seriously examine the discrimination women in business faced—see, for example, "Few Women Reach the Top in Industry" by Peter Greenough (*Boston Globe,* September 19, 1963), which featured a talk with Esther Peterson of the Women's Bureau; see also financial expert Sylvia Porter's syndicated column of August 29, 1967, "Working Wives Fill Labor Force."

31. Mrs. L.R. Scott, "Other Women Hate Me," *New York Herald-Tribune,* March 13, 1966, pp. 8, 18–19.

32. "Women at the Top," *Newsweek,* June 27, 1966, pp. 76–78.

33. Barbara Walters, "Electronic Girl Reporters," *Variety,* January 5, 1966, p. 108.

34. Cokie Roberts, *We Are Our Mothers' Daughters* (New York: Harper and Row, 1988), p. 116.

35. Telephone interview with Charlie Parker in 1990, quoted in my book *Radio Music Directing* (Stoneham, MA: Focal Press, 1991), p. 60.

36. Claude Hall and Barbara Hall, *This Business of Radio Programming* (New York: Billboard Publications, 1977), pp. 75–76.

37. For how women reporters in the early 1960s were treated, see, for example, Marlene Sanders and Marcia Rock, *Waiting for Prime Time* (New York: Harper and Row, 1988), pp. 51–52.

38. Jon Katz, "Battle Lines" (A Review of "Fighting for Air: In the Trenches with Television News" by Liz Trotta), *Columbia Journalism Review* (May/June 1991), pp. 58–61.

39. Susan Douglas, *Where the Girls Are,* pp. 181–184.

40. Ibid., p. 170; also see the cover story in *Newsweek,* March 23, 1970.

41. Nan Robertson, *The Girls in the Balcony* (New York: Random House, 1992), pp. 198–199; see also Susan Douglas, *Where the Girls Are,* pp. 166–167.

42. Susan Douglas, *Where the Girls Are,* pp. 168–173.

43. Ibid., pp. 163–164; see also Susan Faludi, *Backlash: The Undeclared War Against American Women* (New York: Crown, 1991), pp. 3–4, 59–60.

44. Susan Douglas, *Where the Girls Are,* p. 173.

45. Quote by Andrew Hacker in "The American Family: Future Uncertain," *Time,* December 28, 1970, pp. 34–35.

46. For attitudes about women in rock bands, see especially Lucy O'Brien, *She-Bop* (New York: Penguin, 1995), pp. 105–122; Gillian Garr, *She's a Rebel,* pp. 127–132. See also Reebee Garafolo, *Rockin' Out,* pp. 229–230, 269–270.

47. Katherine M. Skiba, "Women Talk over Media Role," *Milwaukee Journal-Sentinel,* August 27, 1996, p. 6. Many of the pioneer women in news began with less-than-auspicious first assignments—Pauline Frederick was first asked to write an article about how to find a husband.

48. Judith Marlane, *Women in Television News Revisited,* pp. 30–31.

49. Ibid.

50. See the research done by Professor Martha M. Lauzen, School of Communication, San Diego State University, San Diego, CA, quoted on the Women in Film website, http://www.wif.org

51. Marlene Sanders and Marcia Rock, *Waiting for Prime Time,* pp. 135–137.

52. "TV News Hens," *Ebony,* vol. 21, no. 12, October 1966, pp. 44–46, 50.

53. For information about Andrea Rhone and other black women in TV journalism, see "Communicating Just Ain't the Same: A Look at Four Black Women in Media," *Baltimore Afro-American,* March 22, 1997. The most detailed biography and interview with Carole Simpson comes from the Oral History Project, Washington Press Club Foundation, Women in Journalism site, http://npc.press.org/wpforal/simint.htm

54. Bruce McCabe, "Women in TV News Game Moving Forward, but . . ." *Boston Globe,* January 4, 1976, p. A9.

55. Jane Bryant Quinn, "A Woman's Place," *Newsweek,* February 26, 1979, p. 73.

56. *Billboard,* February 26, 1978, pp. SW12, SW 21; see also Lucy O'Brien, *She-Bop,* p. 248.

57. *Billboard,* February 26, 1978, p. SW12.

58. Susan Douglas, *Where the Girls Are,* pp. 221–237.

59. Jane Shattuc, *The Talking Cure,* pp. 37–38.

60. CNN's program *Newsstand* did a feature about her on October 25, 1998. She was also featured in *People,* October 19, 1998, pp. 66–68. The NBC show *Dateline* did a feature on her on October 28, 1998; AWRT gave this show a Gracie Award.

61. Jo Foxworth, *Boss Lady* (New York: Warner Brothers, 1979), pp. 223–227. She also spoke at several AWRT during the 1980s on women in sales.

62. Elmo I. Ellis, *Opportunities in Broadcasting* (Skokie, IL: National Textbook Company, 1981), pp. 131–132.

Chapter 7

1. Susan Faludi, *Backlash,* pp. 77–79.

2. Ibid.

3. Marlene Sanders, *Waiting for Prime Time,* pp. 139–140.

4. The story is told by Ms. Craft in her book *Too Old, Too Ugly, and Not Deferential to Men* (Rocklin, CA: Prima Publishing, 1988); the case also received considerable media coverage in most major newspapers in 1983—see, for example, the Associated Press story "Anchorwoman Wins Lawsuit," which ran on August 9, 1983.

5. Jane Shattuc, *The Talking Cure,* pp. 20, 21, 31.

6. Ibid., p. 132.

7. Jack Hilton, *The TV Inquisitors* (New York: Chamberlain, 1981), pp. 42, 50.

8. Linda Ellerbee, "TV Still Pops That Age Old Question," *Newsday,* April 6, 1994, p. A32.

9. Judy Muller, *Now This: Radio, Television . . . and the Real World* (New York: G.P. Putnam, 2000), pp. 113–116; see also Judith Marlane, *Women in Television News Revisited,* pp. 31–32.

10. Judith Marlane, *Women in Television News Revisited,* p. 33.

11. Margaret Zack, "Spencer Trial Bares TV Trivialities," *Minneapolis Star-Tribune,* January 18, 1992, pp. 1, 5B.

12. Marlene Sanders, *Waiting for Prime Time,* pp. 175–176.

13. Susan Faludi, *Backlash,* pp. 118–123.

14. Ibid., p. 112.

15. Ibid., p. 149.

16. Tim Brooks and Earl Marsh, *The Complete Directory to Prime Time Network TV Shows,* p. 152.

17. Susan Faludi, *Backlash,* pp. 149–151.

18. Ibid., p. 152.

19. Elmo Ellis, *Opportunities in Broadcasting,* pp. 131–133.

20. Mark Carreau, "Sally Ride Is Leaving NASA," *Houston Chronicle,* September 21, 1987.

21. In 1993, when *The Nanny* premiered, "Viewers for Quality Television" called it "the 90's version of 'I Love Lucy' . . . it is well written and entertaining." But male critics often found Fran Drescher's character annoying and whiny. Her 1997 autobiography alluded to this—it was called *Enter Whining.*

22. "Quayle Decries Moral Decline in Inner Cities," *Associated Press,* May 20, 1992.

23. Susan Faludi, *Backlash,* pp. 153–163.

24. Interview with Judy Dibble at KSTP Radio, personal correspondence sent to me July 19, 2000.

25. Joseph Wright, "Shirley 'The House Party' Clark Really Likes to Jam in the A.M," *Los Angeles Sentinel,* July 28, 1994.

26. Frank Ahrens, "Female Hosts: Low Frequency," *Washington Post,* March 21, 2000, p. C2.

27. Rush Limbaugh, quoted in Steven Rendell and Jim Naureckas, *The Way Things Ought to Be but Aren't* (New York: New Press, 1995), pp. 51–57, for some of his antifemale quotes.

28. Cathy Hughes, quoted on the Radio One website, http://www.computer-daze.com/RadioOne. See also the profile of her in *Ebony* magazine, May 2000, p. 100.

29. Lynn Norment, "Cathy Hughes: Ms. Radio," *Ebony,* May 2000.

30. Rick Marin, "Coming Up Roses (Rosie O'Donnell)," *Newsweek,* July 15, 1996, pp. 45–48. See also Renee Graham, "Rosie Succeeds as Everywoman," *Boston Globe,* July 5, 1996, p. 37.

31. Jackie Byars and Eileen R. Meehan, "Once in a Lifetime: Constructing 'The Working Woman' Through Cable Narrowcasting," *Camera Obscura—A Journal of Feminism and Film Theory,* vol. 33, no. 4, May 1994.

32. Ellen Goodman, "In Newspapers, a Woman's Place Is Far from Page 1," *Boston Globe,* April 5, 1992, p. 71.

33. George Gerbner, *Casting the American Scene: A Look at the Characters on Primetime and Daytime Television, 1994–1997* (Los Angeles: Screen Actors Guild Publications, 1998).

34. Ibid.

35. Research by Professor Martha M. Lauzen, School of Communication, San Diego State University, San Diego, CA, quoted on the Women in Film website, http://www.wif.org

36. Ibid.

37. Edie Hilliard, quoted in *Radio Ink* magazine, August 16, 1999, p. 62.

38. "The Unforgettable Women of the Century," *People* (Time-Life Books), 1999.

39. Dana Calvo, "Female Anchors on Local TV Paid 28% Less," *Los Angeles Times,* June 1, 2000, p. A1.

40. Mary Mitchell, "It's Not Too Late to Bring Justice to Women in Radio," *Chicago Sun-Times,* April 5, 1998, p. 27.

41. Gloria Cahill, "Class(y) Action," *Radiance,* Fall 1998.

42. Naomi Wolf, *The Beauty Myth* (New York: William Morrow, 1991), especially chap. 7 ("Hunger").

43. Vernon Stone, "Minorities and Women in Television News," University of Missouri School of Journalism website, http://web.missouri.edu, July 1995.

44. Phyllis Stark, "More Women Getting Their Say on Radio," *Billboard,* August 10, 1991, p. 10.

45. Rick Aucoin, "Watching Barbara Walters," *Boston Globe,* May 21, 2000, p. C1.

Selected Bibliography
and Suggested Readings

Ackerman, William C. "The Dimensions of American Broadcasting." *Public Opinion Quarterly* (Autumn 1945): 283–304.

Adamick, Mary. "Heavy Problems for a Little Girl." *Radio Digest* (May 1930): 67–68.

Adams, Dr. Clifford R. "Making Marriage Work." *Ladies' Home Journal* (July 1948): 26; (October 1948): 26.

Ahrens, Frank. "Female Hosts: Low Frequency." *Washington Post,* March 21, 2000, p. C2.

Alesi, Judy J. "Orchids to the Capper Stations' Girl Operators." *Broadcast News—AM/FM/Television* [RCA] (January 1945).

Alicoate, Jack, ed. *Radio Annual and Radio/Television Annual.* New York: Radio Daily Press, 1938–1964.

Allen, Frederick Lewis. *Only Yesterday.* New York: Blue Ribbon, 1931.

Allen, Ida Bailey. "The Man About the House." *Radio Homemakers Magazine* 2, no. 39 (June 23, 1930): 1.

———. "Radio." *Radio Homemakers Magazine* 2, no. 27 (March 31, 1930).

———. "Home-Makers Club Is a Magnet." *Radio Digest* (January 1930): 74, 126.

"All Girl Station." *Tune In* (May 1943): 58.

Altschuler, Glenn C., and David I. Grossvogel. *Changing Channels: America in TV Guide.* Urbana, IL: University of Chicago Press, 1992.

"American Radio Relay League Holds Its Annual Convention; Miss Randall Presents and Assists in Demonstrations." *New Bedford Times*, September 15, 1921, pp. 1–2.

"American Women: Great Changes, New Chances, Tough Choices." *People,* special "Women of the Year" issue (January 5, 1976).

Anderson, Karen Tucker. "Last Hired, First Fired: Black Women Workers During World War II." *Journal of American History* 69, no. 1 (June 1982).

Andrist, Ralph K., ed. *American Heritage History of the 1920s and 1930s.* New York: American Heritage, 1970.

"Anti-Feminist McCarl(and Ruth Hale)." *Time* (August 25, 1924): 5.

"Are Women a Failure in Politics?" *Review of Reviews* (November 1925): 545–546.

Arell, Ruth. "Silent Voices in Radio." *Independent Woman* (November 1937): 342–343, 367–368.

"Army Sweethearts: They Sing and Broadcast to the Troops." *Life* (February 16, 1942): 33.

"At the Ball." *Time* (March 10, 1923): 22.

Aucoin, Rick. "Watching Barbara Walters." *Boston Globe*, May 21, 2000, p. C1.

Baker, Grace. "Price Cutting Under Fire." *The Radio Record* (February 1930): 9.

Baker, John C. *Farm Broadcasting: The First 60 Years*. Ames: Iowa State Press, 1981.

Ball, Rick, and the staff of NBC News. *Meet the Press: Fifty Years of History in the Making*. New York: McGraw-Hill, 1998.

Banning, Margaret Culkin. "Looking Ahead with the Woman Broadcaster." *Independent Woman* (May 1947): 127, 147.

Bantry, John. "Men Souring on Feminism." *Boston Post,* March 22, 1936, pp. 1, 8.

Barnard, Jessie. "You Can't Destroy This Movement." *U.S. News & World Report* (December 8, 1975): 71–73.

Barnouw, Erik. *A Tower in Babel*. New York: Oxford, 1966.

———. *The Sponsor*. New York: Oxford, 1979.

Barrett, Don. *Los Angeles Radio People*. Los Angeles, CA: DB Press, 1997.

Barson, Michael. *Better Dead Than Red*. New York: Hyperion, 1992.

Beach, Rex. "She Tried the Impossible." *Boston Post*, April 21, 1929, Features, p. 6.

Beal, William G., et al. *When Radio Was Young: Early Pittsburgh Radio*. Pittsburgh: Wilkinsburg, Inc., 1995.

Beasley, Maurine H., and Sheila J. Gibbons. *Taking Their Place: A Documentary History of Women in Journalism*. Washington, DC: American University Press, 1993.

Beauchamp, Cari. "Even for Talkies, the Women Who Wrote Worked Silently." *New York Times*, June 22, 1997.

"Beaver, Pa., Girl Is Named 'Miss Radio of 1925.'" *Radio Digest* (September 26, 1925): 7.

Beck, Debra Baker. "The 'F' Word: How the Media Frame Feminism." *NWSA Journal* 10, no. 1 (March 1998).

Beider, Philip D. *Scriptures for a Generation: What We Were Reading in the '60s*. Athens, GA: University of Georgia Press, 1994.

Benderly, Beryl Lieff. *The Myth of Two Minds: What Gender Does and Doesn't Mean*. New York: Doubleday, 1987.

Bernikow, Louise, ed. *The American Women's Almanac*. New York: Berkley, 1997.

Biddle, Mary. "Keep Young and Beautiful." *Radio Stars* (February 1935): 6, 78.

Birkby, Robert. *KMA Radio: The First Sixty Years*. Shenandoah, IA: May Publishing, 1985.

"Birth Control Issue Worries Local Stations." *Variety* (September 23, 1942): 30.

Blair, Emily Newell. "Discouraged Feminists." *Outlook* (July 8, 1931): 302–303, 318.

Blair, Gwenda. *Almost Golden: Jessica Savitch and the Selling of Television News*. New York: Simon & Schuster, 1988.

Blake, Doris. "Airline Hostess Alluring Job for Adventurous Women." *Boston Herald*, June 18, 1933, Magazine section, p. 7B.

"Blushing McBride." *Newsweek* (June 5, 1944): 81.

Bolin, Winifred D. Wandersee. "The Economics of Middle-Income Family Life: Working Women and the Depression." *Journal of American History* 65, no. 1 (June

1978).

Bolstad, Helen. "Rock and Roll: An Evil Influence?" *TV Radio Mirror* (September 1956): 28–30, 85–87.

Borkgren, Edith M. "Sister Aimee." *Radio Doings* 19, no. 7 (June 1931): 24–25.

Borsoli, Mrs. Ralph. "The New Woman Goes Home." *Scribner's* (February 1937): 52–53.

Brainard, Bertha. "Sex No Longer a Factor in Business." *Boston Globe*, December 18, 1927, section 2, p. 7.

———. "Women Listeners Are Good Critics." *New York Times*, September 18, 1927, section X, p.16.

Brindze, Ruth. *Not to Be Broadcast*. New York: Vanguard Press, 1937.

Britten, Loretta, and, Paul Mathless, eds. *Our American Century: The Forties*. Richmond, VA: Time-Life Books, 1999

Britten, Loretta, and Sarah Brash, eds. *Our American Century: The Fifties*. Richmond, VA: Time-Life Books, 1998.

Brooks, Tim, and Earle Marsh. *The Complete Directory to Prime Time Network TV Shows, 1946–present*, 6th ed. New York: Ballantine, 1999.

Brown, Mary Ellen. *Soap Opera and Women's Talk.* Newbury Park, CA: Sage, 1994.

———, ed. *Television and Women's Culture*. Newbury Park, CA: Sage, 1990.

Brown, Wilson. "She Cries for a Living." *Radio Stars* (June 1933): 10, 45.

Buck, Pearl. "Why Shouldn't Women Seek Men in Marriage?" *Radio Mirror* (April 1939): 13, 91.

Burton, Charles W. "A Juvenile Program That Pleases Parents." *Broadcasting* (December 15, 1931): 13.

Burton Jack. *Blue Book of Tin Pan Alley*, 2d ed. New York: Century House, 1965.

Byars, Jackie, and Eileen R. Meehan. "Once in a Lifetime: Constructing 'The Working Woman' Through Cable Narrowcasting." *Camera Obscura—A Journal of Feminism and Film Theory* 33, no. 4 (May 1994).

Cahill, Gloria. "Class(y) Action: An Interview with Camryn Manheim." *Radiance* (Fall 1998).

Calvo, Dana. "Female Anchors on Local TV Paid 28% Less." *Los Angeles Times*, June 1, 2000, p. A1.

Cantor, Eddie. *As I Remember Them*. New York: Duell, Sloan and Pearce, 1963.

Cantor, Louis. *Wheelin' on Beale*. New York: Pharos, 1992.

Carmody, John. "Women, Minorities Still Shut Out." *Washington Post*, June 16, 1993, p. B1.

Carreau, Mark. "Sally Ride Is Leaving NASA." *Houston Chronicle*, September 21, 1987.

"Chicago Link of Mid-Continent Chain." *Radio Digest* (October 31, 1925): 7.

Chinn, Sandra Hardy. *At Your Service: KMOX and Bob Hardy*. St. Louis, MO: Virginia Publishing, 1997.

"Chumsy Sweater Girl." *Newsweek* (July 12, 1943): 83.

Ciolli, Rita. "Suzyn Waldman Invades Male Holy of Holies." *St. Louis Post-Dispatch*, June 17, 1996, p. 3D.

Clines, Francis X. "1000 Watts of Woman Power." *New York Times*, December 21, 1978, p. B7.

Cobb, Irvin S. "What I Think of Nellie Revell." *Illinois State Register*, September 23, 1924.

Cogley, John, ed. *Report on Blacklisting: Radio-Television*. New York: Fund for the Republic, 1956.

"Communicating Just Ain't the Same: A Look at Four Black Women in Media." *Baltimore Afro-American*, March 22, 1997.

Conn, Joseph J. "Making Flying 'Thinkable'—Women Pilots and the Selling of Aviation." *American Quarterly* 31, no. 4 (Autumn 1979).

Coontz, Stephanie. *The Way We Never Were*. New York: Basic Books, 1992.

"Corinne Jordan to Program KSTP." *St. Paul Pioneer Press*, February 19, 1928, p. 10.

Corwin, Norman. *Trivializing America*. Secaucus, NJ: Lyle Stuart, 1986.

Craft, Christine. *Too Old, Too Ugly, and Not Deferential to Men*. Rocklin, CA: Prima Publishing, 1988.

Creedon, Pamela J., ed. *Women in Mass Communication*, 2d ed. Newbury Park, CA: Sage, 1993.

Cremmen, Mary. "Jackie Walks Alone, Then Faces Spotlight." *Boston Globe*, November 10, 1960, p. 4.

"Cure for Cramps." *Newsweek* (October 4, 1943): 88.

Current Biography. New York: H.W. Wilson, various years.

Davidson, Grace. "Prefer Jobs in the Spotlight: Women Especially Influenced by Lure of Publicity." *Boston Post*, February 26, 1933, pp. 1, 4.

Davis, Cynthia J., and Kathryn West. *Women Writers in the United States*. New York: Oxford, 1996.

Deutsch, Sarah Jane. *From Ballots to Breadlines: American Women 1920–1940*. New York: Oxford, 1994.

Dix, Dorothy. "Must a Wife Obey?" *Boston Globe*, March 27, 1916, p. 11.

———. "What Is Equality in Matrimony?" *Boston Globe*, October 30, 1928, p. 23.

Doll, Bob. *Sparks Out of the Plowed Ground: The History of America's Small Town Radio Stations*. West Palm Beach, FL: Streamline, 1996.

Douglas, Susan. *Where the Girls Are*. New York: Times Books, 1994.

Dudar, Helen. "Women's Lib: The War on 'Sexism.'" *Newsweek* (March 23, 1970): 71–75.

Dunning, John. *On the Air: The Encyclopedia of Old Time Radio*. New York: Oxford, 1998.

Dworkin, Susan. *Miss America, 1945: Bess Myerson and the Year That Changed Our Lives*. New York: Newmarket, 1987.

Edelstein, Andrew J., and Kevin McDonough. *The Seventies: From Hot Pants to Hot Tubs*. New York: Dutton, 1990.

Edwards, Evelyn. "Fighting It Out on the Air." *Radio Stars* (May 1936): 42–43, 91.

Ehrenreich, Barbara, and Deidre English. *For Her Own Good: 150 Years of the Experts' Advice to Women*. New York: Anchor, 1978.

Eichberg, Robert. "Too Hot to Broadcast." *Radio Stars* (January 1935): 22–23, 76.

Eisler, Benita. *Private Lives: Men and Women of the Fifties*. New York: Franklin Watts, 1986.

"Eleven Tips on Getting More Out of Women Employees." *Mass Transportation* (July 1943).

Ellerbee, Linda. "TV Still Pops That Age Old Question." *Newsday* (April 6, 1994): A32.

Ellis, Elmo I. *Opportunities in Broadcasting*. Skokie, IL: National Textbook Company, 1981.

Elrod, Bruce C. *Your Hit Parade, 1935–1994*, 4th ed. Ann Arbor, MI: Popular Culture Ink, 1994.

Elson, Robert T. *Time Inc.: The Intimate History of a Publishing Empire, 1923–41.* New York: Atheneum, 1968.

"Enter First Official Woman Umps." *Boston Post*, May 27, 1923.

Entwistle, Guy R. "Citizen Wireless." *Boston Traveler*, May 31, 1921, p. 10.

Erenberg, Lewis A. *Swingin' the Dream: Big Band Jazz and the Birth of American Culture.* Chicago: University of Chicago Press, 1999.

Eskew, Garnett L. "Former Boss of Amos and Andy—Judith Waller of WMAQ." *Radio Digest* (August 1930): 57, 90.

Ewen, Stuart. *PR! A Social History of Spin.* New York: Basic Books, 1996.

Faludi, Susan. *Backlash: The Undeclared War Against American Women.* New York: Crown, 1991.

"Famine in Journalism." *Newsweek* (August 24, 1959): 54.

Farrell, Amy E. "Desire and Consumption: Women's Magazines in the 1980s." *American Quarterly* 46, no. 4 (December 1994).

Feldmann, Linda. "Gains by Women Are Hallmark of Eventful Era." *Christian Science Monitor*, November 25, 1998, p. 1.

Fellman, Anita Clair. "Always the Pragmatist (Margaret Sanger and the Birth Control Movement)." *Reviews in American History* 21 (June 1993): 285–290.

"Fellows New Prexy of Hub Radio Execs." *Variety* (May 10, 1950): 23.

"Feminine Invaders of the Control Room." *Broadcasting* (May 4, 1942): 45.

Fink, John, and Francis Coughlin. *WGN: A Pictorial History.* Chicago, IL: Tribune Press, 1961.

Finkelstein, Norman H. *Sounds in the Air.* New York: Scribners, 1993.

———. *With Heroic Truth: The Life of Edward R. Murrow.* New York: Clarion, 1993.

The First 50 Years of Broadcasting. Washington, DC: Broadcasting Publications, 1982.

"The First Lady's Week," *Time* 35, no. 16 (April 15, 1940): p. 17.

Fleischman, Doris E., ed. *Careers for Women.* New York: Garden City Publishing, 1939.

"The Folk Girls," *Time* (June 1, 1962): 39–41.

Foxworth, Jo. *Boss Lady.* New York: Warner Brothers, 1979.

"Frederick, Pauline." *Current Biography 1954*, pp. 291–292.

Frederick, Pauline. "Red Circle Days on Capitol Hill." *Independent Woman* (November 1938): 351, 363.

Freedman, Estelle B. "The New Woman: Changing Views of Women in the 1920s." *Journal of American History* (September 1974): 372–393.

Friedan, Betty. *The Feminine Mystique.* New York: W.W. Norton, 1963.

———. "What Television Is Doing to American Women." *TV Guide* 12, no. 5 (February 1, 1964): 6–11.

———. "Working Women's Problems." *Cosmopolitan* 158, no. 1 (January 1965): 40–49.

Gaar, Gillian G. *She's A Rebel: The History of Women in Rock and Roll.* Seattle, WA: Seal Press, 1992.

Garofalo, Reebee. *Rockin' Out: Popular Music in the USA.* Boston, MA: Allyn & Bacon, 1997.

Gerbner, George. *Casting the American Scene: A Look at the Characters on Primetime and Daytime Television, 1994–1997.* Los Angeles, CA: Screen Actors Guild Publications, 1998.

Germain, David. "Women Directors Getting Shut Out of TV, Film Work." *Associated Press*, December 10, 1999.

Ginn, Opal. "Lady Bosses—How Tough?" *Parade* (July 10, 1960): 26–28.

Goldman, Golda M. "The Women's Hour." *Wireless Age* 12, no. 6 (March 1925): 34–35.

Goldstein, Norm. *Associated Press History of Television*. New York: Random House, 1991.

Goodman, Ellen. "In Newspapers, a Woman's Place Is Far from Page 1." *Boston Globe*, April 5, 1992, p. 71.

Gordon, Ian. *Comic Strips and Consumer Culture*. Washington, DC: Smithsonian, 1998.

Gordon, Lois, and Alan Gordon. *American Chronicle, 1920–1989*. New York: Crown, 1990.

Gould, Carol C., and Max Wartofsky, eds. *Women and Philosophy*. New York: Putnam, 1976.

Greene, Lloyd. "But 1 in 100 Succeed Who Covet Radio Fame." *Boston Globe*, April 5, 1936, p. E6.

Greenough, Peter B. "Few Women Reach the Top in Industry." *Boston Globe*, September 19, 1963, p. 48.

"A Guest of NBC: Famous European Announcer to Broadcast Here." *Broadcasting* (August 1, 1937).

Hacker, Andrew. "The American Family: Future Uncertain." *Time* (December 28, 1970): 34–35.

Halberstam, David. *The Fifties*. New York: Fawcett, 1993.

Hall, Claude, and Barbara Hall. *This Business of Radio Programming*. New York: Billboard Publications, 1977.

Halper, Donna L. *Radio Music Directing*. Stoneham, MA: Focal Press, 1991.

Hammel, Lisa. "They Meet in Victorian Parlor to Demand True Equality—NOW." *New York Times*, November 22, 1966, p. 44.

Handy, Bruce. "Roll Over, Ward Cleaver and Tell Ozzie Nelson the News (Ellen DeGeneris)." *Time* (April 14, 1997): 79–86.

Harris, Ann P. "Hers: A Forum for Women." *New York Times*, June 14, 1984, p. 2C.

Hatch, Mark. "FCC Lady Member Gives Her Views." *Boston Post*, October 22, 1950, p. A-4.

Haupt, Enid. "How to Win Dates and Influence the Dobie Gillis Type." *TV Guide* (December 5, 1959): 20–23.

Heinz, Catherine. "Women Radio Pioneers." *Journal of Popular Culture* (Fall 1978).

Heldenfels, R.D. *Television's Greatest Year: 1954*. New York: Continuum, 1994.

"Helen (Alvarez) of Tulsa." *Time* (December 12, 1949): 60–61.

"Here's a Girl Farmer Who Is in Real Earnest." *Worcester Telegram*, January 18, 1922, p. 4C.

Herschberger, Ruth. *Adam's Rib*. New York: Harper & Row, 1948.

"Herstory: Women in Television Timeline." *Dallas Morning News*, September 16, 1998, p. 5C.

Herzog, Herta. "Radio—The First Post-War Year." *Public Opinion Quarterly* 10, no. 3 (Autumn 1946): 297–313.

"Higher Education, Lower Wages." *The Survey (*December 15, 1930): 309.

Hilliard, Robert L., and Michael Keith. *The Broadcast Century*, 2d ed. Boston, MA: Focal Press, 1997.

Hilmes, Michele. *Radio Voices: American Broadcasting 1922–1952*. Minneapolis, MN: University of Minnesota Press, 1997.

Hilton, Jack. *The TV Inquisitors*. New York: Chamberlain, 1981.

Hoffman, Joyce. "On Their Own: Female Correspondents in Vietnam." *Quest (The Research Journal of Old Dominion University)* 2, no. 1 (Fall 1998).

Hoopes, Roy. *When the Stars Went to War: Hollywood and World War II.* New York: Random House, 1994.

"How Women Take to the Air." *Literary Digest* (October 26, 1929): 55–56.

Huber, Joan, ed. *Changing Woman in a Changing Society.* Chicago: University of Chicago Press, 1973.

Hughes, Bob. "Feminine Sports Editor Runs into Difficulty." *Miami Herald*, March 6, 1941.

"Hummerts' Mill." *Time* (January 23, 1939): 30.

"Hummerts' Super Soaps." *Newsweek* (January 10, 1944): 79–80.

Hyde, Arthur M. "Farmer Is No Longer Imprisoned on His Acres." *New York Times*, September 22, 1929, p. 2R.

Ingersoll, Fran. Interview with Edythe Meserand. August 31, 1990. Women's Press Club Oral History Project. Oral History Collection, Schlesinger Library, Radcliffe College, Cambridge, MA.

Jeffrey, Ruth. "Radio—Interesting Field for Dramatic Writing." *The Author & Journalist* 15, no. 9 (September 1930): 3–4.

Jonas, Susan, and Marilyn Nissenson. *Going, Going Gone: Vanishing Americana.* San Francisco, CA: Chronicle, 1994.

Jordan, Killian. *Our Finest Hour: Voices of the World War II Generation.* Richmond, VA: Time-Life Books, 2000.

Katz, Jon. "Battle Lines" (A Review of 'Fighting for Air: In the Trenches with Television News' by Liz Trotta). *Columbia Journalism Review* (May/June, 1991): 58–61.

Keith, Michael. *Talking Radio.* Armonk, NY: M.E. Sharpe, 2000.

———. *Voices in the Purple Haze.* Westport, CT: Praeger, 1997.

Keliher, Alice V., ed. *Radio Workers.* New York: Harper & Brothers, 1940.

Kennedy, John B. "Ladies of the Airwaves." *Collier's* 90, no. 2 (July 9, 1932): 14, 44–45.

Kent, George. "Programs for Forgotten Women." *Radio Stars* (May 1935): 48, 60.

Kessler-Harris, Alice. *Women Have Always Worked.* New York: Feminist Press, 1991.

Kismaric, Carole, and Marvin Heiferman. *Growing Up With Dick and Jane.* San Francisco, CA: HarperCollins, 1996.

Klapthor, Margaret Brown. *The First Ladies.* Washington, DC: White House Historical Association, 1999.

Kleinfelder, Rita Lang. *When We Were Young: A Baby Boomer Yearbook.* New York: Prentice-Hall, 1993.

Knight, Ruth Adams. *Stand By for the Ladies.* New York: Caward-McCann, 1939.

Knight, Vic. "First Lady in Radio Sports." *Broadcasting* (May 1, 1934): 14.

Koehler, Joe. "Radio's Dames as Names." *The Billboard* 58, no. 29 (July 26, 1946).

Kossoudji, Sherrie A., and Laura J. Dresser. "Working Class Rosies: Women Industrial Workers During World War II." *Journal of Economic History* 52, no. 2 (June 1992).

Krasne, Belle. "Miami's First Lady of Radio." *Independent Woman* (April 1949): 115–116.

Kutner, Nanette. "Does Radio Rule Women Voters? Fannie Hurst Speaks Her Mind." *Radio Stars* (July 1936): 20–21.

Landay, Lori. "Millions Love Lucy: Commodification and the Lucy Phenomenon." *NWSA Journal* 11, no. 2 (July 1999).

Landry, Robert J. *This Fascinating Radio Business*. Indianapolis, IN: Bobbs-Merrill, 1946.

"Latest in World Sport—A Woman Umpire." *Centralia Evening Sentinel*, May 3, 1922.

Law, Helen. "A New Job for the College Girl." *Review of Reviews* (June 1930): 74, 76.

Lazar, Anne B. "Ladies Must Fly." *Radio Digest* 26, no. 4 (February 1931): 80–81, 105.

Lazarsfeld, Paul F., and Harry Field. *The People Look at Radio*. Chapel Hill, NC: University of North Carolina Press, 1946.

Leach, Eugene E. "Tuning Out Education: The Cooperation Doctrine in Radio, 1922–38." *Current* (January, February, and March 1983).

"Leach, Ruth M." *Current Biography 1948*, pp. 373–374.

Lee, Mabel Barbee. "The Dilemma of the Educated Woman." *Atlantic Monthly* (November 1930); quoted in *Review of Reviews* (December 1930): 71–72.

Levin, Eric, ed. *Unforgettable Women of the Century*. New York: People Books, 1998.

Leuck, Miriam S. "Women in Odd and Unusual Fields of Work." *Annals of the American Academy* 143 (May 1929): 177.

"Little Rock, Take a Bow!" *Independent Woman* (September 1947): 272–273.

Lunardini, Christine. *What Every American Should Know About Women's History*. Holbrook, MA: Bob Adams, 1994.

Lupiano, Vincent de Paul, and Ken W. Sayers. *It Was A Very Good Year*. Holbrook, MA: Bob Adams, 1994.

Lynwander, Linda. "Recollections of a Rock Impresario (Florence Greenberg)." *New York Times*, May 2, 1993, section 13NJ, p. 11C.

"Marble, Alice." *Current Biography 1940*, pp. 557–558.

Makower, Joel. *Boom! Talkin' About Our Generation*. Chicago, IL: Tilden Press, 1985.

Malone, Mary. *Connie Chung, Broadcast Journalist*. Hillside, NJ: Enslow Publishers, 1992.

Maltin, Leonard. *The Great American Broadcast*. New York: Dutton, 1997.

"Man Replaces Woman for Household Talk." *Radio World* (April 9, 1927): 17.

Marin, Rick. "Coming Up Roses (Rosie O'Donnell)." *Newsweek* (July 15, 1996): 45–48.

Marlane, Judith. *Women in Television News Revisited*. Austin: University of Texas Press, 1999.

"Married Women's Jobs in Danger, Women Voters' League Declares." *Boston Evening Transcript,* May 26, 1936, p.5.

Marston, William Moulton. "The Reaction of Man to Woman." *Good Housekeeping* 112 (February 1941): 26–27, 158–159.

Martin, James Kirby, Randy Roberts, et al. *America and Its People*. San Francisco, CA: HarperCollins, 1989.

Martyn, Marguerite. "KSD: Miss Jones Announcing." *Radio in the Home* (September 1923): 5, 29.

Mazie, David. "At 72, She's Still the Voice of the Prairie (Ida McNeil)." *Minneapolis Star-Tribune*, September 25, 1960, p.1.

"McBride, Mary Margaret." *Current Biography 1941*, pp. 540–542.

McBride, Mary Margaret. *Out of the Air*. New York: Doubleday, 1960.

McCabe, Bruce. "Women in TV News Game Moving Forward, but . . ." *Boston Globe*, January 4, 1976, p. A9.

McCall, Michael. *The Best of 50s TV*. New York: Mallard Press, 1992.

McLean, Milly. "TV's Early Days—A Fond Memory." *Gloucester Times*, July 14, 1977, p. 2.

McNeil, Alex. *Total Television*. New York: Penguin, 1996.

"Meet Miss Murphy, 1B". *Boston Globe*, May 24, 1922, p. 11.

"Men Prefer Organ Music, but Women Crave the Orchestra." *The Radio Record* (May 1927): 24.

"Method in Kindness." *Time* (January 21, 1924): 22.

Meyer, Lisa. "Creating G.I. Jane." *Feminist Studies* 18, no. 3 (October 1992).

Meyerowitz, Joanne. "Beyond the Feminine Mystique: A Reassessment of Postwar Mass Culture, 1946–1958." *Journal of American History* 79, no. 4 (March, 1993): 1455–1482.

Millett, Kate. *Sexual Politics*. New York: Avon, 1970.

"Miss Cochran to Train Women Flyers for AAF." *Army Times* (September 19, 1942): 8.

Mitchell, Mary A. "It's Not Too Late to Bring Justice to Women in Radio." *Chicago Sun-Times*, April 5, 1998, p. 27.

Mix, Jennie Irene. "Are Women Undesirable—Over the Radio?" *Radio Broadcast* 5, no. 4 (August 1924).

———. "For and Against the Woman Radio Speaker." *Radio Broadcast* 5, no. 5 (September 1924).

Moskowitz, Eva. "It's Good to Blow Your Top: Women's Magazines and a Discourse of Discontent." *Journal of Women's History* 8, no. 3 (October 1997).

"Most Influential Women of 1999." *Radio Ink* (August 16, 1999): 57–80.

Mulholland, Bland. "The Girl Behind the Men Behind the Mike." *Radio Stars* (January 1935): 68.

Muller, Judy. *Now This: Radio, Television . . . and the Real World*. New York: G.P. Putnam, 2000.

"Musical Clock Girl." *Radio Digest* (November 1929): 57.

Murray, Michael D., ed. *Encyclopedia of Television News*. Phoenix, AZ: Oryx, 1998.

Nash, Alanna. "A Shooting Star Burns Out." *Entertainment Weekly* (October 20, 1995): 80.

"Need for Better Teachers' Salaries." *School and Society* 11 (April 17, 1920): 462.

"Nellie Revell, the Voice of Radio Digest." *Radio Digest* (March 1931): 63.

Norment, Lynn. "Cathy Hughes: Ms. Radio." *Ebony* (May 2000).

"Northwest's Only Lady Mayor Broadcasts." *The Radio Record* 6, no. 1 (February 1926): 35.

"Not Even Bronx Cheer Left After Hays-ites Nix Naughty Lingo." *Variety* (October 2, 1935): 3.

"Number 1 Columnist, Dorothy Thompson." *FM Magazine* 1, no. 2 (December 1940): 3.

O'Brien, John. "Speeds to Discard Her Tomboy Garb." *New Bedford Times*, October 29, 1927, p. 1

O'Brien, Lucy. *She-Bop*. New York: Penguin, 1995.

O'Dell, Cary. *Women Pioneers in Television*. Jefferson, NC: McFarland, 1997.

"Oh Boy! Women Instructors." *Army Times* (September 19, 1942): 7.

Opdycke, Sandra. *The Routledge Historical Atlas of Women in America*. New York: Routledge, 2000.

Packard, Vance. "Married Life in a Goldfish Bowl." *Reader's Digest* (April 1948): 23–25.

Paine, Maggie. "TV Producer Marcy Carsy Garners UNH Alumni Honor." *University of New Hampshire News Bureau*, June 22, 1999.

Palmer, Greta. "What Kind of Wife Has He?" *Reader's Digest* (March 1948): 37–39.

Parks, Lisa. "Watching the Working Gals: 50s Sitcoms and the Repositioning of Women in Postwar American Culture." *Critical Matrix* 11, no. 2 (June 1999).

Pavletich, Aida. *Rock-a-Bye Baby*. New York: Doubleday, 1980.

Pearson, Jo. "Here's Mary Margaret (McBride)." *Radio Television Mirror* (August 1951): 28–31, 85.

Penrose, Margaret. *The Radio Girls of Roselawn*. New York: Cupples & Leon, 1922.

"Perkins, Frances." *Current Biography 1940*, pp. 643–646.

Perkins Jr., Ray. *Logic and Mr. Limbaugh*. Chicago, IL: Open Court, 1995.

Perry, Dick. *Not Just a Sound: The Story of WLW*. Englewood Cliffs, NJ: Prentice-Hall, 1971.

"Philly Mamas Fed Up with Soapers; Too Much Battling on Gleason Show." *Variety* (September 7, 1955): 25.

Polesie, Herbert. "She Plays 1,000 Roles." *Radio Digest* (January 1933): 31.

Pomeroy, Hally. "Housewives Are Happier." *Radio Guide* (May 29, 1937): 11, 18.

"Popular Feminine Announcer." *Radiolog* (October 4, 1931): 17.

"Post-War Horizons." *Newsweek* (August 23, 1943): 52–53.

Power, Helen W. "Suffragists Would Be Amazed at the Progress—and Problems—that Remain." *St. Louis Post-Dispatch*, December 23, 1999, p. B7.

Powers, Jimmy. "Lady Wrestlers—Are They Taboo?" *New England TV Guide* (November 14, 1952): 5.

Press, Andrea, and Terry Strathman. "Work, Family, and Social Class in Television Images of Women." *Women and Language* 16, no. 2 (September 1993).

Quinn, Jane Bryant. "A Woman's Place." *Newsweek* (February 26, 1979): 73.

"Radio Award Is Won by Dorothy Gordon." *New York Times*, December 26, 1951, p. 23.

"Radio Editors Ignore Radio: TeeVee Gets All the Play." *Variety* (October 29, 1952): 31.

"Radio for the Housekeeper." *Literary Digest* (September 9, 1922): 28–29.

"Radio for Women." *Literary Digest* (November 28, 1925): 20.

"Radio Free Babs: Barbara Carlson Says She's Ready for Prime Time." *The City Pages* 18, no. 377 (September 24, 1997): 3.

Read, Phyllis J., and Bernard L. Witlieb, *The Book of Women's Firsts*. New York: Random House, 1992.

Rendell, Steven, and Jim Naureckas, et al. *The Way Things Ought to Be but Aren't: Rush Limbaugh's Reign of Error*. New York: Fair Press, 1995.

Revell, Nellie. "Tells Of Childhood Days in Springfield." *Illinois State Register*, September 28, 1924.

Richardson, David. *Puget Sounds*. Seattle, WA: Superior, 1981.

Rider, John. "Why Is the Radio Soprano Unpopular?" *Scientific American* (October 1928): 334–335.

Riley, Glenda. *Inventing the American Woman*. Arlington Heights, IL: Harlan Davidson, 1986.

Roberts, Cokie. *We Are Our Mother's Daughters*. New York: Perennial, 2000.

Robertson, Nan. *The Girls in the Balcony*. New York: Random House, 1992.

"Roosevelt, Eleanor." *Current Biography 1940*, pp. 691–693.

"Sanders, Marlene." *Current Biography 1981*, pp. 351–354.

Sanders, Marlene, and Marcia Rock. *Waiting for Prime Time: The Women of Television News*. New York: Harper & Row, 1988.

Santoli, Lorraine. *The Official Mickey Mouse Club Book*. New York: Hyperion, 1995.

Savage, Barbara Dianne. *Broadcasting Freedom: Radio, War and the Politics of Race*. Chapel Hill: University of North Carolina Press, 1999.

Savage, Gail. "Fair Sex Inventor." *Radio News* (May 1925): 2089, 2116.

Savitch, Jessica. *Anchorwoman*. New York: Berkley, 1983.

Scharf, Lois. *To Work and to Wed: Female Employment, Feminism and the Great Depression*. Westport, CT: Greenwood Press, 1980

Schiffer, Michael Brian. *The Portable Radio in American Life*. Tucson: University of Arizona Press, 1991.

Scott, L.R., Mrs. "Other Women Hate Me." *New York Herald-Tribune*, March 13, 1966, pp. 8, 18–19.

"Seven Women in Radio and TV Win the McCall's Mike." *McCall's* (January 1954): 9, 58.

"Sex on the Dial (Bill Ballance)." *Newsweek* (September 4, 1972): 90.

Shanley, J.P. "Out of the Kitchen: Betty Furness Welcomes Dramatic Role on TV." *New York Times*, May 12, 1957, section 2, p. 11.

"She-Bang." *Newsweek* (March 27, 1944): 106.

Sheldon, Betty. "To the Ladies." *Radio Doings* 19, no. 9 (September 1931): 12–14.

Shipman, Vera Brady. "KPO—The Voice of the Golden Gate." *Radio Digest* (November 22, 1924): 5.

Shore, Michael, with Dick Clark. *History of American Bandstand*. New York: Ballantine, 1985.

"Should Wives Take Jobs?" *Literary Digest* (January 24, 1925): 23.

Singer, Arthur J. *Arthur Godfrey: The Adventures of An American Broadcaster*. Jefferson, NC: McFarland, 2000.

Sivorinovsky, Alina. "Captain Unconscious: A Parent's Guide to Television Images of Women in Charge." *New Moon Network* 4, no. 4 (May 1997): 8–9.

Skiba, Katherine M. "Women Talk over Media Role." *Milwaukee Journal-Sentinel*, August 27, 1996, p. 6.

Slide, Anthony. *Great Radio Personalities*. New York: Vestal, 1982.

———. *Selected Radio and Television Criticism*. Metuchen, NJ: Scarecrow Press, 1987.

Smith, Sally Bedell. "TV Newswoman's Suit Stirs a Debate on Values in Hiring." *New York Times*, August 6, 1983, p. 1.

Smulyan, Susan. *Selling Radio: The Commercialization of American Broadcasting*. Washington, DC: Smithsonian, 1994.

Sorel, Nancy Caldwell. *The Women Who Wrote the War*. New York: Arcade Press, 1999.

Speece, Wynn, and M. Jill Karolevitz. *The Best of the Neighbor Lady*. Mission Hill, SD: Dakota Homestead, 1987.

Spigel, Lynn. *Make Room for TV: Television and the Family Ideal in Postwar America*. Chicago, IL: University of Chicago Press, 1992.

Stage, Sarah J. "Women." *Journal of American History* 35, nos. 1–2 (Summer 1983).

Stamberg, Susan. *Talk*. New York: Random House, 1993.

Stanovsky, Derek. "Princess Diana, Mother Teresa, and the Value of Women's Work." *NWSA Journal* 11, no. 2 (July 1999).

Stark, Phyllis, "More Women Getting Their Say on Radio." *Billboard* (August 10, 1991): 10

"Station WASN Will Broadcast the Latest Shopping News." *Boston Globe*, January 29, 1927, p. 18.

Stearns, Peter N., and Mark Knapp. "Men and Romantic Love: Pinpointing a 20th Century Change." *Journal of Social History* (Summer 1993): 769–795.

Sterling, Christopher, and J. Michael Kittross. *Stay Tuned*, 2d ed. Belmont, CA: Wadsworth, 1990.

Strasser, Susan. *Satisfaction Guaranteed: The Making of the American Mass Market*. Washington, DC: Smithsonian, 1989.

Sullivan, Elizabeth. "Daughter of Irene Rich to Be a WAVE." *Boston Globe*, May 29, 1944.

———. "What Happened in TV and Radio." *Boston Globe*, January 1, 1954.

"Symphony Goes Co-Ed." *Newsweek* (December 6, 1943): 86–87.

Tavris, Carol. *The Mismeasure of Women*. New York: Touchstone, 1992.

"Texas for Ma." *Time* (September 1, 1924): 5–6.

"They've Got Sales Appeal." *TV Guide* (November 27, 1953): 10–11.

Thom, Mary. *Inside Ms.: 25 Years of the Magazine and the Feminist Movement*. New York: Henry Holt, 1997.

Thompson, Dorothy. "If I Had a Daughter." *Ladies' Home Journal* 56 (September 1939).

———. "On Women Correspondents and Other New Ideas." *The Nation* (January 6, 1926): 11–12.

Thornton, Arland, and Deborah Freedman. "Changes in Sex Role Attitudes of Women, 1962–77." *American Sociological Review* 44, no. 5 (October 1979): 831–842.

Trotta, Liz. *Fighting for Air*. New York: Simon and Schuster, 1991.

Tuchman, Gaye, Arlene Kaplan, and James Benét, eds. *Hearth and Home: Images of Women in the Mass Media*. New York: Oxford, 1978.

"TV News Hens." *Ebony* 21, no. 12 (October 1966): 44–46, 50.

Valentry, Duane. "What Do Executives Have Against Gals?" *Boston Globe*, December 17, 1960, pp. 1–2.

"Video's Dancing Daughters." *New England TV Guide* (March 28, 1952): 4.

"WAAC's First Muster." *Time* (June 8, 1942): 71.

Wagner, Gwen. "A Girl Reporter Speaks Up." *Radio Age* (September 1925): 30, 65, 69.

Wagner, Lilya. *Women War Correspondents of World War II*. Westport, CT: Greenwood Press, 1989.

Wallace, John. "Kind and Unkind Words About Our Friends the Announcers." *Radio Broadcast* 10, no. 2 (December 1926): 159.

———. "Men Versus Women Announcers." *Radio Broadcast* 10, no. 1 (November 1926): 44–45.

———. "Why Is It Difficult to Be Funny over the Radio?" *Radio Broadcast* 9, no. 2 (June 1926): 133–134.

Waller, Judith. *Radio: The Fifth Estate*. Boston, MA: Houghton Mifflin, 1946.

Walters, Barbara. "Electronic Girl Reporters." *Variety* (January 5, 1966): 108.

Watson, Paula. "All Guts for Old Glory: Rosie the Riveter." *Dallas Morning News*, December 29, 1999, p. 5C.

Welles, Kingsley. "Do Women Know What They Want in Radio Programs?" *Radio Broadcast* 8, no. 1 (November 1925): 34.

———. "Meet Mr. Average Radio Enthusiast." *Radio Broadcast* 9, no. 6 (October 1926): 531.

———. "Who Are the Owners of Radio Sets?" *Radio Broadcast* 8, no. 1 (November 1925): 32.

Wenzel, Lynn, and Carol J. Binkowski. *I Hear America Singing*. New York: Crown, 1989.

Wertheim, Arthur Frank. *Radio Comedy*. New York: Oxford, 1979.

Wertheimer, Linda, ed. *Listening to America*. Boston, MA: Houghton Mifflin, 1995.

"What Have Women Done with the Vote?" *Literary Digest* (September 22, 1923): 50, 52.

"What the Farmer Listens to." *Radio Broadcast* 9, no. 4 (August 1926): 315.

"What Women Spend for Their Clothes." *Literary Digest* (August 25, 1923): 57.

Whitcomb, Lewis. "JEK of Station WOR." *Boston Post*, March 25, 1923, p. 27.

————. "JEK to Marry Gloucesterite." *Boston Post*, May 6, 1923, p. 27.

"Who's the Nation's Most Glamorous Disc Jockey?" *Radio Best* (November 1947): 60.

"WHT Makes Scoop: Gets Jean Sargent." *Radio Digest* (July 4, 1925): 7.

"Why Women Change Jobs." *Literary Digest* (November 24, 1923): 27.

Williams, Bob, and Chuck Hartley. *Good Neighbors to the Northwest: WCCO Radio Publications, 1924–74*. Minneapolis, MN: WCCO Publishing.

Wilson, Pamela. "Upscale Feminine Angst: Molly Dodd, the Lifetime Cable Network and Gender Marketing." *Camera Obscura* 33–34 (January 1995): 102–118.

Wise, Mike. "Talking Sports with the Babe." *New York Times*, February 11, 1996, Section 1, p. 59.

WLS Prairie Farmer Family Album. Chicago, IL: WLS Publications, 1948–52.

WNEW: Where the Melody Lingers On. New York: Nightingale Gordon, 1985.

Wolf, Naomi. *The Beauty Myth*. New York: Morrow, 1991.

Wolff, Cynthia Griffin. "A Mirror for Men: Stereotypes of Women in Literature." *The Massachusetts Review* 13, nos.1–2 (Winter–Spring 1972).

Woliver, Robbie. *Bringing It All Back Home: 25 Years of American Music at Folk City*." New York: Pantheon, 1986.

"The Woman 'Pin Money' Worker." *Literary Digest* (March 1, 1930): 12.

"Woman Program Director Comes to Radio Naturally." *Billboard* (August 22, 1964): 32.

"Woman Reporter in Slacks Is Greeted by Pope Pius." *Quincy Patriot Ledger*, June 8, 1944, p. 11.

"Woman Scientist's Guide Used by Army Radio Men." *Chicago Sun*, August 16, 1942.

"Women and Wireless." *Literary Digest* (December 15, 1923): 25.

"Women Are Subject Class, Says Alice Paul Bitterly." *New Bedford Standard*, November 10, 1922, p. 3.

"Women at the Top." *Newsweek* (June 27, 1966): 76–78.

"Women Composers." *Providence Sunday Journal*, June 4, 1922, section 3, p. 9.

"Women Fall Down on the Air." *Variety* (March 11, 1931): 67.

"Women Have Two Squads on Duty." *Boston Sunday Globe*, April 1, 1917, p. 55.

"Women in the News: Engineer and Hockey Star." *Boston Traveler*, September 9, 1925, p. 23.

"Women Listeners Are Good Critics." *New York Times*, September 18, 1927, section X, p. 16.

"Women's Place on the Air." *Broadcasting* (March 30, 1942): 59.

"Women: The Road Ahead." *Time* 136, no. 19 (Fall 1990), special issue.

Wright, John L., ed. *Possible Dreams: Enthusiasm for Technology in America*. Dearborn, MI: Henry Ford Museum, 1992.

Wright, Joseph. "Shirley 'The House Party' Clark Really Likes to Jam in the A.M." *Los Angeles Sentinel*, July 28, 1994.

Wyer, E.B. "The Woman Behind the TV Scene: Could She Be You?" *Cosmopolitan* 216, no. 4 (January 1994).

Yellis, Kenneth. "Prosperity's Child: Some Thoughts on the Flapper." *American Quarterly* 21, no. 1 (Spring 1969).

Zack, Margaret. "Spencer Trial Bares TV Trivialities." *Minneapolis Star-Tribune*, January 18, 1992, pp. 1, 5B.

Zimmerman, Susan. "Rock Writer Jane Scott to Get Achievement Award." *Cleveland Plain Dealer*, March 12, 2000, p. 5L.

Zuckerman, Dianne. "Star Jones Gives You Her Views." *Denver Post*, April 4, 2000, p. E-5.

Also used were numerous issues of the following magazines: *American Heritage, Atlantic Monthly, Billboard, Broadcasting, Current Biography, Ebony, Edison Life, FM, Good Housekeeping, Harper's, Ladies' Home Journal, Independent Woman, Life, Literary Digest, McCall's, Ms., New England TV Guide, Newsweek, The Outlook, Popular Radio, Radio Best, Radio Broadcast, Radio Digest, Radio in the Home, Radio Mirror, Radio News, Radio Stars, Radio World, Record World, Reader's Digest, Review of Reviews, Saturday Evening Post, School and Society, Song Hits, Time, TV Guide, TV/Radio Mirror, Variety,* and *Wireless Age.*

Many clippings in my research came from microfilm of the *Boston American, Boston Globe, Boston Herald, Boston Post, Boston Evening Transcript,* and *Boston Traveler.* I also used the *Baltimore Afro-American, (Boston) Jewish Advocate, Centralia (IL) Sentinel, Chicago Defender, Chicago Sun-Times, Christian Science Monitor, Lynn Daily Evening Item, Los Angeles Times, Minneapolis Star-Tribune, Los Angeles Times, New York Herald-Tribune, New York Newsday, New York Times, Providence Journal-Bulletin, Quincy (MA) Patriot-Ledger, St. Louis Argus, St.Louis Post-Dispatch, St. Paul (MN) Pioneer-Press,* and *Washington Post.*

On the internet, I referred to the websites of *ABC, CBS, NBC, ESPN, Lifetime, American Women in Radio & Television, Society of Professional Journalists,* and *CNN* for biographies of various personalities.

Index

About the Author

Donna Lee Halper is an adjunct professor at Emerson College in Boston in the Journalism Department. Ms. Halper is a well-known radio consultant, with over twenty-five years in broadcasting. She has written two other books, as well as a number of magazine and journal articles. An experienced broadcast historian, she has been a guest lecturer at numerous colleges and is one of the editors of the *Boston Radio Archives*. When not teaching or writing, she is a Big Sister, and she tutors immigrants in English as a second language.